French reflections in the Shakespearean tragic

MANCHESTER
1824

Manchester University Press

French reflections in the Shakespearean tragic

Three case studies

Richard Hillman

Manchester University Press

Published by Manchester University Press
Altrincham Street, Manchester M1 7JA, UK
www.manchesteruniversitypress.co.uk

British Library Cataloguing-in-Publication Data is available

Library of Congress Cataloging-in-Publication Data is available

ISBN 978 0 7190 9989 2 *paperback*

First published by Manchester University Press in hardback 2012

This paperback edition first published 2015

Printed by Lightning Source

Contents

Acknowledgements   *page* vii

Textual notes   viii

1   Introduction   1

2   Hamlet in three French lights   14

3   Nursing serpents: French ripples within and beyond the
    'Pembroke Circle'   94

4   'Rossillion' (*bis*) revisited: five minutes to midnight
    and *All's Well*   150

Works cited   202

Index   221

Acknowledgements

Part of Chapter 3 of this book is adapted from an article published in *Renaissance and Reformation/Renaissance et Réforme* 28.1 (2004), a special issue edited by François Rouget; this material is used by permission. Otherwise, formal thanks for providing me with occasions to present and discuss my ideas on *Hamlet* are due to the Centre d'Études Supérieures de la Renaissance (CNRS/Université François-Rabelais, Tours), the Société Française Shakespeare, and the Institut de Recherches sur la Renaissance, l'Âge Classique et les Lumières (CNRS/Université Paul-Valéry – Montpellier III). Less formally, I have benefited from the wise professional counsel of Andrew Gurr, Michael Hattaway, Gordon Macmullan, Anne Lake Prescott and Greg Walker, as well as from stimulating exchanges with my fellow members of the Équipe Théâtre Européen at the CESR, Pierre Pasquier and Juan Carlos Garrot, who have shared with me unstintingly, over a number of years, their extensive knowledge of early modern French and Spanish drama, respectively. Pierre especially encouraged my pursuit of the elusive Antoine de Bourbon, while Juan Carlos helped my understanding of Garcilaso de la Vega. Finally, the affectionate support of Pauline Ruberry-Blanc has been instrumental in enabling this project (if not necessarily its author) finally to see the light.

Textual notes

Except where otherwise indicated, Shakespeare is cited from *The Riverside Shakespeare*, 2nd ed., gen. eds G. Blakemore Evans and J. J. M. Tobin (Boston: Houghton Mifflin, 1997). Volumes of the *Calendar of State Papers, Foreign Series*, are referred to as *CSPF*, then by period covered. Biblical references are to *The Bible and Holy Scriptvres Conteyned in the Olde and Newe Testament* (Geneva: [n.pub.], 1562 [i.e. 1561]). STC numbers refer to *A Short-Title Catalogue of Books Printed in England, Scotland, and Ireland and of English Books Printed Abroad 1475–1640*, first compiled by A. W. Pollard and G. R. Redgrave, 2nd ed., revised and enlarged, begun by W. A. Jackson and F. S. Ferguson, completed by Katharine F. Pantzer, 2 vols (London: The Bibliographical Society, 1986).

Unattributed translations are my own.

1

Introduction

The present book extends the approach developed in *French Origins of English Tragedy* (2010) through a series of more sustained explorations centred on three plays of Shakespeare: *Hamlet, Antony and Cleopatra* and *All's Well That Ends Well*. (I will explain in due course my decision to include in this trio what is formally a comedy.) The explorations may be more sustained, as well as centred, but the reader should be warned at the outset that the focus is more diffused: hence, 'reflections'. For in each case I take advantage of a particularly rich variety of French intertexts in order to explore exchanges of meaning among the latter, as well as in relation to the English texts that occasion and anchor the discussion.

The enabling premise is that cross-Channel intertextual intervention may cause an apparently 'self-sufficient' textual cluster to signify in new ways, and that criticism may cross the Channel productively in both directions. The crossings are smooth ones in the case of the Roman-Egyptian plays of Étienne Jodelle, Robert Garnier and Nicolas de Montreux, juxtaposed with those of Samuel Daniel and Shakespeare (with Mary Sidney Herbert's translation of Garnier also taken into account). The link there, obviously, is the common subject matter. It may seem a rough and pointless passage, however, to the varied historical, fictional and polemical writings of François de Belleforest – an enormously prolific author, but a 'subliterary' one. (That category carries less weight than formerly, but it remains suggestive that Belleforest does not even figure in the index of Timothy Hampton's 2001 study, *Literature and Nation in the Sixteenth Century: Inventing Renaissance France*.) Indeed, especially by way of Belleforest, major parts of Chapters 2 and 4 depart from the usual geographical preoccupations of Anglo-American literary criticism. The recent historicizing trend in English studies may have led literary scholars to expect extensive deployment of various 'background', even a blurring between background and foreground, but the background is normally not French. If such aspects of this discussion seem beside the point to specialists of English literature, I believe that they would not have done to the English of the period – unless, perhaps, to the extent that they belaboured the obvious.

With due diffidence, I will also be proposing, in the apparent absence of published texts transmitting distinctive and significant details, a few instances in which informally acquired knowledge of French matters seems to have infiltrated dramatic invention. It has long been postulated that Marlowe and Chapman, at least, had independent access through quasi-diplomatic channels, some of them perhaps traversing the large French refugee community in London, to facts and stories in restricted circulation. My explorations of *Hamlet* and *All's Well That Ends Well* suggest that such may also have been the case for Shakespeare, who certainly did have connections with that community.[1]

I

The question of textual origins presents itself in a particularly problematic light when a dramatist might have had access to versions of similar material in different languages: would one necessarily be chosen, the other put aside? In many cases, a negative answer can be given with some confidence, and the point becomes telling for my purposes when an author demonstrably consulted both an English and a French version. This is obviously to touch on the large and nebulous question of linguistic competence, since to choose to work, even in a minor way, in both languages implies a certain ease of access to French.

Among the English authors I have previously approached from a French angle, it is the dominant one, Shakespeare, whose competence in French has most severely been challenged, yet for whose range of French reading I will be making – not for the first time – a notably large claim.[2] This goes against the tradition, which has often seemed curiously anxious to peg him at a beginner's level, inferential though the evidence must always be. The question of his access, in revising the old play of *Hamlet*, to the narrative in Belleforest's *Histoires tragiques* especially shows up the point, since there is no evidence of an English translation prior to 1608, when *The Hystorie of Hamblet* was published; that anonymous rendition, moreover, includes departures from the original that, for many commentators, 'appear to be drawing on Shakespeare's play' (*Ham.*, Jenkins, ed., 1982, p. 89). No certainty is possible, but the natural inference that Shakespeare read Belleforest in French, although occasionally accepted,[3] meets with undue (though mostly passive) resistance – to the point, in one recent instance, where the translation must be 'conjectured to have circulated in manuscript before its printing' (De Grazia, 2006, p. 51).

The immediate (if latent) issue here is less the pinning down of a source – indeed, there is just room for doubt as to whether Shakespeare required recourse to Belleforest in either language[4] – than our sense of what would have been natural and congenial for him. If his linguistic skills were barely adequate to do the basic reading, it seems strange that he would force himself to go to Belleforest in search of details and ideas. And even if we accept the project of revision as his motive, the question remains – and of course remains unanswerable – of who imposed that project in the first place: did the company give him the idea for an updated revival or was it decided on Shakespeare's initiative? Indeed, might the playwright have been inspired independently while reading the *Histoires tragiques* for (dare one say?) 'non-professional' reasons?

The reading of *Hamlet* proposed here would at least allow, as a frank hypothesis, for the latter scenario, while the sheer range of French intertexts that can plausibly be brought to bear on that and other plays – plausibility, I realize, being a matter of judgement and precisely the question at hand – points in the same direction. One does not read in a language for pleasure if doing so is a constant struggle, and I will be arguing that *Hamlet*, as well as *King Lear*, shows that Shakespeare did not confine his reading in Belleforest's volume to the story in question. The level of linguistic comfort thereby implied is consistent with the diversity of the French reading I will be attributing to him elsewhere, most of which cannot simply be consigned to job-related 'research'.

The fact, however, is that there is no need to assume more than rudimentary competence in French on Shakespeare's part in order to account for the 'French' elements hitherto identified in the plays. And such a minimalist *assumption* – the latter term stands out in discussions of the question – exerts considerable interpretative pressure on critics and editors. Thus, with regard to the French and mixed-French scenes in *Henry V*, the poor quality of the language as printed in the First Folio is often taken as corroboration of the author's linguistic mediocrity, whereas the case might be made that even to venture to put so much French on stage bespeaks a privileged relation with the language and presumes an audience's complicity, if hardly its universal understanding. Still less substantive must be any argument from the confused and caricatured Franglais of Doctor Caius in *The Merry Wives of Windsor*, which has nevertheless been held to support the 'assumption' that 'Shakespeare's French was a great deal worse' even than others have supposed (*Wiv.*, Crane, ed., 1997, p. 162). The same editor goes so far as to defend the Folio reading of 'court', as opposed to 'cour', 'on the *assumption* ... that this is an English word put in either for the audience's benefit or because Shakespeare could not recall the French word' (Crane, ed., 1997, n. to I.iv.43–44; my emphasis). In fact, the point is moot, since 'court' was an alternative spelling of French 'cour' in the period – the one given precedence, for instance, in Randle Cotgrave's French-English dictionary of 1611.

A series of discussions of *All's Well*, a play that pushes broadly – insistently, in my reading – in the direction of French knowledge, illustrates the staying (and restrictive) power of the idea of Shakespeare's rudimentary competence. Herbert G. Wright felt compelled to begin his argument for Shakespeare's consultation of the French translation of his source in Boccaccio ('How Did Shakespeare Come to Know the *Decameron?*', 1955) by demonstrating, through circumstantial evidence, the likelihood of the playwright's moderate mastery of French. G. K. Hunter followed suit in his Introduction to the Arden *All's Well*, allowing Shakespeare merely 'some knowledge of French' (1959, p. xxv), and by and large the tradition continues in the same grudging vein. Hunter's conservatism may also be taken as typical when it comes to deciding what the author did when faced with a choice of languages: 'other things being equal ... it seems unlikely that Shakespeare would use a French rather than an English version' (1959, p. xxv). He is duly echoed by the New Oxford editor, who endorses the 'probability that Shakespeare would use a popular English version rather than a less widely available one in French' (Snyder, ed., 1993, p. 1n.1). In the abstract, this seems a perfectly reasonable supposition. Concretely, however, uncertainty as to the 'other things' involved, including the practical question of availability in an era when the circulation of books was less systematic and often personal, undermines such presumptions. Moreover, examination of some prominent cases – for instance, Shakespeare's possible use of Montaigne in French (not just in John Florio's translation) – suggests at least that the eclipse of the original by its translation was sometimes partial, and that the penumbral zone may be intertextually productive (if, by definition, in shadowy ways).

The point is decisively confirmed by one particularly 'unlikely' but revealing discovery – for once I stand by that term – recorded at the end of Chapter 3. It is axiomatic to consider Shakespeare's use of the readily available 'North's Plutarch' for the Roman plays as being exclusive; certainly, his recourse was assiduous and sometimes verbatim. Yet what seems to me irrefutable evidence proves that he also took the trouble, at least in a single local but highly significant instance, to consult Jacques Amyot's French translation – the original of North – as edited and glossed by that indefatigable man of Calvinist letters, Simon Goulart.[5] The text affected involves one of Cleopatra's most prominent and significant speeches as she moves towards her suicide, and the interpretative effect is to signal at a pivotal moment, by the route of 'French' intertextuality, a rejection of the moralistic ('Roman') concept of her tragedy, hence an enlargement of the concept of tragedy itself.

II

Other instances of such 'double consultation' of sources, or possible sources, are far from clear-cut, and many are frankly indeterminate. Even so, it seems worthwhile to raise the issue regularly and to open it up wherever possible. Let me briefly illustrate by a deliberately far-fetched Marlovian example – far-fetched in that the availability of the French text in question remains more than usually hypothetical. The 'official' source of *Doctor Faustus* is, of course, the English translation by 'P. F.' of the *Faustbuch* (*The historie of the damnable life, and deserved death of Doctor John Faustus*), published in 1592 and perhaps available previously in manuscript (the composition of Marlowe's play being of uncertain date). Scholars can probably be trusted in their consensual conclusion that Marlowe owed nothing to the German original (first printed in 1587); they seem never, however, to have considered his possible use of a French translation. Marlowe demonstrably read French, of course – fluently indeed, given his wide range of sources for *The Massacre at Paris*[6] – and a plausible argument has been advanced that the French version of the *Faustbuch* produced by Pierre-Victor Palma-Cayet, although it survives only in an edition of 1598, had first been published in 1589.[7] Palma-Cayet, more than incidentally, was a fascinatingly eccentric and erratic personage, notorious for his magical and alchemical pursuits, unorthodox opinions and religious slipperiness; moreover, he was connected with the court of Navarre (Cazaux, ed., 1982, pp. 19–27) – a court that had multiple if elusive English connections, as this study will further propose. For a period, Palma-Cayet actually served as one of the tutors of the young King Henri. He was precisely the sort of character likely to have come to Marlowe's attention, and to have piqued his interest.

Finally, there is not much distinctive in Palma-Cayet's translation of the *Faustbuch*, although he generally cleaves closer to the original than does 'P. F.' (allowing for a variant source edition and some modifications, including omission of the anti-papal material, which evidently reflect Palma-Cayet's 1595 conversion from Protestantism[8]). But it is at least suggestive to juxtapose the English and French texts with Marlowe's play at one crucial juncture – the core of Faustus's self-torturing final soliloquy:

> Ah, Faustus,
> Now hast thou but one bare hour to live,
> And then thou must be damned perpetually.
>
> ...
>
> Why wert thou not a creature wanting soul?
> Or why is this immortal that thou hast?
> Ah, Pythagoras' *metempsychosis*, were that true,
> This soul should fly from me and I be changed

> Unto some brutish beast.
> All beasts are happy, for, when they die,
> Their souls are soon dissolved in elements;
> But mine must live still to be plagued in hell.
>
> (*Doctor Faustus, A-text [1604]*, ed. Bevington
> and Rasmussen, 1993, V.ii.57–59, 97–104)[9]

For this climactic speech – innovatory within early English tragedy and influential on its subsequent development – the source actually provided a skeletal but directive prototype in Chapter 61 ('How Doctor Faustus bewayled to thinke on Hell …'). Here is the relevant portion from the 1592 English rendering: 'Now thou *Faustus*, damned wretch, howe happy wert thou if as an vnreasonable beast thou mightest die without soule, so shouldest thou not feele any more doubts' (ed. Palmer and More, 1936, p. 224). Palma-Cayet's version is as follows: 'Moy pauvre damné que je suis! pourquoy ne suis nay beste? qui meurt sans ame, au moyen de quoy il ne me seroit necessaire de passer plus oultre' (ed. Cazaux, 1985, p. 205).

On the one hand, Marlowe's 'happy' has clearly been suggested by the English *Faustbuch*, which also has Faustus addressing himself by name. On the other hand, the French offers a closer model for Faustus's direct self-questioning as to his origin: 'Why wert thou not a creature wanting soul?' ('pourquoy ne suis nay beste?'). More significantly, the French concisely defines the point of that question, which is blunted and blurred in the English translation. Marlowe's Faustus, like Palma-Cayet's, explicitly longs to be exempted, not from the vague 'doubts' of *The Damnable Life*, but from immortality itself. If we admit the possibility of Marlowe's access to the French translation, the standard model of a 'creative' encounter with a privileged source yields to one at once more complex and less fraught, for which the term *bricolage* seems ready-made. Obviously, the case of Marlowe and the *Faustbuch/bücher* must remain hypothetical, but that is perhaps all the more reason for it to stand, with that of the 'two Plutarchs' – both of them apparently 'Shakespeare's' to some degree – as an emblem of intertextual potential and a caution against facile linguistic assumptions.

III

Let me conclude these introductory remarks by briefly setting up each of the admittedly lengthy chapters that follow, beginning with the first and longest. Less excuse for prolixity may be needed in the case of *Hamlet*, which has, of course, occasioned many books on its own. These include a recent study by Margreta De Grazia, Hamlet *without Hamlet* (2006), whose objective is to free the text from the 'Modern Hamlet' – the daunting and inhibiting burden of significance that has accrued over the centuries to its central character. Once this is done, it turns out that there is surprising scope for developing issues of diverse kinds, especially political and historical ones.[10] My own approach runs parallel to some extent but posits, in the place of the displaced all-encompassing modern Hamlet, the production of multiple early modern ones – in particular, three with French associations. These are offered, I hasten to add, with no claim whatever to exclusivity. I could not agree more with Eric S. Mallin's perception of 'Shakespeare's most epistemologically unstable play' as deploying 'an extremely murky contagion of referentiality' (1995, p. 22); my aim is to help us understand more fully how, perhaps even why, this is so.

The influence of Montaigne on *Hamlet* is usually assumed, like influence generally, to have left its traces in more or less precise verbal or intellectual correspondences. And since that influence is a widely accepted principle, criticism has got on with the business of debating the degree of precision entailed. This chapter proposes two further sources of French resonance accessible to auditors of the ultimate early modern English tragedy. I begin, however, by revisiting the indebtedness to Montaigne as a dynamic of interpretation rather than a collection of allusions. For it may be argued that all three of the prominent 'Hamlets' that collectively lend the character his precocious modernity come into view respectively – as if by anamorphic perspective – from the three intertextual angles involved. (For the sake of convenience, I refer to them as the philosophical Hamlet – that mandated by Montaigne – the political Hamlet and the psychological Hamlet.) The light that illuminates these figures is refracted by a prismatic 'ungrammaticality'[11] at the generic centre of the play: Hamlet's oblique and shifting attitude toward his revenge, which culminates in his acceptance, despite his better knowledge – despite 'himself' – of the fencing match concealing a plot against his life.[12]

In each case, a certain quantity of 'new' intertextual material needs to be introduced in order to establish the fuller range of contemporary reactions that, in my argument, might have contributed to spectators' reception of the character, hence to the shaping of the play for them. And in the case particularly of the second Hamlet – the political one – such material draws towards the historical and the polemical: its 'literary' directions (not to say its final destinations) need to be found out indirectly, and at some length. As compensation, I can offer the fact that the story is likely to be new to most readers of *Hamlet* criticism. It also makes, I like to think, a good story – or several.

IV

There is general agreement that the story of Cleopatra in *The Legend of Good Women* exerted little influence on subsequent treatments of that heroine, but critics who persist in plunging into the vexed complications associated with the origins of *Antony and Cleopatra* may be tempted to identify with Chaucer's unusual version of her fate: she strips herself naked and jumps into a snake pit. The basic difficulty, paradoxically, is the overwhelming dominance of Plutarch's Life of Antony as the source, not only of Shakespeare's play, but of virtually all the significant prior dramatic 'sources' and 'analogues', as diligently assembled by Geoffrey Bullough (1957–75, vol. 5) – from G. B. Geraldi Cinthio's *Cleopatra* (c. 1542) to Samuel Daniel's (1594–1607).[13] Criticism looking for inter-dramatic relationships has thus found itself seizing on scraps – matches, or near-matches, of plot and language which either short-circuit that common source outright or distinctively adapt it. To a degree, the method is unavoidable, and I will be doing some of the same. But I also want to take a broader view of the intertextual field from the standpoint of French material. My hope is that some patterns may appear rather different from this angle.

Such an approach avowedly bypasses the sporadic Italian adaptations,[14] or at least presumes their assimilation into a more sustained (and highly politicized) French tradition, which in turn feeds into the English one. Encouragement (if not outright justification) may be found in the strong French inflection imparted to Plutarch's compilation itself, as first offered to the English public by Thomas Vautrollier in 1579:

> *The liues of the noble Grecians and Romanes, compared together by that graue learned philosopher and historiographer, Plutarke of Chaeronea: translated out of Greeke into French by Iames Amyot, Abbot of Bellozane, Bishop of Auxerre, one of the Kings priuy counsel, and great Amner [Aumônier] of Fraunce, and out of French into Englishe, by Thomas North.*

The work's Englishing is here presented as anticlimactic, to say the least. The title pages of the subsequent editions printed, from 1595, by Vautrollier's successor, Richard Field (Shakespeare's own publisher and probably his childhood friend), continued to foreground Amyot's mediation of Plutarch, and indeed to cite the other French translators responsible for material added in later years (Charles d'Escluse and Simon Goulart – the latter having impeccable Protestant credentials, unlike Amyot himself). Evidently, such origins were far from being considered a commercial hindrance, and one might further conjecture that the abundant prior encoding of Roman historical material to comment on French affairs was assumed to add a dimension of interest for contemporary English readers. Certainly, English playwrights continued to dramatize those figures and events commonly used by French authors to reflect on their own contemporary reality.[15] It seems quite natural that Chapman's only tragedy not directly concerned with more-or-less recent French history was *Caesar and Pompey*. In this light, too, the cameo appearance of Caesar in that most French of English history plays, *Henry V* (V.Cho.26 ff.) – whomever he is standing in for, and however ambivalently – appears a matter of course. Finally, however the resonance was produced, it cannot have appeared too strange for playgoers to hear Marlowe's Duke of Guise and Shakespeare's Caesar, at the culminating moments of their respective dooms – passing Titanically at nightfall – speaking each other's language.[16]

The latter instances reflect the obvious preeminence of Caesar, with or without Brutus, as a signifying presence on the French political scene, on-stage and off. Antony, my main preoccupation here, remains a more elusive figure, and his recurrence at once in the drama and in the political symbolism is perhaps surprising. The reason may be the particularly rich signifying potential carried by his double identity, as the pivotal link between the two phases, each centred on a Caesar, of Rome's evolution from republic to empire. For if, as I argue, there were at least three 'French Hamlets' conceivably available to English audiences, in French configurations of Roman history – as indeed in both Plutarch and Shakespeare – there are traditionally, in effect, two more-or-less distinct Antonies.

V

My concluding chapter will be even more preoccupied with reflections than I had originally anticipated, including a reflection on methodology. To begin with a fundamental point – the more so because it illustrates the general reluctance of early modern English dramatic criticism to accommodate French facts and fictions – the story of Hélène de Tournon (to be presented below for those who do not know it) has not been integrated into Anglo-Saxon critical or editorial work on *All's Well*. Certainly, it is not included in Bullough's compendium (1957–75, vol. 2) or mentioned in the standard editions. In fact, I had presumed, when I happened upon this narrative by following textual threads picked up from the play itself, that the association had not previously been made. Given scholarship's voracious pursuit of any and all matters Shakespearean, I should not have been surprised to find that this was not the case, and that my concomitant perception of a second Roussillon entering into early audiences' reception of the play had likewise been anticipated.

There are useful lessons to be drawn from this experience. For where I found at least some of my own conclusions already in print was in a 1962 volume of

essays by Georges Lambin (*Voyages de Shakespeare en France et en Italie*).
Lambin's work issues from an early and mid-twentieth century French school
principally inspired by Abel Lefranc (1863–1952), professor at the Collège de
France and a specialist mainly in the French Renaissance. The broad objective
is to discover the 'real' foundations of literature; the orientation is biographical,
the assumptions decidedly 'Old Historicist': texts are presumed to encode
authorial arcana, in which meaning is presumed to consist. A French scholar
regarding *All's Well* from this point of view would be quite likely to realize that
the titles of Count and Countess of Roussillon, in the sixteenth century, were
attached to the family of Tournon and had reference to Roussillon in Dauphiné,
although, as it happens, even Lambin got his information from someone who
knew the region (*Shakespeare et Tournon*, 1954, p. 19). A modicum of genealog-
ical research would then suffice to turn up the Hélène in question – whose life,
in fact, had quite independently become a theme of romantic fiction[17] – as well
as the name of Madeleine (used by Shakespeare for Lafew's daughter).
Evidently, however, such allusion-hunting has failed to engage the imagination
of international Shakespeare scholarship, despite the confidence of certain
practitioners, not only in the particular truths uncovered, but in the imminent
lifting of the veil of Truth itself.[18]

Lambin and myself arrived at our common points – which are telling but
finally not numerous – by very different routes. I preserve the outline of my
own, on the premise that it records lines of textual transmission by which
significance may actually have circulated between author and audience. My
subsequent path, moreover, diverges sharply to pursue a winding course, as
throughout this book, across the indefinite space between textuality and forms
of political and cultural signification. Lambin's allusions claim completeness,
and often forfeit coherence. Thus, since the historical Madeleine (about whom
more will be said) came from the Rochefoucauld family, the father of the
fictional one must be 'LArocheFOUcauld' in disguise ('Lafew' is regularly so
transcribed by Lambin). Likewise, it is not enough that the 'Dumaine' named
in Parolles' denunciations would probably have evoked the Duke of Mayenne;
the whole religious and family politics of the House of Guise must be located
within the scene – with Parolles himself, it turns out, representing the Duke of
Aumale, on the grounds that the latter was also dishonourable and unreliable.
When the mesh is so finely woven, the net is bound to come up full – 'Quel
étonnant coup de filet! [What an astonishing catch!]' (Lambin, 1962, p. 49) –
and Fluellen's 'salmons in both' argument echoes insistently. To take another
example, we have the name of Lavatch evoking 'la vache à Colas' – an expression for Huguenots – yet his intended Isbel somehow stands in for the daughter
of Philip II (pp. 50–51). At least equal precision, moreover, must be imposed

on fictional geography. Thus, the itinerary of Helena en route from Roussillon (*bis*) to Italy, then within Italy, even Florence itself, is tracked with near-electronic exactitude (pp. 34–38). The entire exercise finally serves to demonstrate the familiarity with both geography and history imparted to the playwright by his *Voyages … en France et en Italie* – imparted not, however, to William Shakespeare from Stratford-upon-Avon, but to the 'veritable' author: William Stanley, sixth Earl of Derby.

Obviously, my own study is less concerned with the identities and personal politics of authors than with the ways in which texts acquired meaning for their audiences – even if the means by which authors acquired certain kinds of knowledge sometimes obtrude unavoidably. My final chapter, indeed, might encourage the theory of a Jesuit connection for Shakespeare – hardly a novel idea, but one equally compatible with a knowledge of anti-Jesuit government operations.[19] As my explorations of Hamlet and Antony seek to demonstrate, textual games of multiple identity may entail the kind of meaningful shift in perspective associated with anamorphic effects in painting. Interpretation depends on the angle of vision, and in this respect Shakespeare's method remains as carefully poised as when, in what may be seen as his first venture into morally ambiguous political tragedy, he suspended judgement over the competing claims, by right and by merit, of Richard II and Bullingbrook. By means of its generic disclaimers, *All's Well* may purport to reassure an audience, freeing it from, amongst other burdens, that of political engagement. Yet this book finally offers no more concise instance of the more fundamentally destabilizing potential of anamorphic technique than the coexistence of two contrasting but overlapping Roussillons.

Notes

1   At least through Richard Field, who married Thomas Vautrollier's widow, and the Mountjoy family. See Schoenbaum, 1975, pp. 130–32, 208–13 *et passim*, and Maguin and Maguin, 1996, pp. 306–8, 473–75 *et passim*.

2   Apart from *French Origins* (2010) and *Shakespeare, Marlowe and the Politics of France* (2002), see my articles, 'Des *Champs faëz* de Claude de Taillemont au labyrinthe du *Songe* shakespearien' (2004), and '*A Midsummer Night's Dream* and *La Diane* of Nicolas de Montreux' (2010).

3   As, with enthusiasm, by Hadfield: 'This French collection [the *Histoires tragiques*], used by many English writers in the late sixteenth century, was undoubtedly Shakespeare's principal source' (2005, p. 187).

4   See Jenkins, ed., 1982, p. 96, and Ann Thompson and Neil Taylor, eds, 2006, pp. 66–77.

5   Much will be said of Goulart in the ensuing chapters; he also figures in my *French Origins*, 2010, pp. 9, 14–15n.8 *et passim*.

6   See *Shakespeare, Marlowe and the Politics of France*, 2002, p. 75. I have more recently ('Marlowe's Guise', 2008) proposed a further French dramatic source (one which would advance the *terminus a quo* of the play's composition): *Le Guysien*, by Simon Belyard (pub. 1592).

7   See *L'histoire prodigieuse du doctor Fauste*, Cazaux, ed., 1982, p. 19.

8   On these two points, respectively, see Cazaux, ed., 1982, pp. 16–18 and 120–21n.90.

9   The complex question of the variant 'A' and 'B' texts is not to the point here.

10 See De Grazia, 2006, esp. pp. 45–204 (chapters 3 and 4, entitled, respectively, 'Empires of World History' and 'Generation and Degeneracy').

11 The notion of 'ungrammaticality', borrowed from intertextual theory, as a stumbling-block to linear and unitary reception of a text is fundamental to my critical practice in this study and its predecessor volume. See *French Origins*, 2010, pp. 4 and 14n.4.

12 Hamlet's self-destructiveness has been viewed from many angles but never, I think, through any of the three intertextual lenses interposed here; cf. my own 'Hamlet and Death' (1986); *Shakespearean Subversions*, 1992, pp. 181–85; and *Self-Speaking*, 1997, pp. 133–38, 267–79.

13 The downplaying of French dramatic precedents on the grounds of 'universal dependence' on Plutarch was established early in modern Shakespeare criticism – see Sidney Lee's 1915 biography, p. 410 and p. 410n.1.

14 On the Italian treatments, see Bullough, ed., 1957–75, 5: 222–27.

15 Hopkins's recent exploration of 'The use of the Caesars to discuss contemporary issues' (*The Cultural Uses of the Caesars on the English Renaissance Stage*, 2008, p. 11) ranges widely in its textual and cultural juxtapositions, some of which compel more conviction than others, but never in a French direction. In this regard, my approach through the political baggage carried by Roman material in French texts, though developed before her work appeared, may be taken as a supplement to it.

16 See *French Origins*, pp. 10–11, 46–51 (esp. 48) and 60n.19.

17 See Lefranc, 1926, pp. 17–19.

18 Thus Lefranc effuses:

> Le lien qui jusqu'à présent n'avait jamais pu être établi entre la réalité et les grandes œuvres dramatiques de Shakespeare commence à être entrevu. … Dans la nuit des commentaires traditionnels … un trait de lumière nous apparaît. Suivons-le d'une marche confiante. C'est l'étoile qui nous conduira sans nul doute, comme les rois mages, vers la révélation.
>
> [The connection which till now could never be established between reality and the great dramatic works of Shakespeare begins to be glimpsed. … In the night of traditional commentaries … a beam of light appears to us.

Let us follow it with confident steps. It is the star which undoubtedly shall lead us, like the three kings, to the revelation.] (1926, p. 34)

19 The most notable recent proponent of a Catholic Shakespeare is Richard Wilson; see esp. *Secret Shakespeare* (2004) and his reading of *AWW* in 'To Great St Jaques Bound' (2004). That William Stanley, Earl of Derby, was gathering intelligence on the Tournon Jesuits is Lambin's conjecture to explain 'Shakespeare's' presumed visit (1954, p. 29).

2

Hamlet in three French lights

Part I – The philosophical Hamlet

With respect to Montaigne, the argument can at least start on familiar ground. A number of verbal correspondences – some widely classed as decisive, others as suggestive – establish that Shakespeare drew on the *Essais*, at least in the translation of Florio (in manuscript until 1603), and perhaps also in the original.[1] (The co-influence of the French text is far from universally conceded, but my analysis tends to support the idea.) Most of these correspondences belong to the meditations often loosely termed 'philosophical' of the protagonist – to such a degree, indeed, that Hamlet's thought has come to epitomize the influence of Montaigne on Shakespeare, and especially the impact of the 'Apologie de Raymond Sebond'. That major essay opposes in sustained fashion the two perspectives on the human being – as 'beauty of the world' and as 'quintessence of dust' (II.ii.307–8) – that are contrasted by Hamlet himself. It is the irony of this juxtaposition that, for Robert Ellrodt, 'discloses a kinship in spirit not traceable in the other analogues' (1975, p. 40).

Towards the beginning of the 'Apologie', Montaigne establishes the fragility of the idea that 'ce branle admirable de la voute céleste [this admirable moving of heavens vault]' was made for man, 'cette misérable et chetive creature [this miserable and wreched creature]' who believes himself 'estre seul, en ce grand bastimant, qui ayt la suffisance d'en recognoistre la beauté et les pièces [to be the onely absolute creature in this huge worlds-frame, perfectly able to know the absolute beautie, and severall parts thereof]' (ed. Villey and Saulnier, 1978, II, 12, 450A; trans. Florio, ed. Harmer, 1965, 2: 139). This is the illusion that appears to have collapsed for Hamlet, who complains to Rosencrantz and Guildenstern that he has recently 'lost all my mirth, foregone all custom of exercises' (II.ii.296–97), so that 'this goodly frame the earth seems to me a sterile promontory, … this brave o'erhanging firmament … a foul and pestilent congregation of vapours' (298–303). In the abstract, however, he well knows that man is a 'piece of work' unparalleled:

how noble in reason, how infinite in faculties, in form and moving how express and admirable, in action how like an angel, in apprehension how like a god: the beauty of the world, the paragon of animals. (303–7)

Across Hamlet's appropriation of it, the vocabulary of Montaigne (and/or Florio) slips away from the creation ('huge world's-frame', 'admirable moving', 'beauty' – even 'pièces') towards the creature, ironically driving home the essayist's point regarding human vanity. But Hamlet's intellectual manœuvres also enact the essay's essential paradoxical procedure with regard to reason. Hamlet presents his pessimistic thoughts as a deviation from his reason (itself very much in question at this point), even as he is busily deploying reason as a weapon against his adversaries. To employ reason against reason – that is the tactical method of the 'Apologie'; but in the end, is it not to make an opponent of oneself?

For Hamlet at this point, as in the soliloquies where he more openly squares off against himself, it is reason, assimilated to 'discourse', that raises man above the beasts and brings him closer to the divine: 'a beast that wants discourse of reason' (I.ii.150); ' … A beast, no more. / Sure he that made us with such large discourse, / … gave us not / That capability and godlike reason / To fust in us unus'd' (IV.iv.35–39). The same commonplace, however, less optimistically informs the sceptical heart of the 'Apologie', whose premise is that 'nos raisons et nos discours humains, c'est comme la matière lourde et sterile: la grace de Dieu en est la forme [our reason and humane discourse, is as the lumpish and barren matter; and the grace of God is the forme thereof]' (ed. Villey and Saulnier, 1978, II, 12, 447A; trans. Florio, ed. Harmer, 1965, 2: 136).[2] 'Sterile', of course, as in the French – not Florio's 'barren', and a rare word in Shakespeare – is Hamlet's term for his perception of the earth.

It is in terms of such innate deficiency that the essayist issues his challenge to mankind, using a highly pertinent image:

Considerons donq pour cette heure l'homme seul, sans secours estranger, armé seulement de ses armes, et despourveu de la grace et cognoissance divine, qui est tout son honneur, sa force et le fondement de son estre. … Qu'il me face entendre, par l'effort de son discours, sur quels fondamens il a basty ces grands avantages qu'il pense avoir sur les autres creatures.

[Let us now but consider man alone without other help, armed but with his own weapons, and unprovided of the grace and knowledge of God, which is all his honour, all his strength, and all the ground of his being. … Let him with the utmost power of his discourse make me understand, upon what foundation, he hath built those great advantages and ods, he supposeth to have over other creatures.] (ed. Villey and Saulnier, 1978, II, 12, 449–50A; trans. Florio, ed. Harmer, 1965, 2: 139)

Later, in his letter to Claudius, Hamlet will represent himself as similarly unprovided: "'High and mighty, you shall know that I am set naked on your kingdom'"
… And in a postscript here he says "Alone"' (IV.vii.42–51). He will even declare
himself converted to the principle – common ground between Montaigne and
Saint Paul (1 Cor. 3:19) – that 'nostre sagesse n'est que folie devant Dieu [all
our wisdome is but folly before God]' (ed. Villey and Saulnier, 1978, II, 12,
449A; trans. Florio, ed. Harmer, 1965, 2: 138), when he affirms to Horatio, by
way of Montaigne/Florio, that 'There's a divinity that shapes our ends, /
Rough-hew them how we will' (V.ii.10–11). But at the same moment he will
boast of the eminently rational stratagem by which he has rid himself of Rosencrantz and Guildenstern, while his acceptance of the fencing match hardly
demonstrates that he is well able to separate wisdom from folly. For that matter,
if 'l'homme qui présume de son sçavoir, ne sçait pas encore que c'est que sçavoir
[man, who presumeth of his knowledge, doth not yet know what knowledge
is]' (ed. Villey and Saulnier, 1978, II, 12, 449A; trans. Florio, ed. Harmer, 1965,
2: 138),[3] how can one distinguish between hope and despair? The argument
is as well adapted to suicide as to the leap of faith prescribed by Montaigne's
fideism. To entrust oneself to 'a divinity that shapes our ends', or to 'a special
providence in the fall of a sparrow' (V.ii.215–16), might amount to embracing
nothingness: 'Since no man of aught he leaves, knows, what is't to leave betimes'
(218–20).[4]

I

We are so thoroughly accustomed to a reflective Hamlet that we underestimate
the disorientation probably experienced by early audiences. Not that the
running commentary on his grievances and prospective vengeance would have
surprised: these were already present in the narrative of Belleforest, while
Thomas Nashe's mocking allusion to 'whole Hamlets … of tragicall speeches'
(Preface to *Menaphon*, cited Jenkins, ed., 1982, p. 83) suggests that they
abounded also in the so-called *Ur-Hamlet*, presumably by Kyd. To judge from
The Spanish Tragedy, the original play may also have exploited the imputation
of madness that Belleforest inherited from Saxo Grammaticus. But nothing
suggests that in any precursor version the hero does other than pursue his
vindictive course in the face of concrete obstacles: such may be considered the
'grammar' of the revenge-play genre.[5]

In Shakespeare, by contrast, that grammar is multiply disrupted. The Mousetrap, which might have led to the murderer's public exposure and punishment,
is placed near the middle of the play and fulfils neither of those functions. The
protagonist disconcertingly agrees to be shipped off to England at the very

moment when he declares himself ready to act. Most flagrantly, the plot by which the revenge is accomplished is not his own but that of his enemies, and he walks into the trap with no apparent plan but with a strong presentiment of imminent death. That Hamlet achieves his revenge before succumbing to the double treachery deployed against him depends on mere chance – to the point of recalling the heavy authorial hand that imposes tragedy on the story of Lear. Decidedly, to accept an invitation to a fencing match from the two men who Hamlet well knows have every reason to see him dead seems anything but an exercise of reason.

What a strange notion, finally, to end a story of revenge with a counter-plot of which the revenger was likely to have been the only victim. And where could such a notion have come from? Not from Saxo or Belleforest: in their versions the hero directly confronts the royal murderer, having first taken every measure to assure success. The device might have come from Kyd, but there is a sharp contrast with the eminently logical conclusion of that author's surviving revenge play, not to mention the models of Seneca. There is only one element in the source-tale that appears to have been reworked for the fencing match and might conceivably have inspired it: in Saxo and Belleforest, the hero tricks the king by replacing the latter's sword with his own, which had been nailed to its scabbard to prevent him from harming himself in his supposed madness. This deception may lie behind the exchange of rapiers that improbably makes possible Hamlet's revenge.

Yet if the conclusion violates the story's logical 'grammar', it simultaneously fulfils a contrary logic of character put in place almost from the start. The fencing match to which Hamlet commits himself reluctantly, despite an inner voice urging the contrary, serves as the metaphor *par excellence* for his ambiguous moves with regard to the task imposed by his father's spirit – for the double game with others and himself by which he pursues his goal on one level, while, on another, drawing closer to destruction. His acceptance thus enacts his fundamental self-division between being and not-being, between man conceived as the 'beauty of the world', for whom action is possible, and as the 'quintessence of dust', drawn to annihilation. To provoke his own death at the hands of his self-produced *semblable* ('For by the image of my cause I see / The portraiture of his' [V.ii.77–78]) amounts to suicide – his initial desire, after all – but within the role of dedicated revenger.

II

The *Essais* intervene intertextually virtually from the start in Hamlet's self-negotiations. One of the first 'ungrammaticalities' associated with the role of revenger recalls a specific weakness avowed by Montaigne. When the father's Ghost urges the son to 'Remember me' (I.v.91), the latter spontaneously declares that he will retain nothing but that 'commandment' (102) in 'the table of my memory' (98), then immediately, in a bizarre gesture, takes out his actual 'tables' to write on. If this already suggests a fear, not only of forgetting, but of having his will to act subverted, such a sequence of ideas is resonantly confirmed by the words of Montaigne, when the latter complains of his untrustworthy memory:

> Je ne sçaurois recevoir une charge sans tablettes. ... Cecy que je sens en la memoire, je le sens en plusieurs autre parties. Je fuis le commandement, l'obligation et la contrainte. Ce que je fais ayséement et naturellement, si je m'ordonne de le faire par une expresse et prescrite ordonnance, je ne le sçay plus faire.

> [I cannot receive a charge, except I have my writing tables about me. ... And what I feele in my memorie, I feele in many other parts of mine. I eschew commandement, duty, and compulsion. What I doe easily and naturally, if I resolve to doe it by expresse and prescribed appointment, I can then doe it no more.](ed. Villey and Saulnier, 1978, II, 17, 649–50A; trans. Florio, ed. Harmer, 1965, 2: 375–76)

Thus an image drawn from Montaigne at once takes centre-stage to announce the de-centring of vengeance. This intertextual ill-omen is borne out through the debates that the hero initiates with himself on the subject of fulfilling his 'charge', as he is far from doing 'easily and naturally'.

The *Essais* likewise frame Hamlet's self-reorientation towards the vanity of heroic effort in the face of death. In the graveyard he allows his 'imagination' – contrary to the advice of Horatio ("Twere to consider too curiously to consider so' [V.i.199]) – to follow the 'noble dust', first of Alexander, then of Caesar, to the basest of uses. The association of these two heroes is commonplace enough; so is the allusion to Alexander, at least, as a *memento mori*.[6] But Montaigne's extended comparison between the two heroes (II, 34) has already made itself felt in Hamlet's meditations. '[T]o take arms against a sea of troubles / And by opposing end them' (III.i.59–60) perhaps evokes, as editors record, the practice of desperate Celtic warriors.[7] In any case, the suggestion of action leading to death is imbricated with the motif of encountering one's doom sword-in-hand. A hero, then, may himself take on the elemental force of rushing water – at least until reason intervenes, after which

> ... the native hue of resolution
> Is sicklied o'er with the pale cast of thought
> And enterprises of great pitch and moment

> With this regard their currents turn awry
> And lose the name of action.
>
> (86–88)

In his own deliberations on heroism, Montaigne reckons Caesar

> un peu plus retenu et consideré en ses entreprinses qu'Alexandre: car cettuy-cy
> semble rechercher et courir à force les dangers, comme un impetueux torrent
> qui choque et attaque sans discretion et sans chois tout ce qu'il rencontre.
>
> [somewhat more warie and considerate in his enterprises, than *Alexander*; for
> the latter seemeth to seek out, and by maine force to runne into dangers, as an
> impetuous or raging torrent, which without heede, discretion, or choise, shockes
> and checkmates what ere it meteeth withall.] (ed. Villey and Saulnier, 1978, II,
> 34, 739A; trans. Florio, ed. Harmer, 1965, 2: 468)

Even in Caesar, 'resolution' seems to have possessed a fatalistic, if not suicidal, dimension: 'il me semble lire en plusieurs de ses exploits une certaine résolution de se perdre, pour fuyr la honte d'estre vaincu [me seemeth I reade in diverse of his exploits, a certain resolution rather to lose himself, then to abide the brunt or shame to be overthrowne]' (ed. Villey and Saulnier, 1978, II, 34, 740A; trans. Florio, ed. Harmer, 1965, 2: 469) – that is, in effect, 'to suffer / The slings and arrows of outrageous fortune' (III.i.57–58).[8]

Montaigne continues: 'Et quant aux entreprinses qu'il a faites à main armée, il y en a plusieurs qui surpassent en hazard tout discours de raison militaire [And concerning the enterprises he underwent with armed hand, there are divers of them, which in respect of the hazard, exceed all discourse of military reason]'. Besides, again, the lexical overlap, it is worth emphasizing the conclusion that such courage, which might otherwise be accounted the 'hardiesse temeraire [rash fond-hardinesse]' (ed. Villey and Saulnier, 1978, II, 34, 741A; trans. Florio, ed. Harmer, 1965, 2: 471) of youth, signals that 'Ces gens là ont eu je ne sçay quelle plus qu'humaine confiance de leur fortune [such men have had a kinde of more than humane confidence of their fortune]' (ed. Villey and Saulnier, 1978, II, 34, 740A; trans. Florio, ed. Harmer, 1965, 2: 469). Hamlet, by contrast, while in the grip of indecision, deems fortune his 'outrageous' adversary.

Yet before he accepts the proposition of Laertes and Claudius, Hamlet re-imagines his relation with fortune – or, rather, re-images 'fortune' as 'a divinity that shapes our ends' (V.ii.10). He convinces himself, as he explains to Horatio, that 'rashness' has saved his life (6–9). This change of perspective is all the more striking because it contrasts with his praise of Horatio in Act III. There, he was still putting a premium on Stoical endurance:

> ... thou hast been
> As one, in suff'ring all, that suffers nothing,
> A man that Fortune's buffets and rewards
> Hast ta'en with equal thanks; and blest are those
> Whose blood and judgement are so well commeddled
> That they are not a pipe for Fortune's finger
> To sound what stop she please.
>
> (III.ii.65–71)

Again, the 'Apologie' provides an intertextual measure of Hamlet's intellectual evolution:

> Nostre esprit est un util vagabond, dangereux et temeraire; il est malaisé d'y joindre l'ordre et la mesure. ... Certes il est peu d'ames si reiglées, si fortes et bien nées, à qui on se puisse fier de leur propre conduicte, et qui puissent, avec moderation et sans temerité, voguer en liberté de leurs jugements au delà des opinions communes. ... C'est un outrageux glaive que l'esprit à son possesseur mesme, pour qui ne sçait s'en armer ordonnément et discrettement.

> [Our spirit is a vagabond, a dangerous, and fond-hardy implement; it is very hard to joyne order and measure to it. ... Verily, there are few soules, so orderly, so constant, and so well borne, as may be trusted with their owne conduct, and may with moderation, and without rashnes, saile in the liberty of their judgments beyond common opinions. ... *The spirit is an outragious glaive, yea even to his owne possessor, except he have the grace, very orderly and discreetly to arme himself there-with.*] (ed. Villey and Saulnier, 1978, II, 12, 559A,B,C; trans. Florio, ed. Harmer, 1965, 2: 271–72)

In deciding finally that 'Our indiscretion sometimes serves us well' (V.ii.8), Hamlet has found another model, that of Alexander, who 'seemeth to seek out, and by maine force to runne into dangers, as an impetuous or raging torrent, which without heede, discretion, or choise, shockes and checkmates what ere it meteeth withall' – and why not, since, after all, the common destiny is dust? In taking up 'rash fond-hardinesse' as his weapon, he reveals himself to be armed with a 'spirit' that is 'an outragious glaive, yea even to his owne possessor' – all the more so because his 'madness' has made him behave outrageously to the 'image of [his] cause'. He now sees himself reflected, not in Horatio, but in Laertes, whom he has put on guard: 'though I am not splenative and rash, / Yet have I in me something dangerous, / Which let thy wiseness fear' (V.i.254–56).[9] Hamlet has found out that new self-image by exercising his 'discourse of reason', the 'continual practice' (V.ii.207) of intellectual fencing that has replaced 'all custom of exercises' (II.ii.296–97) under the influence of his melancholic thought. There is more divergence than he admits from

Laertes, who is endowed, as Claudius has learned from the Frenchman Lamord, with a 'masterly report / For art and exercise in [his] defence / And for [his] rapier most especial' (IV.vii.95–97).[10]

III

Montaigne's description of the mind as an 'outragious glaive' marks an exceptional turn taken by the 'Apologie' at its conclusion, a *mise-en-abyme* exposing the danger of giving free rein to reason in order to devalue reason. He urges a learned lady (probably Marguerite de Valois[11]), 'en vos opinions et en vos discours, autant qu'en vos mœurs et en toute autre chose, la moderation et l'attrempance et la fuite de la nouvelleté et de l'estrangeté. [*I persuade you, in your opinions and discourses, as much as in your customes, and in every other thing, to use moderation and temperance, and avoide all newfangled inventions and strangeness*]' (ed. Villey and Saulnier, 1978, II, 12, 558A; trans. Florio, ed. Harmer, 1965, 2: 271). In thus pursuing the middle way – like Horatio, without 'consider[ing] too curiously', for Montaigne agrees that 'il ne faict mie bon estre si subtil et si fin [it is not good to be so subtill, and so curious]' – she may 'maintenir vostre Sebond par la forme ordinaire d'argumenter dequoy vous estes tous les jours instruite, et exercerez en cela vostre esprit et vostre estude [maintaine your Sebond, with the ordinary form of arguing, whereof you are daily instructed, and will therein exercise both your mind and study]' (ed. Villey and Saulnier, 1978, II, 12, 557–58A; trans. Florio, ed. Harmer, 1965, 2: 270). Otherwise, she runs the following risk, to which Montaigne, like Hamlet, subjects himself:

> car ce dernier tour d'escrime icy,[12] il ne le faut employer que comme un extreme remede. C'est un coup desesperé, auquel il faut abandonner vos armes pour faire perdre à vostre adversaire les siennes, et un tour secret, duquel il se faut servir rarement et reservéement. C'est grand temerité de vous perdre vous mesmes pour perdre un autre.
>
> Il ne faut pas vouloir mourir pour se venger …
>
> [For this last trick of fence, must not be employed but as an extreme remedy. It is a desperate thrust, gainst which you must forsake your weapons, to force your adversary to renounce his, and a secret slight, which must seldome and very sparingly be put in practise. *It is a great fond-hardinesse to lose our selfe for the losse of another*. A man must not be willing to die to revenge himself …] (ed. Villey and Saulnier, 1978, II, 12, 558A,B; trans. Florio, ed. Harmer, 1965, 2: 270)

Is Montaigne, who was a thorough connoisseur of fencing, referring here to some veritable 'tour secret'? On the one hand, specialists in the sword-play of the period appear unaware of such a manœuvre; on the other hand, a true secret would not necessarily be disclosed in the published manuals.[13] Whatever the case, this imagistic distillation of Montaigne's thought, like his mention of the writing tablets, effectively takes concrete form on stage to represent a protagonist who indeed appears determined to 'die to revenge himself'. For while the original staging must remain obscure in its finer details, it seems highly probable that, at one moment or another, Hamlet is intended to disarm himself.

Almost certainly, the match is played with rapier and dagger (V.ii.142). After the wound revealing the treachery, a desperate Hamlet might well rid himself of one of his weapons, or even both, in order to wrest the dangerous foil from the hands of Laertes, who would then take up that of the prince. A reader of Florio might also have transferred the desperation to Laertes, as would suit the latter's initial failures to score a hit and Claudius' sceptical, 'I do not think't' (299). Florio's dubious translation of 'auquel' (meaning 'whereby'[14]) as 'gainst which' suggests that it is a 'coup desesperé' received from an adversary that might provoke the tactic of disarming. Such a reading would mandate the common staging in which Laertes initiates the mutually fatal sequence with a sudden treacherous stroke. In any case, for Hamlet to render himself more vulnerable for the sake of his revenge constitutes the next eminently logical step in the series of blows delivered with the 'outrageux glaive à son possesseur mesme' that his 'spirit' has become under the influence of his father's. Hamlet thus finally resolves his famous 'question' rather as Alexander dealt with the Gordian knot, by *rashly* enacting a refusal to choose that enables him at once 'to suffer / The slings and arrows of outrageous fortune' and 'to take arms against a sea of troubles / And by opposing end them.'

Part II – The political Hamlet

The metaphysical complications attached by Shakespeare to the protagonist of Saxo/Belleforest are rooted in an essentially political dilemma. Hamlet's malcontent and menacing behaviour, projected into the Mousetrap, is presumed to revolve around his anomalous position vis-à-vis the throne of Denmark; the 'mystery' whose 'heart' his erstwhile friends would 'pluck out' (III.ii.356–57) is understood as his political intention. For Rosencrantz and Guildenstern are spies, first and foremost, and of a kind eminently recognizable for an audience familiar with the game of statecraft as played throughout early modern Europe. Such recognition is enforced, I will be suggesting, by gestures towards situations and paradigms familiar from contemporary political and historical discourse. The effect is to set in motion a referential dimension which, while hovering beyond the confines of the text, imposes a shifting of perspective: Hamlet is alternatively focused as a precociously modern tragic subject – a site of self-struggle – and as a political actor.

I

Whether or not we give literal credence to the Gravedigger's 'thirty years' (V.i.157),[15] the prince certainly does not begin the play as Belleforest's (and folklore's) wily child, feigning the fool until old enough to accomplish his long-planned revenge. Amleth takes refuge in political non-entity, even if later, in his justificatory oration to the people, he speaks of being pitied for the loss of his heritage along with his personal sufferings (Gollancz, ed., 1926, pp. 275–76).[16] As this would suggest, the rules of the political game in Belleforest are reductively feudal, assimilating the honour of the royal family to the general welfare. It is taken for granted, not least by the prince himself, that Amleth will emerge as 'legitime successeur du Royaume [lawfull successor in the kingdom]' and liberator from 'le joug du tyran [the yoke of the tyrant]' at the same moment when he becomes the 'juste vengeur d'un crime sur tout autre le plus grief et punissable [just revenger of a crime above al others most grievous and punishable]' (1926, pp. 280–81). Confident in his 'fortune', certain that 'la gloire' is 'la couronne de vertue et le prix de constance [glorie is the crown of vertue, and the price (prize) of constancie]', and disdaining 'la poltronnerie ... qui retarde le cœur des gaillardes entreprises [villany ... that withholdeth the heart from valiant interprises]', the prince takes for granted his right and capacity to punish the murdering usurper: 'mon vassal, qui s'est forfait desloyaument contre son seigneur, et soverain Prince [my subject, that hath disloyaly behaved himselfe against his lord and soveraigne prince]' (1926, p. 226–27). His confidence proves justified, even if the story will carry on through new twists and turns and ultimately to an unhappy ending, with Amleth betrayed to his death by his second wife (as it happens, the Queen of Scotland).

Amleth's triumph over Fengo, at least, is in conspicuous contrast to the failure of the Shakespearean hero. Hamlet manages to fulfil his revenge only at the cost of his family's ruin and his country's loss of sovereignty. Personally, he is left with only enough breath to bestow his 'dying voice' in the prospective 'election' (V.ii.361) on the same foreign prince whose menace of invasion the murderer had successfully forestalled. In Shakespeare's version, moreover, the prince's other victims are far from ciphers, or even unequivocal villains. A primitive warrior culture is updated to a recognizably early modern political society, in which personal grievance and familial honour take on destabilizing potential within the 'state of Denmark' (I.v.90).

The potential of Shakespeare's Hamlet to have succeeded at his father's death, as is not the case in Belleforest, immediately makes him a factor on the political scene. So Claudius acknowledges in publicly proclaiming him 'the most immediate to our throne' (I.ii.109), then later (disingenuously or not) in blaming his tolerance of Polonius' murder on the prince's popularity (IV.vii.16 ff.). Gertrude's role, however indefinite, as 'imperial jointress to this warlike state' (I.ii.9) gives her remarriage a political dimension lacking in the original – one that ties in, however indistinctly, with Hamlet's later complaint that Claudius 'Popp'd in between th'election and my hopes' (V.ii.65). Finally, the 'deux ... fideles ministres de Fengon [two of Fengons faithfull ministers]' (pp. 232–33) who accompany Amleth to England are, of course, made over into Hamlet's former friends and called upon earlier by Claudius to ferret out his inner thoughts, as they do on the assumption (far from discouraged by Hamlet himself) that he suffers from 'ambition' (II.ii.252 ff.), despite having 'the voice of the King himself for your succession in Denmark' (III.ii.332–33). On this level, too, the natural trajectory of the source is thwarted, since he is never 'put on', never enabled 'To have proved most royal' (V.ii.404–5). The loud speaking of 'The soldier's music and the rite of war' (404) offered as his epitaph carries the ironic resonance of anticlimax.

It is the political dimension, too, that provides the most objective measure of that notoriously vexed question of character: Hamlet's 'delay' – likewise a question that does not arise in Belleforest. Of course, an entire school of criticism banishes that question from the play by making practical and moral excuses for Hamlet (excuses that he never makes for himself – on the contrary). But when the broad political outcome is considered, it is at least difficult to clear the prince of gross misjudgement and mismanagement. Again, the source tale throws the change into relief, giving the protagonist not just the cunning to succeed in his private affair but the sophistication to capitalize publicly on his success. Shakespeare himself, just a year or so before he wrote *Hamlet*, had adopted from Plutarch the contrast between Brutus's communicative failure and Antony's resounding success; he had also just portrayed, in Henry V, a particularly effective translator of personal ambition into public policy. Yet of Hamlet he chose to make a conspicuous failure in public relations.

Regarded specifically as a politician, Hamlet exemplifies a fatal combination of activity and passivity, impetuosity and irresolution, simplicity and over-cleverness, credulity and cynicism – in short, in his own terms, of 'rashness' and 'discretion'. As surely as 'indirections find directions out' (II.i.66) – to cite Polonius, another would-be political 'calf' who finds himself in the abattoir when he thinks he is in the theatre (see III.ii.102–5) – Hamlet's indecision decidedly writes him out of the effective political role that he began with the power to play. And his final decision seals the preceding ones. When he refuses

Horatio's sensible proposal of a tactical delay – 'If your mind dislike anything, obey it. I will forestall their repair hither and say you are not fit' (V.ii.213–14) – and instead entrusts himself to the 'special providence in the fall of a sparrow' (215–16), Hamlet chooses the worst possible moment to be reborn out of scepticism into faith.

The traditional compendia of political *exempla* (even if one adds Machiavelli to the corpus) offer no obvious precedent for a prince of Hamlet's peculiar stamp. The elusive but sustained portrayal of Hamlet as a political (non-)actor thus finally feeds back into his larger 'mystery' and, for criticism, becomes assimilable to the playwright's originality in character-drawing. To this solution I wish to offer resistance in the form of a large material move: I propose the intertextual intervention of a particular historical model, one sufficiently familiar to a contemporary audience to switch its perceptions – though in a teasing and indefinite way – onto a different imaginative track. The model is bound up, again, with the 'ungrammaticality' of the fencing match.

II

Hamlet's grossly inopportune discovery of a faith in providence that overrides prudence has often been taken as suddenly and strangely at odds with his metaphysical doubting. His formulation is so indistinct, however, and the 'readiness' that is 'all' (V.ii.219) so strongly smacks, in the urgent context, of a doubtfully Christian wish to be rid of it all, that, once again, his 'mystery' tends to prevail. True, when Amleth uses an analogous image, it is to cast himself in an active, not a passive, role: 'c'est sottement faict, que de cueillir un fruict avant saison [it is foolishly done to gather fruit before it is ripe]' (pp. 226–27). Still, partisans of an heroic but Christian Hamlet may take comfort in his near-citation of scripture, for, as is universally recognized, the 'fall of a sparrow' alludes to Matthew 10:29.

Arguably, however, the biblical context is more richly pertinent than is usually noticed – to the point of uncannily anticipating Hamlet's own mixture of cunning and naïveté, his conciliatory address to the 'brother' (V.ii.240, 249) who will betray him, and the play's preoccupation with the mutual destruction of parents and children. In the full gospel passage, Christ is warning the apostles about the dangers they will face and enjoining them to courageous resolution for the sake of the faith:

> Beholde, I send you as shepe in the middes of wolues: be ye therefore wise as serpentes, and innocent as doues.
> But beware of men, for they will deliuer you vp to the Councils, and will scourge you in their Synagogues.

And ye shall be broght to the gouernours and Kings for my sake, in witnes to them and to the Gentiles.

But when they deliuer you vp, take no thoght how or what ye shal spake: for it shal be giuen you in that houre, what ye shall say.

For it is not ye that speake, but the spirit of your Father whiche speaketh in you.

And the brother shall betray the brother to death, and the father the sonne, and the children shall rise against (their) parents, and cause them to dye.

...

And feare ye not them which kil the bodie but are not able to kill the soule: but rather feare him, whiche is able to destroye bothe soule and bodie in hel.

Are not two sparrowes solde for a farthing and one of them shall not fall on the ground without your Father?

Yea, and all the heeres of you[r] heade are nombred.

Feare ye not therefore, ye are of more value than manie sparrowes.
                                        (Matt. 10:16–31)[17]

In so far as Hamlet accompanies the fulfilment of his vengeance by his only direct verbal attack on Claudius, might not an auditor be tempted to adapt verse 20 as a gloss: 'For it is not ye that speake, but the spirit of your Father whiche speaketh in you'?[18] For when Hamlet explodes, 'Here, thou incestuous, murd'rous, damned Dane ...' (V.ii.330), he at last delivers the message of his 'father's spirit – in arms!' (I.ii.255).

Yet, finally, to overlay Hamlet's situation on the biblical text confirms the template as fundamentally askew. It is indeed not the Hamlet we have previously heard who speaks here. And neither his earlier image of himself as the 'scourge and minister' of 'heaven' (III.iv.175–77), nor his belated submission to providence, nor his posthumous commendation by Horatio to 'flights of angels' (V.ii.365) convincingly assimilates his vindictive worldly 'cause' (77) to that of the apostles. For that matter, while Claudius is undoubtedly a villain, and arguably an abusive governor, he is no pagan tyrant bent on martyring the faithful; on the contrary, his pangs of conscience strike the closest thing to an authentically Christian note in the play. Stubbornly, this tableau of personal and political intrigue resists translation onto the religious plane.

III

For these very reasons, the scriptural echo might well have struck Shakespeare's auditors as multiply, and ironically, apposite. As has been observed, Hamlet's reference to 'special providence' – providence, that is, on the level of particular events – evokes Calvin.[19] It is indeed to illustrate this point that Calvin cites Matthew 10:29–31 in the *Institution of the Christian Religion*.[20] The term itself does not figure, however, in the biblical passages (or, for that matter, in their Genevan glosses), and to this extent the play-text is technically 'ungrammatical'. By contrast, 'providence' is similarly integrated into the biblical reference at an analogous climactic moment in a cluster of French narratives likely to have been familiar to many Elizabethans and significant for a fair number.

The *Histoire de l'estat de France, tant de la république que de la religion, sous le règne de François II*, published pseudonymously in 1576, is presumably the work of Louis Régnier de La Planche, secretary to the son of Anne de Montmorency, Constable of France. It thus originated in the milieu that opposed the powerful House of Montmorency to that of the Guises, a struggle intensely focused during the brief reign (1559–60) of the young François II, whom the Guises succeeded in dominating, as they plotted to destroy enemies and rivals, real and potential, including the Princes of the Blood descended from the House of Bourbon. Régnier has just narrated the story of the latest and most spectacular – almost incredible, as he affirms (*Histoire*, 1576, p. 707) – of a series of plots by which the Guises (principally François, Duke of Guise, and his brother Charles, Cardinal of Lorraine) sought to entrap the life of Antoine de Bourbon, Count of Vendôme and King of Navarre. The latter had seemed poised to play an Apostolic role on behalf of Reformed religion ever since his public participation in Protestant hymn-singing and processions in the Pré-aux-Clercs outside the walls of Paris on 16 May 1557 – an event that rocked the court of Henri II.

The Guises' first plot had involved poison, the second a pistol-shot. For the third attempt, they arranged for the fifteen-year-old monarch to conceal a knife, summon Navarre to his private chamber, then provoke him by accusation and insult into violent anger; at this point, the king was supposed to stab Navarre, whereupon the others would finish him off. This plot, however, petered out – providentially:

> Il ne faut nullement douter, que la vertu de Dieu, qui bride la rage des meschans, & tient en sa main le cœur des Roys, ne sestendist sur l'vn & sur l'autre: Sur le Roy, pour ne luy permettre estre parricide, commettant en son sang vn si lasche tour: & sur le Roy de Nauarre aussi, pour luy faire paroistre, qu'vn seul cheueu de nostre teste ne peut tomber sans sa prouidence, quelques asseurances que puissent prendre les meschans de leurs coniurations.

> [There is no doubt that the power of God, who restrains the hearts of evil-doers and holds in His hand the hearts of kings, extended itself upon one and the other: upon the king, lest he be permitted to become a parricide, committing such a cowardly slight against his own blood; and also upon the King of Navarre, to

make it manifest to him that a single hair of our head cannot fall without His providence, whatever assurances the wicked might harbour regarding their conspiracies.] (Régnier, *Histoire*, 1576, pp. 710–11)

The opening of the passage draws on the much-cited Proverbs 21:1 – 'The Ki[n]g's heart is in the hand of the Lord …' – while the invocation of providence draws the conclusion towards Hamlet's variant on Matthew 10:29, although Hamlet is more accurate in applying the 'fall' to the sparrow. Obviously, we are dealing with a cluster of Calvinist intertexts.[21] What is specifically likely to have activated the French narrative for audiences of the play – and Régnier's version is far from isolated, as will be shown – is the context: the 'coniurations' of 'meschans'.

The situational parallel with the conspiracy of Claudius and Laertes is supported by the suspenseful charging, in closely overlapping terms, of the liminal moment when the prospective victim decides to obey the summons despite his foreboding. For in Navarre's case, as well, there is a faithful companion, his friend since childhood (one Jacques de Ranty[22]), to whom he confides his fear. He is advised not to go and at first agrees, but, 'A la fin poussé d'vn cœur magnanime, & aussi que la pureté de sa conscience en ce fait, l'empeschoit d'apprehender ceste mort, il se resolut d'y aller', affirming, 'S'il plaist à Dieu, il me sauuera' (Régnier, *Histoire*, pp. 709–10). Hamlet, too, is sure of his 'perfect conscience' (V.ii.67); for him, too, the heart is the site of struggle with fear and of self-mastery: 'Thou wouldst not think how ill all's here about my heart' (208–9). And its recovered courage resounds at least in Horatio's epitaph: 'Now cracks a noble heart' (364).

There are enough contemporary references in French and English to establish this episode, though pre-dating *Hamlet* by forty years, as thoroughly integrated within Huguenot mythology, having been multiply recycled. And its authority was impeccable, for the section of Régnier's *Histoire* in question was based, with relatively slight variations in wording – though one of them is especially telling, as I will argue – on the *Mémoires* of Antoine's wife, Jeanne d'Albret, Queen of Navarre.[23] (The latter, of course, who survived her husband by ten years, independently developed a far more deeply rooted commitment to Reform and emerged as a major political and moral force.) The incident received the endorsement of, amongst other authorities, the *Histoire ecclésiastique des églises réformées du Royaume de France* (1580), widely attributed to the Calvinist theologian and man of letters, Théodore de Bèze (Baum and Cunitz, eds, 1974, 1: 391 [p. 437]).[24] An abridged account, without the biblical reference but crediting 'la prouidence de Dieu' ['mercifvll prouidence'] and supplying the gloss 'miracvleusement', is also contained in Goulart's *Histoire des choses mémorables* (1599, p. 117; *An historical collection*, 1598, p. 83).[25] It is Régnier, however – the tireless enemy in other propaganda, too, of the House of Lorraine[26] – whose narrative verve and passionate sense of the stakes involved still make for compelling reading, all the more so because he supplies an explicit dramatic perspective:

> Durant ce regne, la France seruit de theatre où furent jouées plusieurs terribles tragédies, que la posterité à juste occasion admirera & detestera tout ensemble.
>
> [During this reign, France served as a theatre in which a number of terrible tragedies were played, which posterity with good reason will at one and the same time marvel at and abhor.] (*Histoire*, 1576, p. 765)[27]

Régnier was not only a narrator but a subject of narrative. He was, in fact, sufficiently implicated in key events of the time to have been personally interrogated by Catherine de Medici regarding the abortive Protestant uprising in March 1560 known as the 'tumulte' or 'conjuration' of Amboise.[28] On that occasion also he reportedly made a spirited defence of the Princes of the Blood to the detriment of the House of Lorraine. This is according to Pierre de La Place, whose *Commentaires de l'estat de la religion et république* were published in 1565, with an English translation (*The fyrst parte of commentaries, etc.*) – or, rather, the translation of a Latin abridgement (*Rervm in Gallia ob religionem gestarvm libri tres*, 1570) – appearing in the post-Bartholomew year of 1573.[29] La Place does not deal with the particular moment of drama evoked by Régnier, but like the latter he vividly evokes the reigning atmosphere of plotting, counterplotting and espionage: in fact, during Régnier's first interrogation by the Queen Mother, the Cardinal of Lorraine and others are said to have been eavesdropping, 'cachez derrière vne tappisserie [hidden behind a wall-hanging]' (1565, fol. 66ᵛ); the English version makes him a solitary spy and draws even the vocabulary in the direction of *Hamlet*: 'But all the whyle that he had this talke with the Queene, the Cardinal of *Loraine*, was hydde behinde the Tapistrie clothes ['post tapeta' in the *Rervm in Gallia … libri tres*, 1570, p. 33] that hung before the wall of the Closet' (1573, p. 60).[30] This story, too, made its way into Goulart's *An Historical Collection*, with 'the Cardinall standing behinde the tapistrie' (1598, p. 73).

To the extent that 'providence' may be implicated in both the cases of Hamlet and Navarre, the former was apparently marked for death, the latter for miraculous survival. In Régnier's full narrative, however, the miracle takes on a distinct tarnish. For the pacific outcome more practically depended on Navarre's utter refusal to be provoked. As soon as he entered the chamber, the Guises leapt to close the door and the king launched into his rude assault, but Navarre, using to greater effect the mollifying tactic that Hamlet employs (half-heartedly?) with Laertes, remained so mild in his replies that the king was denied any pretext for violence. There is at least a contrast with Antoine's heroic resolve, if not an acceptance of dishonour hardly befitting a nobleman, much less the first Prince of the Blood – honour being notably, of course, the point on which Laertes openly holds out (V.ii.242–46). The furious and frustrated Guises had no doubt that the 'cœur' thus displayed before them was far from 'magnanime': 'Voyla le plus poltron cœur qui fut jamais [Behold the most cowardly heart that ever was]' (Régnier, *Histoire*, 1576, p. 710).

Some such pronouncement figures in most narratives of this incident. What is not necessarily clear is whose 'cœur' is the object of such disdain. The ambiguity bears indirectly on any association an audience might have made with Hamlet, given that his behaviour overall teeters precisely between the 'noble' and the cowardly. The latter image, when the Danish prince applies it to himself, conforms exactly to Navarre's refusal to be provoked:

> Am I a coward?
> Who calls me villain, breaks my pate across,
> Plucks off my beard, and blows it in my face,
> Tweaks me by the nose, gives me the lie i' th' throat
> As deep as to the lungs – who does me this?
> Ha!
> 'Swounds, I should take it: for it cannot be
> But I am pigeon-liver'd and lack gall
> To make oppression bitter . . .
>   (II.ii.566–74)

Jeanne d'Albret herself, however, pointedly presents the target of the Guises' contempt as being François II, whom they were blaming for being insufficiently aggressive; the same reading is offered in the Prologue to the 1570 collection (*Histoire de nostre temps*) that first printed her memoirs (there, indeed, Navarre's submissiveness is not even mentioned).[31] More generally, Navarre's widow is notably generous in presenting him as ensnared by the Guises to the point of helplessness – witness her poignant conclusion:

> Voilà ce que j'ai peu entendre du faict seulement en passant de la propre bouche du feu Roy mon mary, & du Capitaine Ranty. Mais en voulant depuis rafreichir ma memoire, lesdicts de Guyse auoyent desia commencez à le posseder de telle façon que ie n'en peuz plus rien sçavoir de luy.
>
> [That is what I could gather of the matter simply from the mouth of the late king my husband, and from Captain Ranty. But since then, when I sought to refresh my memory, the said Guises had already begun to possess him to such a degree that I could never learn more from him]. (Albret, *Ample Declaration*, 1570, p. 179)

Régnier, by contrast, while otherwise closely imitating Jeanne d'Albret's narrative, suppresses her statement that the contemptuous remark applied to the French king.[32] In general, moreover, his *Histoire* tells rather a different story, one likely to recall for his readers the enumeration of the apostles with which Matthew 10 begins and which arrives at its conclusion in verse 4 with 'Iudas Iscariot, who also betrayed him'. Such disillusion was in proportion to the hopes Antoine had aroused and the importance accorded him by Calvin himself, at least prior to the Amboise debacle:

> Le roi de Navarre est, à son avis, le pivot de toute action légitime; c'est lui qui doit solliciter la convocation des états généraux, c'est lui qui doit s'opposer aux Guise, en vertu de la suprême magistrature que sa naissance lui confère. Pour le décider, pour l'aider, pour l'encourager, Calvin ne néglige rien; même, il lui fait offrir l'appui de l'Allemagne réformée. Mais, le jour où il s'aperçoit qu'on ne peut pas faire fond sur le premier prince du sang, il se désintéresse d'une cause, qui, sans lui, estime-t-il, n'est défendable ni par le droit ni par la coutume.

> [The King of Navarre was, in his view, the pivot of all legitimate action: it was he who must press for the convocation of the Estates General; it was he who must oppose the Guises, by virtue of the supreme judicial function conferred by his birth. To get him to decide, to assist him, to encourage him, Calvin spared no effort; he even caused the support of Protestant Germany to be offered him. But as soon as he perceived that one could not count on the first Prince of the Blood, he withdrew his engagement from a cause that without Navarre, in his estimation, was defensible neither by law nor by custom.] (Naef, 1922, pp. 90–91)

By early 1562, the King of Navarre had become Julian the Apostate in the eyes of Bèze.[33] Finally, he forfeited all credit by condoning the so-called massacre of Wassy on 1 March 1562, in which the Guises slaughtered dozens of Protestants holding religious services.[34] An analogous sense of blind vindictiveness unleashed irrupts into *Hamlet*: Laertes storms back from France, not only with the commendation of 'Lamord' (IV.vii.91) – 'la mort' making itself heard – and the Guises' weapons of sword and poison, but also with vengeful determination sufficient, regarding his enemy, 'To cut his throat i' th' church' (125). Wassy proved the spark for the first War of Religion, and Antoine was almost immediately killed at Rouen, fighting alongside the Guises.

Even the casual reader of Régnier would have been regularly 'edified' (*Ham.*, V.ii.152) by marginal comments that help to skew the culminating accusation of cowardice in Navarre's direction. From the first, these comments mark Navarre as 'trompé par soy-mesme, trahi des siens, et mocqué de ses ennemis [deceived by himself, betrayed by his own people and mocked by his enemies]' (*Histoire*, 1576, p. 40); they signal his 'Belles promesses [pretty promises]' (p. 46), his 'Desseings inutiles [useless schemes]' (p. 52), for which he is 'payé de ses peines de la même fumée dont il auoit repue les autres [paid for his pains with the same smoke on which he had fed others]' (p. 91). Ultimately, he is 'trahi comme de costume [betrayed, as usual]' (p. 600). The narrative elaborates these traits across situations and in language that recurrently intersect with *Hamlet*. Thus, at the beginning of the section, one reads that the Constable Montmorency, anticipating the death of Henri II, urged Navarre to seize the government at once, but 'ce Prince peu desireux d'honneur et du maniement d'afaires [this prince, little desirous of honour and the management of affairs]' (p. 40) hung back from action, suspecting an attempt to sound out his intentions. In fact, his most trusted adviser was in the Guises' pay and urged him to keep his thoughts to himself, to ingratiate himself with them and 'rien hasarder par trop entreprendre [not to risk anything by undertaking too much]' (p. 44). Navarre's withdrawal from 'enterprises of great pitch and moment' (*Ham.*, III.i.186) of which he is only half-believed to be capable is a leitmotif in the observations regarding his character, which relentlessly record ambition and promise self-subverted by wavering, flashes of heroism collapsing into cowardice, self-defeating cunning, opportunities forfeited by – obviously, I use the term advisedly – delay.

The discourse surrounding the unstable character of Antoine de Bourbon is inextricable from his shifting politics and religion. His initiatives, intrigues and ambitions remain surrounded by much mystery, but the key political facts suffice to show the 'heart' of that mystery as overlapping with what Rosencrantz and Guildenstern suspect about Hamlet. The vaguely and ineptly aspiring Navarre was a 'loose cannon', who, at various moments and to varying degrees, posed a threat not only to the Guises but to Catherine de Medici, Philip II of Spain, and, as seems very much to the point, the King of Denmark. As the first Prince of the Blood, Antoine enjoyed a status within the realm of France second only to that of the king and his direct successors – at least in theory. When the accidental death of Henri II (10 July 1559) left the throne to François II, his potential influence suddenly expanded, and his brother, the Prince of Condé, among others, encouraged him to assume the regency, even though, at fifteen, the new king had achieved majority under French law. This Antoine was unwilling to envisage – hence, his vulnerability to Guisean counter-moves. Condé was soon a prisoner, to be saved from execution only by the king's death on 5 December 1560. That event left a more conspicuous power vacuum, since Charles IX was only ten years old, but again Antoine allowed himself to be shunted aside – this time by Catherine de Medici, who had herself hurriedly declared 'gouvernante de France'. Still, Catherine was keen to break the stranglehold of the Guises and found it expedient to accord Antoine a measure of prestige and power by appointing him Lieutenant-Général.

Antoine's position within France was rendered still more equivocal by his shadowy title of King of Navarre, acquired in right of his wife, Jeanne d'Albret. For Antoine very much thought of himself – and it's the thought that counts – as a king without a kingdom. While the region of Béarn and so-called Basse-Navarre to the north of the Pyrenees remained under his sovereignty, most of the ancient kingdom had been annexed by Ferdinand II of Aragon in 1511. The evidence abundantly witnesses Antoine's obsession with regaining his full heritage or acquiring some compensatory seat of sovereignty. In this cause he dreamed and plotted; for it, he sacrificed religious principle. And although his plots were ultimately no more effectual than his dreams, they caused concern, and provoked active counter-measures, from foreign as well as domestic adversaries. According to the Venetian ambassador, Michele Suriano, reporting to his political masters on the state of France in 1562, Antoine was known as a prince 'très faible et irrésolu [most weak and irresolute]', wavering in religion, despite possessing 'de la noblesse, de l'agrément, du brillant dans l'esprit, et même beaucoup de courage [nobility, attraction, brilliance of mind, and even a great deal of courage]'; he is said to nurture two projects: to recover Navarre or receive compensation; and to get himself elected King of the Romans (a stepping-stone to the Holy Roman Empire), with the assistance of his ally the Elector Palatine. He is supposed by some to aim at the crown of France and to be enlisting the Protestants in this cause, but this is far-fetched: 'Ce prince ne donne aucune preuve d'où l'on puisse conclure qu'il ait ce désir, et il n'est pas capable de tramer une aussi grande trahison [This prince manifests nothing from which one might conclude that he has such a desire, and he is not capable of plotting such a great treason]' (Suriano, 1836, pp. 391–92).

I will return to Antoine's imperial dreaming, which matches the odd political spin given by Hamlet to another existential commonplace recalling Montaigne's 'Apologie': 'A certain convocation of politic worms are e'en at him. Your worm is your only emperor for diet' (IV.iii.19–21).[35] But I hope that enough has been said to establish Hamlet's vague but insistent posture of political grievance, the very condition his precursor in Belleforest takes such pains to conceal, as rich with recent historical resonance still in discursive circulation. Antoine de Bourbon, a veritable chameleon, might readily be imagined as quibbling provocatively on Claudius' question as to how he 'fares': 'Excellent, i' faith, of the chameleon's dish. I eat the air, promise-crammed. You cannot feed capons so' (III.ii.93–94). And he was imprudent enough to let on to spies of various stripes that, however 'immediate' to the French throne he might, or might not, be, he acutely felt himself to 'lack advancement' (331).

Philip II had particular reason to worry about a resolute Navarre. During the negotiations leading to the peace of Cateau-Cambrésis (signed March-April

1559), Henri II had given Navarre permission, and lent him the military services of Blaise de Monluc, for an expedition aimed at recovering his lost territory. Navarre was hoping at least to put pressure on the negotiations for some recognition of his claim, and the failure to obtain anything of the kind was particularly grating.[36] Predictably, and as the French king had certainly foreseen, the adventure was futile, and in late July Monluc, too, was serving as an errand boy to the Guises, informing them of the 'intentions pacifiques [pacific intentions]' of Navarre, along with his naïve hope to be received in grand style at court so that Spain might be convinced to make him a concession.[37] Philip might have had just cause, then for warning the newly acceded François II about this potential trouble-maker. But Régnier insists that he did so just to maintain fear in Navarre, who had already 'conclu de ne rien entreprendre [concluded to undertake nothing]' (*Histoire*, 1576, p. 61).

The situation took a new turn when Navarre became Lieutenant-Général under Charles IX. Certainly, the correspondence of Catherine de Medici over 1561 and 1562 becomes palpably nervous with regard to his disruptive potential, and she puts increasing pressure on Philip to offer compensation. Likewise, Margaret of Parma, *gouvernante* of the Low Countries on Philip's behalf, warned the Spanish king that Antoine might recklessly risk something, 'comme celuy qui n'a rien ou peu, pour veoir si, durant la minorité de ce roy, et de l'autorité qu'il a pris en France comme roy, il se pouvait avancer à quelque chose [like one who has nothing or little, to see if, during this king's minority, he could advance to something]' (cited de Ruble, 1881–86, 4: 305–6). As it turned out, any rash action that Navarre may have seriously entertained was effectively turned back against him, thanks again to his passive irresolution and lack of principles, and this time the outcome was not his miraculous escape, thanks to the 'volonté de Dieu', but a catastrophe at once inevitable and accidental, noble and absurd – like Hamlet's, and with analogous repercussions for the rot-infected state that he had failed to redeem from disaster.

IV

Before returning to politics pure and simple (obviously, neither term applies), I wish briefly to open a wider perspective on contemporary portrayals of Navarre. This involves moving beyond material known to have been accessible in print, but it also fills in the discursive space, and the fuller picture is likely to have corresponded more closely with that current in the period. With regard to Shakespeare, moreover, one case in particular suggests the possibility of access to a manuscript source, perhaps by way of his contacts in the milieu of Huguenot politics and publishing. Such access would be consistent – although the details necessarily remain out of reach – with the proposition I will be making in Chapter 4 for a direct relationship between *All's Well* and the autobiography of Marguerite de Valois (1553–1615), the first queen of Henri IV. These are rare cases that seem to me not only to go beyond commonplaces, at least cumulatively and in context, but to call for an explanation in terms other than intertextuality. Still, we simply do not possess at the moment, and may never do, the information needed to define those terms.

Régnier's *Histoire*, which does not extend beyond François II, was incorporated, expanded and continued by Nicolas de Bordenave, a Protestant minister commissioned by Jeanne d'Albret to write the history of Béarn and Navarre from their beginnings to the present moment (the narrative ends with her death in 1572). Bordenave, himself resident in Béarn, evidently worked on this mammoth project virtually until he died, sometime within the first seven months of 1601.[38] This date agrees with the probable insertion of the War of the Theatres material in an earlier version of *Hamlet*,[39] when other elements may conceivably have been added as well. The coincidence is probably no more than that, although it seems just possible that the manuscript became known at that point in circles overlapping with those of Shakespeare. It was, after all, an important dynastic document, latterly produced under the direct auspices of the ruling French monarch. Perhaps the best measure of its importance, paradoxically, is the fact that it was not published until 1873, when excerpts (including the relevant portions) appeared in a highly competent edition prepared by a local antiquary for the Société de l'Histoire de France.

Bordenave's successor as official historiographer of Navarre, Paul Olhagaray, definitely had access to the manuscript, since he acknowledges borrowings in his *Histoire de Foix, Béarn et Navarre* (1609), which carried the narrative further forward.[40] The point becomes interesting when the treatment of Antoine de Bourbon in the two versions is compared – an especially sensitive matter for Henri IV on two counts: at stake was not only his father's general reputation but a history of religious wavering that might recall his own. Certainly, too, the now officially Catholic monarch could hardly have countenanced Bordenave's insistently Protestant point of view, including his bold justification of the Amboise rising.

In general, Olhagaray rebalances the standard portrait of Henri's father without completely eliminating its ambiguity. The solution, it turns out, is to play him up as the upright and innocent victim of the 'cauteles [tricks]' and 'audaces [bold strokes]' (Olhagaray, 1609, p. 531) of the Guises, while playing down his lack of conviction, his wavering and lapsing.[41] Although Bèze's rebuke for his feeble attempt to excuse the massacre of Wassy is recorded (1609, p. 530), the tragic loss associated with Antoine is no longer that of true religion but – in a way closer to Shakespeare's prince – of personal promise, the evaporation of 'ses grandes esperances [his great hopes]' (1609, p. 531). This is a hero who really did conceive grand 'enterprises' but was led astray by the Guisean will-o'-the wisp, chasing after the 'vent de leurs promesses, iusqu'à ce qu'il eust trouué la mort au bout de ses immortelles entreprinses [wind of their promises until he met death at the end of his immortal enterprises]' (1609, p. 531). As for the spectacular conspiracy sequence, much is made in general terms of Antoine's heroism and faith in the divine will, but the key scriptural passage is not cited, as if to avoid any implication of a 'special providence' that might also have to be presumed in subsequent events. The moment of confrontation itself is actually rendered more dramatic – to the point where the plotters of 'ceste tragœdie [that tragedy]' (1609, p. 527) do not shut the door behind Navarre as he enters but instead conceal themselves behind a tapestry.

Evidently, the tapestry motif has a habit of insinuating itself into this cluster of texts: it even makes one of the points on which the translator of *The Hystorie of Hamblet*, published in the previous year, apparently took his cue from Shakespeare's Polonius rather than Belleforest's 'intelligencer'.[42] Olhagaray was doubtless quite innocent of *Hamlet*; he may instead have been gesturing towards the providential parallel often perceived between the nefarious practices of the Guises and the spectacular retribution meted out to the later Duke and Cardinal of Guise, when Henri III had them murdered in the royal château of Blois in 1588: the standard account has the royal assassins concealed behind a doorway tapestry.[43]

What is thoroughly remarkable – and I cannot pretend to account for it – is that in several distinctive details Bordenave's unpublished portrayal of Antoine de Bourbon comes closer to the depiction of Hamlet than do the published versions. Simply, there are more frequent, and more substantial, correspondences, including verbal ones, than coincidence or commonplace would warrant in this compact narrative (of about thirty-five pages). Most suggestive – not only in itself but as a methodological signal – is a change in the climactic scene of confrontation: only in this version do we find the biblical verse transferred from the narrator's commentary after the fact to the character's anticipatory thought. For at the moment corresponding to Hamlet's entrusting of himself to God, who bears sole power over life and death (although Bordenave does not name 'providence'), Navarre is said to be 'asseuré qu'il ne tombe un seul cheveu de nostre teste que par la disposition de ce grand Dieu qui seul fait mourir, et vivre, et démène les cœurs des Roys à son plaisir [assured that not a single hair of our head may fall without the assent of that great God who alone causes to die, and to live, and directs the hearts of kings at his pleasure]'

(Bordenave, 1873, p. 105). More broadly, this change also manifests a shift in narrative procedure from traditional portraiture and Christian *exemplum* to interiority; the intertextual effect is to align the 'political' Hamlet with the 'philosophical' one.

To this novelty may be added what seems the novel representation of Navarre as a would-be revenger – an incompetent, conflicted and self-defeating one. The point is accompanied by astute analysis (after all, Bordenave presumably had the benefit of Jeanne d'Albret's privileged insight), and from this point of view he appears decidedly more petty than noble. To begin with, we are told that Navarre probably rejected the prudent injunction of the Constable to act opportunely against the Guises less out of mere indolence, or because he suspected a device to 'sonder et descouvrir sa volonté [to probe and discover his will]' (Bordenave, 1873, p. 71), than because he took pleasure in imagining Montmorency's own fall at their hands – and this because he held the Constable responsible for his exclusion from the treaty of Cateau-Cambrésis. In consequence,

> mal avisé et suivant plus la passion que la raison, se voulant venger d'autruy, se vengea de soy-mesmes, et vuidant honnir et abaisser autruy, se deshonnora et perdit soy-mesmes, car outre qu'il tomba en hazard très éminent de perdre vie et biens, jamais depuis ses affaires n'allèrent qu'en décadence.

> [poorly advised and following passion rather than reason, seeking to avenge himself on others, he took vengeance on himself, and aiming to shame and put down others, dishonoured and ruined himself, for besides incurring a great risk of losing his life and possessions, never since did his affairs go anywhere but downhill.] (1873, pp. 71–72)

This behaviour is linked to a Hamlet-like mixture of mental agility, self-centredness and inconstancy:

> Et comme la promptitude et vivacité de l'esprit de ce Roy surpassoit les plus vifs esprits, aussi sa vanité et inconstances naturelles surpassoient la vanité et l'inconstance mesmes.

> [And as the quickness and liveliness of mind of that king surpassed the most agile intelligences, so his vanity and natural inconstancies surpassed vanity and inconstancy themselves.] (1873, p. 72)

The incongruous result, as in Hamlet's case, is a pattern of vaguely threatening behaviour that puts his enemies on guard – the opposite effect to that of the pretended folly of Amleth. Not daring to act directly against Navarre after the Amboise affaire, out of 'doubte d'embraser un feu qui les consumât eux mesmes [fear of enkindling a fire that might consume themselves]' (Bordenave,

1873, p. 81), the Guises sent someone of higher rank than Rosencrantz and Guildenstern, the Marshal Saint-André, 'pour sonder la volonté et espier les actions du Navarois et de son frère le Prince [de Condé] [to sound out the desire and spy on the actions of the Navarrois and his brother the Prince]', although the Marshal is at similar pains to affirm that he has come of his own accord 'en fidèle serviteur qui désiroit leur repos, bien et grandeur, sans qu'il en eust recue charge ne commandement, car il n'estoit venu là que pour les visiter seulement et leur offrir son service [as a faithful servant who sought their peace, well-being and greatness, without having received instructions or command, for he had come there merely to visit them and offer them his service]' (1873, p. 82). (The parallel protests of Rosencrantz and Guildenstern likewise fly in the face of their evident willingness to be 'commanded' [II.ii.32].) The response of Navarre is a Hamlet-like mixed message: professions of good will (towards the king and queen) mingled with reckless provocations (directed at the Guises). By Hamlet, of course, such self-defeating doubleness will be pursued to the point where, having just threatened Laertes, he finally talks himself into his submission at once to divinity and to his enemies' scheme on the premise that 'Our indiscretion sometime serves us well / When our deep plots do pall' (V.ii.8–9). He might have done better to heed Bordenave's practical advice:

> C'est une grande indiscrétion de menacer celuy qu'on ne peut abattre ne luy apporter aucun dommage important, car cela luy sert d'avertissement pour se tenir en garde et le provoque pour le tenir en garde et le provoque pour son propre salut de prévenir le menaçant et luy faire le premier cela de quoy il l'aura menacé.
>
> [It is a great indiscretion to threaten someone whom one cannot strike down or do any real harm, for it serves as a warning to keep him on his guard and provokes him to keep on his guard and provokes him for his proper safety to anticipate the threatener and do to him first that with which he has been threatened.] (1873, p. 83)

At this point Navarre had two further agents of the Guises (d'Escars and Nicolas Dangu, Bishop of Mende) posing as loyal advisers but actually encouraging his 'irresolution', for 'ils luy fesoient les choses, non seulement de dificile et dangereuse exécution, mais aussi du tout impossibles et jointes à son entière ruine [they presented these matters to him as not only of difficult and dangerous execution, but also as completely impossible and tending to his total ruin]', given the combined forces arrayed against him by the Guises and the Spanish king, who was determined not to allow him to recover the lands 'sur lesquels … il pouvoit prétendre droit [upon which … he might pretend a claim]'

(Bordenave, 1873, p. 74). The mixture of prying into political intentions and cautioning against wrath from on high is by no means alien to the confrontation between Hamlet and his two spying friends in Act III, Scene ii (289 ff.). While Hamlet may indirectly flatter himself on his 'native hue of resolution' even in deploring the 'pale cast of thought' that inhibits 'enterprises of great pitch and moment' (III.i.86–88), Bordenave knows better with regard to Navarre's 'propre irrésolution', which thwarted the 'grandes entreprises' (1873, pp. 74–75) of the reformers and put their persons in peril. Meanwhile, Navarre ostentatiously temporized. He did not exactly ask his friends to indulge an 'antic disposition' (I.v.180), but he requested that they accept as a stratagem his contradictory religious deportment – attending both Protestant services and the mass. In his commentary, Bordenave decries the alienating effect of such wavering and affirms the Apostolic model of forthright action, as Hamlet will finally seem to accept it:

> ses propos firent penser aux meilleurs et plus sages qu'il avait aussi peu de religion que de résolution et de courage, car quand il est question des choses de la foy, il faut marcher rondement et rejetter simplement ce que Dieu défend et faire ce qu'il commande, quelque danger qui se puisse présenter du costé du monde.

> [his words caused the better and wiser ones to think that he had as little religion as he had resolution and courage, for when it is a question of matters of faith, one must march boldly and simply reject what God prohibits and do what He commands, whatever danger may present itself on the part of the world.] (1873, p. 75)

Practically speaking, moreover, there is a point of no return: Navarre 'reconnoissoit lors la faute qu'il avoit fait de s'estre venu mettre à la discrétion de ses enemies. ... C'est la coustume des inconstans de se r'aviser hors tems [then recognized the fault he had made in putting himself at the discretion of his enemies. ... For the custom of the inconstant is to change their mind when it is too late]' (Bordenave, 1873, p. 76). However, having yielded the advantage, it was neither the time nor the place

> de faire le mauvais garçon et faloit avoir commencé plus tot et ailleurs et mis tout autre ordre à ses affaires qu'il n'avoit, mais l'esprit de ce Prince estoit incapable de toute hazardeuse résolution.

> [to act the bad boy, and he should have begun earlier and elsewhere and ordered his affairs wholly otherwise than he did, but the mind of that prince was incapable of all hazardous resolution.] (1873, p. 76)

As the story tends towards its conclusion, Bordenave becomes still further inclined to character analysis, and two such passages have a particularly close rapport with *Hamlet*. The first, dealing with Navarre's ultimate apostasy, actually applies Hamlet's self-label 'chameleon' in such a way as to link changeability, a secondary implication in Hamlet's case, with a predilection to 'eat the air, promise-crammed' in the form of flattery and ambition (the latter termed by Rosencrantz 'of so airy and light a quality that it is but a shadow's shadow' [II.ii.261–62]). The effect is fatally to impair the judgement and, especially, the will:

> Mais ce Prince estoit tellement commandé par son inconstance naturelle, ambition, voluptez, lubricitez et flateries qui (tout ainsi que le caméléon reçoit toutes les couleurs des choses sur lesquelles il est posé) n'ayant autre conception, jugement ni volonté que celles que l'ambition, la lubricité et la flaterie luy mettoient en teste ou plus tot luy commandoient, changeoit plus souvent de déliberations que d'habillemens, ne demeura guère long tems en volonté de favourir la dite religion.

> [But that prince was so commanded by his natural inconstancy, ambition, pleasures, lubricities and flatteries (just as the chameleon takes on all the colours of the things on which it is placed), having no other conception, judgement or will than those that ambition, lubricity and flattery put into his head, or rather dictated to him, changed his deliberations more often than his garments, and hardly remained for long in a determination to favour the said religion.] (Bordenave, 1873, p. 109)

As for the sensuality said to enter into Antoine's case,[44] the two intelligencers in *Hamlet* are fully prepared to add this dimension to their picture ('Man delights not me – nor woman neither, though by your smiling you seem to say so' [309–10]), as is Hamlet himself: witness the ambiguous sexual games he plays with, and around, Ophelia.

The second passage that stands out in Bordenave is in the nature of an epitaph and a summary. The historian goes against most reports in having the dying Navarre waver for the last time in the wrong religious direction, so that 'Il ne donna pas moins de tesmoignage de son inconstance en sa mort qu'il avait fait en sa vie [He showed no less testimony of his inconstancy in his death than he had done in his life]' (Bordenave, 1873, p. 114). Yet this leads into a generous assessment of his potential, in effect, 'To have prov'd most royal' (*Ham.*, V.ii.403), had it not been for the same 'vicious mole of nature' (I.iv.24) – lack of resolution – that arguably proves Hamlet's downfall. The author reflects with detachment on the 'mole of nature' phenomenon, much as Hamlet does himself, and arrives at essentially the same conclusion that 'The dram of evil / Doth all the noble substance often dout / To his own scandal' (36–38):

> Ce prince estoit d'un esprit fort gentil, vaillant de sa personne, bien disant et libéral et avoit beaucoup d'autres vertus dignes d'un grand prince qui le rendoient

bien voulu de tous, et si la constance eut accompagné ces vertus, il eut esté l'un des plus princes accomplis de son tems; mais il n'y a rien de parfait en l'inperfection de ce monde et le plus souvent les plus grands vices logent avec les vertus plus héroiques et communément ès plus entiers le vice surmonte la vertu.

[This prince was of a most noble mind, valiant of his person, full of fair words and generous, and he had many other virtues worthy of a great prince which rendered him desired of many, and if constancy had accompanied those virtues, he would have been one of the most accomplished princes of his time. But there is nothing perfect in the imperfection of this world, and most often the greatest vices lodge with the most heroic virtues, and commonly in the most absolute men, vice surmounts virtue.] (Bordenave, 1873, p. 114)

Here again the parallel is a matter less of content than of narrative development. The power of inconstancy to vitiate all the virtues is certainly a commonplace; the device of a concluding character summary is likewise conventional.[45] But not only is Bordenave's eulogy conditional (like that of Fortinbras); it modulates into regretful qualification akin to Hamlet's own, which is itself triggered, of course, by the image of Claudius as king. It is irresistible to note that the 'mole of nature' speech, which seems never to have been attributed to a particular source, appears only in the Second Quarto of 1604–5; the passage thus at least makes a candidate for composition after the manuscript of Bordenave passed into his inheritors' hands – and perhaps beyond them.

In sum, Bordenave's narrative goes well beyond its analogues in drawing the central figure towards the status of a tragic protagonist, fatally flawed. Played down, by comparison, is an element more prominent in other accounts and by no means unparalleled in Shakespeare: the immediate social consequences of Navarre's chronic ineffectuality. For according to the highly codified practices of court etiquette, Navarre attracted widespread disdain and mockery for forfeiting his rightful dignity. So reports Régnier, for one, who adds that even those who owed their places and prosperity to him turned to scorning him, 'tant est muable et variable la condition des Courtisans [so changeable and variable is the condition of courtiers]' (*Histoire*, 1576, p. 724). Goulart's retelling, in *Histoire des choses mémorables*, has him 'remettant sa vie ès mains de Dieu [committing his life into the hands of God]' (1599, p. 120) after being warned, but also mocked. It is not, perhaps, sufficiently appreciated by modern audiences, who tend to see the play's 'waterfly' (V.ii.82–83) through Hamlet's own disdainful eyes, that Osric, in his addresses to Hamlet, is being not merely ridiculous but insolent, and in a way that reflects a change in the political wind – the same wind that nearly carried Laertes to the throne. It is hardly for an upstart courtier to greet the first Prince of the Blood with the haughty condescension of 'Your Lordship is right welcome back to Denmark', as Hamlet himself surely registers in ironically replying, 'I humbly thank you sir' (81–82). And when Osric evokes Laertes as 'an absolute gentleman, ... the card or calendar of gentry' (106–10), it could not be clearer 'who's in, who's out', to cite Lear on similar 'gilded butterflies' (*Lr.*, V.iii.15, 13). The court has just witnessed, after all, if not fully grasped, Hamlet's degrading display of impotent rivalry with Laertes in Ophelia's grave.

Another contemporary with much to say about Antoine de Bourbon, especially in *Grands Capitaines François*, was Pierre de Bourdeille, *abbé* de Brantôme, although here too any knowledge on Shakespeare's part would have depended on hearsay or circulation of manuscripts.[46] As a partisan but not fanatical Catholic, as well as a long-standing witness of religious vacillations amongst aristocratic acquaintances, Brantôme was not personally invested in Navarre's betrayal of the Huguenots, although he registers the intensity of their resulting scorn, which extended to calling Navarre 'Thony', the name of the king's fool (Lalanne, ed., 1864–82, 4: 366n.2). Brantôme also regards in a cold light the political manoeuvres of the Guises and others in relation to Navarre's unfulfilled ambitions. As a member of the *noblesse d'épée*, however, what Brantôme plays up is Navarre's jealousy of the military glory of François de Guise. Such jealousy enters the play generally through Hamlet's rivalry with Laertes, more specifically through his self-accusatory reaction to the army of Fortinbras, 'a delicate and tender prince, / Whose spirit, with divine ambition puff'd, / Makes mouths at the invisible event' (IV.iv.48–50), and who exemplifies the chivalric capacity 'to find quarrel in a straw / When honour's at the stake' (55–56); he will also, of course, survive to rule over Denmark. In what amounts, then, to another plausible – necessarily partial – 'take' on the play's politics, Brantôme effectively shunts aside the discourse of religion and traces to such rivalry the factionalization of the court and the subsequent struggle for power:

Ce brave roy et M. de Guyze contendoient si tresfort ensemble en compétance de gloire, que toutes leurs actions de guerre tendoient à l'envy à qui fairoit mieux. ... Les petites æmulations pourtant se convertirent amprès en innimitiéz sourdes, sans se descouvrir pourtant, et mesmes quand il vist M. de Guyze si ennobly de beaux faictz et qu'on ne parloit que de loy, et qu'il le voyoit si bien advancé et favory de son roy; sie bien que parmy leurs pages et laquays des uns et des autres on voyoit faire des quadrilles et des parties. ... Ces petites choses picquent quelquesfois autant ou plus que des grandes. ...

Le roy François venant en règne, là fut la grand' picque et innimitié, à cause que M. de Guyze ne luy céda l'autorité et prééminance de tout l'Estat, mais non qu'il en vint grande rumeur et esclandre descouverte.

[This brave king and Monsieur de Guise contended so strongly in distinction for glory that all their actions in war related to jealousy as to who should do better. ... Nevertheless, their petty rivalries afterward converted to stubborn hostilities, though still without disclosing themselves, even when he saw Monsieur de Guise so ennobled by his splendid deeds, and that one spoke only of him, and when he saw him so thoroughly advanced and favoured by his king – to such a point that among their pages and lackeys one saw divisions and parties. ... These little matters sometimes annoy as much as or more than great ones. ...

When King François acceded, there the great offence and hostility arose, because Monsieur de Guise did not yield him the preeminence and authority of the whole state, but not so that noisy confusion and open outrage resulted.] (ed. Lalanne, 1864–82, 4: 371–72)

While Brantôme is at pains to grant Antoine due credit for personal valour and noble qualities as a 'tout bon et gentil prince' (1864–82, 4: 367), it says much that his greatest act, in the memorialist's view, remains his fathering of 'nostre grand roy d'aujourd'huy Henry IV' (1864–82, 4: 372).

Finally, Brantôme's account of Navarre's fatal wounding at the siege of Rouen invests that event with something very like the complex mixture of valorous resolution, heroic display, jealous rivalry, absurd accident and futile banality that is crystallized by the play's fencing match. Navarre exposed himself freely to danger, we are told, and was preparing for the assault, 'moytié mené du brave et généreux courage qu'il a toujours possédé, moytié d'ambition et æmulation qu'il portoit de tout temps à M. de Guyze [half led by the brave and noble courage that he always possessed, half by ambition and envy which he bore at all moments towards Monsieur de Guise]' (1864–82, 4: 366), when he was shot in the shoulder after turning aside to urinate. That circumstance occasioned an epitaph rather less reverent than those provided for Hamlet by Horatio and Fortinbras. One might readily imagine it intoned, however, by the Gravedigger: 'Ami françois, le prince ici gissant / Vécut sans gloire et mourut en pissant [French friend, the prince who lies here lived without glory and died having a piss]' (Lalanne, ed., 1864–82, 4: 367n.1).[47]

V

Whatever may have been happening with Navarrois texts in 1601 – and it seems highly likely that some were circulating across the Channel – Antoine de Bourbon's character had been of more active concern to Englishmen some forty years earlier. Given the particularly high political, religious and military stakes for England in the years 1558–62, English diplomats and 'intelligencers' were naturally much interested in the King of Navarre, who seemed fated, if not self-determined, to remain at once in the centre and at the margins of power. 1558, it should be recalled, saw the capture of Calais by François de Guise, as well as the death of Queen Mary and the return of England to Protestantism under Elizabeth. In the spring of the following year, the English participated in the negotiations and treaty of Cateau-Cambrésis, which provided for their eventual recovery of Calais (though on conditions no one expected to be met); they well knew that Navarre was 'offended' by the omission of his interests.[48] With the accession of François II in July 1559, the English suddenly found themselves faced with a young French Queen, dominated by her Guisean relations, who was also indubitably Queen of Scots and in the view of many the rightful Queen of England. In autumn of 1560, the English were, if not materially implicated, at least keenly interested, in the Conspiracy of Amboise[49] – an ambiguous position analogous to that of Antoine himself. Only a few months later, the Queen of Scots became a remarriageable wild-card, while Navarre emerged as the man on whom war or peace between French Catholics and Protestants, hence potentially between the Catholic and Protestant powers of Europe, appeared to hinge. Finally, with his recommitment to Catholicism and the Guisards in 1562, Navarre briefly rose to the status of England's declared adversary.

The dealings of the English with Navarre throughout this period soon convinced them of his inveterate double-dealing. On 22 May 1560, the English Ambassador, Nicholas Throckmorton, wrote to the Queen of his frustration at finding that the King of Navarre had shared a letter of his with the Cardinal of Lorraine, who supplied an answer of his own to accompany that of Navarre. Throckmorton's concluding comment bespeaks considerable prior experience: 'Wherein, for some confirmations of that I have heretofore tolde your Majesty of the said King, I say no more; but that the prince is more happy that hath such a subject to command, than such a friend to stay upon' (cited Forbes, 1740–41, 1: 472). Apparently, the English had quickly acquired an understanding of the man on whom they were then dependent for advancing the Protestant cause in France, and their estimation was essentially that of the modern political historian Lucien Romier:

> Dans sa génération, a[u] milieu de personnalités puissantes et vives, Antoine représente un type extraordinaire de médiocrité. Changeant d'opinions à tout instant, maladroit avec insouciance, incapable de comprendre et d'exécuter, n'obéissant qu'aux fantaisies d'un cœur puéril et d'une ambition sans suite, il fut un triste chef dans le camp où le poussa Jeanne d'Albret.

> [In his generation, in the midst of forceful and lively personalities, Antoine represents an extraordinary type of mediocrity. Changing his opinions at every moment, carelessly clumsy, incapable of understanding or of executing, heeding

nothing but the fantasies of a childish heart and a fruitless ambition, he was a sad leader in the camp into which Jeanne d'Albret thrust him.] (Romier, 1974, 2: 257)

VI

English intelligence seems also to have known more than can now be clearly discerned about one of Navarre's futile projects of particular interest in Shakespearean terms. A number of documents for the years 1559–61 converge on his apparent attempt to get himself elected King of Denmark. The matter seems to have come to a head in late 1561, to judge from a dispatch from Thomas Shakerley to Throckmorton dated 14 December:

> ... the Emperor asks to keep diet, ... but the Duke of Saxony, the Count Palatine, the Landgrave and many others will not consent. So that King Philip, understanding the secret working of these Princes with the King of Navarre, to make him King of Dakia (which kingdom pertends to the King of the Romans) and afterwards Emperor, to take clean away from the house of Austria the empire, for the great injury received of Charles V., – most hotly pricks forth that the Emperor makes this diet in such places as the Princes cannot but choose to come, as Mentz [Mainz] in High Almaine. The Princes understanding this have sent to the King of Navarre their Ambassadors, giving out that they are come for money lent to the late King Henry, but the truth is that they are come to offer to the King of Navarre 20,000 men, paid for six months, to aid himself and maintain their religion. It appears by a letter sent to the King of Navarre that the King of Spain knows how the matter goes, who [i.e., Navarre] this morning talked with the Queen and the Cardinal two great hours, and showed himself in great travail. (*CSPF, 1561–62*, No. 724, p. 441)[50]

'Dakia' (more often 'Dacia') is here the Latin name for Denmark.[51]

The story is now little known, but the handful of historians who have followed the lead of this dispatch have no doubt that Denmark is intended: 'Vers le milieu de l'année 1561, il se forma à la diète un parti qui voulait porter Antoine de Bourbon sur le trône de Danemarck pour le faire arriver un jour à l'empire [Toward mid-1561, a party formed at the Diet which wished to place Antoine de Bourbon on the throne of Denmark in order that he might some day become Emperor]' (de Ruble, 1881–86, 2: 264).[52] It is useful to bracket Shakerley's report between two other surviving documents. The first is a letter to Navarre from François Hotman of almost a year earlier (31 December 1560), in which that tireless Protestant activist, jurist and propagandist urges him, in near-apocalyptic terms, to fulfil his promises by leading the forces of truth against the bloody tyrants. He heralds the assembly of German Protestant

princes planned for late January 1561 in Nuremberg as an unparalleled oppor-
tunity, naming all twenty-one expected there and offering to negotiate 'de
quelque affaire', if only Navarre will give him instructions right away.[53]

As for the 'letter sent to the King of Navarre' showing the Spanish king's
knowledge of the matter, this was almost certainly written on 15 November
1561 by a colourful minor player on the political stage, the military man Nicolas
de Bolwiller, *bailli* of Haguenau in Alsace, who was in the service of Philip II.[54]
In it, Bolwiller cautions Navarre about extravagant claims he is supposed to
have made about changing the religion of France, indeed of all Christianity,
and offers to help him obtain satisfaction from the Spanish king if only he will
firmly embrace the Catholic faith (Hauser, 1891, p. 58). Such satisfaction obviously relates to the perennial question of compensation for the Spanish annex-
ation of Navarre, but there were further insinuations sufficiently provocative
to induce Catherine de Medici to send an agent to Bolwiller, who, however,
remained evasive (Hauser, 1891, p. 59; de Ruble, 1881–86, 2: 255–56). That
Navarre disclosed Bolwiller's letter to Catherine matches the double-dealing
complained of by Throckmorton; so does the fact that, to mollify the Protestant
faction, he had the king and Catherine certify that he had corresponded
with Bolwiller only at their behest (Hauser, 1891, p. 59). It was not until after
the massacre at Wassy that he openly threw in his lot with the Guises, thereby
occasioning Cecil's report (to Christopher Mundt, or Mont, Elizabeth's
Strasbourg-based agent) that 'France waxes faint, and the King of Navarre is
carried from his conscience with ambition and fear' (*CSPF, 1561–62,* 22 March
1562, No. 946 [3], p. 562 [Cecil to Mundt]). He had by this point been decisively outmanoeuvred.

The manoeuvres are unlikely ever to be known in detail,[55] but it is clear that
the ultimate prize for Navarre – whether seriously aimed at or a bargaining chip
for remedying the omissions of Cateau-Cambrésis – was nothing less than the
imperial crown. That monarchy, of course, was elective, and the succession was
established by electing the so-called King of the Romans. It is as a stepping-
stone to the latter title that Shakerley presents Navarre's potential acquisition
of the throne of Denmark (again, necessarily, by some form of election). (His
word 'pertends' is not in the *OED* but obviously derives from the Latin
pertendere, meaning 'to lead on to'.) The so-called Peace of Augsburg in 1555,
which allowed for religious variation within the Empire on the principle of
'*regio cujus, religio ejus*', had obviously not resolved tensions between the powerful Lutheran princes and the Catholic Hapsburgs, especially given the refusal
of Pius IV to confirm the 1558 election of Emperor Ferdinand I on the grounds
of his excessive tolerance. In 1561, Ferdinand began to provide for the succession of his son Maximilian by arranging his nomination as King of the Romans.

This project met with Protestant resistance, notably from the Elector Palatine, Frederick III, and it was not until late in 1562 that Maximilian, after protracted negotiations, was declared first King of Bohemia, then King of the Romans.[56]

The interval obviously allows for the possibility of an alternative election, and the prominent role of the Elector Palatine corresponds to his particular alliance with Navarre, according to Suriano.[57] It is in this context of politico-religious gamesmanship that Navarre's sponsorship of the contemporaneous Colloquy of Poissy should be seen, as well as the Guises' counter-moves, including their efforts to exploit the divisions between the Lutheran princes, who adhered doctrinally to the Confession of Augsburg (1530), and the Calvinist French Protestants.[58] The split had just been painfully confirmed, together with the consequent fragility of any anti-Catholic political alliance, at the Colloquy of Worms (late 1557) in the Palatinate, despite the efforts at compromise undertaken by Philip Melancthon and his followers (prominently including Hubert Languet) from Wittenberg in Saxony.[59] (Note that Hamlet's apparently haphazard quip links 'worms' with 'convocation', a theological gathering, then evokes the Imperial 'diets' held for political purposes.) What also emerges vividly from the historical accounts is that the brokering of influence was on all sides accompanied by large-scale bribery (de Ruble, 1881–86, 2: 261 ff.).

VII

The potentially pivotal role of Denmark in these events has not been formally explained, as far as I know, but the known facts form a partial picture. As early as 24 May 1561, Cardinal Granvelle (a marginal note by the translator in La Place, *The fyrst parte of commentaries*, adds that the latter 'might rather be called Granvillan, or greate villane' [1573, p. 166][60]) was writing from Brussels to his master Philip II that he feared a Protestant move to take the throne from the Hapsburgs, and that the Duke of Saxony, perhaps even the King of Denmark, had his eye on it (Granvelle, 1841–52, 6: 320 [No. 51]). In late August, Catherine de Medici cited the rumour in a letter to her ambassador at the imperial court, although by the end of November, she was sceptical that 'la pratticque du roy de Danemarc avec l'électeur de Saxe [the scheming of the King of Denmark with the Elector of Saxony]' could interfere with the succession of the King of Bohemia (*Lettres*, 1880–1943, 1: 231, 255). The association of the Duke of Saxony with the King of Denmark confirms that the king envisaged here as a possible contender is the one actually on the throne: Frederick II, whose sister Anna was married to August of Saxony (and whose daughter – also Anna – would later marry James VI of Scotland, Shakespeare's future sovereign).[61]

Frederick had, indeed, been active recently on the diplomatic front, not least with respect to France. In mid-March 1561 he sent his ambassador to Paris, where he met with Antoine de Bourbon (de Ruble, 1881–86, 2: 268).[62] The immediate occasion was the death of François II and accession of Charles IX. Naturally, then, Frederick offered the French at once 'condolence and congratulation', but he also proposed an alliance, to be sealed by his marriage with the late king's widow, Mary Stuart (*CSPF, 1561–62*, No. 77 [2], p. 42 [31 March 1561, Throckmorton to the Queen]). If this lends him a structural resemblance to Claudius, he had, in the English view, the morals to match.[63] In any case, while she did not leap at his proposal for Mary's hand,[64] Catherine de Medici was anxious to placate Frederick, as well as the other Protestant princes; she assured him that there would be no religious persecution in France and arranged for him to receive the order of Saint Michel.[65] Meanwhile, her letters show anxious interest in having Antoine receive some gratification from the King of Spain.[66]

Regardless of any imperial prospects, which came to nothing, as Catherine de Medici had foreseen with her usual acumen, Frederick II had particular reason to be uneasy with respect to France. His title was, in the eyes of many, usurped, and he had powerful enemies. Frederick's grandfather, Frederick I, acceded on the deposition of his own nephew, Christian II, in 1523; the latter had attempted to take the throne back eight years later but was defeated and imprisoned until his death in 1559. The latter year also saw the death of Frederick's father, Christian III, so that, while the succession of Frederick had been technically provided for by his father from the age of two, in the eyes of those who denied the usurper's right, the throne was now up for grabs – or, more technically, open for election. This was certainly the view of the deposed king's family, which included two daughters and a range of lofty connections, for Christian II's wife had been the Infanta Isabella of Spain.

The elder of those two daughters, Dorothea of Denmark, had married the Elector Palatine, Frederick II, in 1535, and her husband, with the support of Charles V and the Pope, had energetically pursued his wife's claim to the three northern countries, to the point of planning an invasion of Sweden in 1543.[67] He died in 1556 without direct descendants, however, and the Palatinate passed into another branch of the family. The other daughter was now a more formidable foe. The second husband of Christina of Denmark had been François I, Duke of Lorraine; on his death in 1545 she assumed the regency of Lorraine on behalf of their son Charles, now also the heir, in her view, to the Scandinavian kingdoms, which she never ceased to dream of recovering. In order to draw Lorraine firmly into the French political orbit, Henri II had deprived Christina both of her son, who was brought up in the French court (and married to

Claude de France in 1559), and of her political base: she lived in virtual exile in the Low Countries from 1552 to 1559. She then became an active power-broker again, however, and was instrumental in the negotiations at Cateau-Cambrésis.[68]

It is in the same busy year of 1559 that we have evidence of a large-scale scheme, principally organized and financed by the Guises, to dethrone Frederick II of Denmark at the very outset of his reign and install Christina's son.[69] At the same time, Frederick's brother-in-law, Duke August of Albertine electoral Saxony, was to be overthrown in favour of the so-called Ernestine branch of the family, headed by John Frederick II, Duke of Saxe-Weimar, which had been much reduced in status and territory under the Empire and which adhered to a conservative Lutheranism unmitigated by the influence of Melanchthon, hence uncompromisingly hostile to Calvinism. In the shadow of this threat, Frederick seems to have begun intensive counter-manœuvring. As early as 14 February 1559, Mundt sent Cecil the following news, which turned out to be somebody's wishful-thinking:

> The young King of Denmark shall marry the Emperor's daughter, which seems to be practised by Augustus the Elector of Saxony, who has married this King's sister. For all that the French King will not be pleased with this marriage, but it will not be unmeet for Denmark, for the establishment of the realm to this King and his posterity, and the exclusion of Christiern's daughters. (*CSPF, 1558–59*, No. 327, p. 134)

Similar rumours were circulating as late as the end of 1560,[70] but in August of the following year Frederick was evidently trying another tack, again matrimonial (in fact, despite offering himself on all sides, he would not marry until 1572):

> The Count of Swartzenburg, a vassal of the Elector Augustus, was lately in Lorraine, as was thought to seek the sister of the Duke of Lorraine as wife for the King of Denmark. (*CSPF, 1561–62*, No. 399, p. 247 [12 August 1561, Mundt to Cecil])

The latter initiative was probably part of an attempt by Frederick at reconciliation with Christina that her biographer places in 1562 – an attempt she roundly rebuffed (Duvernoy, 1940, p. 287).

Perhaps more effectually, Hubert Languet, in service to August and at the behest of Melancthon, undertook in 1560 the first of two secret diplomatic missions from Wittenberg to France. His principal contact was the King of Navarre, the would-be King of the Romans to whom all roads momentarily led:

C'est vers lui que convergeaient, en cette année 1560, les envoyés des diverses tendances évangéliques: Bèze se rendit à Nérac en été 1560, tandis que Hotman était officiellement chargé par le roi de Navarre de ses relations avec les princes évangéliques allemands.

[It was towards him that, in that year of 1560, the envoys of various evangelical tendencies converged: Bèze journeyed to Nérac in the summer of 1560, while Hotman was officially entrusted by the King of Navarre with his relations with the evangelical German princes.] (Nicollier-De Weck, 1995, p. 105)

Navarre's role at this point remains shadowy, as Nicollier-De Weck stresses, but clearly enough Languet's main objective was to head off the Guisian threat to Frederick II and his own political master.[71] And the Danish turn that Navarre's interests subsequently took, as well as a curious set of connections already in place, suggests somebody's attempt to enlist that 'velléitaire [wishful-thinker]' (Nicollier-De Weck, 1995, p. 106) as a counter-weight.

Was Navarre perhaps induced to dream of adapting the Guises' machinations to his own advantage? Documents prove that he had already been in contact, for the purpose of contracting mercenaries on behalf of the French crown, both with the son of John Frederick of Saxe-Weimar and with a key player in a number of projected and executed armed adventures in the Germanic states, a thoroughly unscrupulous and formidable soldier-of-fortune called Wilhelm von Grumbach, who was under sanction within the Empire for having murdered the Bishop of Würzburg in May 1558.[72] Grumbach was a player over a number of years in schemes for 'liberating' Denmark and Sweden (the latter from Gustave Vasa – here a marriage with a daughter of Christina was contemplated); he was suspected of engineering assassination attempts against August of Saxony; and, while he was technically in the service, at least off and on, of the King of France, he was most immediately in the employ of the Guises.[73] This may well have been the case even when he tempted the impetuous François Hotman to accept his services as 'Brutus' in anticipation of the Amboise affair.[74] It is hardly to reduce *Hamlet* to political allegory – on the contrary, destabilizing new resonances are thereby introduced – to note that Horatio, newly come from Wittenberg, is at the outset strangely cast in the role of a political intelligencer along the lines of Languet ('Who is't that can inform me? ... That can I. / At least the whisper goes so ...' [I.i.82–83]), and to recognize the likes of Grumbach behind the sort of mercenary adventurers associated with Fortinbras, who,

> Of unimproved mettle, hot and full,
> Hath in the skirts of Norway here and there,
> Shark'd up a list of lawless resolutes

> For food and diet to some enterprise
> That hath a stomach in't. . . .[75]
>
> (98–123)

Grumbach may conveniently serve to document another condition of political allusion-making on the late-Elizabethan stage: in part, no doubt, because of the prevailing analogical habits of thought and the persistence of the same basic issues, even short-term historical memory in the period was longer than it generally seems to be today. In 1585, when Elizabeth was attempting to forge an anti-Guisean alliance among the Protestant Germanic states, it evidently seemed to her natural to instruct her ambassador, Thomas Bodley, to advise them that they should –

> as they have often done in the civil wars of France – inhibit levies of men to go into France or the Low Countries to serve any of the 'contrary religion'; which might be afterwards employed against the peace of Germany and of the Catholics themselves, for revenge of private quarrels, 'as Grumback did against the Bishop of Würzburg'. (*CSPF, August 1584–August 1585*, p. 433 [27 April 1585, Instructions for Thomas Bodley 'for such matters as he is to communicate to the Duke of Brunswick')

A word to the wise, then, was evidently considered sufficient in referring to an event almost thirty years prior. The ambassador's instructions, incidentally, extended to delivering a warning to the King of Denmark that the House of Lorraine's pretensions to his throne had survived the recently defunct Christina of Lorraine (p. 434).

Obviously, since the Danish plots of the Guises turned on the pretensions of their kinswoman, during her lifetime she would necessarily have been implicated. There survive, in fact, four of what today would be called feasability studies, apparently prepared for Christina, in which the prospects of recovering these realms through military action are assessed. The date of these documents is uncertain – 1564 has been proposed, but at least one is prior to the death of Gustave Vasa in 1560; two were authored, respectively, by Grumbach and Bolwiller (Duvernoy, 1940, pp. 288–89). This connection makes it particularly suggestive that the latter would have approached Antoine de Bourbon to dissuade him from actions on behalf of the Protestants and to hold out the prospects of Spanish compensation. It is also on record that when Christina was reunited with her son Charles in May 1558 at Péronne, on the occasion of preliminary peace negotiations between Henri II and Philip II, she anxiously and sternly warned him to be on his guard against Navarre, citing the latter's heretical leanings (Duvernoy, 1940, p. 268).[76] Could she already have had some inkling of a Danish ambition on his part – a reaction, perhaps, to the early signs that his loss of Navarre would not be compensated under the eventual treaty?[77]

VIII

The question remains: how could Antoine de Bourbon plausibly have nurtured such a hope for himself? The obvious (if necessarily conjectural) answer is through marriage, and the obvious candidate was Christina's sister Dorothea, who, being the elder, was actually one degree closer to their father's royal right. In fact, she had been widowed (childless) in 1556 at the age of thirty-six; she was thus two years younger than Navarre. She might have seemed to offer, on the political level, something of the practical value that Gertrude possesses for Claudius. And she might be supposed to have been susceptible to influence by the current ruler of her former husband's state, the Elector Palatine, Frederick III, the principal backer of Navarre as King of the Romans.

As to Christina's general relations with her sister, there seems to be little evidence. Her biographer records, however, that in the summer of 1560 she paid a visit to Dorothea in order to discuss Danish affairs, and that she returned disappointed (Duvernoy, 1940, p. 287). Thanks (as not infrequently) to English intelligence, we can fill in the picture somewhat:

> The Dowager of Lorraine is come to Heidelberg, to try to persuade her elder sister, the old [i.e., former] Countess Palatine, to give over to her and her children the right and title to the realm of Denmark, as her aforesaid sister has no children; and also to make a marriage with the Palsgrave's second son and one of her daughters; which marriage will be very commodious for her son, seeing the troubles that are like to come over France if 'thir' enterprises get the upper hand, or with Almaine [i.e., Germany], whensoever they make war for the liberty of Metz. (*CSPF, 1560–61*, No. 328, p. 189 [12 July 1560, J. Melville to Kellegrew])

This looks rather like a desperate bid to outflank a stratagem in the course of execution, and in September of the same year her son was suspected of being used to advance presumably similar interests: 'The Duke of Lorraine, with the consent of the French and Spanish Kings, shortly goes into Almain; whether his going be touching the matter of Denmark or some other matter is not known as yet' (*CSPF, 1560–61*, No. 534, p. 303 [17 September 1560, Throckmorton to the Queen]). At the same time, the Elector Palatine was in correspondence with the ubiquitous Grumbach, seemingly with a caution that, given the enmity between the Guises and the King of Navarre, the German colonels in the French royal service were likely to be admonished ('vermahnt würden').[78]

True, Antoine de Bourbon was a married man. It says much about him, however, that, once his prospects of acquiring his wife's heritage of Navarre were thwarted, he began to think of himself as less than securely married. Apart from various infidelities, which apparently resulted in real alienation, after the outbreak of war he, too, proposed himself for the hand of Mary Stuart, who is reported to have dismissed the proposition as immoral (Brantôme, 1864–82, 7: 420–41; Bordenave, 1873, p. 110; Cazaux, 1973, p. 209). At that point, he was prepared to have his wife put away on the grounds of heresy; earlier he had thought, like Henry VIII, of invoking her brief youthful marriage, which had been annulled on the grounds of non-consumption. Navarre's multiple tergiversations finally left him not only empty-handed politically but personally isolated. In the last months of his life, as he saw the succession of the Empire assured to Maximilian II and the throne of Denmark increasingly secure in the hands of Frederick II, despite the latter's 'insolency and monstrous manners', he would have had multiple targets for Hamlet's frustrated sense that others had 'Popp'd in between th'election and my hopes'.

IX

To reconsider the possible routes by which information might have been transmitted to an English playwright in 1600, it seems to the point that one of the most deeply engaged and best informed figures in the events surrounding Antoine de Bourbon from 1558 until his death was, again, Hubert Languet.[79] Languet's first mission to France, undertaken after six months in Wittenberg gathering intelligence for the Elector of Saxony, lasted from May until autumn 1560; in January 1561 he travelled to Nuremberg for the Diet which appeared to offer Navarre such high hopes. His subsequent stay in Wittenberg was short, and in June he undertook a second mission to France, which lasted over a year – that is, until well after the outbreak of war. About this second mission, too, there is much mystery, but again no doubt about the central role of Navarre (Nicollier-De Weck, 1995, pp. 122–24). And one of Languet's 'secret' letters, dated 1 July 1561, suggests his involvement in discussions including the Cardinal of Lorraine over the Danish king's offer of marriage to Mary Stuart – an aspect, evidently, of that monarch's self-protective manœuvring.[80] The point, from the perspective of English literary history, is that Languet also stands out for his extensive network of English acquaintances (Nicollier-De Weck, 1995, p. 227 *et passim*). During the period in question, Languet was regularly in collaborative contact with Christopher Mundt, who was likewise present at the Nuremberg conference (Nicollier-De Weck, 1995, p. 114).[81] A prominent friend in later years, of course, was Philip Sidney, and through him the Sidney family and Fulke Greville.[82] (The latter, while on a political mission, accompanied Languet and Robert Sidney on the first stage of a Continental tour in 1579.[83]) All in all, Languet (who lived until 1581) might well have figured vividly enough in stories passed on about the period, with the support of his voluminous diplomatic correspondence,[84] to have been fictionally recycled as the well-informed, studious and loyal supporter of the would-be king of Denmark: a friend who somewhat mysteriously arrives from Wittenberg, keeps that fickle and unhappy prince faithful yet circumspect company, provides him with a charitable epitaph, and, while perhaps not fulfilling the desire to 'Report me and my cause aright' (V.ii.344) so as to preclude a 'wounded name' (349), could indeed 'truly deliver' (391) to posterity things otherwise 'unknown' (350). Certainly, Horatio's summary of the action shifts the focus from the protagonist's downfall to tangled political intrigues consistent with the historical moment I have been exploring – a bizarre compound of courtliness, religious fervour and gangsterism, in which the cunning Guises rub shoulders with the gun-for-hire Grumbach, while the ineffectual likes of Antoine de Bourbon are liable quite simply to get rubbed out:

> So shall you hear
> Of carnal, bloody, and unnatural acts,
> Of accidental judgments, casual slaughters,
> Of deaths put on by cunning and forc'd cause,
> And, in this upshot, purposes mistook
> Fall'n on th' inventors' heads.
>   (385–90)

Certainly, too, one distinctly hears in Horatio's final words the voice less of a sentimental confidant mourning the tragic hero than of a shrewd political adept, urging that Fortinbras' election should quickly be confirmed: 'But let this same be presently perform'd / Even while men's minds are wild, lest more mischance / On plots and errors happen' (398–400).

Part III – The psychological Hamlet

It is a salutary saw that when he composed his plays on English and Roman history, Shakespeare did not have handy for consultation the volumes of pertinent excerpts entitled, respectively, *Shakespeare's Holinshed* and *Shakespeare's Plutarch*. I do not recall ever being reminded, however, that when he was presumably remaking the so-called *Ur-Hamlet*, and perhaps consulting Belleforest's elaboration of Saxo for its treatment of Amleth, he also lacked access to such compilations of sources as those of Gollancz and Bullough. On these, however, scholars have even more heavily relied, given that there exists to date no critical edition of any complete volume of the *Histoires tragiques*. Such is not the case for either Holinshed or Plutarch.

The bibliographical record with regard to Belleforest's vast narrative œuvre is bafflingly complex: Belleforest was one of the first early modern authors in any language to 'vivre de sa plume [live by his pen]' – I allude to Michel Simonin's 1992 monograph, which is largely, in fact, bibliographical – and the volume of the *Histoires tragiques* containing the story of Amleth (properly volume five, but for commercial reasons sometimes issued as number six) was published in Paris and Lyons in at least twelve editions between 1570 and 1601, several of which were split between different publishers.[85] Still, only minor variants have been identified among the different printings of the tale itself; none of these seem decisively to privilege one edition over another as that consulted by Shakespeare – that is, of course, if he consulted any.[86]

The fact remains that compilations do not deliver 'Shakespeare's Belleforest' any more than the pre-selected 'sources' of the English and Roman plays constitute the playwright's Holinshed or Plutarch. For Shakespeare obviously found the story of Amleth in a volume containing other stories, probably eleven of them. Almost immediately – as early as 1572 – Belleforest had supplemented his original 1570 *Cinquiesme tome* of eight *histoires* (including that of Amleth) with four additional tales, although the original edition also continued to be republished, presumably for reasons of *privilège* (copyright). The expanded collection prints the stories in two different orders: in some editions that of Amleth remains the third, as it was in the original collection of eight; in others it becomes the fifth. For reasons that will become apparent, it appears to me virtually certain that Shakespeare read the tale of Amleth in an augmented collection (of which there were seemingly seven editions prior to 1601, as opposed to five of the original[87]) – hence in one containing the story of the 'Mort pitoyable du prince de Foix'. That tale appears in some editions as the eleventh, but in others, apparently beginning with that published in Paris by Jean Hulpeau in 1572, it is inserted as number four, immediately preceding that of Amleth.[88] It would therefore have furnished a sort of lens for reading the latter if one were making one's way through the volume systematically. We need by no means assume that Shakespeare did so, but in attempting to recover a fuller sense of *his* Belleforest, we should at least feel free to range as widely as he might have done: systematic reading is not particularly Shakespeare's hallmark, but eclectic and associative reading very much is; he cannot be presumed to have ignored everything in a volume that was not directly related to an immediate authorly purpose.

When we look at the *Cinquiesme tome* in any edition, we are likely first to be struck by the fact that among the original eight tales is a second one concerning Denmark: this presents the unquiet rule and ultimate martyrdom of the saintly King Canute IV (d. 1086).[89] Still, despite its vivid picture of power-struggle within the ruling family, there is finally little that bears specifically on Shakespeare's play. Belleforest's contrast (1572, fols 360^r–62^v) of the valiant Canute to his unwarlike but smooth-talking brother Harold, who initially indeed 'popp'd in between the election and [his] hopes', is arguably to the point ('taschant d'auoir par cauteleuse tyrannie, ce que brauement il n'ose entreprendre [seeking to obtain by deceitful tyranny what he dared not boldly undertake]' [1572, fol. 362^v]). So is the author's disparaging of elective monarchy (1572, fol. 382^{r-v}), which he judges vulnerable to manipulation and likely to breed discontent. But – in contrast, I believe, with the tale of Gaston de Foix – these points do not more actively engage *Hamlet* than do the various more commonplace messages of political morality, which cumulatively provide a bland sauce for the *crudité* of Canute. As is typical of the *Histoires tragiques*, such interventions insistently issue from a conservative royalist Catholic bias: the Danes' perennial backwardness in religion is proved by their current susceptibility to Lutheranism (1572, fol. 365^{r-v}); Calvinist 'boute-feuz [fire-brands]' (1572, fol. 376^v) are blamed for France's domestic strife. The author wishes, after recounting Canute's triumph over a dangerous rival, that France's own kings had been 'aussi rusez ou egaux en seueri[t]é à ce Roy à l'endroit des conspirateurs [as artful or equal in severity as that king was with regard to the conspirators]' (1572, fol. 369^v). He can only fall back on the usual consolation (which matches Hamlet's self-justification – but also Tamburlaine's) that God permits 'que ces fleaux de nostre desbauche ... soient les ministres de la vengeance de Dieu sur nos iniquitez & insolences [that these scourges of our corruption ... should be God's ministers of vengeance for our iniquities and presumptions]' (1572, fol. 370^r).

A late sixteenth-century English reader of Belleforest would have associated such rhetoric with the early period of the French civil wars. The author is thus confirmed as a long-standing supporter of royal power and Catholic exclusivity. In 1567, Belleforest translated a Latin poem (by Léger Duchesne) exalting the House of Guise and urging all-out war against the heretic rebels. The following year saw his polemic against schismatics in the same spirit, *Remonstrance av peuple de Paris, de demevrer en la foy de leurs Ancestres*, as well as a widely diffused pamphlet, *Discours des presages et miracles advenuz en la personne du Roy et parmy la France*, characterized by Denis Crouzet as 'étonnant [astonishing]' for its contribution to the 'sur-sacralisation [hyper-sacralization]' of the monarchy, with Charles IX figured as 'le vengeur de Dieu et le zélateur de la Loi [the avenger of God and the zealous guardian of the Law]' (1990, 2: 54–55).

Obviously, these activities were not independent of political sponsorship – witness, more concretely, Belleforest's role in producing a 1572 pamphlet, probably commissioned by Catherine de Medici, to counter Protestant propaganda against Mary Queen of Scots.[90] It was, of course, under Charles's auspices that Belleforest's *privilège* for the *Cinquiesme tome* was granted and that, some months after its publication in 1572, the Saint Bartholomew's massacre would be seen by some as proving that French monarchs could be 'aussi rusez ou egaux en seueri[t]é à ce Roy à l'endroit des conspirateurs'; that event, after all, was proclaimed triumphantly to the world by Camillo Capilupi as *Le Stratagème, ou la ruse de Charles IX, Roy de France, contre les Huguenots rebelles à Dieu et à luy* (1574).

Arguably, the sensational story of Gaston III, Count of Foix (1331–91) – self-styled 'Gaston Phoebus'[91] – interpellates the political context of France in the early 1570s even more dynamically than does that of Canute, while inflecting the potential reception of Shakespeare's *Hamlet* at a more basic level. It does the latter by bringing into focus, by a further anamorphic shift, another potent image of the tragic prince. For Shakespeare's construction of his protagonist has caused the folklore-derived wily youth of Saxo/Belleforest to be reimagined by audiences and commentators not only as the successful philosopher and the failed politician, but also as the notably innocent victim of a family struggle involving a vengeful father, a wicked royal uncle, and a mother haplessly torn between the two. This is likewise, in essence, the structural mechanism of Belleforest's *histoire tragique* concerning the Count of Foix, who is inadvertently responsible for destroying his own son.

Remarkably, this narrative, too, harks back imagistically to Shakespeare's climactic ungrammaticality: the rigged fencing match, where the hero effectively agrees to play by his uncle's underhanded rules and sacrifices himself to his father's vindictive spirit. Spectators (or readers) of *Hamlet* who were also readers of Belleforest – and we may at least presume some overlapping of those categories – might well have assimilated the scheming Claudius to the villainous royal uncle of the 'Mort pitoyable du prince de Foix': 'Ce Roy ayant tenu le bec en l'eau à son neveu [That king, having strung his nephew along]', finally had recourse, we are told with blunt irony, to his preferred weapon, 'à sçauoir du poison, car s'estoient les armes les plus coustumieres desquelles ce vaillant Prince souloit s'escrimer [namely, poison, for these were the customary weapons with which that valiant prince was wont to fence]' (1572, fol. 121ʳ).[92]

'Escrimer [fence]' is metaphorical here, as in Montaigne, and although the poison – not a factor at all in the tale of Amleth – is quite real, it is twice given a metaphorical packaging that recalls Claudius' proffer of the presumably poisoned 'union' to Hamlet:[93] 'il se reseruoit le ioyau le plus delicat pour le presenter à son neveu en secret [he kept to himself the most precious jewel to present it to his nephew in secret]' (1572, fols 121ᵛ–22ʳ); 'Ainsi mon neueu, mon amy, prenez ce present comme le plus cher ioyau que ie sçauray vous donner [So, nephew, my friend, take this present as the most precious jewel I could give you]' (1572, fol. 124ʳ). This is a plot that thoroughly succeeds – as, perhaps, that of Claudius is also seen to do – because God conspicuously keeps his hands off the princely hearts involved: 'Voyez combien peut la fureur, & le soupçon au cœur des Princes [See how much the fury and suspicion in the hearts of princes are capable of doing]' (fol. 132ᵛ). Moreover, to the extent that Hamlet might have shadowed forth Antoine de Bourbon as a political disaster case, it becomes especially ironic that the wicked uncle in the story retailed by Belleforest is the King of Navarre.

I

Not that Belleforest is writing here about Antoine de Bourbon. Rather, his unmitigated villain is Charles II of Navarre – known to history as 'le Mauvais [the Bad]'[94] – who flourished (if that is the right word) in the mid-fourteenth century (1332–87). There is, however, a tense interplay between past and present that would have lent Belleforest's narrative as much ideological punch as entertainment value, and at least some turn-of-the-century English readers would have been alert to this dimension – some French ones, too, undoubtedly including the current King of Navarre, Henri. (More than commercial vicissitudes may underlie the fact that, when the pertinent volume of the *Histoires tragiques* was reissued, beginning in 1601, after an interval of seventeen years, the tale of the Prince of Foix was invariably omitted.) If only to account for the predisposition of Shakespeare's audience to recognize features of the story behind the situation in *Hamlet*, the probable political resonances are worth some attention here.

For Belleforest, the purifying apocalypse inaugurated by Charles IX's accession to the throne of France effectively renewed the medieval perfection of the French chivalric ideal. Of this ideal Charles II of Navarre had been literally and symbolically a poisoner, beginning with an attempt on the life of Charles V ('le Sage') of France (1338–80). It is for that ideal that Gaston Phoebus is allowed to stand in his glory before succumbing to the malignant influence of Navarre, and his initial portrait is as idyllic as Hamlet's image of his father:

> Si iamais la Gascongne a veu vn prince bon iusticier, cestuy aimoit l'equité, & ne denioit iustice à homme du monde, charitable, doux à ses suiets. ... En somme ce Prince sembloit estre vne chose feée, & son palais vn paradis de son temps.

[If ever Gascony has seen a prince who was a good dispenser of justice, he was a lover of equity and never denied justice to any man in the world, charitable, mild to his subjects. ... In sum, this prince seemed to be a thing enchanted, and his palace a paradise of his age.] (1572, fols 107ᵛ–8ʳ)

Belleforest's contemporaries might have been expected to supply the knowledge that the equivalent threat to the French national 'paradis' of the present time was none other than Charles II's descendant and the current bearer of his title. Henri of Navarre would have been the candidate for the role of chief 'boute-feuz' – at least symbolically, even if the epithet was more plausibly applied to the Admiral Coligny, as by Chantelouve in his 1574 tragedy (ed. Cameron, 1971, l. 828). Certainly, Belleforest's rhetoric in the *histoire tragique* closely matches that commonly applied to the Huguenot leaders:[95]

lequel Charles estant Roy de Nauarre, fut aussi celuy, qui iamais n'eut plaisir qu'a troubler le repos d'autruy, ny contentement qu'à mescontenter tout le monde: & lequel estoit lors a son aise, quand il voioit le sang espandu par tout, & ouioit la nouuelle du saccagement des villes & prouinces de ses voisins.

[the which Charles, being King of Navarre, was also he who never took pleasure except in troubling the peace of others, nor contentment except in discontenting everyone; and who was at his ease when he saw blood shed everywhere, and heard of the ravaging of the towns and provinces of his neighbours.] (1572, fol. 108ᵛ)

Henri's marriage into the royal family in the person of Marguerite de Valois had come into prospect during negotiations over the Peace of Saint-Germain (8 August 1970), as Belleforest himself would later record in his monumental – and eminently official – history, *Les Grandes Annales et histoire générale de France* (1579, 1: fol. 1682ʳ).[96] That matrimonial event of 1572, which Crouzet terms 'l'achèvement [fulfilment]' of 'la pacification de 1570 [the pacification of 1570]' (1990, 2: 50), was destined, of course, to furnish the occasion for the Saint Bartholomew massacre. Although publicly promoted by the royal family, chiefly Catherine de Medici, the marriage was seen by many Catholics as a concession to heresy – one doubly dangerous because of Henri of Navarre's claim to the crown should the Valois line fail. The dark underside of the celebrations is epitomized by the festive ballet – proof, retrospectively, for many Protestants that the cataclysm was in planning – in which King Charles and his brothers defended the 'paradis d'amour' from Huguenot assailants, led by Henri of Navarre, who were repulsed, then dragged by devils into hell.[97] However remote Henri's inheritance of the crown might have seemed in 1572, it loomed as all but inevitable from 1584 (with the death of François, Duke of Anjou), and Matthieu, in *La Guisiade* (1589), would make his Clergy deplore the idea that 'un superbe Apostat' might 'ravisse le lis, la perle de l'Estat [an arrogant apostate / Ravish the fleur-de-lys and the pearl of the state]' (1990, ll. 1151–52; trans. Hillman, 2005) – images that combine the symbolism of sovereignty with that of Marguerite.

Such a perspective would be hard to exclude from Belleforest's insistence, in the tale of Gaston, that the latter's fatal error was his marriage into the family of Navarre: 'Ce Prince estant si heureux en toutes autres choses, fut en cecy infortuné, que d'auoir aliance au plus fin & malicieux Prince de son siecle, à celuy Charles [That prince being so happy in all other things, was in this unfortunate, in being allied by marriage with the most cunning and devious prince of his age, with that Charles]' (1572, fol. 108^{r-v}). The self-recriminations of the Count himself reiterate the taint, assimilating the past poisoning of French royalty to his present cursed 'alliance':

> Tellement qu'il maudissoit en son cœur, le Roy de Nauarre, comme celuy, qu'il soupçonnoit auteur de quelque meschanceté contre sa vie, veu qu'il sçauoit comme c'estoit luy qui auoit voulu faire empoisonner le Roy de France Charles le quint, & qui ne faisoit non plus d'estat des meurtres, que d'autres font de la conseruation de leur semblable: destestoit, & maudissoit l'heure que iamais il s'estoit allié de ceste maison, non pour le respect de la race, qui estoit des plus anciennes, & illustres de l'Europe, mais à cause de la lascheté de celuy qui en estant le chef, faisoit tout à la posterité par le memoire de ses vices & forfaits.

> [So greatly did he curse in his heart the King of Navarre as he whom he suspected to be the author of some wickedness against his life, since he knew that it was he who had sought to have the King of France Charles V poisoned, and who made no more account of murders than others do of preserving their fellow-man. He detested and cursed the hour when he had ever allied himself with that house, not on account of the family, which was one of the most ancient and illustrious of Europe, but because of the base-mindedness of him who, as its leader, determined all for posterity by way of his vices and crimes.] (1572, fol. 128^{r})

Indirect evidence for Belleforest's use of Charles of Navarre to stigmatize Henri in the *histoire tragique* is provided by another of the author's politico-historical interventions – one that illustrates more straightforwardly, however, his sense of 'what's in a name'. This work's orientation is amply conveyed by its title: *Histoire des neuf roys Charles de France, contenant la fortune, vertu et heur fatal des Roys, qui sous ce nom de Charles ont mis à fin des choses merveilleuses* (1568). Yet here the fourteenth-century Navarre's machinations against Charles V (pp. 174–77), while serving to oppose the latter's glory ('O heureux siècle de ce bon & sage Roy Charles le Quint! [O happy age of that good and wise King Charles the Fifth!]' [p. 176]) to the former's 'sagesse, ruses & subtilitez [cunning, ruses and subtleties]' (p. 177), stops well short of demonizing Henri's ancestor: even allowing for the difference in genre (Gaston's story finds no place here), there is no suggestion that Navarre brought moral pollution to the realm of France.

The radical difference of Belleforest's project here may be gathered from what may seem a surprising treatment of Henri's much closer relative, Antoine de Bourbon. I have earlier viewed that figure mainly through the lens of Protestant disillusion. Obviously, though, there was room for treating his death in the Catholic cause in a positive way, and Belleforest resolutely does so, picking up the element of personal valour noted by Brantôme and others, attaching it to royalist fervour, and referring with the greatest discretion to earlier lapses, which are conveniently blamed on misleading advisers. It is, indeed, as if Belleforest is deliberately countering the degrading squib that circulated after Antoine's death, denying that the latter 'vécut sans gloire' (and suppressing the less-than-ennobling fact that he 'mourut en pissant'):

> Durant ces entrefaites, comme le Roy de Nauarre faisant l'office d'vn bon chef allast autour de la ville pour veoir le lieu plus commode afin d'y donner l'assaut, voicy vne balle mortelle qui le frappe en l'espaule, & le blesse à mort au grand regret de tous, & dommage de toute la France. Car ce Prince tant qu'il a vescu a esté orné de toutes les parties dignes d'vn si genereux chef, & vaillant homme de guerre, lequel pour le seruice du Roy, n'espargna onc ne biens, ne vie, & à la fin pour inceluy il y a glorieusement finy ses iours: en vne chose esto[it] il à vituperer de ce que trop facilement il se laissoit mener & croyoit plus de leger que sa grandeur & reng ne le requeroient point: & c'est pourquoy plusieurs choses se passoient indignes de son nom à cause qu'il prestoit par trop l'oreille a ceux qui luy estoient familiers desquels ne se pouuoit tirer conseil qui luy fust par trop profitable. Mais qui est celuy qui est sans vice, ou sur lequel on ne trouue que reprendre tant iuste soit-il?

> [While these things were going on, as the King of Navarre was performing like a good leader in going round the town in order to see the most convenient place to make the assault, behold a fatal bullet came to strike him in the shoulder and give him his death's wound, to the great regret of all and the injury of all of France. For that prince, while he lived, had been adorned with all those parts worthy of such a noble leader and valiant man of war, who, in his king's service, spared neither goods nor life; and for him, in the end, he gloriously finished his days there. In one thing he was to be condemned: that he allowed himself to be led too easily and believed more credulously than called for by his greatness and rank. And that is why many things took place unworthy of his name, because he lent his ear too readily to those familiar to him, from whom he could not receive advice that was overly profitable for him. But who is he who is without vice, or in whom one cannot find something to reproach, however righteous he may be?]
> (1568, p. 522)

It seems to the point that, while the *Histoire des neuf roys Charles de France* was published in 1568, not only does its *privilège* date from 1566, but a contract is extant, dated 5 August 1561 and terming the book 'composé', in which Belleforest promises his publisher, L'Huillier, to deliver the completed manuscript within eight days. In fact, the work covers events through 1567, and the author concludes with a frankly arbitrary decision to end at that point and await royal reaction:

> Icy donc mettray-ie fin pour ce coup a ma Carliade, n'ayant en deliberation de passer plus auant, iusqu'à ce que ie cognoisse si mon labeur est aggreable a celle puissance, a qui ie l'addresse.

> [Here then I shall make an end for this time to my Carliad, not having the intention to go further forward until I may know whether my work is agreeable to that power to whom I address it.] (1568, p. 684)

The facts suggest that Belleforest had written all or most of his history of the preceding reigns by 1561 and that he continued to chronicle events of the current one more or less as they occurred. The account of Charles of Navarre thus almost certainly precedes the first civil war, while Antoine's death may have been described not long after the event. At that point, Henri de Navarre was the nine-year-old son of a fallen Catholic prince, living at court in Paris, separated from his mother and by no means acquired for the Protestant cause.[98] As such he also made a suitable dedicatee for a translation of an Italian conduct manual published in the same year, a work in which Belleforest seemingly had a hand and which bears his initials (Simonin, 1992, pp. 67–71). By 1570, the political situation had changed drastically, and Henri might be taken to have betrayed his father's noble example. At the same time, Belleforest had become more deeply implicated in promoting royalist Catholic mythology. It is in these circumstances that the current King of Navarre's disreputable ancestor appears to have stepped from the historical shadows into an *histoire tragique* as a ready-made vehicle for deploring 'alliance' with a 'race, qui estoit des plus anciennes, & illustres de l'Europe ... à cause de la lascheté [de son] chef'.

Charles le Mauvais would also have made a particularly appropriate vehicle for blackening the House of Navarre because, at least intermittently, he had been England's ally against France in the Hundred Years War, just as Henri de Navarre was the new champion of English Protestants. Indeed, English sensibilities would likely have bristled at one scandalous connection: Charles's daughter, Joan of Navarre, had been the second wife of Henry IV, and although she had had a particularly good relation with the youthful Prince Hal, she was imprisoned for some time by the mature Henry V for attempting to destroy him by witchcraft – a charge, according to historians, almost certainly trumped up for financial motives and belatedly renounced by Henry to salve his conscience.[99] That Belleforest was far from unconscious of the English dimension is signalled by his depiction of Gaston, with more than a touch of patriotic exaggeration, as a sort of inverted King Arthur: 'de son logis sortoyent les braues cheualiers pour le seruice des Roys desquels il estoit amy, tels qu'estoyent le François, & l'Espaignol, car bon Anglois ne fut ce Comte en sa vie [from his lodging went forth those brave knights for the service of the kings whose friend he was, such as the French and the Spaniard, for never in his life was that Count a good Englishman]' (1572, fol. 108ʳ).

Just how useful Charles of Navarre historically was to the English is a point hammered home by another extremely curious product of Belleforest published in the massacre year: *Recueil diligent et profitable auquel sont contenuz les choses plus notables à remarquer de toute l'histoire de Jean Froissart ... abrégé et illustré de plusieurs annotations, par François de Belle-Forest*. In fact, this is a translation – generally quite close but with suggestive colourations – of the Latin *Epitome* of Froissart's chronicle that was first produced by Johannes Sleidanus in 1537. It is notable, first, that Belleforest is translating Froissart back into French, when the *Chroniques* themselves were readily available, having been regularly republished since the late fifteenth century. Perhaps more remarkable is that, while the *Epitome* itself was a popular work, Belleforest does not acknowledge Sleidanus. On the contrary, he claims, in his introductory epistle, that he is himself the epitomizer: 'Froissard ... estant presque fasceux, & trop long, ie vous l'ay abregé y faisant choir de ce qui est le plus remarquable & digne d'y estre noté [Froissart ... being almost tedious, and too long, I have abridged him for you by choosing in it what is most remarkable and worthy in it to be noted]' (Sleidanus, trans. Belleforest, 1572, sig. aiiijʳ). The most obvious explanation is that Belleforest was aiming at a quick commercial success with a proven product among a 'down-market' readership, but it may be equally pertinent that Sleidanus was a staunchly Protestant translator and historian.[100]

We are some distance from the *histoire tragique*, but the *Epitome* and Belleforest's cooptation of it deserve a passing word. Sleidanus distils to its essence Froissart's account of the Hundred Years War over most of the fourteenth century. Detail is stripped down and narrative played up, with attention to the most colourful characters. A major actor for much of the period is Charles of Navarre, whose name virtually leaps off page after page, usually in connection with nefarious schemes that put his self-interest ahead of that of France and ally him with the English. His name is all the more conspicuous in Belleforest's version because of its recurrence in the added marginal notes, usually to signal some wicked action, as when 'Le roy de Nauarre voulut faire empoisonner le Roy Charles [The King of Navarre sought to have King Charles poisoned]' (Sleidanus, trans. Belleforest, 1572, fol. 93ʳ). It seems probable that readers in late 1572 would have made a reflexive association with the current King of Navarre, the current King Charles. There is even an attempted massacre in Paris sponsored by the treacherous Navarre, and Belleforest's translation grabs attention in a way that reminds us that we are dealing with the master of the *histoire tragique*.

The Latin recounts dryly, with consummate concision, the Dauphin's deft foiling (with the Church's help) of the bloody designs of Navarre, who had corrupted the Provost of Paris:

> Regis filius, inter Nauarrium & vrbis præfectum tacitam esse conspirationem videns, Lutetia cessit, collectis copiis. & spectabat res ad tumultuosum exitum, obsidebat enim vrbem. Sed Episcoporum quorundam intercessione, reconciliati sunt principes.
>
> Cæterum præfactus vt misceret omnia, nocte quadam statutum habuit eos, qui sequerentur aduersas partes, opprimere.
>
> [The king's son, seeing that there was a silent conspiracy between Navarre and the mayor, left Paris, having gathered forces. And he looked for a violent issue, for he was besieging the city. But by the intercession of certain bishops, the princes were reconciled.
>
> Yet the mayor, that he might throw all into confusion, decreed that on a certain night those who followed the adverse parties should be taken by surprise.] (Sleidanus, 1537, fol. 16ᵛ)

By contrast, Belleforest's version of the last sentence is spectacular and, for good measure, names the arch-villain again: 'Mais le Prevost des marchans [i.e., the mayor], qui prenoit plaisir à troubler tout, delibera de faire tailler en pieces de belle nuit tous ceux qui suyuoyent le party contraire du Nauarrois [But the mayor, who took delight in causing trouble, determined to have cut to pieces during the night all those who followed the party opposed to Navarre]' (Sleidanus, trans. Belleforest, 1572, fol. 43ᵛ). It is to the point that the official justification of the Saint Bartholomew massacre was precisely the accusation that the party of Navarre was planning its own. Belleforest's vivid account is no less eerily suggestive in retrospect – on the contrary – for having been written at least five months before the event (the dedicatory epistle is signed 20 March 1572). One thinks again of the uncannily accurate prophecy of Henri of Navarre's fall from the 'paradis d'amour'.[101]

It suggestively highlights the more cautious procedures of official historiography that in the magisterial retrospective offered in the *Grandes Annales*, the marriage of Henri de Navarre and Marguerite is presented positively – as an 'alliance tant bonne et nécessaire [such a good and necessary alliance]' (1579, 2: fol. 1682ʳ), whose celebration was spoiled by the insolence and rebellious machinations of the Huguenots. In fact, the positive view is pointedly extended to Henri, Duke of Guise, widely singled out by Protestants (as in Marlowe's play) as an engineer of the massacre: he is said to have approved of the union. Meanwhile, in its proper historical moment the blackening of the character of Charles of Navarre can proceed apace (and to be fair, the evidence is not far to seek) by way of dispassionate narrative, and with special attention to his subversion of French national unity in the face of the English enemy.[102]

To round out the sense of Belleforest's interventions as at once literary and political – a point that will figure again in connection with *All's Well* – there may be a more personal reason why the relations between Gaston de Foix and Charles II of Navarre were invested with a particular charge in his *histoire tragique*. Belleforest habitually identified himself on his title pages as 'Comingois', with reference to his origin in Comminges, the former province of Gascony situated in the Pyrenees. Clearly, he possessed a strong sense of local identity to counterpoint his ostentatious devotion to the French crown and its traditional religion. His most significant literary enterprise has a regional connection: the prime mover of the *histoire tragique* as a genre was Matteo Bandello, of Piedmontese origin but at his death (1561) Bishop of Agen, where he had spent many years. That city, which was the centre of a flourishing Humanist culture, under strong Italian influence, during the second quarter of the sixteenth century,[103] is located just outside the domains of Foix-Béarn. (In fact, it was the site of a tense diplomatic encounter at which the Count of Foix deftly managed to avoid paying formal homage to Edward the Black Prince [Tucoo-Chala, 1993, pp. 117–20].) The region, then, is very much the territory of the events in question, and the central circumstance of the *histoire*, the ill-starred marriage between Agnès de Navarre and Gaston III, was largely the project of the latter's mother, Aliénor de Comminges (Tucoo-Chala, 1993, pp. 52–54, 208). Belleforest shows himself highly sensible of the taint attaching to the House of Foix from the widely received French account of the episode, according to which Gaston's son deliberately sought his father's death in order to seize his inheritance and was duly executed in consequence. The author's version redeems the family's honour together with its Frenchness, and in support he deploys the credentials at once of the learned, and the local, historian:

> mais quand à nous, ayant lue & les annales de Foix, & Froissard, & Fulgose, qui discourent l'histoire ainsi que vous l'auons iusqu'icy deduite, laisserons en cest endroit nostre annaliste, qui peut estre s'est laissé informer tout au contraire de ce qui passe en Bearn sur cest affaire.

[but as for us, having read the annals of Foix, as well as Froissard and (Fregoso), which relate the history as we have set it down for you, we shall depart on this point from our annalist, who perhaps has let himself be quite misinformed as to what happened in Béarn in this matter.] (*Cinquiesme tome*, 1572, fol. 125ʳ)[104]

II

Let me return now from the political charge with which Belleforest loads the tale of Gaston Phoebus to its intertextual engagement by *Hamlet*. The narrative of Froissart is extremely spare and furnishes none of the interpretive embel-lishment – the sense of drama, the psychology of character, the moral signifi-cance – that is introduced by Belleforest in the *Cinquiesme tome*.[105] An English playwright might also have read Froissart's account, of course, and he could have found it, in closely similar versions, not only in Froissart's original French and the English of John Bourchier, Lord Berners,[106] but also in Sleidanus' *Epitome* (1537, fols 69ʳ–71ᵛ) and the translation of the latter back into French by Belleforest (Sleidanus, trans. Belleforest, 1572, fols 155ʳ–89ᵛ). Without the rich additions of the *histoire tragique*, however, there would be only a glancing relation to *Hamlet*, and it is the enriched text that Shakespeare would most naturally have encountered. The broad tendency of the elaboration is obviously to render the *histoire* veritably *tragique*, both in its aesthetic design and as a morally significant structure. Of this strategy Belleforest shows himself fully conscious in his summarizing address to the reader:

> Ainsi fut poursuiuie la sanglante tragedie en la maison de Foix, que ie vous ay deduite, quoy qu'ailleurs vous la puissiez trouuer assez au long escrite: mais non auec tels enrichissemens, ny accompaignée de tant de succez, ny de la vengeance que Dieu print de ceux qui auoient causé la mort de l'innocent, et poursuiuy la ruine de toute vne maison, par celle de l'heritier principal d'icelle.

> [Thus was fulfilled the bloody tragedy in the House of Foix which I have set down for you, although elsewhere you may find it written out at length – but not with such enrichments, nor accompanied with such development, nor with the vengeance that God took upon those who have caused the death of the innocent, and pursued the ruin of an entire house by that of its principal inheritor.] (1572, fol. 145ᵛ)

This is a summary, incidentally, that anticipates the trajectory of Shakespeare's tragedy far more closely than does the limp encomium of the virtues of Amleth with which the latter's *histoire* concludes.

At the moral and affective core of Belleforest's tale is the young prince's inno-cence, which is bound up with his affection for his father. Precisely this point becomes complicated in *Hamlet*, of course, and it is intriguing to learn, from

Olhagaray's (post-*Hamlet*) *Histoire de Foix, Béarn, et Nauarre*, that a proto-Freudian explanation is advanced by those who accept the prince's murderous intention: Navarre supposedly induced him to punish his father for ill-treating his mother (1609, pp. 292–93). (Olhagaray rejects such theories on the basis of 'nos origineaux [our originals]' [1609, p. 293].) There is evidently plenty of room within the shifting narratives of this family situation for emotional ambiguity – ambiguity such as the Shakespearean hero himself, in psychological readings, projects upon his father's ghost:

> The spirit that I have seen
> May be a devil, and the devil hath power
> T'assume a pleasing shape, yea, and perhaps,
> Out of my weakness and my melancholy,
> As he is very potent with such spirits,
> Abuses me to damn me.
> (II.ii.594–99)

As it happens, the archival evidence abundantly demonstrates that the real Count had little affection for his wife (to put it mildly), and that he welcomed an excuse to get rid of her in humiliating fashion.[107] Even in Belleforest, the shimmering innocence of the young man is set off against the Count's distinctly forbidding character.

I hasten to acknowledge that the story of the Count of Foix intersects little with the plot of *Hamlet*. The basic circumstances are these – in simplified form, which makes any accidental explanation of the prince's death stand out as intrinsically improbable, to say the least.[108] Against his better judgement, the noble Gaston accepts the word of Navarre, his brother-in-law, to pay the ransom of a prisoner-of-war. When the deceitful king defaults, the Count sends his wife to deal with him, but to no avail. The Count's son suffers greatly at the resulting alienation between his parents and obtains his father's reluctant permission to visit his mother. Before returning, he is tricked by the uncle into accepting a powder, to be secretly administered to his father, which will supposedly act magically to restore the Count's love for his wife. (Charles's 'ioyau' – seemingly derived from a rare ironic touch in Sleidanus' account[109] – thus matches not only Claudius' poisoned 'union' but the attendant play on words; nowhere else does Shakespeare use this term for a rare pearl.) Before he can act, however, the boy's bastard brother discloses the powder's existence. The Count seizes it, proves it to be deadly, and is restrained only with difficulty from killing his son on the spot. He imprisons the boy, has a number of his companions put to death, and convokes the Estates of the realm in order to sanction his son's execution.

Meanwhile, the boy becomes melancholic and refuses to eat. When the Count is so informed, he visits his son's cell, torn between love and anger, and grabs him in such a way that, unbeknownst to him, the paring knife he happens to be holding wounds the boy's neck. This proves sufficient, given the latter's weakness and low morale, to provoke his death shortly afterwards. When the father is notified, he is grief-stricken. There is, then, no concealed murder, usurpation, or ghost; the young prince's mother is his uncle's true sister, and not linked with him sexually or morally; the father outlives the son. Yet, in transforming *histoire* into *histoire tragique*, Belleforest lavishly sensationalized, moralized and embellished – not least the Count's enigmatic and contradictory behaviour – in ways that resonate with Shakespeare.

In fact, the father's transformation, by way of his blind insistence on vengeance, from intended victim of his treacherous brother-in-law to victimizer of his son lends him at least a structural affinity with *Hamlet*'s ghost. It is as if Claudius' attempt on Old Hamlet had failed but conjured a similar spirit of vengeance, and several details are attached to the transformation which provocatively extend the resemblance. Of course, the *Ur-Hamlet*'s ghost miserably crying, 'Hamlet, revenge', has credentials as a pre-Shakespearean addition to Saxo/Belleforest (Jenkins, ed., 1982, pp. 82–83); it is hardly probable, however, that the distinctive ambiguities of Shakespeare's version, which intimately interplay with the doubts and ambivalence of his protagonist, were anticipated there, and these are the elements that suggest colouration by Belleforest's tale of Gaston.[110]

The play's accent on the sinful state of Hamlet's notably virtuous father at his death has often appeared 'ungrammatical' and certainly has no counterpart in the story of Amleth. The point is made first by the ghost himself, who speaks of having to purge 'the foul crimes done in my days of nature' (I.v.11), having been 'sent to my account / With all my imperfections on my head' (78–79). Hamlet returns to the theme when he recalls that Claudius 'took my father grossly, full of bread, / With all his crimes broad blown' (III.iii.80–81), and vows to do likewise. This is already to assume the role of heaven's 'scourge and minister' to which he will lay claim after dispatching Polonius, similarly unprepared; later he boasts of sending Rosencrantz and Guildenstern to their doom, 'Not shriving-time allow'd' (V.ii.47).

Belleforest's *histoire tragique* is nowhere truer to its genre than in dwelling with gruesome relish on the sudden deaths justly visited on the perpetrators of evil, Gaston and Charles, deadly enemies but finally unwitting accomplices, 'pour satisfaire les ombres du fils du Comte occis à tort [to satisfy the shades of the Count's son wrongfully killed]' (1572, fol. 145ʳ). (The Bastard is thrown in for good measure.) Still, demonstrating heaven's justice poses rather a challenge, given the long and prosperous lives enjoyed by both wrong-doers. It is gratifying, at least, that the Claudius-like Navarre, the 'second Neron de son aage [the second Nero of his age]' (1572, fol. 144^r), guilty of chronic 'paillardise [wantonness]', 'concupiscence [lust]', 'gloute, & pillarde conuoitise [gluttony and greedy avarice]', not to mention numerous 'massacres, brusle-mens & empoisonnemens [murders, burnings and poisonings]' (1572, fols 144^r–45^r), finally goes up in flames when his valet accidentally sets fire to his bandages, which had been soaked with *eau-de-vie* as a medical measure. By contrast, Gaston's end comes stubbornly close to anticlimax: aged almost ninety, he takes a chill after a morning's hunting on a hot day.

The excitement of the latter death must therefore be supplied rhetorically. Thus the death-chamber is abundantly decked with greenery – to the point of evoking the orchard in which Old Hamlet took his fatal nap (another addition to the Amleth tale) – and the reader is warned:

> la mort ne craignit de s'y loger auec sa face hideuse, & espouuentable, & se cachant souz la frescheur de de [*sic*] cest ombrage, conduisit le Prince aux obscurs riuages d'Acheron, d'ou aucun ne peut repasser …
>
> [death did not fear to lodge itself there with its hideous and terrible face, and, hiding beneath the freshness of those shadows, conducted the Prince to the dark banks of Acheron, whence no one may return …] (1572, fol. 142^r)

Hamlet's 'undiscover'd country, from whose bourn / No traveller returns' (III.i.79–80) has, of course, ample precedent elsewhere,[111] but the note may have made the greater impression on Shakespeare for being sounded twice in quick succession: 'il estoit allé en lieu d'o[u] le retour n'est facile [he had gone to that place whence the return is not easy]' (1572, fol. 143^r).

Not 'facile', but not necessarily impossible. For, thanks to a dying call for mercy, the Count's sin-laden soul is not simply left to sink away. Rather, theological niceties aside (as indeed they seem to be for Shakespeare), his spirit gives the impression of entering a purgatorial state akin to that of Hamlet's father:

> Mais quoy? Il falloit qu'il allast payer la rançon de son forfait, qui luy estoit sur la teste, dés [*sic*] la mort violente commise en la personne de son fils innocent: & que comme il l'auoit contraint de mourir sans auoir loisir de penser au salut de son ame, aussi bien [Dieu][112] le priua de la lumiere de ceste vie, pour, au milieu de ses aises, luy rauir, & plaisirs, & vie, sans qu'il eust moyen de faire la recong-noissance deuë au chrestien à telle heure, si pressée & effroyable: bien qu'il criast mercy à celui, la main duquel il sentoit le punir, & chastier ce corps afin (comme ie pense) que l'ame n'allast en perdition eternelle.

[But what of that? He had to go pay the ransom of his crime, which lay upon his head since the violent death committed on the person of his innocent son. And since he had compelled him to die without having the time to think of the salvation of his soul, even so (God) deprived him of the light of this life so as to ravish from him pleasures and life without his having the means to make the due acknowledgement of a Christian at such an hour, so urgent and terrible, although he cried for mercy to Him whose hand he felt punishing and chastizing his body, so that the soul, as I take it, should not pass into eternal perdition.] (1572, fol. 143^r–^{v})

Indeed, as further titillation, Belleforest assimilates Gaston's vindictive evil to supernatural suasion:

ie ne veux pas dire que ceste punition luy escheut, à cause qu'il s'aidoit du conseil d'vn malin esprit familier, qui luy racomptoit tout ce qui se faisoit, car s'il est veritable qu'il s'adonnast à telle folie, il est impossible que ce meschant secretaire ne l'aye conduit à sa ruine, & n'ait esté cause de ses folies, comme ainsi soit que iamais homme n'eust familiarité à tels fantosmes, qui ne sentist en fin pour qu'elle [sic] occasion est-ce que Satan se monstre amy de l'homme, & qu'il ne le caresse sinon pour le tromper, & ne se communique à luy que pour l'attirer à sa perdition.

[I do not wish to say that such punishment came upon him because he made use of the advice of an evil familiar spirit, who dictated to him all that he did to himself, for if it is true that he gave himself over to such madness, it is impossible that that evil instrument did not lead him to his ruin and was not the cause of his outbursts of madness, as never does it happen that a man has familiarity with such ghosts who does not finally realize for what occasion Satan shows himself the friend of man, and that he soothes him only in order to deceive him and reveals himself to him only so as to draw him to his perdition.] (1572, fols 143^v–44^r)[113]

These are precisely the terms in which Hamlet doubtfully weighs the ghost's authority.

Divine vengeance, obviously, abounds as spectacularly as possible in Belleforest's *tragique* evocation of Gaston's death. The contrast could not be more striking with the version offered in the *Grandes Annales* (1579, 2: fol. 999^v). There, not only is the episode of his son, which was recounted some sixty pages earlier, not reintroduced, but Gaston expires, however suddenly, in a spirit approaching saintly tranquillity: 'si heureusement il auoit vescu plus de soisante douze ans ... craint, & honnoré de chascun, aimé, & reueré de ses suiets [thus happily he had lived more than seventy-two years ... feared and honoured by all, loved and revered by his subjects]' (1579, 2: fol. 999^v). The *histoire tragique*, on the other hand, pulls out all the vindictive stops, and it does so in order to support the moral preoccupation of its Argument: the destructive potential of human retribution – 'la vengeance, qui excede la raison [vengeance which exceeds reason]' (1572, fol. 104ᵛ). This makes a sharp swerving from the broad endorsement of the heroic code in the Amleth tale, whose pagan setting Belleforest stresses in his conclusion. The world of Gaston Phoebus is inexorably Christian, and reflection and careful weighing of evidence are strenuously recommended to ensure that any revenge of a public injury is compatible with justice. As for private injuries, it is simply not 'au chrestien à prendre vengeance [for a Christian to take vengeance]' (1572, fol. 104ᵛ). But this, too, is part of Hamlet's dilemma: where do public and private start and stop?

In order to 'sweep to my revenge' (I.v.31) as he first anticipates doing, Hamlet would need the very 'fureur [furor]' that is unequivocally condemned in the story of Gaston as 'vne estrange imperfection de l'ame, et vn transport brutal de l'esprit ... [qui] ne peut aussi ouurer que follement, ny donner ou engendrer que des effects de mauuaise consequence [a strange imperfection of the soul, and a brutal transport of the mind ... (which) cannot act other than madly nor give or engender effects other than of evil consequence]' (1572, fol. 104ᵛ). Hamlet's determination to 'have grounds / More relative than this' (II.ii.599–600) conforms precisely to the principle that justice 'ne venge que les forfaits euidents, & ne punit que les choses apparentes, sans se laisser aller apres les simples coniectures [avenges only evident crimes, and punishes only things that are apparent, without letting itself go according to simple conjectures]' (1572, fol. 104ᵛ). And whereas Amleth gains points for playing the fool so that his sword is nailed to its scabbard, then turning that trick against the king in a climactic display of cleverness, here Belleforest comes down on the side of 'les loix [qui] ostent le couteau aux fols, & deffendent a chascun de iuger en sa propre cause [laws (that) deprive fools of the knife and forbid everyone to judge in his own cause]' (1572, fol. 105ʳ). Finally, there is less than might be supposed to distinguish the 'perturbed spirit' (I.v.190) of Hamlet's father, to which Hamlet swears his memory and service, from the 'esprit inexorable [inexorable spirit]' of a desire for vengeance that must be subjected to protracted pondering: 'la raison nous comande de penser vn fait longuement, auant que l'executer [reason commands us to ponder a deed at length before executing it]' (1572, fol. 105ʳ).

From this perspective, precisely the second thoughts that impede his 'resolution', the 'regard' that causes to 'turn awry' the forceful 'currents' (III.i.86–87) set in motion by the Ghost's 'Remember me' (I.v.91), appear as a salutary check to the tormenting goad of obsessive memory:

> Car quelque equité qui reluise en leur fait, quelque droit qui paroisse en leur cause, si est ce que le transport les guide de telle sorte, & le souuenir de se sentir

outragéz bourrelle tellement leurs esprits, qu'il n'y a raison qui les destourne [cf. 'turn awry'] de leur premiere conception, & pretente, ny iustice tant seuere, qui puisse contenter leur felonnie.

[For whatever justice appears in their deed, whatever right appears in their cause, so is it that transport so guides them and the memory of feeling outraged so greatly torments their minds, that there is no reason that turns them aside from their first conception and purpose, nor justice severe enough that might satisfy their criminal intent.] (1572, fol. 105^r)

The model of the 'impetuous or raging torrent' borrowed from Montaigne's Alexander thereby reveals itself as morally bereft.

Accordingly, for Hamlet finally to discern 'divinity' in his 'indiscretion' (V.ii.8–10) is falsely to elevate his father's vindictive spirit to the status of godhead and to effect his own destruction, as surely as if he had taken his impious cue from the Count of Foix, 'vsant plus indiscretement que de raison de sa puissance [making use of his power more indiscreetly than was reasonable]' and perhaps even, like him, incurring the ultimate responsibility 'de ceste tragedie':

Il auoit beau qu'accuser les actes cruels, & traistres du Roy son beau frere, ... car bien que ce fussent des accessoires de ceste tragedie, si est ce que de luy, & par luy estoit sorty le principal, qui sans raison, ny consideration emprisonna vn innocent, & poursuiuit celuy, le sang duquel criant vengeance deuant Dieu, fut à la fin exaucé.

[In vain might he accuse the cruel acts and treacheries of the king his brother-in-law, ... for although they were the accessories of that tragedy, still it was from him and by him that the essential had proceeded, who without raison or consideration imprisoned an innocent and pursued him, whose blood crying for vengeance before God in the end was granted it.] (1572, fols 140^v–41^r)

Nothing Belleforest has to say on the subject of revenge (and little on other matters) goes beyond the commonplace. The point is that he furnished drastically contradictory commonplaces in the two stories, and that these precisely define the double bind that transforms the primitive heroism of Amleth into the self-destructive tragic variety.

It is worth returning to the familial context in which Belleforest develops the victimization of his young prince of Foix (whose stated age of sixteen [1572, fol. 116^v] resonates with the 'impression the play conveys of the hero's youth'[114] in spite of all calculations). There is no question of conflicting loyalties or divided sentiments in Amleth, who is as active and positive in this respect as in the social and political spheres. His sole confrontation with his mother – the direct original of the closet scene – is accordingly unambiguous: he browbeats and cajoles; she repents outright and thoroughly. By contrast, the relations among father, mother and uncle in the story of Gaston anticipate 'young Hamlet' as wavering, if not torn, at a basic emotional level – the entire dimension, in short, that modern commentary tends to assimilate to Oedipal psychology.

Paradoxically – and there may be a lesson for *Hamlet* criticism here – the tale of Gaston ties sentiment to the codes governing loyalties within aristocratic families. Thus even the young prince's mother has, despite her brother's flagrant villainy, a double allegiance that, however obliquely, casts Gertrude's ambivalence in a more comprehensible light. The prince himself is likewise emotionally split between mother and father, though he bows to the latter's authority, as when he asks to visit her:

> ... apres vne grande reuerence luy proposa son desir, le fondant sur celle affection naturelle & seruice que les enfans doiuent à ceux qui les ont engendrez: le priant luy donner congé, & et ne trouuer mauuais si luy, estant le fils commun de luy, & de madame, ne vouloit toutesfois participer au diuorce qui estoit entr'eux: & s'il estoit marry de ce que, tout ainsi que son cœur estoit esgalement lié à tous les deux, il ne pouuoit les seruir auec vn mesme effect & esgal deportement. Se rapportoit neantmoins du tout en cecy au bon vouloir de monsieur le Comte, aimant mieux viure encore toute sa vie absent de sa mere, quoy que le regret luy en fut presque insupportable, que de faire la moindre chose de ce monde, sans son expres congé & consentement.
>
> [... after a great bow proposed his desire, founding it on that natural affection and service that children owe to those who have begot them, beseeching him to give him leave, and not to find it bad if he, being the common son of him and his lady, wished in no way to participate in the divorce which existed between them, and if he was dejected at the fact that, just as his heart was equally tied to the two, he could not likewise serve them with the same effect and equal behaviour. Nevertheless he referred himself in all of this to the good will of Monsieur the Count, preferring to live his entire life absent from his mother, although his regret was almost insupportable, rather than to do the least thing in this world without his express leave and consent.] (1572, fols 116^v–17^r)

It is, ironically, the prince's naïve sincerity in wishing the reuniting of his parents that renders him vulnerable to his uncle's machinations; the narrator ominously intones, 'mieux luy eut valu ne voir iamais ny mere, ny oncle, que d'en acheter la veuë si cherement que depuis il feit [it would have been better for him never to see mother or uncle than to pay for the sight of them as dearly as since he did]' (1572, fol. 116^v). That sincerity first produces, however, a version, *mutatis mutandis*, of *Hamlet*'s closet scene, in which the young man, 'mon deuoir me le comandant [my duty commanding me]' (1572, fol. 119^r), attempts to detach his mother from the 'ruses du Roy mon oncle [ruses of the king my uncle]', to revive her loyal affection for his father, and to persuade her to return to her husband – '& à moy qui ne vis qu'en languissant [to me, who live but in languishing]' (1572, fol. 119ᵛ). His words, like Hamlet's ('O Hamlet, thou hast cleft my heart in twain' [III.iv.158]), strike her to the emotional core:

> Ces parolles de l'enfant outrerent tellement le cœur de la bonne dame, qu'à peine qu'elle ne se pasma entre les bras de son fils, & si sur l'heure elle luy eut respondu, & qu'il eut encore donné vne autre charge, il eut esté pour la gaigner.

> [These words of the child so charged the heart of the good lady that she all but collapsed in the arms of her son, and if she had answered him at once, and he had urged her again once more, he would have succeeded in winning her over.] (1572, fols 119ᵛ–20ʳ)

There is overlap with the 'official' precursor scene in the history of Amleth, but also divergence from melodrama towards Shakespearean ambiguity: this 'bonne dame' is not an accomplice in evil ripe for repentance at the discovery of her son's true heroic state.[115] Rather, like Shakespeare's Gertrude, the Countess soon regains control of herself, thinks the better of her momentary weakness and asserts the claims of her own family, telling her son that 'le Roy seroit marry, s'il s'en alloit sans le visiter [the King would be disappointed if he departed without visiting him]' (1572, fol. 120ʳ), as duty, moreover, required. The young man proves less acute than Hamlet and is led to trust 'en l'enemy mortel de son pere [in the mortal enemy of his father]' (1572, fol. 120ᵛ), a smooth-talker who knows how to strike a high moral tone in fabricating a show of favour:

> ayant tenu de beaux, & sages propos à son neueu en leur presence, comme le Prince le plus eloquent de son aage, & qui auoit la plus sage malice d'autre qui vesquit pour lors, il tira son neueu à part l'exhortant à tout ce que l'homme de bien peut inciter celuy qu'il desire que luy soit semblable: puis feit de beaux, & rares presens. ...

> [having addressed fine and wise words to his nephew in their presence, as the most eloquent prince of his time, who possessed the wisest cunning of any who lived then, he drew his nephew apart, exhorting him to everything that an honest man can urge upon one whom he desires should be like him: then made him splendid and rare presents. ...] (1572, fol. 121ᵛ)

All in all, the picture makes a reasonable model for the rather less successful attempts of Claudius to ingratiate himself with his nephew – a further element without precedent in the tale of Amleth.

It is not quite the case that there is no hint in that tale of the melancholy of

Shakespeare's prince, but the mention is all but technical: 'la vehemence de la melancholie [his over great melancholy]'[116] explains Amleth's power of divination. The playwright may have elaborated the character's 'philosophical' melancholy by way of Montaigne, but the idea of making it the core of his alienation and introversion – not at all Amleth's style – might well have been inspired by Gaston's son. For no sooner was that young man back in his father's court than things began to go wrong, beginning with his brother's discovery of the bag containing the powder, from which point, we are told, 'le Prince deuint ... plus melancolique [the prince became ... more melancholic]' and irritable, '& prenoit sa resolution de iouer son personnage le plustost qu'il luy seroit possible [and took the resolution to play his part as soon as he possibly could]' (1572, fol. 126[r–v]). It is when he is brutalized by his father and cast into prison, however, that the theme comes into its own, amidst a welter of dark ideas anticipating the disaffection and resentment of Hamlet, for whom all 'Denmark's a prison' (II.ii.243):

> L'enfant n'ayant homme qui luy parlast, ou qui le conseillast en prison, y auoit desia demeuré dix ou douze iours sans prendre que bien peu de substance, il se commença à se melancolier plus que iamais, & desperant sa vie, maudissoit l'heure de sa naissance, accusoit, & pere, & mere, & oncle: l'vn pour le rudoyer ainsi sans son merite, l'autre pour l'auoir conseillé d'aller voir le Roy, & sur cestuy vomissoit il toutes les maledictions du monde pour estre cause de son desastre, & pour luy auoir dressé le piège qu'il ne pensoit pas si nuisible: destestant les grandeurs & les aises de ce monde, puis que pour en iouyr quelque peu de temps, on est tousiours en crainte de les perdre.

> [The young man, having no one who might speak to him, or counsel him in prison, had already remained there ten or twelve days without taking much of any sustenance; he began to become more melancholy than ever, and, despairing of his life, cursed the hour of his birth, accused father, mother and uncle: the one for treating him so harshly without desert; the other for advising him to go and see the king; and upon him he poured forth all the curses of the world for being the cause of his disaster, and for having laid the trap that he did not suspect so harmful, detesting the grandeurs and pleasures of this world, since, for the sake of enjoying them for a little while, one is forever in fear of losing them.] (1572, fol. 138[r])

And here the *historien tragique* has a *coup de théâtre* in store: it turns out that the prince, rather than merely reflecting morbidly, is speaking his thoughts aloud. The discursive dislocation announces itself abruptly: 'Or fault il entendre que celuy qui ordinairement luy portoit à manger, ouyt tout ce discours [Now it must be understood that he who ordinarily brought him his food heard all this discourse]' (1572, fol. 138ᵛ). Not only are we mere inches away from Hamlet's initial despair ('How weary, stale, flat, and unprofitable / Seem to me all the uses of this world!' [I.ii.133–34]; ' ... detestant les grandeurs & les aises de ce monde'), but for an imposing moment we are projected out of the narrative frame into a virtual dramatic space conditioned by the concept of soliloquy. That is far from any space occupied by Amleth, a prolific orator of great efficacity, but no more a soliloquizer than a *penseur*.

III

If any doubt remains that the dramatist knew the story of the Count of Foix as recounted in the *Cinquiesme tome*, it may be dispelled, I think, by looking briefly through the same lens at *King Lear*. It is generally agreed that when Shakespeare added the Gloucester subplot to the old play of *King Leir*, he drew the basic outline from the narrative in Sidney's *Arcadia* (Bk. II, Ch. 10) of the Paphlagonian king dispossessed and blinded by his bastard son.[117] What the playwright found there, however, included a notable, indeed self-declared, gap, which had to be filled somehow to make the action stageworthy. For while the sequel of the king's sufferings and succour by his true son is fully enough presented, the operations of the deceitful bastard are not only left unstated but pointedly excluded from the narrative:

> I was caried by a bastarde sonne of mine (if at least I be bounde to believe the words of that base woman my concubine, his mother), first to mislike, then to hate, lastly to destroy, or doo my best to destroy this sonne (I thinke you thinke) undeserving destruction. What waies he used to bring me to it, if I should tell you, I should tediously trouble you with as much poysonous hypocrisie, desperate fraude, smoothe malice, hidden ambition, and smiling envie, as in any living person could be harbored. But I list it not, no remembrance (no, of naughtiness) delights me, but mine own; and me thinks, the accusing his trains might in some manner excuse my fault, which certainly I loth to doo. (ed. Bullough, 1957–75, 7: 404)

For a reader who recalled Gaston's destruction of his son according to Belleforest, the literally 'poisonous hypocrisy' of Charles II of Navarre would furnish an ample model for such villainy.

Commentators have generally traced Edmund's central machination to a subsequent story in the *Arcadia* (Bk. II, Ch. 15), in which the wicked second wife of the King of Iberia weaves an elaborate plot to make her husband jealous of his son Plangus; the latter is then trapped into the appearance of seeking the king's life and subsequently banished.[118] But while this parallel intertextually supplies the 'missing' deception, it takes a further step away from *Lear* by foregrounding the scheming woman and eliminating the motifs of bastardy and fraternal rivalry. By contrast, while he kept the basic premise of the father's gullibility, Shakespeare chose to put the female villain, whether 'concubine' or wicked queen, harmlessly in the background and to develop instead, as a parallel to the Lear-plot, superficially amical relations both between the father and the bastard and between the bastard and his legitimate brother. In fact, these are all features of what might be considered the subplot of the story of Gaston Phoebus (which, for that matter, Sidney himself is likely to have known), and as with the main plot's relation to *Hamlet*, they tend to translate fairy-tale and melodrama onto a human scale.[119]

According to Belleforest's concise exposition, the Count had two bastard sons, although only one figures in the story: 'Bastards qu'il aimoyt fort, & les cherissoit presque autant que son fils & heritier legitime [Bastards whom he loved greatly, and he cherished them almost as much as his legitimate son and heir]' (1572, fol. 125ᵛ). 'Our father's love is to the bastard Edmund as to the legitimate' (I.ii.17–18), repeats Edmund scornfully in soliloquy, recalling Gloucester's claim to Kent in the first scene (I.i.19) and going on to play on the rankling term, 'legitimate'. The word recurs in Belleforest's account, which evokes the intimacy, tainted with an essential inequality, that the Count himself encouraged between his elder bastard and his lawful son:

> cest aisné estoit presque de mesme aage, grandeur, & proportion que Gaston l'enfant legitime: qui estoit cause que le pere les faisoit vestir de mesme, & vouloit qu'ils fussent touiours ensemble, voire mangeassent, & couchassent en mesme lict, sauf, que le gouuerneur auoit charge d'instruire le Bastard à recognoistre le legitime comme son Seigneur, & duquel il faudroit qu'vn iour il eut soustien, & auancement.

> [that elder was nearly of the same age, height and proportion as Gaston the legitimate child, which was the reason that the father had them dressed alike and wished that they should always be together; indeed, they ate together and slept in the same bed, except that their governor had the charge of instructing the Bastard to recognize the legitimate as his Lord, from whom one day he would have to have support and advancement.](1572, fol. 125ᵛ)

Precisely such an intimate relation is evoked by the initial bantering encounter between Edgar and Edmund (I.ii.138 ff.), while its false premise looms in the latter's private resentment:

> Wherefore should I
> Stand in the plague of custom, and permit
> The curiosity of nations to deprive me?
> For that I am some twelve or fourteen moonshines
> Lag of a brother? Why bastard? Wherefore base?

> When my dimensions are as well compact,
> My mind as generous and my shape as true
> As honest madam's issue?
>   (I.ii.2–9)

Belleforest adds a quasi-sociological reflection on bastardy that, far from restating commonplaces, seems to have supplied specific verbal hints for Gloucester's lax talk about his bastard and legitimate sons, although the moralism of the genre frowns on the 'good sport at [their] making' (I.i.22):

> nous ne sommes point en païs ou la bastardise se soit respectée, ains nous suffit de contempler les illegitimes comme fruits outre saisonnez [cf. 'came something saucily to the world before he was sent for' (*Lr.*, I.i.20–21)], desquels on se sert par faute de meilleurs [cf. 'Do you smell a fault?' (15)], & que lon ne doibt reiecter [cf. 'the whoreson must be acknowledged' (22–23)], puis que nature les a produit, quoy que la production [cf. 'his making' (22)] en soit maudicte, estants engendrez hors la licence de la loy [cf. 'by order of law' (18)], & auec le violement de la couche sans macule, hors laquelle tout accouplement est defendu.

> [we are by no means in a country where bastardy is respected, but it is sufficient for us to consider the illegitimate as fruits out of season, which we make use of in the absence of better and which should not be rejected because nature has produced them, although the production of them is condemned in itself, since they are engendered outside the permission of the law and with violation of the pure couch outside of which all copulation is prohibited.] (1572, fols 125ᵛ–26ʳ)

Edmund's appeal to 'nature' is anticipated by Belleforest, even as Gloucester's rash reversal ('Loyal and natural boy' [II.i.84]) echoes the furious outburst of the Count, likewise over-ready to believe his 'fils si desnaturé [son so unnatural]' (1572, fol. 130ʳ) as to seek his death. Yet Belleforest's bastard is no villain, and his positive side is true to the tragically thwarted potential with which Shakespeare, without warrant in Sidney, also endows Edmund: 'il estoit fin & subtil, comme aussi il eut esté grand personnage, si le desastre ne l'eut suiuy en la fortune commune de la maison de Foix [he was clever and subtle, so that he too would have had high standing if the disaster had not occurred in the common fortune of the House of Foix]' (1572, fol. 126ʳ).

'Disasters' (I.ii.120) is the word Edmund plays on in scorning the tendency of human beings – his father chief among them – to shun responsibility for their own vices and follies, and the parallel between the two rash fathers extends to the point of suggesting Gaston as a model for Gloucester. Like Gloucester, Gascon hardly needs encouragement to believe in his true son's guilt: 'Le Comte, qui estoit le plus soupçonneux homme du monde, & le soupçon duquel auoit pris plus d'accroissement en ces parolles du Bastard … [The Count, who was the most suspicious man in the world, and whose suspicion had grown with these words of the Bastard ...]' (1572, fol. 127^v). Like Gloucester after the disinheriting of Cordelia, he is already – before his 'discovery' of the poison, 'hard' evidence like Edmund's forged letter – in the grip of tormenting fantasies, couched in elemental terms:

> le Comte ... s'en alla pourmener seul resuant, et fantasiant mille discours, & formant autant de caprices en sa teste qu'il y a d'atomes, & parties indiuisibles en la composition du monde d'Epicure, tant ceste occurence le tourmentoit. ...
>
> [the Count ... went off to walk by himself, sweating over and fantasizing a thousand speeches, and forming as many whims in his head as there are atoms, and indivisible particles in the composition of the world of Epicurus, this occurrence so tormented him. ...] (1572, fol. 128^r)

Accordingly, once seized by the delusion of his son's guilt, Gaston, like Gloucester, whose general judgement and compassion show in his treatment of Lear, becomes violently committed to destroying the basis of his personal happiness:

> cetuy-ci, qu'on louoit d'equité, modestie & debonnaireté sur tous ses voysins, soit en vn instant si changé en vn autre naturel, que la raison luy est odieuse, & la mesme iustice, luy semble estre du tout inique. Aussi depuis que l'apprehension d'embusche s'enracine en l'esprit d'vn homme qui à [*sic*] puissance, tant plus il est genereux, & plus elle y iouë ses folies, & luy oste la mesme ioye qui luy est presente.
>
> [he who was praised for equity, modesty and benevolence above all his neighbours was in an instant so changed into another sort of nature that reason was hateful to him, and even justice appeared to him to be wholly unfair. So since the discovery of the plot took root in the mind of a man possessing such power, by as much as he was noble-spirited, by so much did it produce follies in him and deprive him of the very joy that was present to him.] (1572, fol. 132^v)

Unlike Edmund, the Count's bastard is not actively the cause of his brother's or his father's destruction, but he is likewise sensible of injustice and looking for paternal recognition when he complains of being struck by the young prince: 'voicy le Bastard, qui se presente à luy tout espleuré, gemissant, & esmeu de grande colere: auquel le Comte demanda l'occasion de ce pleur, & et qui estoit celuy qui l'auoit offencé [here the Bastard comes, who presents himself to him all teary-eyed, complaining and moved with great anger: at which the Count asked the occasion of this weeping, and who it was who had offended him]' (1572, fol. 127^r); we may compare the scheming Edmund's 'Look, sir, I bleed' (II.i.41). And it is a further irony in both cases that the father, by his very

disposition to favour the bastard – 'qu'il aimoit sur toute chose [whom he loved
above all]' (1572, fol. 136ᵛ) is the phrase in Belleforest – entails him in their
mutual destruction. Indeed, to the dispassionate subjects of Gaston Phoebus,
the situation appears to be such as it actually is in *Lear*; their suspicion of a plot
is strong: 'plusieurs murmuroient que cecy fut dressé pour faire bonne la cause
des bastards, & les auancer [many murmured that it was set on foot to justify
the cause of the bastards and advance them]' (1572, fol. 136ʳ). This is the point
at which the story of Gaston switches back onto the track of that of the Paphlagonian king. It would have been a natural move for Shakespeare to follow, and
to mark the conjunction by assigning to Edmund himself the advocacy of his
'cause': 'Now gods, stand up for bastards!' (I.ii.22).

Part IV – Brief (and very tentative) conclusion

It is not Edmund but Hamlet who deserves these few final words. If, after criss-
crossing this complex intertextual territory, we seem to find ourselves in the
presence of three more-or-less distinct Princes of Denmark, that perception is
true, I suggest, not only to the critical record but to the theatrical dynamic. The
latter, unless artificially truncated by performance practice (and regardless of
Q2-F1 choices), tends to render the anamorphic effect kaleidoscopic: Hamlet
really does appear as now one sort of prince, now another; if the cumulative
result is the 'modern subject', that subject is arguably produced, like the original
'moving picture', by a succession of 'stills'.

If it is not my critical project to identify the 'real' Hamlet, it is well beyond
my capacity to explain how the confluence of an existing dramatic treatment
of Hamlet, a recent encounter with Montaigne, an association with a potent
myth of the lost Huguenot cause, and a reading of Belleforest's *histoire* of the
Count of Foix might have issued in distinguishable intertextual streams rather
than mere muddy water. The only certainty is Shakespeare's active familiarity
with the discursive representation of the French Wars of Religion, which I have
abundantly documented elsewhere (especially in *Shakespeare, Marlowe and the
Politics of France* [2002]), and which presupposes special sensitivity to narratives bearing on the royal House of Navarre and its relation to both France and
England. When Shakespeare turned to 'update' the old play of *Hamlet*, the
Treaty of Vervins and the Edict of Nantes (both dating from 1598) had just
imposed a provisional closure on these issues, but he himself had indirectly
reopened them – and at a moment when England's own succession crisis
seemed to be looming – by representing England's greatest anti-French hero,
Henry V, in terms calculated to recall, and to problematize, the Huguenot
discourse of Henri de Navarre's divine entitlement.[120]

In these circumstances, might it not have seemed natural to use the tale of Amleth, the dispossessed rightful Prince, as a vehicle for recuperating the House of Navarre from Belleforest's slander, reversing the positions of victim and villain implicitly assigned in the story of Gaston de Foix? The structural reversal was already built into Protestant accounts of the persecution of Antoine de Bourbon by the Guises, and, intertextually, there were specific points of contact to develop as points of contrast: the tainting of the very emblem of the *noblesse d'épee*; the hypocritical abuse of honour and religion; the betrayal of personal trust. Indeed, someone who knew those stories might have been struck by the fact that Navarre's double-dealing adviser, the Count of Escars, one of the Guises's treacherous agents, has a nominal counterpart in a shady ecclesiastical ally of Charles II of Navarre: the 'Euesque de Lescar, qui du viuant du Comte n'osa onc reuenir en Bearn, lequel aussi on soupçonnoit fort, comme grand amy du Roy de Nauarre [Bishop of Lescar, who during the Count's lifetime never dared return to Béarn, and who was strongly suspected as a great friend of the King of Navarre]' (Belleforest, *Cinquiesme tome*, 1572, fol. 132ʳ). A reversal would presumably return throat-cutting, poisoning and dishonour generally to the politico-religious camp to which they were popularly supposed to belong.

Yet to cast Antoine de Bourbon as Hamlet would also have meant, inevitably, warping the original trajectory of the triumphant hero and relating the deviation not only to the failed career but also to the notoriously irresolute character of that unhappy prince. There would remain, then, the generic challenge of recuperating irresolution in the service of tragic heroism – a task entailing the transformation (it is tempting to say the *modernization*) of the latter concept. This is where Montaigne might have come in: last, perhaps, but certainly not least. Such a paradoxical project lay beyond the scope of political analysis; it called for the interweaving of sceptical philosophy, a doubting perspective on the possibilities of humanity itself such as one who lived through the worst of the Wars of Religion – himself a Catholic but far from an extremist or an enemy of the House of Bourbon – was uniquely qualified to supply.

Notes

1   The list of proposed correspondences is long, their classification inevitably subjective (the term 'decisive' goes back at least to Robertson, 1909, p. 34). Among the specific echoes of Florio that resonate for most commentators, one might cite the parallel between 'divinty … rough-hew' (V.ii.10–11) and 'roughly hew … heaven' (trans. Florio, ed. Harmer, 1965, 3: 171), which renders III, 8, 934B (ed. Villey and Saulnier, 1978), as well as that between 'consummation … dreams'

(III.i.63–66) and III, 12, 1053C (ed. Villey and Saulnier, 1978), which Florio translates as follows: 'If [death] be a consummation of one's being, it is also an amendment and entrance into a long and quiet night. We find nothing so sweet in life, as a quiet rest and gentle sleep, and without dreams' (ed. Harmer, 1965, 3: 309). The first parallel is especially important for Ellrodt, 1975, p. 40, the second for Levin, 1959, pp. 72–73. See *Ham.*, Jenkins, ed., 1982, pp. 557 and 489. (Jenkins's edition is used for citations throughout this chapter, in view of the complex textual issues involved.)

2   On the tendency in the 'Apologie' of the link between 'raison' and 'discours' to render problematic the distinction between man and the animals, see Demonet, 2003, pp. 81 ff.

3   Cf. 1 Cor. 8:2.

4   Here I adopt the version of Q2, which Jenkins emends ('of aught he leaves, knows aught'), even as he argues convincingly (1982, pp. 565–66) against the reading of F1: 'ha's ought of what he leaues'. Certainty will never be possible, but the 'Apologie''s conjunction of fundamental human ignorance, suicide and duelling constitutes compelling evidence. Towards the culmination of the essay, where the last two of these themes unite, Montaigne returns to the first:

> Vrayement Protagoras nous en comtoit de belles, faisant l'homme la mesure de toutes choses, qui ne sceut jamais seulement la sienne. ... Or, luy estant en soy si contraire et l'un jugement en subvertissant l'autre sans cesse, cette favorable proposition n'estoit qu'une risée qui nous menoit à conclurre par nécessité la néantise du compas et du compasseur.
>
> Quand Thales estime la cognoissance de l'homme tresdifficile à l'homme, il luy apprend la cognoissance de toute autre chose luy estre impossible.
>
> [Truely *Protagoras* told us prettie tales, when hee makes man the measure of all things, who never knew so much as his owne. ... Now he being so contrary in himselfe, and one judgement so uncessantly subverting another, this favorable proposition was but a jest, which indused us necessarily to conclude the nullity of the Compasse and the Compasser. *When* Thales *judgeth the knowledge of man very hard unto man, hee teacheth him the knowledge of all other things to be impossible unto him.*] (ed. Villey and Saulnier, 1978, II, 12, 557C; trans. Florio, ed. Harmer, 1965, 2: 270)

Ironically, a long-standing argument in favour of reading 'has' is based on a passage from another essay (ed. Villey and Saulnier, 1978, I, 20, 95A; trans. Florio, ed. Harmer, 1965, 1: 89 [I, 19]), which may lie behind *MM*, III.i.32 ff. See Feis, 1970, p. 111, and Hooker, 1902, pp. 319–20.

5   With most recent critics, I believe that the *Tragoedia der bestrafte Brudermord*, whose plot corresponds in general to that of *Hamlet*, derives from Q1's version of Shakespeare's play. See esp. Jenkins, ed., 1982, pp. 112–22, and Wells, Taylor *et al.*, 1997, p. 398.

6   See Jenkins, ed., 1982, nn. to V.i.191, 191–94, 206–9.

7   Jenkins, ed., 1982, pp. 491–92.

8   Florio's 'abide' renders the translation closer to Shakespeare's text at this point.

9   His aggression has conspicuously failed to have the calming effect that 'résolution' can sometimes produce, according to Montaigne (ed. Villey and Saulnier, 1978, I, 1, 7A; trans. Florio, ed. Harmer, 1965, 1: 17), on those who seek vengeance. Notably, too, he fails to take responsibility for his actions – on the contrary – even in asking pardon of Laertes before the match, when he regrets the acts committed, not just in, but by, his madness (IV.ii.233).

10 The 'Frenchness' of this report is enhanced in Q2 by the borrowing – *OED* records no other occurrence – of '*escrimeurs*' (in the form of 'Scrimures', hence 'scrimers'): 'The scrimers of their nation / He swore had neither motion, guard, nor eye, / If you oppos'd them' (IV.vii.99–101).

11 Another candidate is Catherine de Bourbon, sister of Henri de Navarre; see Villey and Saulnier, eds, 1978, p. 1290, n. to p. 557, 35.

12 Villey and Saulnier gloss as follows: 'à savoir de refuser toute valeur à la raison humaine [that is, to refuse all value to human reason]' (1978, p. 558n.1).

13 On this point I have profited from the expert knowledge of my colleague Pascal Brioist. On Montaigne's interest in fencing, see Brioist, Drévillon and Serna, 2002, pp. 67–68. I have not found in Montaigne criticism any suggestion that an actual manœuvre might been involved. Certainly, the expression remains metaphorical for Limbrick, 1981, pp. 53–64, who simply concludes that 'Montaigne renoncera aux armes de la raison [Montaigne will renounce the arms of reason]' in order to 'arriver à la doctrine paulinienne par excellence [arrive at the perfect Pauline doctrine]' (p. 64). On the other hand, Rigolot, 1990, pp. 261–90, detects an authorial stratagem calculated to exclude the female addressee: 'La métaphore militaire, banale en apparence, a donc son importance, et cela d'autant plus que, loin d'être simplement occasionnelle, elle se "file" tout au long de l'adresse à la Princesse [The military metaphor, banal in appearance, thus has its importance, all the more so because, far from being simply occasional, it 'threads itself' all through the address to the Princess]' (p. 284).

14 '[P]ar lequel' (Villey and Saulnier, eds, 1978, p. 558n.2).

15 Jenkins, ed., 1982, pp. 551–54, Longer Note to V.i.139–57, concludes that the numbers (including 'three and twenty years' for Yorick's corpse at V.i.167–68) are not to be taken literally. They do squarely block, however, any notion that Hamlet is too young to be a full political player in Renaissance terms.

16 For the reader's convenience, I refer to Belleforest's story of Amleth, which first appeared in *Le cinquiesme tome des Histoires tragiques* (1572), in the form of the reprint of the 1582 edition given by Gollancz, ed., 1926; translations are taken from the anonymous *The Hystorie of Hamblet* (1608), also in Gollancz's edition.

17 Shaheen compares the various English biblical versions and concludes that in coining Hamlet's 'the fall of a sparrow', 'Shakespeare no doubt had the Geneva in

mind' (1999, p. 561). The last verses correspond to Luke 12:6–7, where, however, no falling is mentioned.

18   That this verse was running in Shakespeare's mind around the time of the composition of *Hamlet* is suggested by its echo, in a not wholly unrelated context, by the disaffected Orlando: 'the spirit of my father, which I think is within me, begins to mutiny against this servitude' (*AYL*, I.i.22–24).

19   Jenkins, ed., 1982, n. to V.ii.215–16.

20   I.16.1–2, I.16.5, and I.17.6. See Calvin, 1578, fols 69^v, 72^r, and 78^{r-v}.

21   It is again intriguing to find an analogue in *AYL*, although Adam's expostulation is significantly different: 'He that doth the ravens feed, / Yea, providently caters for the sparrow, / Be comfort to my age!' (II.iii.43–45). The context here particularly evokes Luke 12:24 (with an echo of Job 38:41), while 'providently' seems to enter by way of Calvin's affirmation in the *Institution*: 'howe much we be more worth than sparrowes, with so much nyer care doth God prouide for vs' (1578, fol. 78^r [1.17.6]).

22   See Jeanne d'Albret, *Mémoires*, ed. de Ruble, 1883, p. 10n.1.

23   See de Ruble, ed., 1883, p. 7n.3 and pp. 9–12. The *Mémoires* originally appeared within a collection of diverse texts published in 1570, either, as de Ruble supposes, in La Rochelle or in England: *Histoire de nostre temps, contenant vn recveil des choses memorables passées & publiées pour le faict de la Religion & estat de la France, depuis l'edict de pacifification du 23. iour de Mars, 1568 iusques au iour présent*. Within this volume, for which editorial responsibility is conjecturally attributed to Christophe Landré (or Landrin) and Charles Martel, the *Mémoires* carried the obscure heading, *Ample Declaration des lettres precedentes*.

24   In citations, the first page number refers to the original edition, that in brackets to the current one. I continue to cite this work under the name of Bèze, who at least prepared material for it; see, however, Geisendorf, 1967, pp. 340–45.

25   On this work, see my *French Origins*, 2010, esp. pp. 9–11. In addition, *A general inuentorie of the history of France*, 1607, pp. 582–83, translated by Edward Grimeston from Jean de Serres (for this period), contains what looks like a displaced and toned-down version of the episode: the Guises are shifted to the background, and, after attempts on his life by 'both poison and sword' engineered by the marshals Brissac and Saint-André, which fail because 'God had otherwise decreed', Navarre is summoned 'into her closet' by Catherine de Medici herself, acting for the Guises, to what might have proved a fatal confrontation, had he not been warned 'As he was entring' by a 'Ladie of the Court' and agreed to the queen's terms; at this point, the king is already in his last illness. Multiple editions of the French original, the *Inventaire général de l'histoire de France depuis Pharamond jusques à présent*, were published in 1600.

26   Cf. *Response à l'épistre de Charles de Vaudémont, cardinal de Lorraine* (1565), in which Antoine de Bourbon is posthumously evoked as the dupe and victim of the Guises ('La play du Roy de Navarre est si fraiche, quelle seigne encor [The wound of the King of Navarre is so fresh that it bleeds still]' [sig. Ei^v]), as well as *La Legende*

de Charles, Cardinal de Lorraine, et de ses freres (1576), *passim*, esp. fols 52^v, 62^r, 65^v–66 [misnumbered 96]^v. The latter attack was swiftly translated into English and published anonymously: *A legendarie conteining an ample discovrse of the life and behauiour of Charles Cardinal of Lorraine* (1577); see esp. sig. Fvii^r.

27 The *Legende*, too, regularly resorts to dramatic metaphor; thus with respect to the incident at Wassy, the Guises and their adversaries are described as 'iouans en vne mesme tragedie chascun son personnage, d'vne estrange sorte [eche played his part after a strange maner, and al in one tragedy]' (*Legende*, 1576, fol. 73^v; *Legendarie*, 1577, sig. Hvii^r). Likewise, speaking of the first civil war, the author includes himself among the 'spectateurs des horribles tragœdies que le Cardinal & ses freres iouoyent à la ruine du Roy Charles & du Royaume [beholders of such horrible tragedies as the Cardinal & his brethren played to the confusion of King Charles & his kingdome]' (*Legende*, 1576, fol. 77^r; *Legendarie*, 1577, sig. Ii^v).

28 The most thorough and solid account of this complex affair remains that of Naef, 1922; for a more recent view, with close attention to the ring-leader, La Renaudie, see Brown, 1996, pp. 451–74.

29 The translator (Thomas Tymme) claims to be working from the original Latin of the martyred Petrus Ramus ('The Translator to the Reader' [*The fyrst parte of commentaries*, 1573, sig. Lliv^v]) – evidently, a name to conjure with, while the true author's identity is nowhere indicated in the French, Latin or English editions. The account of the King of Navarre here extends to his enticement into the Catholic camp after the 1561 Colloquy of Poissy (1573, p. 261), whereas the *Commentaires* mention him last (1565, fol. 302^r) in association with the ministers sent to encourage him in the Reformed faith by the Duke of Wittenberg (Saxony) and the Count Palatine.

30 The militant Protestant colouration of *Hamlet*'s discourse may also be gathered by the account here of the Prince of Condé's defence before the Parliament of Paris, by which he was finally cleared of involvement in the Conspiracy of Amboise: 'It is (saith he) a special token of Gods prouidence, by whiche I being deliuered from the secret platformes and traps of my enemies, shall get vnto my selfe an euerlasting testimonie of my innocencie in those thynges layde to my charge' (p. 145).

31 Albret, *Ample Declaration*: 'le Duc de Guyse & son frere retirez en vne fenestre, vserent de ces mots dignes de leur impudence, parlants du Roy [the Duke of Guise and his brother, having withdrawn to a window, used these words, worthy of their impudence, in speaking of the King]: Voilà le plus poltron cœur qui fut iamais' (p. 178); cf. Prologue, *Histoire de nostre temps*: 'Dieu ne permit lors qu'il eust aucun mal, parquoy le Cardinal & son frere saschez de ce que le Roy n'avoit executé leur rage & fureur, vserent de ces mots parlant du Roy Françoys [God did not then permit him to be harmed, wherefore the cardinal and his brother, when they knew that the King had not executed their rage and fury, used these words in speaking of King François], voyla le plus poltron cœur qui fut iamais' (sig. BBvii^r).

32 Evidently, the issue is particularly sensitive, and the 'hard' and 'soft' lines may be

traced into post-*Hamlet* accounts – by which time Antoine de Bourbon was being recalled chiefly as the father of the reigning Henri IV. The diplomatic historian Jacques-August de Thou hedges his bets as to both the historicity of the encounter itself and the reason for its peaceful outcome, but in his version the Guises' remark ('O l'homme timide & lâche! [What a timid and cowardly human being!]' [*Histoire universelle*, 1740, 2: 832]) was clearly aimed at François II. Agrippa d'Aubigny, on the other hand, who remained a fierce critic of compromisers with Catholicism, including Henri IV, associates the comment with Navarre's kissing of the king's hand and leaves it to float suggestively free: '*ô que voilà un Prince poltron* [O what a cowardly prince!]' (*Histoire universelle*, 1981–99, 1: 300).

33   Jouanna *et al.*, eds, 1998, p. 109. On Bèze's evolving relations with Navarre, see notably Geisendorf, 1967, pp. 120, 192–94, 196 *et passim*. Bèze's own account of the attempt to provoke Navarre omits the scornful remark attributed to the Guises.

34   On this key and controversial event, see Jouanna *et al.*, eds, 1998, pp. 1376–77 ('Wassy').

35   See below, p. 47. Montaigne's version of the commonplace reads, 'c'est le desjeuner d'un petit ver que le cœur et la vie d'un grand et triumphant Empereur [The heart and life of a mighty and triumphant Emperor, is but the break-fast of a seely little Worme]' (ed. Villey and Saulnier, 1978, II, 12, 462A; trans. Florio, ed. Harmer, 1965, 2: 155).

36   See his thinly veiled letter of complaint to Henri II of 25 April 1559 (*Lettres d'Antoine de Bourbon et de Jehanne d'Albret*, 1867, No. 131 [pp. 176–77]).

37   Monluc, *Commentaires et lettres*, ed. de Ruble, 1864–72, No. 46 (Verteuil, 22 juillet 1559 à M. de Latou), 4: 108–9.

38   Bordenave, Raymond, ed., 1873, p. v.

39   See Jenkins, ed., 1982, pp. 2, 6.

40   Both Bordenave and Olhagaray refer to Jeanne d'Albret's *Mémoires* (de Ruble, ed., 1883, p. i).

41   Still, more equivocation remains than in the 1596 history of Navarre by Gabriel Chappuys, a work whose 'official' status is reflected in its anti-Spanish title and fulsome praise of the reigning monarch – for Catholic piety, among other qualities. Here the account of Antoine de Bourbon (1596, pp. 659–71) is thoroughly sanitized, with a bare mention of the Guises and none of their plots. Antoine's irresolution is glossed over blandly ('il estoit Prince sans ambition et facile à contenter [he was a prince without ambition and easy to content]'), while, inevitably, his death in battle is made heroic.

42   Ed. Gollancz, 1926, p. 207.

43   See, e.g., the dramatisation by Pierre Matthieu in *La Guisiade*, ed. Lobbes, 1990, l. 2058. On the Guises and retributive providence, with specific reference to *The Massacre at Paris*, in which Marlowe conflates the Cardinal of Lorraine responsible for the persecutions of the 1560s and 70s with his nephew, Louis, murdered in 1588, see my *Shakespeare, Marlowe and the Politics of France*, 2002, pp. 72–97, and 'Marlowe's Guise', 2008.

44 On this point, cf. Régnier, *Legendarie*, 1577, sigs Hi^v–ii^r.

45 Indeed, Belleforest concludes by deeming the excellencies of Amleth 'blemished' by 'one onely spot' (*The Hystorie of Hamblet*, ed. Gollancz, 1926, p. 309) – in this case, concupiscence.

46 There is some indication that portions of the vast manuscript memoirs of Brantôme, who maintained English contacts, were known at least to George Chapman. See my article, 'The Tragic Channel-Crossings of George Chapman, Part I', 2004, pp. 27–28 and n. 28. Brantôme, who had grown up in the court of Marguerite de Navarre, became an intimate of Marguerite de Valois.

47 Brantôme withholds the verses, as he says, out of 'révérance [respect]'; they are recorded by the editor.

48 *CSPF, 1558–59*, No. 833, p. 310 (13 June 1559, Throckmorton to the Queen).

49 See Sutherland, 1984.

50 Shakerley was an English musician very well connected in Roman church circles, who had offered his intelligence services to Throckmorton; see *CSPF, 1561–62*, No. 750, p. 458 (28 December 1561, Throckmorton to the Queen).

51 The term is common, for instance, in Hakluyt's *Principal Voyages of the English Nation* (1598–1600), vol. 1, and figures in a gloss to the initial geographical table in the 1567 Basel folio of the reworking of Saxo by Olaus Magnus (a work Shakespeare might have consulted for *Hamlet*, according to a recent suggestion by Maxwell [2004]). The gloss gives a sense of the country's political weight at the time: 'Dania, siue Dacia, regnum insulare, & potens [Dania, or Dacia, an island kingdom, and a mighty one]' (Olaus Magnus, 1567, n.p.).

52 Cf. Cazaux, 1973, p. 242.

53 See Hauser, 1891, pp. 60–61; cf. Dareste, 1876, p. 26. Hotman's modern biographer, Donald R. Kelley, provides a useful general outline of Hotman's activities over this period (1973, pp. 99–167), but the specifics remain elusive.

54 For an outline of Bolwiller's career, see Sitzmann, 1909–10. He is mentioned in a dispatch of 3 June 1561 (*CSPF, 1561–62*, No. 222, p. 128, Mundt to Cecil) as 'a vassal of the empire who two years ago was employed by King Philip' and has recently 'had two interviews with the Cardinal of Lorraine' (p. 128).

55 The 'promesses mirifiques [amazing promises]' that definitively gained Antoine de Bourbon for the Catholic cause are at least contextualized in Jouanna *et al.*, eds, 1998, p. 109. On Saint-André's particularly unsavoury role in mediating Antoine's rapprochement with Catholicism, see Romier, 1909, pp. 342–56.

56 A still-useful summary is by Heinrich, 1797–1805, 5: 788–91.

57 For an overview of the Palatinate's role in the French religious question, see Vogler, 1965.

58 The Elector Palatine himself had Calvinist leanings and formally adopted Calvinism in 1573 (Vogler, 1965, p. 53). The manipulations of Navarre by the Catholics around the time of the Colloquy, and his subsequent apostasy, are at least suggestively outlined in the extended narrative of La Place, *Commentaires*, 1565, fols 234^v ff. (*The fyrst parte of commentaries*, 1570, pp. 244–61). Cf. Régnier,

Legende, 1576, esp. fols 74^v–75^r (*Legendarie*, 1577, sigs Hi^r–Ii^r), who maintains that the Guises' visit to Saverne just before the massacre at Wassy aimed at pressuring the Duke of Württemberg to accept the confession of Augsburg on the understanding that the House of Lorraine's traditional position within the Empire would enable them to destroy Protestant power. Cf. Muntz, 1856.

59   See Nicollier-De Weck, 1995, pp. 64–68.

60   The pagination is erroneous, pp. '166–67' being inserted between pp. 156–57 and pp. 160–61; a second pp. 166–67 appears in proper sequence.

61   For further confirmation, see Richard, 1910, pp. 46–47.

62   Cf. the account in La Place, *The fyrst parte of commentaries*, 1573, pp. 139–40, where Navarre is cited only as wishing that the Protestants, despite the differences between Lutherans and Calvinists, would first remain united against the Catholics.

63   See *CSPF, 1561–62*: 'the King of Denmark is a dissolute and insolent Prince' (No. 151 [18], p. 85 [29 April 1561, Throckmorton to the Queen]); 'the Dane (who in insolency and monstrous manners exceeds all his predecessors)' (No. 692, p. 421 [28 November 1561, Robert Jones to Throckmorton]).

64   This despite her intense opposition to the far more consequent marriage being promoted by the Cardinal of Lorraine between Mary (who was his niece) and Don Carlos of Spain; Catherine's power, however, was limited. See Chéruel, 1975, pp. 17–28.

65   See *CSPF, 1561–62*, No. 399 (1), p. 247 (12 August 1561, Christopher Mundt to Cecil), and No. 425 (2), p. 264 (19 August 1561, Thomas Gresham to Cecil).

66   See Chéruel, pp. 22–25, who cites (p. 23) a letter to her ambassador in Spain (21 April 1561) explicitly linking the threat of religious strife with Navarre's discontent – 'lesquelles deux choses peuvent, avec le temps, apporter incommodité et danger [which two things may, over time, bring disadvantage and danger].'

67   See Johannesson, 1991, pp. 34, 139–40, 142.

68   For Christina of Denmark, I draw chiefly on Duvernoy, 1940.

69   See Barthold, 1848, pp. 297–98, and Nicollier-De Weck, 1995, pp. 98–99. Reflections of the scheme may be found in Mundt's intelligence; see *CSPF, 1559–60*, No. 405, p. 182 (12 December 1559, Mundt to Cecil) and No. 729, p. 377 (15 February 1560, Mundt to Cecil).

70   See *CSPF, 1560–61*, No. 834 (6), p. 475 (31 December 1560, Throckmorton to Cecil).

71   Cf. Nicollier-De Weck, 1995, p. 107:

> Quant à l'objet de sa mission, Languet rassura d'emblée ses interlocuteurs saxons: le duc de Lorraine était à la cour avec sa femme, mais il n'y avait rien à craindre de ce côté; les choses étaient si tendues en France, qu'on ne songeait pas à soutenir une guerre au Danemark ou en Saxe.

> [As for the objective of his mission, Languet at once reassured his Saxon correspondants: the duke of Lorraine was at court with his wife, but there was nothing to fear from that side; things were so tense in France that there was no thought of sustaining a war in Denmark or Saxony.]

72 See Hauser, 1891, p. 55, and Nicollier-De Weck, 1995, pp. 105, 98.

73 See Nicollier-De Weck, 1995, pp. 98, 99, 163–67 *et passim*; Pariset, 1981, pp. 178–82; Barthold, 1848, p. 297; Waddington, 1890, pp. 253–54; and Fröbe, 1912, p. 97.

74 See Naef, 1922, pp. 150–52, 156. Political discourses in these circles were conducted largely through classical allusions – a practice that must have influenced readings of neo-classical drama. Hence Hotman's collaborator Jean Sturm, rector of the Academy of Strasbourg, opined, 'Je m'étonne que la mort de Néron ne s'ensuive pas. … Il achèverait la guerre celui qui achèverait Antoine; tu sais de qui je veux parler [des Guise] et quel fut l'avis de Cicéron [I will be astonished if the death of Nero does not ensue. … He who finishes off Antoine will put a successful end to the war; you know whom I am talking about (the Guises) and what Cicero's advice was]' (cited Naef, 1922, p. 152).

75 The atmosphere, the milieux and the activities of the second-string political actors over this period (which obviously extended well beyond the death of Antoine de Bourbon in 1562) are effectively evoked by Nicollier-De Weck, 1995, pp. 85–182.

76 It gives a sense of the intertwining of these aristocratic circles to realize that, in all probability, Antoine de Bourbon had himself been a possible candidate for marriage with Christina in 1539 (Duvernoy, 1940, p. 12).

77 According to Régnier, the Cardinal of Lorraine profited from the peace negotiations conducted under the Duchess's auspices to suggest to Granvelle the hopes of certain Protestant French princes of obtaining the French crown, as well as to disclose 'ce qu'il sauoit de quelques offres faites au Roy Henry par les Princes protestans, & des allees & venues sur ce faites entre le Roy de Nauarre & eux [all that he knew touching certaine offers which the Protestante Princes had made to King Henry, togither with the meetings thereupon between the King of Nauarre and them]' (*Legende*, 1576, fol. 28^v; *Legendarie*, 1577, sig. Diiij^v).

There is reason to suppose that, by late summer 1558, Navarre was in significant political contact with the German Protestant electors – and, perhaps, that he was already playing a distasteful double-game. An agent of Navarre, Gaspard de Heu, seigneur de Buy (the brother-in-law of La Renaudie, who would lead the abortive uprising at Amboise), was captured by the Guises on his way back from delivering dispatches, tortured over several days, and hanged on 1 September 1588. This dramatic episode, effectively recounted by Rahlenbeck, 1880, pp. 165–66, is alluded to (presumably by Hotman, who succeeded Heu as Navarre's agent) in the notorious polemic, *Epistre envoyée au tigre de la France*, 1560, sigs Av^v–vi^r, and recorded by La Place, *Commentaires*, 1565, fols 69^v–70^r. Obviously, it became widely known, although the precise political game being played remains obscure; cf. Pariset, 1981, pp. 186 and 196n.124. Masson (1876) prints a chilling first-hand account of the execution, although the authenticity of this document remains uncertain. The event is cited as an injury to Navarre in the same dispatch by Throckmorton that mentions his dissatisfaction with the treaty of Cateau-

Cambrésis (*CSPF, 1558–59*, No. 833 [5], p. 310 [13 June 1559, Throckmorton to the Queen]).

Perhaps the most disturbing of all the evidence bearing on Navarre's character, however, is the possibility that he himself betrayed Heu. This, at least, is a plausible inference from a dispatch by the Italian agent, Guido Giannetti, to the English queen, in which Navarre is said to have informed the Pope, as proof of his sound Catholicism, that 'He had moreover caused one of his men to be taken by the Lords of Guise as being a promoter of a sect in communication with Geneva' (*CSPF, 1560–61*, No. 815, p. 452 [21 December 1560]). The impression is not inconsistent with Hamlet's near-sadistic destruction of Rosencrantz and Guildenstern ("'tis the sport' [III.iv.208], "'tis most sweet' [211]). For Navarre, too, the obverse of his chronic ineffectuality was a self-inflating contempt for the 'baser nature' caught 'Between the pass and fell incensed points / Of mighty opposites' (60–62). The dispassionate observer in both cases is likely to be morally revolted – witness Horatio's sober reflection: 'So Guildenstern and Rosencrantz go to't' (56).

78 This appears to be the gist of the Elector's enigmatic letter of 21 September 1560; see Frederick III, *Briefe*, 1868–70, 1: 148–49 (No. 106) and 149n.2.

79 I draw here on Nicollier-De Weck, 1995, esp. pp. 85–149.

80 Languet, *Huberti Languet … Epistolae secretae*, 1699, part II, p. 123; this letter is discussed by Nicollier-De Weck, 1995, p. 138n.88.

81 For an outline of the lengthy diplomatic career of the ingenious and seemingly indefatigable Mundt, see Hildebrandt, 1984.

82 For an intriguing glimpse of the Sidney-Leicester circle in relation to Dutch humanism, see Dorsten, 1962, esp. pp. 84–85. The French connection was maintained notably through Jean Hotman, the son of François, who had tutored the children of Amyas Paulet, the English ambassador to France, and who became Leicester's secretary.

83 See Millicent V. Hay, 1984, p. 32.

84 This began to be published towards the end of the seventeenth century, so its prior accessibility in manuscript is not inconceivable.

85 See Simonin, 1992, p. 310. On the bibliographical picture, which is more complex than might be gathered even from Simonin, see also Stone, 1972, pp. 492–93, who, with respect to volumes five and six, comments that 'the history … defies simplification' (p. 492).

86 See Gollancz, ed., 1926, pp. 318–21. There is, however, one variant pretty clearly signalling the Lyons edition of 1576 as known to the author/adapter of *Der bestrafte Brudermord*; see Gollancz, ed., 1926, pp. 319 and 320 (n. to p. 210, l. 6). On the perennial doubts regarding Shakespeare's use of Belleforest, which I hope my discussion may put to rest, see above, Chapter 1, pp. 2–3 and nn. 3, 4.

87 For the publication history of the volume containing the story of Amleth, I draw on the table provided by Simonin, 1992, p. 311.

88 Apart from the story of Amleth, I cite Belleforest in this edition, published under

the title of *Le cinquiesme tome des histoires tragiques, contenant vn discours memorable de plusieurs Histoires, le succez & euenement desquelles est pour la plus part recueilly des choses aduenuës de nostre temps.* See the description by Simonin, 1992, p. 257, who lists the edition as No. 97; it was shared with Gervais Mallot, whose imprint thus appears in certain copies.

89 This *histoire tragique* was also adapted theatrically – as *La tragédie française du bon Kanut, roi de Danemark* (see my *French Origins,* 2010, pp. 40–41), whose editor, Lauvergnat-Gagnière, comments pertinently on its political implications (1999, pp. 7–8). The play was clearly intended for the stage, although the rebellions of the Duke of Alençon against his brother Henri III in 1574 and 1575 could obviously not have been part of Belleforest's original meaning. Cf. Simonin, 1992, p. 66n.24, and Le Hir, 1979, p. 193.

90 *L'innocence de la très illustre, très chaste et débonnaire princesse Madame Marie, royne d'Escosse, etc.* (1572); see Simonin, 1992, pp. 142–45.

91 See Tucoo-Chala, 1993, p. 10; this is the principal modern biography of the flamboyant historical personage in his time and place.

92 The accusation that Charles II of Navarre had weakened the health of the French king, Charles V, by poison was widespread at the time of the latter's death in 1380, and is recorded by Froissart; see Leroy, 1995, p. 28.

93 Most critics, like Hamlet himself, associate the king's pearl with the poison ('Drink off this potion. Is thy union here?' [V.ii.331]), and to make difficulties over the staging, as does Jenkins, ed., 1982, n. to V.ii.284, seems to me otiose. The evocation of a pearl dissolved in drink appears to resonate with the well-known story of Cleopatra drinking a dissolved pearl in front of Antony.

94 The sobriquet was actually introduced into French historical discourse by Belleforest himself (who probably picked it up from a Spanish chronicle published in 1571) in his *Grandes Annales* of 1579; see Honoré-Duvergé, 1951, pp. 345–50, esp. 349. If Belleforest deliberately avoided the epithet in his *histoire tragique* of 1572, this may have been to avoid the remotest ambiguity concerning Charles IX.

95 See my *French Origins,* 2010, pp. 39–46.

96 See also Jouanna *et al.,* eds, 1998, p. 969.

97 See Crouzet, 1990, 2: 60–61.

98 See Jouanna *et al.,* eds, 1998, p. 968.

99 See Seward, 1987, pp. 177–78.

100 Cf. Simonin, 1992, p. 139n.73.

101 It matches the pattern that the 'sçavant [learned]' Belleforest was invoked by Jean Le Masle to help him do poetic justice to the glorious overthrow of Coligny when it occurred; see Margolin, 1974, p. 500.

102 See esp. *Grandes Annales,* 1579, 2: fols 882^r–85^r, on Navarre's subtle manœuvres and schemes, supported by his considerable eloquence, to seduce the people from their proper royal allegiance.

103 At the centre of this phenomenon was Julius Caesar Scaliger, whom Monluc may have known during his time in Agen; see Sournia, 1981, pp. 206–7.

104 This judgement is repeated in the *Grandes Annales* (1579, 2: fol. 970^r), where the version exonerating both Gaston Phoebus and his son is explicitly given the nod over the alternatives. Indeed, a further palliating detail is added: the Count is said to have wounded his son accidentally in the gums while using his little knife to pry the child's mouth open in order to make him eat.

105 See Froissart, *Here begynneth the thirde and fourthe boke* ... , trans. Bourchier, 1525, fols 30^r–31^r (Bk. III, Ch. 26).

106 Belleforest's *Recueil* adds very little to Sleidanus' version of the episode, with the notable exception of the sudden chill preceding Gaston Phoebus's death (1572, fol. 259^r; cf. Sleidanus, 1537, fol. 99^r) – apparently a trace of the *histoire tragique*. No morals are drawn from the deaths of either the Count or Charles II of Navarre (*Recueil*, 1572, fols 234^v–35^r; Sleidanus, 1537, fols 88^v–89^r), although a marginal gloss labels the latter event as 'merueilleuse'. Navarre is engaged in typically villainous activity at the time (extorting money by force), but his fatal accident is much less sensational than in the *histoire tragique*: he is sordidly burned in his bed, not flambéed in *eau-de-vie*.

107 Tucoo-Chala, 1993, pp. 206–9; see also 'La destinée de Gaston Fébus', a well-researched Internet document produced under the auspices of the Archives Départementales des Hautes-Pyrénées: www.passion-bigorrhp.org/febus.html (accessed October 2011).

108 Strangely, it is preferred by Tucoo-Chala, 1993, pp. 214–15, despite his scepticism regarding the claim in Froissart's version that the young man – in reality, eighteen years old and married – was Navarre's dupe rather than his accomplice.

109 'Offerens adolescenti hoc tam venustum munus ... [Offering the youth this charming present ...]' (Sleidanus, 1537, fol. 70^r); cf. Belleforest, *Recueil*: ' ... cest execrablement beau don [this execrably beautiful gift]' (1572, fol. 175^r). The irony is expunged from Belleforest's *Grandes Annales*, which reports simply that Navarre 'luy feit plusieurs beaux presens, mais sur tout luy donna vne petite bourse, en laquelle y auoit certain pouldre mortelle [made him many attractive presents, but especially gave him a little purse, in which there was a certain mortal powder]' (1579, 2: fol. 970^r).

110 If a hint for the dramatic ghost may be detected in the Amleth tale according to Belleforest, the eschatological mechanism is restricted to vaguely Christianized neo-Senecanism of the kind adopted by Kyd (see my *French Origins*, 2010, pp. 33–35): as he dispatches Fengon to hell, Amleth urges him to give a report there to his father, whose soul will henceforth repose among the blessed in heaven, thanks to his son's discharging of the obligation to revenge (ed. Gollancz, 1926, pp. 256–58).

111 See Jenkins, ed., 1982, pp. 491–92 (Longer Note to III.i.80).

112 The subject of the verb is missing here, and the deity seems best qualified to supply it. The poor quality of the printing is responsible for gross errors throughout.

113 Belleforest's rhetoric should not obscure his opinion, which appears in a marginal

gloss: 'Comte de Foix auoit vn esprit familier [The Count of Foix had a familiar spirit]' (1572, fol. 143ᵛ).

114 Jenkins, ed., 1982, p. 551 (Longer Note to V.i.139–57).

115 Cf. the equivalent moment in the tale of Amleth:

> Quoy que la Royne se sentist piquer de bien pres, et que Amleth la touchast vive-vivement ou plus elle se sentoit interessee, si est-ce qu'elle oublia tout le desdain qu'elle eust peu conceuoir, se voyant ainsi aigrement tancee et reprise, pour la grande joye qui la saisit, cognoissant la gentilesse d'esprit de son fils, et ce qu'elle pouvoit esperer d'une telle et si grande sagesse.

> [Although the queene perceived herselfe neerly touched, and that Hamlet mooved her to the quicke, where she felt herselfe interested, nevertheless shee forgot all disdaine and wrath, which thereby she might as then have had, hearing her selfe so sharply chiden and reprooved, for the joy she then conceaved, to behold the gallant spirit of her sonne, and to thinke what she might hope, and the easier expect of his so great policie and wisdome.] (ed. Gollancz, 1926, pp. 218–19)

116 Ed. Gollancz, 1926, pp. 236–37.

117 Yet cf. Mueller, 1994, who leaves Sidney, but also bastardy, out of the picture.

118 See Bullough, ed., 1957–75, 7: 284–85, who excerpts the story (pp. 408–11), classing it as a 'source'.

119 I would suggest that Belleforest's remarkable narrative, together with his comments, adds to the range of attitudes towards bastardy documented by Findlay (1994) and broadens our understanding of Edmund's position, especially as concerns his relations with father and brother.

120 See my *Shakespeare, Marlowe and the Politics of France*, 2002, pp. 33–36, 188–90 *et passim*.

3

Nursing serpents:
French ripples within and beyond
the 'Pembroke Circle'

I spoke in my Introduction of there being two French Antonies. One is the steadfast friend of Caesar and avenging Triumvir, as heralded in Jacques Grévin's *César* (1561)[1] and vividly evoked in Garnier's *Porcie* (1568). The other seems an essentially different figure: the hedonist who ruins himself for Cleopatra, as first brought on stage in France (at least in ghostly form) by Étienne Jodelle in *Cléopâtre captive* (performed 1553), then substantially fleshed out in Garnier's own *Marc Antoine* (1578).

Even in his early treatment of the post-assassination Antony, however (*Porcie* was his first published tragedy), Garnier depicted a contrast between Antoine and Octave on the question of vengeance – the great preoccupation of the French Roman plays (with the behind-the-scenes encouragement of Seneca),[2] but also of civil war polemic. In a conventional debate with the philosopher Arée (*Porcie*, ed. Lebègue, 1973, ll. 841–936), Octave shows himself relentlessly bloody-minded. Later, in response to the danger of Pompey, his ruthlessness is seconded by Lepide. Antoine, however, is allowed a lengthy rebuttal displaying disdain for attacking an enfeebled opponent, in keeping with his 'magnanime cœur [magnanimous heart]' (l. 1233). Ironically, this capacity to rise above vengefulness affiliates Antoine with Porcie herself, who so deplores the Triumvirs' depredations that she actually wishes Caesar had not been assassinated:

> J'affecte plustost voir nostre dolente Romme
> Serve des volontez de quelque Prince doux
> Qu'obeir aux fureurs de ces Scythiques Lous,
> De ces trois inhumains, qui n'ont en leur courage
> Que l'horreur et l'effroy, que le sang et la rage.

[I would rather see our suffering Rome in servitude to the desires of some mild prince than obey the fury of these Scythian wolves, these three cruel monsters, who have nothing in their hearts but horror and fear, blood and rage.] (ll. 564–68)

Such stigmatizing of the Triumvirs had formed part of Garnier's ideological project even before he took to drama. His first published work, the 1567 *Hymne de la Monarchie*, had cited the ravages of 'ces trois Tyrans, ces Tygres affamés [these three tyrants, these famished tigers]' (ed. Chardon, 1970, p. 266 [sig. Ci^v]) as an instance of the cruelty to which the rule of 'quelque doux Prince' is far preferable. The 'doux Prince' in question was Charles IX, who in 1563 had been proclaimed (in his fourteenth year) as being legally of age to govern. This move was part of Catherine de Medici's effort to promote the monarchy as a transcendent unifying force and thereby restrain the radical Catholic faction, whose persecutions of Protestants had provoked the first civil war. At the head of that faction were three intransigent advocates of Catholic exclusivism who, putting their differences aside, had joined together in highly symbolic fashion at Easter 1561: François, Duke of Guise; the Constable, Anne de Montmorency; and the marshal Jacques d'Albon de Saint-André. They were re- (or de-)christened the 'Triumvirs' by the Huguenots, on the grounds that, as Louis de Bourbon, Prince of Condé, put it, they resembled 'Auguste, Marc Antoine et Lépide, quand par leur Triumvirat meschant et infâme ils suvertirent les loix et la République Romaine [Augustus, Marc Antony and Lepidus, when by their wicked and contemptible Triumvirat they subverted the laws and the Roman republic]'.[3] The name stuck and passed into widespread use. Hence, perhaps, the drastic revision made by Grévin to the ending of his Latin source-play: for Marc-Antoine Muret's apotheosis of Caesar, he substituted the arousal of the soldiers to vengeance by a Marc Antoine who invokes all the powers of the underworld on his behalf.[4] The highly unorthodox lack of a final Chorus leaves that bloodthirsty resolution hanging in the air.

In the late 1560s, then, Garnier's royalism mandated his condemnation of the politics of vengeance in the *Hymne* and *Porcie*. The overriding theme of the latter, as the original subtitle made explicit, was the civil war that had broken out anew: '*tragédie françoise, représentant la cruelle et sanglante saison des guerres civiles de Rome, propre et convenable pour y voir dépeincte la calamité de ce temps* [a French tragedy, representing the cruel and bloody season of the civil wars of Rome, appropriate and suitable for seeing depicted the calamity of this age]' (1568). Paradoxically, however, French royalism began to express itself quite differently in the aftermath of the Saint Bartholomew massacre, with Charles emerging as the instrument of a divine vengeance launched, in a preemptive strike, against the tyrannical menace of Coligny and his allies: hence, as proposed in *French Origins* (2010, p. 47), the cosmic vindictiveness invoked against Caesar in the *Cornélie* of 1574 (by both the heroine and the resident philosopher – in that case, Cicero).

When the first version of *Marc Antoine* appeared in 1578, the national situation had again evolved: that year offered a brief and unstable interlude between the sixth and seventh civil wars; Henri III was now the monarch, but a notably weak one, unable to impose his authority and setting the tone for a court widely regarded as pleasure-loving and dissolute, even if the League's most ferocious accusations of perversity against him lay some years in the future. The ambitions of his brother François d'Anjou were a source of pressure, while the Catholic extremists were regrouping under Henri, Duke of Guise, son of the assassinated 'Triumvir' François. In May 1578, the Guises and their followers flaunted their discontent by deserting the court. All in all, it might seem a suitable (if not necessarily receptive) milieu into which to launch a fable of the completing claims of virtue and pleasure, Mars and Venus.[5] Or, rather, this was to relaunch the fable, since Plutarch's Life of Antony had been perennially popular in France well beyond the other Lives, with successive translations appearing virtually from the first edition of the Greek text in the early sixteenth century.

Moreover, the posthumous publication in 1574 of Jodelle's *Cléopâtre captive* had recently defined a gap for Garnier to fill. As his title indicates, Jodelle's attention is on the Egyptian queen, whose story, I will suggest, he develops in ways more closely anticipating Shakespeare than has been realized.[6] His Antony, however, is redeemed from being a caricature of Roman moralization – the 'strumpet's fool' (*Ant.*, I.i.13[7]) of Philo – only by being also a Senecan ghost seeking revenge on the woman who corrupted and destroyed him. Garnier, on the other hand, develops the contrast with Octave that he had roughly sketched in *Porcie*. His defeated Antoine harks back with bitter nostalgia to the ruthless Triumvir he once was:

> J'ay, vengeur de Cesar ton oncle, ingrat Octave,
> Teint de sang ennemy les rivages que lave
> Le rougeâtre Enipee, et ses flots empeschez
> De cent monceaux de corps l'un sur l'autre couchez.

[Avenger of your uncle Caesar, ungrateful Octave, I have stained with enemy blood the banks that bathe the reddish Enipeus and blocked its floods with a hundred heaps of corpses stacked one upon another.](*Marc Antoine*, ed. Lebègue, 1974, ll. 952–55)

The hero goes on, however, to flagellate himself more severely for his susceptibility to Cleopatra than the audience is cued to do. His reconciliation with her and pitiful death come close to purging the moral stigma and leaving the poetic field clear for Cleopatra's love to take on redemptive overtones. By comparison with Jodelle, this is to return to the letter of Plutarch (although Garnier stops the action short of Cleopatra's suicide, recounted in the earlier play), but it is also to inflect Plutarch's spirit in directions that Jodelle had actually anticipated. The essence of my argument is that the English plays – of Mary Sidney Herbert, Countess of Pembroke (as translator of Garnier), Samuel Daniel and Shake-speare – are far from standing above or outside this dynamic. Indeed, while these works undoubtedly, as commentators have increasingly stressed,[8] counted on English contexts to lend fresh resonances to the political stances, shifting moral messages, even the dramatic and emotional intensity of their French precursors, they also laid intertextual claim to – and to some extent took refuge in – their multiple French heritage.

I

That heritage was still vibrant in France itself. Apart from frequent reissues of Garnier's play (at least ten editions of his complete tragedies appeared between 1585 and 1609), a further contribution appeared no later than 1595, perhaps somewhat earlier. (For reasons that will become apparent, the question of date is especially pertinent here.) The *Cléopâtre* of Nicolas de Montreux amounts to a more rigorously neo-classical, if in some ways more fanciful, rewriting of *Cléopâtre captive* – the latter title is echoed in Montreux's Argument (1595, p. 3) – with, arguably, its own topical political application. This work has, I think, been unduly neglected by specialists in both English and French drama. Given his obscurity today, it is striking how widely Montreux's extremely varied works in verse, prose and drama were diffused in his own time.[9] Montreux was the secretary, librarian and court-poet of the last powerful hold-out of the League against the triumphant Henri IV: Philippe-Emmanuel de Lorraine, Duke of Mercœur. Following Henri IV's conversion, Mercœur had withdrawn, with his militant and flamboyant wife, Marie de Luxembourg (known as 'la belle Nantaise'), if not into an Egyptian monument, at least into the ducal palace at Nantes in his fiefdom of Brittany. There, with Spanish support, they resisted for some years the hegemony of the contemporary equivalent of the conquer-ing Caesar.[10] Roman analogies were (it must be said) legion: appended to Goulart's *An historical collection* (1598) is a four-page exhortation, translated from a pamphlet attributed to Antoine Arnauld (*Libre discours sur la delivrance de la Bretagne*, 1598), which calls upon the French king to lead a glorious expe-dition for the taking of Nantes from Mercœur and upon the French people to support him (*A trve discovrse concerning the deliuerie* of Brittaine, *in the yeare* 1598 [sigs Bbb3ʳ–4ᵛ]). The inexorable conquering force of Henri IV is there evoked, as it regularly was,[11] in Caesarean terms ('the whole course of your life, haue beene no other but triumphs, garlands, and trophees, brought from your enemies'), and he is urged to emulate 'those great heroes of antiquitie' (*A trve discovrse*, 1998, sig. Bbb4ᵛ), while Mercœur is excoriated as a 'Cateline [*sic*]' (sig. Bbb3ʳ).

Montreux was an extraordinarily prolific producer of texts on the other side of the fence, and in this phase of his career there is no hard-and-fast distinction between his propandistic and his literary output. In 1591 he published in Nantes *La miraculeuse délivrance de Monseigneur le duc de Guise Henry* [properly Charles] *de Lorraine, naguère prisonnier au château de Tours* [The miraculous deliverance of my lord the Duke of Guise Henri de Lorraine, formerly prisoner in the Castle of Tours], a year later *L'Heureuse et entière victoire, obtenue ... sur les ennemis de Dieu à Cra[o]n, par le grand, victorieux et catholique prince Philippe Emanuel de Lorraine* [The happy and entire victory obtained ... over the enemies of God at Craon by the great, victorious and Catholic prince Philippe-Emmanuel of Lorraine].[12] Around 1594, as the writing on the wall grew increasingly legible, it seems clear that he made a further political intervention, at once timely and timeless, by appropriating the model of Antony and Cleopatra for his patron's (and perhaps especially his patroness's) consumption.[13]

It is worth paying attention to Montreux's predilection for heroines who prefer liberty by glorious death to slavery and humiliation. The potential for such a treatment of Cleopatra exists in Jodelle, and no doubt Montreux, in this respect as in others, was inspired by Garnier,[14] but the fact remains that he seized on the model to portray a series of women who fuse political, indeed quasi-religious, engagement with personal dignity. And in the case of Cleopatra, known elsewhere for her courage but hardly for her chastity, that traditional crowning female virtue is invoked to signal an honour essentially masculine. Indeed, *Cléopâtre*'s first known publication (1595) presents it as an annex to Montreux's neo-Hellenistic prose romance, *Œuvre de la chasteté*.

The chastity of the dramatist's two other tragic heroines is by definition beyond question but no less politically fraught. One is Sophonisba, brought on stage around 1600, when the political crisis was past but hardly forgotten. (Meanwhile, the Protestant Antoine de Montchrestien had staged and published his own *Sophonisbe* – in revised versions entitled *La Carthaginoise, ou la Liberté* – at Caen, where the culture of Reform was particularly active, in 1596.[15]) More surprising, perhaps, is Montreux's adaptation of Ariosto in *La tragédie d'Isabelle* (a work I have related to *Othello* in *French Origins* [2010, pp. 76–77]), which was seemingly composed prior to *Cléopâtre*.[16] For the encounter that in the original simply represents the moral victory of Christian chastity over pagan sensuality there acquires an insistant political dimension.

The transformation extends to appropriating Ariosto's Fiordiligi, the devoted spouse of Brandimart, to become Isabelle's sister Fleurdelys, so that she may serve, like Cleopatra's waiting-women, as the interlocutor indispensable in Humanist tragedy for counselling would-be suicides. The *Didon se sacrifiant* of Jodelle (composed around 1555) had provided an early model by adapting Anna from the *Aeneid*; Garnier's Antoine confides in Lucile; then, of course, there are Jodelle's and Montreux's own Cleopatras, who have their waiting-women. Across the board, suicide asserts at once amorous fidelity and political independence.

The politicized *rapprochement* of Isabelle and Cleopatra remains especially striking in Montreux, even if Garnier had generally pointed the way (Mouflard, 1961–64, 3: 212–18). Montreux's Cléopâtre specifically recalls his Isabelle (and echoes Jodelle's *Cléopâtre*) by sounding the same lugubrious keynote: 'Non, non, il faut mourir [No, no, it is needful to die]' (Montreux, *Cléopâtre*, 1595, Act I [p. 15]) resonates with Isabelle's 'Ie veux ie veux mourir [I wish, I wish to die]' (*Isabelle*, 1595, I [p. 31] and 'Il vaut bien mieux mourir [It is worth far more to die]' (p. 38). Remarkably, Montreux gives second billing to Isabelle's chastity, nominally her *raison d'être* (or *de non-être*): she will die for love of her Zéobin and to preserve her 'foi [faith]', rather than become the 'Esclaue d'vn Tyran plain d'infidelité, / Ennemy de mon los & de ma chasteté [Slave of a tyrant full of infidelity, enemy of my fame and of my chastity]' (II [p. 35]). There is a further allusion to Jodelle, for Rodomont is finally obliged to render homage to a woman he would have rendered 'au deshonneur captiue' (V [p. 91]). For Leaguers, the evocation of Henri IV, complete with womanizing and expedient conversion, would have been hard to miss, especially since this infidel is endowed with royal pretensions: 'Par ce Dieu que tu sers, par ceste saincte foy, / Qui doit estre l'honneur & le los d'vn grand Roy [by that God whom you serve, by that holy faith which must be the honour and the glory of a great king]' (IV [p. 77]).[17] Montreux's Caesar is likewise a violator of 'la saincte foi': he is bluntly told by one of his own that Cléopâtre took action on learning that he intended 'de la traisner contre la saincte foi / Que jadis tu juras captiue deuant toy [to draw her (in triumph) contrary to the sacred faith you pledged when she stood captive before you]' (*Cléopâtre*, 1595, V [p. 108]).

To pursue Montreux's Cléopâtre, several variants on Plutarchian themes seem especially significant. First, this heroine is more distanced than either Jodelle's or Garnier's from both paganism and sexuality: she speaks only vaguely of having led Antony into error. On the contrary, she anticipates in chapter and verse the resolution of Shakespeare's queen to emulate her 'Husband': 'Now to that name my courage prove my title!' (*Ant.*, V.ii.286, 287). In Montreux, Cléopâtre vows to render herself worthy 'de sa vive constance, /

De son fidelle amour, & de sa vive Foy [of his fervent constancy, his faithful love and his ardent faith]' (1595, I [p. 15]), leaving the last term resonating in the contemporary Catholic air.[18] Then, Cleopatra's effective victory over Caesar is played up even beyond the model in Jodelle: the conqueror at the end appears in person to deliver a long lamenting speech, not remote from Rodomont's, in which he concedes himself morally vanquished and overshadowed by her tragic heroism. He vows in apostrophe to build a splendid tomb 'Où tu seras enclose avecque ton Antoine [Where you shall be enclosed with your Antony]' (1595, V [p. 116]). The command to bury the lovers together comes from Plutarch, but apart from Montreux, only in Shakespeare is the moved Caesar brought on stage to give it – and to acknowledge, pronominally, that Antony remains her conquest rather than his own: 'She shall be buried by her Antony' (*Ant.*, V.ii.357). And in Montreux, as in Shakespeare, this marks an especially sharp defeat for a Caesar whose slipperiness is habitually tricked out in third-person grandiosity: 'Il combat pour l'honneur [He combats for honour's sake]' (1595, IV [p. 87]); 'Caesar cannot lean / To be ungentle' (V.i.59–60).

About Cleopatra's heroism there is no equivocation in Montreux, beginning with the Argument, in which 'Ceste reine courageuse [That courageous queen]' is said to have acted 'desirant plustost vne mort honorable & courte qu'vne vie seruile & cruelle, tant pour euiter le seruage prochain & pour suiure son Antoine [desiring rather an honourable and brief death than a life servile and cruel, both to avoid the imminent servitude and to follow her Antony]' (1595, sig. A2ʳ). Her action proves that, as her Shakespearean counterpart claims in her last moments, she has 'nothing / Of woman' (V.ii.237–38) in her: 'Encor qu'elle portast d'vne femme la face, / Le cœur braue & hardy, & l'ame d'vn heros / Affamé de l'honneur, & cupide du los [Although she bore the face of a woman, she had a heart brave and bold, the soul of a hero hungry for honour and desirous of glory]' (1595, V [p. 108]).[19] Moreover, her women 'la suiuirent en cest acte courageux & loüable [followed her in that courageous and praiseworthy act]' (1595, sig. A2ᵛ).

Nor is there any doubt as to the means of death: the Argument describes her as 'ioyeusement [joyously]' greeting the serpent hidden in the figs, whose biting 'endort les esprits vitaux des hommes & les faict doucement mourir [puts to sleep the vital spirits of men and causes them to die gently]' (1595, sig. A2ᵛ). This is to anticipate the encounter of Shakespeare's Cleopatra with the Clown, from her initial question regarding the 'worm ... / That kills and pains not' (V.ii.242–43) to his benediction: 'I wish you joy o' th' worm' (278). The asp itself, not death in the abstract, is addressed: 'Ha, dit-elle, és-tu [*sic*] là remede à mon tourment? / Je vay te voir, Antoine, ô l'heure bienheureuse! [Ah, she said, are you there, remedy of my torment? / I shall see you, Antony, O happy hour!]' (1595, V [p. 111]). These details richly embellish Plutarch – 'Art thou here then?' (ed. Bullough, 1957–75, 5: 316) makes the closest precedent – and seem novel in the dramatic tradition. There is a notable correlation also with the treatment of Daniel, whose heroine greets the asp similarly ('Such was her joy', 'as one over-joyed' [1594, ll. 1482, 1485][20]) and introduces the metaphor of sleep in addressing it:

> Better then Death, Deaths office thou dischargest,
> That with one gentle touch canst free our breath:
> And in a pleasing sleepe our soule inlargest,
> Making our selves not privie to our death.
> (ll. 1500–3)

II

Apart from North's translation of Amyot's Plutarch, Antony and Cleopatra had recently re-entered the English discursive field by way of Herbert, whose translation of Garnier's *Marc Antoine* (entitled *Antonius*) was first published in 1592 (it would be reprinted in 1595 as *The tragedie of Antonie*). Daniel professed in his 1594 dedication to the Countess that he was supplying a supplement to *Antonius* at her behest and counting on her inspiration to help him invest the character with sufficient 'glory', 'maiestie' and 'courage' (*The tragedie of Cleopatra*, 1594, sig. H5ᵛ) to make her recognizable to the Countess's Antony. Given Herbert's Protestant militancy and close connections with the Huguenot cause, it has puzzled some commentators that she should, as Anne Lake Prescott puts it, 'turn to so Catholic and so royalist a writer as Garnier' (2008, p. 68). On the other hand, the argument of Paulina Kewes (2012) that both Herbert's and Daniel's plays were intended to condemn Elizabeth, in the guise of Cleopatra, for neglecting the succession, ruining her country (to the profit of Philip of Spain, figured in Octavius) and even promoting lasciviousness at the English court implies that the pathos and heroism developed in the French figurations of the Egyptian queen and invoked by Daniel's dedication serve as a mere smokescreen. (So then do, presumably, his introductory compliments to Elizabeth, who is structurally associated with the Countess herself.[21]) One can hardly deny that images of a land bereft of native succession would have resonated politically in the England of the 1590s, but I will be proposing that the political question as such may not have been preeminent in the Countess's response to Garnier. Moreover, the unqualified renewal of the heroine's qualities of 'glory', 'maiestie' and 'courage' in Montreux's tragedy makes it tempting to suspect, despite the impossibility of proving its priority, that in commission-ing Daniel the Countess was concerned to seize the heroic feminine initiative from the ultra-Catholic camp.

We are increasingly appreciating the imbrication of aesthetic and political interests in early modern literary production, and in this case there is conceiv-ably a personal link: instrumental as Henri IV's agent in the protracted negoti-ations with the ducal couple in Brittany during 1594–95 – negotiations which failed to effect their capitulation to royal authority – was Philippe de Mornay, seigneur du Plessis-Marly, the close friend of the late Philip Sidney, who almost certainly remained in affectionate contact with the latter's sister.[22] Robert Sidney, the brother of Philip and Mary, was in Brittany as Elizabeth's envoy with the English expedition of John Norris in 1593–94:[23] a letter from Mornay dated 4 March 1594 speaks of recently coming from a stay in Nantes with much to report and asks his correspondent (one La Fontaine), with whom he evidently has secret political dealings, 'd'asseurer M. de Sidney de mon tres affectionné service, et estre instrument que l'amitié qui estoit entre feu son frere et moi se perpetue [to assure my lord Sidney of my most affectionate service, and that he is the instrument by which the friendship that existed between his late brother and myself may continue]' (Mornay and Arbaleste, *Mémoires et correspondance*, 1824–25, 6: 16 [No. 9]).

The Mornay correspondence also offers a tantalizing glimpse of a network of Protestant noblewomen mingling political and literary affairs.[24] During the same period, Madame de Mornay (Charlotte Arbaleste) received a letter (dated 30 July 1594) from the Duchess of Rohan, the same Catherine de Parthenay who had composed the militant tragedy of *Holoferne* during the 1572 siege of La Rochelle. The Duchess complains of the Duke of Mercœur's exactions, and certain details in the letter are sensitive enough to have been written in cipher.[25] Yet the conclusion moves seamlessly (if also inexplicitly) onto an apparently different plane: 'Je vous envoye ung livre qui a esté faict nouellement, que je crois que vous trouverés fort joliement et plaisamment faict [I send you a book which has recently been made, which I believe you will find most handsomely and pleasantly turned out]' (Mornay and Arbaleste, 1824–25, 6: 85 [No. 56]). Obviously, news of literary productions blends into information of other kinds in such milieux. This picture of the channels and registers of communication is not incompatible with the idea that the Countess of Pembroke may have commissioned 'her' version of the Egyptian queen's tragic heroism as a riposte to that provided by Montreux for his patroness in Nantes.

III

One demonstrable point not acknowledged by Daniel is that he was tracing in reverse the original supplementation of Jodelle by Garnier.[26] There are, obviously, divergences and differences of emphasis – the English play is a loose adaptation, not (except occasionally) a translation – but it is fair to say that in reworking the *Cléopâtre captive* (hence conceivably reappropriating it from Montreux), Daniel conformed to its moral and political contours, including its fundamental ambivalence regarding the heroine: she is guilty but heroic, destructive to her kingdom (not least by her example of pride and viciousness),[27] yet victorious in her courage, which sets the seal on her 'gloire'/'glorie' (Jodelle, 1990, l. 1532; Daniel, ed. Bullough, 1957–75, 5: l. 1640). Daniel's indebtedness is virtually signalled by his inclusion of Seleucus, a minor figure who appears in no other pre-Shakespearean staging except Jodelle's; Jodelle is the obvious dramatic precedent, too, for the direct representation of the scene at Antony's tomb and the subsequent report of Cleopatra's suicide.

With regard to the key Seleucus scene, the affinity is clinched by a common element taken not from Plutarch but from the *Roman History* of Dio Cassius:[28] both Jodelle and Daniel make Cleopatra, prior to producing the statement of her wealth that elicits Seleucus' contradiction, plead for Octavius' favour on the grounds of her relationship with Julius Caesar and mention the latter's letters to her. The passages culminate in a line that Daniel all but translated:

> Ne t'ont donc pu les lettres émouvoir
> Qu'à tes yeux j'avais tantôt fait voir,
> Lettres, je dis, de ton père reçues,
> Certain témoin de nos amours conçues?

[Could not then the letters move you which I just caused to be shown you, letters, I say, received from your father, certain testimony of the loves we shared?] (Jodelle, ed. Charpentier *et al.*, 1990, ll. 869–72)

> Great Cæsar me a Queene at first did make,
> And let not Cæsar now confound the same,
> Reade here these lines which stil I keepe with me,
> The witnes of his love and favours ever.
>   (Daniel, ed. Bullough, 1957–75, 5: ll. 659–62)

The climactic scenes of Cleopatra's sacrifice at the tomb are not only generally parallel in their rhetoric of lament, which broadly derives from Plutarch, but linked through an intense evocation of Antony's spiritual presence, for which Daniel appears to take his cue from Jodelle: 'Antoine, ô cher Antoine! Antoine ma moitié! [Antoine, O dear Antoine! Antoine, half myself!]' (1990, l. 1281).

And in a line that virtually references his precursor's title, Daniel has Cleopatra implore, 'Then heare thy ghost, thy captive spouse complaine' (Daniel, ed. Bullough, 1957–75, 5: l. 1104), where Jodelle had written: 'Entends la faible voix d'une faible captive [Hear the feeble voice of a feeble captive]' (1990, l. 1284).

A further move in the direction of the multiply synthetic achievement that is Shakespeare's *Antony and Cleopatra* occurred when Daniel, for his heavily revised version of 1607, reincorporated the death of Antony in Cleopatra's story by way of Dircetus' account to Caesar in Act I, Scene ii. This account derives from Garnier, as Ernest Schanzer established in rebutting the hypothesis of revision based on Shakespeare's play (1957). The inference is natural that Daniel would have used the Countess's translation, but nothing in the language confirms this, and it is disappointing that Schanzer takes Garnier's original to have been not only Englished but naturalized out of existence: it becomes 'the Countess of Pembroke's play' (1957, p. 377). I will shortly be focussing on that play in its own right – that is, as the translation it is – and suggesting that although Shakespeare undoubtedly knew it, to judge from a couple of incidental echoes, there are closer verbal links between Shakespeare and Garnier's French, while the most essential elements of *Marc Antoine* informing *Antony and Cleopatra* are ones that Herbert's translation resists. At the same time, Daniel's rendering is freer than would warrant Schanzer's affirmation that he 'follows [Dircetus' account] step by step' (1957, p. 376) before returning to Plutarch to supply Antony's last words.

When Daniel does return to Plutarch, he produces some wording very close indeed to Shakespeare: 'And none about *Octauius* trust, said he / But *Proculeius*, he's an honest man' (*The Tragedie of Cleopatra*, 1607, V.ii [sig. H^r]). Together with a couple of other verbal echoes and the notion, not found in Plutarch or Garnier, that Eros was Antony's freedman,[29] this is conclusive evidence for influence in one direction or another: Shakespeare may have read Daniel (Schanzer, 1957, pp. 379–81); Daniel may have seen a performance of Shakespeare's play[30] or, conceivably, a manuscript, while he was licenser for the Queen's Revels – necessarily before 28 April 1605, a date that would make *Antony* earlier than is generally supposed (Wilders, ed., 1995, p. 73). There is no settling the issue of priority, but likewise no questioning the inter-referentiality of the two texts, and the corollary, again, is Shakespeare's dependence on the French dramatic predecessors – the plays of Jodelle, Garnier and, I would add, Montreux – of which Daniel's version was itself, in part, a vehicle.

To this phenomenon must be added Shakespeare's less ambiguous borrowing of details and expressions found only in Daniel's earlier version, notably the allusion to Cydnus (ed. Bullough, 1957–75, 5: ll. 1460–61; cf. *Ant.*, V.ii.227–28) and the description of Cleopatra's fall:

> And sencelesse, in her sinking downe she wries
> The Diademe which on her head shee wore,
> Which *Charmion* (poore weake feeble maid) espies,
> And hastes to right it as it was before.
> (ed. Bullough, 1957–75, 5: ll. 1634–37)[31]

The latter passage makes itself felt in the words of Shakespeare's Charmian, 'Your crown's awry; / I'll mend it' (V.ii.317–18), and behind it lies an impulse to clarify and strengthen Plutarch's original. North's translation has Charmian discovered 'trimming the Diademe which Cleopatra ware upon her head' (ed. Bullough, 1957–75, 5: 316) – 'trimming' translates the equally bland 'raccoutrait' of Amyot – and Daniel follows suit in summing up the scene some lines later, when Caesar's messengers rush in to find 'dying *Charmion* trimming of her head' (ed. Bullough, 1957–75, 5: l. 1653). Shakespeare too repeats the detail in narrative, using North's term (but sharpened), when the guard reports, 'I found her trimming up the diadem / On her dead mistress' (V.ii.340–41). There is no equivalent in Jodelle, but the sharpened picture has its close precedent in Montreux, who writes of Carmian 'd'une main loyalle / R'addressant doucement la coiffure royalle / De sa maistresse morte [with a faithful hand gently setting upright the royal headdress of her dead mistress]' (1595, V [p. 112]).

IV

Before dealing with Shakespeare's direct use of Jodelle, it remains to look briefly at the poem by Daniel that immediately preceded his *Tragedie of Cleopatra* in both the 1599 and the 1607 collections, namely, 'A Letter sent from *Octauia to her husband* Marcus Antonius *into Egypt*'. Bullough (1957–75, 5: 237–38) singles out two stanzas as particularly evoking the behaviour and temperament of Shakespeare's heroine. These are Stanza 2, in which Octavia imagines the scornful reception of her letter, and Stanza 36, where the wiles of 'the Inchanters [i.e., enchantress]' ('Letter', 1607, fol. 5ʳ [St. 35.7]) are epitomized, much as the audience sees them in action:

> Shee armes her teares, the ingins of deceit,
> And all her battery to appose my loue,
> And bring thy comming grace to a retreayt
> The power of all her subtilty to proue:
> Now pale and faint she languishes, and straight

> Seemes in a sound, vnable more to moue:
> Whilst her instructed followers plie thine eares
> With forged passions mixt with fained teares.
> ('Letter', 1607, St. 36 [fol. 5ʳ])

It is worth adding the words of those 'followers' in the succeeding stanza:

> Hard harted lord, say they, how canst thou see
> This mighty Queene a creature so diuine,
> Lie thus distrest, and languishing for thee,
> And onely wretched but for being thine?
> Whilst base *Octauia* must intitled bee
> Thy wife, and shee esteem'd thy concubine:
> Aduance thy heart, raise it vnto his right,
> And let a scepter baser passions quite.
> ('Letter', 1607, St. 37 [fol. 5ʳ])

The undoubted resonance with Shakespeare's character needs, as elsewhere, to be taken with a Plutarchian grain of salt. *The Life of Marcus Antonius* anticipates not only Cleopatra's general flair for flattery (the 1579 edition of North marginally crowns her the 'Queene of all flatterers' [Bullough, ed., 1957–75, 5: 276n.4]), but also the specific account (ed. Bullough, 1957–75, 5: 288–89) at the root of Daniel's in the 'Letter'. Indeed, Plutarch describes Cleopatra as adopting these stratagems in jealous response to a report praising Octavia, so it is hard not to think as well of Shakespeare's queen reacting to the messenger in Act II, Scene v, and Act III, Scene iii. But the Shakespearean resonance must also be read across the fact – hitherto unnoticed, it seems[32] – that here again Daniel, in his familiar manner of condensed paraphrase slipping into translation, was most immediately adapting Jodelle.

The French original is found in the Séleuque scene (Act III) of *Cléopâtre captive*, where it forms part of Octavian's rebuke of Cléopâtre for luring Antoine from Octavienne by manipulative tricks amounting to enchantment:

> Vous le paissiez de ruse et de finesses,
> De mille et mille et dix mille caresses[.]
> Tantôt au lit exprès emmaigrissiez,
> Tantôt par feinte exprès vous pâlissiez,
> Tantôt votre œil votre face baignait
> Dès qu'un jet d'arc de lui vous éloignait,
> Entretenant la feinte et sorcelage.
> Ou par coutume ou par quelque breuvage,
> Même attitrant vos amis et flatteurs,
> Pour du venin d'Antoine être fauteurs,
> Qui l'abusaient sous les plaintes frivoles,

> Faisant céder son profit aux paroles.
> 'Quoi! disaient-ils, êtes-vous l'homicide
> D'un pauvre esprit qui vous prend pour sa guide?
> Faut-il qu'en vous la Noblesse s'offense,
> Dont la rigueur à celle-là ne pense
> Qui fait de vous le but de ses pensées?
> O qu'[elles]³³ sont mal envers vous adressées!
> Octavienne a le nom de l'épouse,
> Et cette-ci, dont la flamme jalouse
> Empêche assez la vite renommée,
> Sera l'amie en son pays nommée,
> Cette divine à qui rendent l'hommage
> Tant de pays joints à son héritage.'

[You fed him with ruse and subtleties, a thousand and a thousand, ten thousand, caresses. Now in bed you deliberately emaciated yourself; now you expressly feigned to grow pale; now your eye bathed your face when he distanced himself from you by a bow-shot, making use of feigning and spell-casting – whether by habitual usage or some potion, even commissioning your friends and flatterers to help poison Antony, they who abused him with frivolous complaints, causing him to yield his profit to their words. 'What, they said, will you be the murderer of that poor soul who takes you for her guide? Must in you Nobility be blemished, whose harshness thinks not of her who makes of you the object of her thoughts? O they do wrong to direct themselves towards you! Octavienne has the name of wife, and this lady here, whose jealous flame stands in the way of a rapid fame, shall be called your mistress in her country, this divine creature, to whom so many lands joined in her heritage render homage.'] (ed. Charpentier *et al.*, 1990, ll. 909–32)

Since the scene in question, minus the cited lines, was in fact included by Daniel in his tragedy, we are effectively dealing with an 'out-take', for which the author found a related use. And Shakespeare seems to have followed suit, for he likewise chose to drop Caesar's accusatory character analysis from the Seleucus sequence and, in effect, to redeploy it otherwise – though, as usual, with a twist. For while his Cleopatra does indeed do her share of ostentatious languishing, she is shrewder than Jodelle or Daniel – or indeed Plutarch – imagined her: 'If you find him sad, / Say I am dancing; if in mirth, report / That I am sudden sick' (I.iii.3–5). So she tells Charmian, who can conceive of no other flattery than that which proclaims dependence. The power of paradox is captured, by contrast, by Enobarbus, for whom her charms transcend the notion of feigning and fully recuperate Jodelle's 'sorcelage', Daniel's 'Inchanter', even – most paradoxically – Montreux's 'chasteté':

> Age cannot wither her, nor custom stale
> Her infinite variety; other women cloy

> The appetites they feed, but she makes hungry
> Where most she satisfies; the vilest things
> Become themselves in her, that the holy priests
> Bless her when she is riggish.
>
> (II.ii.242–47)

V

The evidence is more than circumstantial, if not quite beyond a reasonable doubt, that Shakespeare did not merely take his cue in the Seleucus scene from Daniel but responded in his turn, as Daniel had done, to the pioneering version of Jodelle. There is, first, the fact that only in Shakespeare and Jodelle is the fate of Cleopatra's children both raised as an issue within this scene and confined to it. Daniel reserves the subject for detailed development (based on Plutarch) both before and after – inspired, perhaps, by the staging of Cleopatra's tearful parting with them in Garnier's final scene. Shakespeare essentially transfers to the meeting between Caesar and Cleopatra, and recasts in veiled form, the direct threat that Plutarch reports Caesar as having earlier conveyed to deter her from self-starvation. At that time, she was so 'overcome with sorow and passion of minde' that she had abused her body and worked herself into a fever:

> But Cæsar mistrusted the matter, by many conjectures he had, and therefore did put her in feare, and threatned her to put her children to shameful death. With these threats, Cleopatra for feare yelded straight, as she would have yelded unto strokes. (ed. Bullough, 1957–75, 5: 313)

Shakespeare's Caesar is typically subtler – more calculating, cold-blooded and careful of the magnanimous image behind and through which he applies his power:

> ... if you seek
> To lay on me a cruelty by taking
> Antony's course, you shall bereave yourself
> Of my good purposes, and put your children
> To that destruction which I'll guard them from,
> If thereon you rely.
>
> (V.ii.128–33)

On the surface, the matter is quite differently handled in *Cléopâtre captive*, but in this respect, as in others, Jodelle's rudimentary dramaturgy proves surprisingly rich in hints that Shakespeare may have taken up. In the first place, by introducing Cléopâtre in her abject physical and mental state, Jodelle likewise incorporates Plutarch's previous narrative, tying the queen's plea for her children to her battered condition:

> Prends donc pitié; tes glaives triomphants
> D'Antoine et moi pardonnent aux enfants!
> Pourrais-tu voir les horreurs maternelles,
> S'on meurtrissait ceux qui ces deux mamelles,
> Qu'ores tu vois maigres et déchirées,
> Et qui seraient de cent coups empirées,
> Ont allaité?

[Take pity, then. Spare the children your swords, which triumph over Antony and me. Could you sustain the horrors a mother would feel if one murdered those whom these two breasts, which now you see thin and torn, and harmed by a hundred blows, had given suck?] (ed. Charpentier *et al.*, 1990, ll. 879–85)

Besides becoming, more than incidentally, the only Cleopatra besides Shakespeare's who bares her breasts in maternal self-display – a point I will return to – Jodelle's figure thus uses her concern for her children to prove the sincerity of her submission. Such sincerity is the key issue in this climactic confrontation, as is confirmed by Octavian's reproaches of her emotional tricks. From the outset, he accuses her of feigning – she underscores the point by reacting as if struck ('Feindre, hélas! ô! [Feign, alas! O!]' [1990, l. 803]) – and when he returns to her children, rejecting her excuses and repeating his scepticism, he is clearly using their fate, like his Shakespearean counterpart, to keep her under control:

> Contentez-vous, Cléopâtre, et pensez
> Que c'est assez de pardon et assez
> D'entretenir le fuseau de vos vies,
> Qui ne seront à vos enfants ravies.

[Be contented, Cléopâtre, and consider that it is sufficient to pardon and sustain the spindle of your lives, which shall not be ravished from your children.] (1990, ll. 949–52)

So she acknowledges by throwing herself wholly on his mercy, pronouncing herself humbly grateful that he has spared her life and theirs, then sealing her submission by proffering her treasure.

With Cléopâtre's sincerity explicitly at stake in Jodelle and, as in Shakespeare, at once tied to her children's fate and kept momentarily in suspension for both on- and off-stage audiences,[34] the surprising contradiction of Séleuque has much broader application than in Daniel to the game of cat-and-mouse played out between conqueror and captive. That contradiction also carries greater impact. The 'many things' (ed. Bullough, 1957–75, 5: 314) that Plutarch records her as withholding are reduced to 'some things' by Daniel in two bare lines assigned to Seleucus (ed. Bullough, 1957–75, 5: II. 671–72) . By contrast, Jodelle's Séleuque gets a long speech evoking her immense wealth and concluding, 'Crois, César, crois qu'elle a de tout son or / Et autres biens tout le meilleur caché [Believe, Caesar, believe that of all her gold and other possessions, she has concealed much the best]' (1990, ll. 1010–11) – a far closer anticipation of his dramatic revelation in Shakespeare: 'Enough to purchase what you have made known' (V.ii.148).

Daniel also flattens to a mere menacing gesture, to judge from Caesar's single line restraining her – 'Holde, holde; a poore revenge can worke so feeble hands' (ed. Bullough, 1957–75, 5: l. 675) – the violent reaction signalled by Plutarch: 'Cleopatra was in such a rage with him, that she flew upon him, and tooke him by the heare of the head, and boxed him wellfavoredly' (ed. Bullough, 1957– 75, 5: 314). The English dramatist's decorum is all the more conspicuous by comparison with Jodelle, and it gains the approval of Joan Rees: 'Jodelle's treatment of the scene strikes a note out of harmony with the play as a whole', while 'Daniel was not, by temperament, liable to fall into the same error' (1952, p. 6). By contrast, the 'error' is one that Shakespeare grasps and exploits, even if he also picks up Daniel's wording when Cleopatra excuses herself.[35] The point bears more largely on Cleopatra's sincerity, which in all three plays remains equivocal in itself but within the general framework, supplied by Plutarch, of her outmanœuvring of Caesar: '... and so he tooke his leave of her, supposing he had deceived her, but in deede he was deceived him selfe' (ed. Bullough, 1957–75, 5: 314). Only the dynamic stagings of Jodelle and Shakespeare effectively call attention to that framework.

Most exceptionally, Jodelle here not only allows action to intrude on discursive exchange but dares to show kings descending to the level of clowns in a flagrantly indecorous manner for a sound French Humanist. The astonishing slapstick encounter proceeds over twenty-five lines of brisk interchange, including an intervention by the panicked Séleuque that momentarily produces threeway dialogue – a further technical rarity – and ironically calls attention to the behind-the-scenes stakes: 'Retiens-la / Puissant César, retiens-la donc! [Hold her back, potent Caesar, do hold her back!]' (1990, ll. 1019–20). An audience would automatically attribute Caesar's amusement to his heightened sense of security and masculine superiority:

> Ô quel grinçant courage!
> Mais rien n'est plus furieux que la rage
> D'un cœur de femme. Et bien, quoi, Cléopâtre?
> Etes-vous point jà soûle de le battre!
> Fuis-t'en, ami, fuis-t'en.

[O what squeaking courage! But nothing is more furious than the rage of a woman's heart. So then, Cleopatra, have you already had enough of beating him? Flee, my friend, flee.] (1990, ll. 1025–29)

This is arguably not a clumsy lapse but a daring metadramatic effect. By breaking the confines of convention, Jodelle throws Cléopâtre's 'performance' into relief precisely as such; tragic decorum is violated in the cause of dramatic irony.

The effect may be linked with that in *Antony and Cleopatra*, where Shakespeare has Cleopatra initiate a virtual scene-within-the-scene, cueing Seleucus to speak and thereby giving herself the occasion to lose her self-control: 'What, go'st thou back? Thou shalt / Go back, I warrant thee! But I'll catch thine eyes / Though they had wings!' (V.ii.154–56). This recapitulation of the outburst against the messenger who reported Antony's marriage ('Hence, / Horrible villain, or I'll spurn thine eyes / Like balls before me!' [II.v.63–64]) has much the same effect as the evocation immediately preceding, in Jodelle's scene, of Cléopâtre's jealous response to Octavienne. The character's stereotypically feminine behaviour functions, paradoxically, to assimilate the masculine heroic model. Shakespeare's Cleopatra, fulfilling her resolution to do 'what's brave, what's noble, / ... after the high Roman fashion' (IV.v.90–92), will shortly announce, 'I have nothing / Of woman in me. Now from head to foot / I am marble-constant' (V.ii.237–39); Jodelle's will compel the rueful Roman recognition 'que l'espérance / Que nous avions cède à cette constance [that the hope we possessed yields to that constancy]' (1990, ll. 1547–48). And both dramatists self-reflexively set the enactment of that gender-transcending reality against the sexually degrading mimicry threatened by Caesar's triumph. When Cleopatra conjures the image of the 'quick comedians' (V.ii.215), including a 'squeaking Cleopatra' who will 'boy my greatness / I'th' posture of a whore' (219–20), she effectively recycles Charmium's welcome (on her mistress's behalf) of the 'remède de mort [remedy of death]' (Jodelle, ed. Charpentier *et al.*,1990, l. 1197), given that 'dans trois jours préfix, cette douce contrée / Il nous faudra laisser pour à Rome menées / Donner un beau spectacle à leurs efféminées [in three days appointed, this sweet land we must leave to be led to Rome so as to offer a pretty show to their effeminates]' (1990, ll. 1204–6).[36] In her last pathetic monologue she bristles at the thought of the attempt to 'orner de moi [adorn with me]' (1990, l. 1295) the Roman triumph. It seems to have been Montreux's initiative, in adapting Jodelle, to lend particularly vivid imagining to Cleopatra herself in dialogue with her women, though in a version that privileges the rude humiliations of Shakespeare's 'Mechanic slaves' and 'Saucy lictors' (V.ii.208, 213) over theatrical self-referentiality; she asks Iras whether a queen of Egypt could conceivably

> Serve de passetemps, cruellement seruile,
> Et menée en triomphe à la troupe inciuile
> Des superbes Romains?

[Serve as a pastime in cruel servility and led in triumph before the uncivil crowd of haughty Romans?] (Montreux, *Cléopâtre*, 1595, I [p. 15])

The theatrical image put into play by Jodelle becomes indispensable to Shakespeare's version, where the power mimetically to renew Cleopatra's humiliation would appropriate her 'infinite variety' as a reflection of Caesar's immortality. The conqueror's assurance of mercy ('Caesar cannot lean / To be ungentle' [V.i.59–60]) is transparently inextricable from his conviction that 'her life in Rome / Would be eternal in our triumph' (65–66). It is a point that Montreux's counterpart likewise makes in an affirmation thinly masking self-interest behind magnanimous clemency: 'la douceur rend nostre los immortel [mildness renders our praise immortal]' (1595, V [p. 100]). These are the terms – essentially those of the world-as-stage – in which the counter-triumph of Shakespeare's Cleopatra emerges as most richly ironic, when she fulfils 'Immortal longings' (V.ii.280) that project her beyond the 'fleeting moon' (239) into 'fire and air' (288), and into the company of an Antony 'Condemning shadows quite' (100). Part of that irony is the backdrop of the Ruins of Rome, as Renaissance audiences and readers would have supplied it – and as it is explicitly developed by the Egyptian Chorus in Garnier's *Marc Antoine*, which vividly evokes the downfall of the 'eternal city' as a function of Time itself:

> Le Temps abbat toute chose,
> Rien ne demeure debout,
> Sa grande faulx tranche tout,
> Comme le pié d'une rose:
> La seule immortalité
> Du ciel estoilé s'oppose
> A sa forte deïté.

[Time strikes down all things; nothing remains upright. His great scythe cuts all like the base of a rose. The immortality of starry heaven alone stands up against his potent deity.] (ed. Lebègue, 1974, ll. 824–30)

As is also the case in Plutarch, Seleucus simply disappears after he has played his Shakespearean scene, thereby assuring that scene's ambiguity. Both Jodelle and Daniel, however, treat Seleucus as a loose end needing to be tied up. The procedure of Daniel is literal-minded, not to say heavy-handed: Seleucus has been rewarded by Caesar, as traitors usually are, with scorn and disfavour. So he laments, obligingly pointing the proverbial moral ('Princes in this case / Do hate the Traitor, though they love the treason' [ed. Bullough, 1957–75, 5: ll. 837–38]); he then serves as interlocutor for its seconding by Rodon, who recounts at length his own shameful betrayal of Caesarion to his death. By contrast, Jodelle, although his dramaturgy is equally naïve, cuts poetically to the imaginative and moral bone, and again in a way that suggests the deeper appeal of his version to Shakespeare. Séleuque encounters the Chorus, which asks him why he is still fleeing when he is safely out of the way of Cleopatra's rage. The answer is that his punishment is now inward rather than outward – that he is vainly fleeing from his conscience, which so torments him that death would be preferable:

> S'elle m'eût fait mort en terre gésir,
> Elle eût prévu à mon présent désir,
> Vu que la mort n'eût point été tant dure
> Que l'éternelle et mordante pointure,
> Que jà déjà jusques au fond me blesse
> D'avoir blessé ma Reine et ma maîtresse.

[If she had caused me to lie dead on the ground, she would have anticipated my present desire, given that death would not have lasted as long as the eternal and biting sting that already wounds me most deeply for having wounded my Queen and my mistress.] (ed. Charpentier *et al.,* 1990, ll. 1077–82)

This is, of course, the punishment of Cain, the 'guilt of conscience' that Henry IV seeks to impose on Exton after invoking a variant of Daniel's proverb: 'They love not poison that do poison need' (*R2*, V.vi.41, 38). But it is also, in Jodelle's representation, living testimony to Cléopâtre's tragic grandeur. Séleuque is not merely internalizing his violation of a code of loyalty but reacting to what he – contrary to the mocking César – has truly recognized as dignity in extreme distress: 'Lorsque la reine et triste et courageuse / Devant César aux cheveux m'a tiré ... [When the queen both sad and courageous dragged me before Caesar by the hair ...]' (1990, ll. 1074–75). He has, in a sense, offended against the divinity implanted within, and inextricable from, her vulnerable humanity. This is to anticipate the fate of Enobarbus, when, for down-to-earth reasons, he turns against a master who 'Continues still a Jove' (IV.vi.30) and is inwardly driven to 'seek / Some ditch wherein to die' (38–39), expiating his impiety ('I am alone the villain of the earth' [31]) through the melancholic sacrifice of a life that has become 'a very rebel to my will' (IV.ix.17).

The sense that Shakespeare reaches within and behind the text of Jodelle is sustained by Antony's ghost, who is as relentlessly moralistic and vengeful as he is garrulous (the speech extends over one-hundred-and-six Alexandrines). His chief crime, he insists, the one that arouses the Furies against him ('Echauffant les serpents des sœurs échevelées [Inflaming the serpents of the discheveled sisters]' [1990, l. 41]), was the one for which César also rebukes Cléopâtre – the abandonment of his legitimate wife and children:

> C'est que jà jà charmé, enseveli des flammes,
> Ma femme Octavienne, honneur des autres Dames,
> Et mes mollets enfants je vins chasser arrière,
> Nourrissant en mon sein ma serpente meurtière,
> Qui m'entortillonnant, trompant l'âme ravie,
> Versa dans ma poitrine un venin de ma vie,
> Me transformant ainsi, sous ses poisons infuses,
> Qu'on serait du regard de cent mille Méduses.

[It is that, already charmed, enveloped in flames, my wife Octavienne, the honour of all other women, and my tender children I chased to the rear, nourishing in my breast my murderous serpent, which, enfolding me, deceiving the ravished soul, poured into my bosom a poison against my life, so transforming me, under the poisons it infused, as if it were the gaze of a hundred thousand Medusas.] (1990, ll. 43–50)

Obviously to the point are the intertwined images of deceitful enchantment and serpentine poisoning, for which the allusion to Aesop's fable of the viper in the bosom serves as the pretext (in both senses). In the intertextual light of Jodelle's ghostly monologue, the pining of Cleopatra for her absent lover takes on a stronger colouration of spell-casting:

> He's speaking now,
> Or murmuring 'Where's my serpent of old Nile?'
> For so he calls me. Now I feed myself
> With most delicious poison. Think on me …
> (I.v.25–28)

At the same time, Shakespeare's treatment makes it clear that, at least, the delicious poisoning is mutual, and Cleopatra gets an anamorphic (and gender-transgressing) glimpse of her lover as a transfixing Medusa – at the very moment, moreover, when she learns that he has deserted her for Octavia:

> Let him for ever go! Let him not, Charmian.
> Though he be painted one way like a Gorgon,
> The other way's a Mars.
> (II.v.115–17)

If this is, almost literally, a pivotal moment in the (re)deployment of such imagery, by the end of *Antony and Cleopatra* it is Cleopatra who is nourishing a serpent at, if not exactly in, her bosom: 'Dost thou not see my baby at my breast, / That sucks the nurse asleep?' (V.ii.308–9). There was precedent for having Cleopatra apply the asp to her breast instead of to her arm, as she does in Plutarch and the other dramatic versions, as well as for the image of the nursing baby.[37] But the image gains greater force when it is set off against the

Roman denigration of her sexuality and femininity. Jodelle's Senecan Antoine lurks in the intertextual background, endorsing that reading, and to this extent Jodelle's Cléopâtre remains captive, her death according to Plutarch. But Jodelle also opens the issue up – not least by having Cléopâtre bare her breasts to César in an appeal for her and Antoine's children, and symbolically for recognition of their love. And therein, as the impact on Séleuque confirms, lies the glimpse of a nurturing divinity that fulfills itself imagistically in Shakespeare but remains, for Jodelle, in the shadow of moralistic denial. The central irony of *Cléopâtre captive* is that the engagement and persistence of the heroine on her tragic path free her from César but not Antoine. The ghost lulls her with desire for death so that she may spend eternity with him 'en ma peine et tristesse [in my pain and sorrow]' (1990, l. 105); Cléopâtre begins her lengthy rhetorical journey by acknowledging that summons: 'Antoine jà m' appelle, Antoine il me faut suivre [Antoine already calls me, Antoine I must follow]' (1990, l. 117).

VI

Garnier, by contrast, provided a living Antoine, who, like Shakespeare's, expiates his self-blame through suicide and, by narrative implication, is lovingly reconciled to Cléopâtre. His starting point, however – the aftermath of Actium – coincides with the posture of shame and hostility fixed for eternity in Jodelle's character. Thus he similarly excoriates himself for submitting to Cléopâtre's charms, even if he also takes credit for having temporarily extricated himself:

> Tu t'arraches en fin, comme un homme charmé
> S'arrache à l'enchanteur, qui le tient enfermé
> Par un forçable sort: Car ta raison premiere,
> Debrouillant les poisons de ta belle sorciere,
> Reguarit ton esprit. ...

[You tear yourself away, finally, as a man under a spell tears himself from the enchanter who keeps him confined by a compelling destiny. For your first reason, shaking off the poisons of your beautiful sorceress, restores your mind. ...]
(*Marc Antoine*, ed. Lebègue, 1974, ll. 79–83)

The effect is subtly to shift his inevitable relapse, morally reprehensible as it is ('Lascivement vivant d'une femme abusé, / Croupissant en ta fange [Lasciviously living off a dissipated woman, stagnating in your slime]' [1974, ll. 119–20]), in the direction of a loving constancy, which in turn contrasts with his lover's wavering and offers a model to which she can aspire in her mourning. His very powerlessness to resist emerges as a positive marker of identity – and for eternity: 'Si l'aymé-je tousjours, et le premier flambeau / De sa meurtriere amour m'ardra dans le tombeau [But I love her still, and the first torch of her deadly love shall inflame me in the tomb]' (1974, ll. 139–40).

Soon thereafter – and this innovation served as a precedent for Shakespeare – the scene is shifted to Cléopâtre, who in dialogue with her women is allowed unambiguously to establish her constant love and announce her own resolution to die. She blames herself for leading Antony to disaster and defeat, given her womanly weakness and her fatal influence over him – 'Ma beauté trop aimable est notre adversité [My too-appealing beauty is our adversity]' (1974, l. 430) – but the idea that she has betrayed him, or could do so, by coming to terms with César is solemnly (and relentlessly) repudiated. Indeed, her elemental invocations lie close behind those of Shakespeare's Cleopatra after Antony's encounter with Thidias (although Shakespeare felicitously transmigrated Garnier's revamped plagues of Egypt into flies and gnats, preferring to put the crocodile's tears to comic purpose elsewhere [II.vii.50]):

> Plustost un foudre aigu me poudroye le chef,
> Plustost puissé-je cheoir en extreme mechef,
> Plustost la terre s'ouvre et mon corps engloutisse,
> Plustost un Tigre glout de ma chair se nourrisse,
> Et plustost et plustost sorte de nostre Nil,
> Pour me devorer vive, un larmeux Crocodil.

[Rather let a violent thunderbolt turn my head to dust; rather may I fall into extreme distress; rather may the earth open and swallow up my body; rather may a greedy tiger feed on my flesh; and rather may a tearful crocodile emerge from our Nile to devour me alive.] (1974, ll. 393–98)

> Ah, dear, if I be [cold-hearted],
> From my cold heart let heaven engender hail
> And poison it in the source, and the first stone
> Drop in my neck; as it determines, so
> Dissolve my life! The next Caesarion smite,
> Till by degrees the memory of my womb,
> Together with my brave Egyptians all,
> By the discandying of this pelleted storm
> Lie graveless, till the flies and gnats of Nile
> Have buried them for prey!
> (III.13.163–72)

Garnier's audience thus has an ironic distance on Antoine's interpretation when he next appears to lament the fatal relationship in Act III. His three-hundred-line debate with Lucile – of the standard *adversité/félicité* kind, without precedent in Plutarch – also cushions his rancour, although suicide still looms as necessary self-punishment for the 'deshonneur [dishonour]' (1974, l. 1241) of his 'lascives amours [lascivious loves]' (1974, l. 1239).

Finally, Dircet's account of Antoine's last moments returns to a bare transcription of Plutarch, likewise recording his brief outburst against apparent betrayal, then, when the queen's death is reported, his despair at having lost 'La seule cause ... desirer la vie [the only reason to desire his life]' (1974, l. 1589). A significant shift is introduced after the bungled suicide, however, for, where Plutarch merely states that he requested 'verie earnestlie' (ed. Bullough, 1957–75, 5: 309) to be carried to her when he learned she was alive, Dircet reports that 'le pauvre homme' was 'esmeu de grande joye [moved with great joy]' (1974, l. 1624). The rest of the narrative is pure pathos, and it breaks off before the reunion of the lovers, so Garnier allows Antoine to fade out, as it were, on the same mingled sense of love as destructive and exalting that Cléopâtre will take up and sustain to the end. From Shakespeare's perspective (and perhaps Daniel's in preparing his 1607 revision), it is clear that the ambivalence of Antoine developed by Garnier provided, as a single-mindedly vindictive spectre could not have done, the basis for presenting Cleopatra's final achievement as synthesis, resolution and transcendence.

The initial representation of Cleopatra as a witch by Garnier's Antoine supplies one of the very few moments at which Herbert's translation pretty clearly influenced Shakespeare's wording, since she has, 'Thou breakest at length from thence, as one encharm'd / Breakes from th'enchaunter' (1998, ll. 79–80), for 'Tu t'arraches en fin, comme un homme charmé / S'arrache à l'enchanteur' (1974, ll. 79–80);[38] Shakespeare makes Antony say, 'I must from this enchanting queen break off' (I.ii.128). Most of the points adduced to show such influence are less definitive. (Thus Herbert's verb 'hauntst' at line 1995, where Cleopatra imagines joining Antony in the underworld, might – but need not – have led Shakespeare to have the dying Antony use the noun 'haunt' [IV.xiv.55] for the Elysian fields he will share with her.[39])

In any case, it is virtually certain that Shakespeare knew Garnier's original as well. I will be dealing systematically below with the translation's wary handling of terms that, in Garnier, lend a quasi-religious dimension to Cléopâtre's attraction – an element positively developed by Shakespeare. Less prominent but more decisive, in its way, is Antony's reference to sending 'to the boy Caesar ... this grizzled head' (III.xiii.17), about which there is a surprisingly large point to be made. The phrase occurs in a sequence leading to his challenge of Caesar to single combat and opposing Caesar's 'youth' (21) and 'gay caparisons' (26) to his own mature experience. The imagery picks up Antony's earlier reminiscence of Octavius at Philippi ('kept / His sword e'en like a dancer' [III.xi.35–36]; 'no practice had / In the brave squares of war'

[39–40]), with its defensiveness directly linked to his sense of age: 'My very hairs do mutiny, for the white / Reprove the brown for rashness, and they them / For fear and doting' (13–15). Anticipated, by contrast, is Antony's momentary renewal of confidence that, 'Though grey doth something mingle with our younger brown' (IV.viii.19–20), he 'can / Get goal for goal of youth' (22). Behind all this must lie Antoine's complaint to Lucile, which contains a precise equivalent of 'grizzled head' in 'chef grison' (1974, l. 1058) (translated by Herbert more loosely as 'gray hayres' [1998, l. 1069]):

> Je luy ay de nous deux le combat presenté,
> Bien qu'il soit en sa force, et que ja la viellesse
> M'oste en m'affoiblissant et la force et l'addresse:
> Si l'a-til refusé, tant son cœur est couard,
> Vilainement craintif d'un louable hasard.
>
>   C'est dequoy je me plains, et dequoy je m'accuse,
> C'est en quoy la Fortune outrageusement use
> Contre mon chef grison: c'est en quoy, malheureux!
> Les immortels je blasme, à mon mal rigoureux:
> Qu'un homme effeminé de corps et de courage,
> Qui du mestier de Mars n'apprist oncque l'usage,
> M'ait vaincu …

[I challenged him to single combat, although he is in his strength, and age has already weakened me by depriving me of strength and agility. But he refused, so cowardly is his heart, shamefully fearful of a praiseworthy risk.

It is of that I complain, of that I accuse myself; it is in this that Fortune commits outrage against my grizzled head. It is in this, unhappy man! The immortals I blame, harsh in my unhappiness – that a man effeminate in body and spirit, who never mastered the art of Mars, should have vanquished me …] (1974, ll. 1051–62)

The issue of fortune is likewise very much to the point in Shakespeare, not only generally (beginning with the Soothsayer in Act II, Scene iii), but in connection with Antony's futile challenge. Enobarbus perceives at once that Caesar will not 'Unstate his happiness' to answer it, and that 'men's judgements are / A parcel of their fortunes' (III.xiii.30–32); later he will explain Caesar's refusal – 'Let the old ruffian know / I have many other ways to die' (IV.i.4–5) – on the grounds of his being 'twenty times of better fortune' (IV.ii.3). A significant thematic strand, then, is spun out from the single allusion to the challenge in Plutarch, where Caesar simply answers 'that he had many other wayes to dye than so' (ed. Bullough, 1957–75, 5: 307). It seems clear that attaching to this minor detail the interrelated issues of age, manliness and fortune was originally – like much else that made its way into *Antony and Cleopatra* – Garnier's idea.

VII

Before attempting a final measure of the 'Frenchness' of *Antony and Cleopatra*'s textual heritage by taking up Herbert's translation as such, I wish, with due caution, to indicate the possible participation of a slight and obscure tributary stream. This is the *Tragedie de Jeanne-d'Arques* composed by a certain Jean de Virey, seigneur Du Gravier, which first appeared in Rouen in 1600 from the busy press of Raphaël du Petit Val.[40] Virey has long since been forgotten as an author (deservedly, no doubt, although a contemporary reader would not necessarily have anticipated posterity's judgement), and this work is hardly likely to attract critical attention as an 'Antony play' for the simple reason that its subject is Jeanne d'Arc. On the other hand, Shakespeare had a long-standing interest in the latter, obviously manifested in *Henry VI, Part 1*, but reflected, as I have argued elsewhere, across both tetralogies of English history plays, as well as in relation to the first Jeanne d'Arc tragedy, that of Fronton Du Duc (1580).[41] If this interest led him to pick up Virey's stilted neo-classical exercise, he is likely to have been struck by its multi-faceted absurdity, not least in an original variation on the confrontation between Jeanne d'Arc and Talbot. Both he himself and Fronton Du Duc had developed that confrontation in ways that subordinate historical accuracy to symbolism, but Virey went a large step farther: in Act IV of the *Tragedie de Jeanne-d'Arques* – ironically, just before La Pucelle is captured – 'Le Seigneur Talbot Anglois' experiences a drastic access of melancholy, overwhelmed by the reverses the English have suffered because of her, and stabs himself to death.[42]

More to the point here, however, is this scene's close resemblance to the dialogue between Antoine and Lucile that occupies Act III of Garnier's play. Talbot is given a corresponding interlocutor, Allide, with whom he conducts an exchange touching on many of the same points and likewise turning on an attempt to dissuade the discouraged warrior from suicide. The outcome is different, however; in a sort of inversion of the deception of Eros, Talbot finally pretends to be persuaded and tricks Allide into leaving the stage (to prepare the army to sail back to England). Thereupon he kills himself – a fairly unusual on-stage event for contemporary French theatre – leaving Allide with nothing to do when he returns but express surprise and grief, vow the death of Jeanne, and get the body off-stage in the style of Fortinbras: 'Vous, soldats ce pendant pour office dernier / Leuez auecque moy ce corps fort & guerrier [You, soldiers, meanwhile, as a last service, bear along with me this body, strong and warrior-like]' (Virey, 1600, Act IV [p. 41]).

As if concerned that the Roman analogy did not speak loudly enough for itself, Virey invoked it directly. The Chorus ending the previous act drones on

in the usual way about the vicissitudes of fortune but offers the following pertinent illustration:

> Ainsi le Romain vainqueur
> Deuant les forces d'Actie
> Fut contraint perdant le cœur,
> En fin se couper la vie.

[Thus the Roman conqueror, before the forces at Actium, was constrained, losing
heart, finally to cut off his life.] (1600, III [p. 33])

Moreover, Antony (if not by name, at least generically) is appropriated as a role
model by Talbot himself: 'Aussi le fier Romain de son propre couteau / S'enfile
pour ne voir vn triomphe nouueau [Thus the proud Roman with his own knife
does away with himself so as not to see a new triumph]' (1600, IV [p. 40]).

All in all, these commonplaces effect an imaginative fusion of Talbot and
Antony, arguably in such a way as to claim a place in the intertextual story. For
the melancholic mixture of shame, rage and despair evinced by Shakespeare's
character just before his suicide simply has no closer precedent in the
analogues. The indirect narratives of this sequence in Garnier and Daniel (the
latter in the version of 1607) follow Plutarch closely, adding little. Only Shakespeare actually puts Antony on stage at this point and fills in the outline of his
agony with an imaginative loss of that heroic essence that conferred identity.
Such is, however crudely, the case of Talbot. If Antony presents himself to Eros
as an insubstantial image, unable to 'hold this visible shape' (IV.xiv.14), Talbot
laments to Allide,

> Helas ie ne suis plus qu'vne morte stature?
> Je ne suis qu'vne Idole ou qu'vn chesne Indien
> A qui les aquilons inspirent le moyen
> De parler en sa mort, ie ne me sens moy mesme
> Pasle defiguré plus que la Parque blesme.
> Le sang gelle en mes nerfs: la force me deffaut:
> Ie suis cil qui mourant, de mourir ne se chaut.

[Alas, I am no more than a dead statue! I am nothing but an idol, or an Indian
oak, in whom the northern blasts inspire the means to speak in death; I no longer
feel myself, pale, more disfigured than livid destiny. The blood freezes in my
nerves; my strength deserts me; I am one who, in dying, is not troubled to die.]
(Virey, 1600, IV [p. 34])

Of course, Antony is reliving the agony of his mythical ancestor, that of the
'shirt of Nessus' (IV.xii.43); as if in the grip of destructive magic, he curses the
'charm' (16, 25) whose 'death / Might have prevented many' (41–42). The loss

of his gallant friends profoundly afflicts Talbot, too, and attracts him to their company. 'Vous reposez mollement sur les fleurs [You repose gently on flowers]' (1600, IV [p. 35]), he sighs, anticipating Antony's eventual hope to rejoin his queen 'Where souls do couch on flowers' (IV.xiv.52). Yet as for the unreconciled Antony, Talbot's chief shame is that of having 'pris la fuite [taken flight]' because of a woman: 'Chacun nous pensera craintifs, coüards, infames / De nous laisser dompter par les mains d'vne femme [Everyone will think us fearful, cowardly, shamed, for having let ourselves be overcome by a woman's hands]' (1600, IV [p. 39]). For both, that woman is (falsely) a witch – for Talbot a mistress of poisons ('Et mille autres poisons, sorciere que tu sçais [And a thousand other poisons, witch, that you know]' [p. 37]), as well as a serpent, if not of 'old Nile', then of the river of Hades:

> ... ô fille d'Acheron!
> O monstre serpentin espouse de Charon
> Qui quittas tous les morts despouillé [*sic*] de la parque
> Par tes enchantemens dans la fatale barque.

[O daughter of Acheron! O serpentine monster, spouse of Charon, who leave all the corpses destined to death by your enchantments in the fatal boat.] (1600, IV [p. 36])

As for Antony, never has the discourse of witchcraft been so fully realized, so acutely internalized, as at this point, although it is quite absent from the corresponding moments in the other analogues: 'Ah, thou spell! Avaunt!' (IV.xii.30); 'The witch shall die' (47). In the event, both he and Talbot die first, although the latter leaves Allide behind to enact his thwarted revenge:

> ... pour son forfait
> Elle doit endurer en fin ce qu'elle a fait
> Souffrir à tant de nous: & sorciere execrable,
> Etaindre dans son feu son charme detestable.

[... for her crime she must finally endure what she has caused so many of us to suffer, and, execrable witch, extinguish in her flames her detestable charm.] (1600, IV [p. 41])

Yet only superficially do the English prevail in their suppression of Jeanne, as Caesar does with Cleopatra, and before she finally turns to conventional Christian prayer in her final speech, she embraces her death as a victorious transcendence that resounds with the Egyptian queen's, although in a bizarrely discordant key. At first, Jeanne laments the shame of defeat and capture ('Pour vn char de triomphe, ou quelque verd laurier / Suis-ie trainee icy par vn barbare fier? [Instead of a triumphal car or some green laurel, am I dragged here by a fierce barbarian?]' [1600, V [p. 42]). Quickly, however, like all the Cleopatras since Jodelle, if not Plutarch, the captive turns to glorying in a paradoxical triumph. That triumph will likewise have a political aspect: Jeanne urges France, for whom today her soul will be 'froidement [coldly]' freed from her body 'par les feux [by fire]' (1600, V [p. 43]), forever to remember her victories, her willing sacrifice. But the *joyful* eternity she anticipates for that soul intersects more notably with Cleopatra's, if thanks only to the heavy hand of Humanist classicizing:

> ... les ombres saintes
> M'attendent sur l'émail de leurs fleurettes peintes
> Aux beaux champs d'Elizee, & que tarday-ie tant?
> La mort m'est vne vie, où ie vais soulageant
> Mes peines par plaisirs, par ioye ma tristesse[.]

[... the holy shades await me on the enamel of their painted flowerets in the beautiful Elysian fields, and why do I so delay? Death is life to me, where I will soothe my pains with pleasures, and with joy my sadness.] (1600, V [p. 43])

There is no proving, of course, that the points of contact between Virey's text and *Antony and Cleopatra* amount to more than a coincidence of common-places. In any case, however, these serve intertextually to highlight Shakespeare's supplementation of perceptible gaps in his more direct dramatic precursors, as well as in Plutarch. In particular, the transformation in Virey of the putative witch into the virtual saint by way of her accuser's self-immolation figures a thorough purgation of the false projection, such as Shakespeare's dying Antony also experiences, and without the ambivalence retained by his counterpart in Garnier. Antony succeeds, that is, in killing the part of himself that has hated Cleopatra. He thereby frees himself to accept the numinous force of his 'great fairy' (IV.viii.12) on its (or her) own terms – no longer as destructive but as 'holy' and redemptive: 'I will o'ertake thee, Cleopatra, and / Weep for my pardon' (IV.xiv.45–46).

VIII

Alexander Witherspoon was breaking new ground in 1924 when he wrote *The Influence of Robert Garnier on Elizabethan Drama*, and while his views are outmoded in many respects (including the narrow notion of 'closet drama'), his study (reprinted in 1968) has had considerable carrying power. It remains a widely received notion, at least, that Mary Sidney Herbert sought, in translating Garnier, to impose neo-classical decorum on the populist Elizabethan stage, in keeping with her brother's strictures in *An Apology for Poetry*.[43] The only direct evidence for such an aim was the disdain expressed by Daniel for 'this tyrant of the North: / *Gross Barbarism*', in the dedication of his *Cleopatra* to the Countess, coupled with his profession of aesthetic devotion: 'Loe heere the worke the which she did impose, / Who onely doth predominate my Muse' (1594, sigs H5^v and H5^r). The hypothesis, however, also depended on – and was used to reinforce – the notion, if not quite of a salon on the European model, at least of a 'circle' of patronage and influence with the Countess at its centre.

The existence of any such structure has increasingly been called into question, notably by Mary Ellen Lamb and Michael Brennan, the latter qualifying the premise of his own study, *Literary Patronage in the English Renaissance: The Pembroke Family*, in a persuasively argued section entitled, 'The Myth of Patronage'.[44] At the same time, Brennan's conclusion, which again aligns him with Lamb, offers a framework for reassessing the translation of Garnier. In the place of one myth Brennan reads another, this one self-created – that of the surviving sister of 'an honorary Protestant saint', an idealized identity conferring an 'aura of semi-divinity' akin to Queen Elizabeth's (1988, p. 82). The latter myth is abundantly documented, being rooted in the Countess's highly public role, not just as Philip's literary executor, but as the manager of his immortal memory. Hence, her revision of his (and nominally *her own*) *Arcadia*, accompanied by touchiness about the competing version published by Fulke Greville and, perhaps, by a concern to chastize its eroticism. Hence, too, her completion of the Psalms, an act that, as Margaret P. Hannay has demonstrated (1990, pp. 84–105), effectively recuperates Sidney's association with both the political and spiritual ethic of French Protestantism.[45]

Hannay's assimilation of the translation of Garnier to such a picture, however, is less than convincing, in part because she seeks to place the Countess's dramatic initiatives at the cutting edge, both ideologically and culturally. In translating Garnier and sponsoring Daniel, she believes, Herbert was not merely 'combatting formal weaknesses of the early English drama' and promoting the 'salutary' importation of 'a drama of character, not of action', but also showing the English 'that drama could be used for political statement' (Hannay, 1990, pp. 120–21). Garnier suited that purpose because he was 'a magistrate who used his drama to criticize the state' and whose 'dramas were at the forefront of the contemporary movement in Continental historical tragedy, the avant-garde of the theater' (1990, pp. 126, 119).

Yet Garnier is unlikely to have recognized his political reflection in such a light. Of course, the playwright readily admitted to deploring the civil wars through his classical and biblical tragedies. But he was also a dispenser of the king's justice, and apart from the *Hymne de la Monarchie*, he contributed (with

Pierre de Ronsard and Amadis Jamyn) to *Le Tombeau du feu Roy Tres-Chrestien Charles IX* (1574), a funeral collection celebrating the latter's struggle against heresy, whose high point was the Saint Bartholomew massacre. Garnier seems never to have doubted that the problem lay, not with the divinely sanctioned 'state', but with Huguenot challenges to it and the Catholic impiety that had induced God's wrath. His adherence to the League in 1588 (two years before his death), however belated and lukewarm, manifested a continuing conviction that only a state committed to religious repression could pretend to legitimacy. This position is confirmed by the recurrent political refrain of the plays, which places human suffering against a background of divine displeasure and ultimate vengeance.[46] It is worth recalling that Garnier's mentor and model, to whom he addressed the *Hymne* and dedicated *Marc Antoine*, was Guy Du Faur de Pibrac, who, on the one hand, enjoyed a similar reputation as a humane intellectual and, on the other hand, produced the pack of lies comprising the quasi-official justification of the 1572 massacre. We falsify literary history (and much else besides) when we offer such figures excuses they never asked for and obscure their belief in a higher truth which sometimes must be cruel in order to be kind.[47]

As for the 'avant-garde' status of Garnier's drama, not only does the label imply far more of a 'movement' than is consistent with the spotty records of theatrical activity in contemporary France – composition, publication and staging alike – but *Marc Antoine*, which was Garnier's last Roman play, dates from twelve years before the Countess began her translation (in 1590) and *Les Juifves*, his final dramatic composition, from 1583. Further, it is misleading to term Garnier's a 'drama of character', unless character is understood as a sequence of moral and emotional postures, mainly conveyed through elaborately rhetorical monologues and stichomythia. One cannot claim that even the Shakespeare of the early comedies and history plays had much to learn from Garnier with respect to the theatrical imitation of human thought and behaviour. What I take to be the manifold engagement of *Antony and Cleopatra* with Garnier, whether directly or through Herbert, is of a different order.

It might also be suggested that if political critique had been her primary concern, the Countess could have chosen works that were more politically engaged. These notably include the play to which Garnier's was effectively a supplement (and which Daniel knew so well), *Cléopâtre captive*, where Jodelle develops the queen's personal and political triumph as a belated counterpoint to her destructive immorality and royal irresponsibility. Even if the literary prestige of Garnier was a determining factor, other tragedies of his might have claimed priority. To take only the Roman plays, *Porcie* and *Cornélie* (the latter due to be translated by Kyd in 1593 or 1594 on the warrant of Herbert's example) are more directly and forcefully concerned with questions of power and resistance, the tyrannical tendencies of ambition, and indeed the suffering of the innocent. (The Chorus of Egyptians in *Marc Antoine* makes a perfunctory gesture by comparison.) As for warning rulers about the dangerous public consequences of private passions, *Marc Antoine* was hardly breaking new ground: that eminently Senecan truism had been at home on the English stage at least since the early 1560s, with *Cambyses* and *Gorboduc* (the latter considered by the Countess's brother, of course, as a promising, if imperfect, model for an English neo-classical drama [Sidney, *Apology*, 1973, pp. 133–34]). It is not quite true that there was nothing notably pungent about the political point of *Marc Antoine* in its French context: Henri III may have had reason to feel admonished (see above, n. 5). So may Elizabeth, by aspects of the translation. Still, the affective centre of Garnier's work is unquestionably the Egyptian queen's suffering in her bereavement. For that matter, Daniel, following Jodelle, pulled out the poetical stops in investing his more problematic heroine with 'glory', 'maiestie' and 'courage' (indeed, 'honour' is a key term in the Nuntius' culminating account [ed. Bullough, 1957–75, 5: ll. 1557, 1562, 1572]). Whatever lent Greville's dramatization of the story such affinity with the case of Essex that he chose to destroy it, it remains notable that even Daniel's *Cleopatra*, unlike his *Philotas*, got that author into no trouble whatsoever.[48]

Rather than blurring the affective centre of *Antonius* by making its politics paramount, I prefer to follow the lead of Lamb (1990, pp. 115–45) in tracing the Countess's particular interest in Cleopatra to the figure of the nobly mourning heroine. Such a view also opens a further perspective on the thematic connection, first pointed out by Willard Farnham (1936, p. 59),[49] between *Antonius* and its companion translation in the 1592 volume: that of the *Excellent discours de la vie et de la mort* (1576) of Philippe de Mornay, Philip Sidney's personal friend. This treatise is as relentlessly neo-Stoical as it is devout, and Lamb finds not only continuity in the preoccupation with dying well but a development from the treatise to the play in a feminist direction (accompanied by suppressed anger at the patriarchal structure). Cleopatra, Lamb proposes, exemplifies a female form of the Stoic ideal, an 'heroics of constancy' acceptably tied to the memory of a beloved man (p. 130). Thus, too, in dedicating the Psalms to her brother's 'spirit', the Countess conveys her aspiration to follow him in death. Another step takes place with her sponsorship of Daniel's *Cleopatra*, in which the 'violent emotions' beneath her own Stoicism find indirect expression in the Egyptian queen's surmounting of male tyranny and shaming of male cowardice (Lamb, 1990, p. 135). Lamb, I am convinced, has identified an important dynamic here. Closer examination of the several texts involved, however, reveals a less stable portrait of the Countess both as a translator and as her brother's survivor, as well as a more complex relation between the two component pieces of her volume, which in turn emerges as a meta-translation, so to speak, of a partly obscured original.

IX

Let me begin with the extraordinary poetic address 'To the Angell spirit of the most excellent Sir Philip Sidney', whose revelatory interest is heightened by the contrast between its two extant versions. One is found as the dedicatory poem in the Tixall manuscript of the Psalms; the other was published in 1623, after being recovered among Daniel's papers. As a number of commentators have observed, the manuscript version lavishly invests the relation of supplementarity between sister and brother with an immediate, intense and personal – indeed, highly erotic – energy, of which there is far less in the measured, stately and sober printed version, universally presumed to represent an early draft.[50] This contrast turns out to be germane to the translation of Garnier, so I will briefly document it, and if the main idea is familiar, it may be lent new energy by detaching it from the standard narrative of Herbert's development of a distinctive poetic voice.

Comparison of the opening and closing stanzas of the two versions succinctly introduces the point.[51] The Tixall manuscript text begins as follows:

> To thee pure sprite, to thee alone's addres't
> > this coupled worke, by double int'rest thine:
> > First rais'de by thy blest hand, and what is mine
> inspird by thee, thy secrett power imprest.
> > So dar'd my Muse with thine it selfe combine,
> > as mortall stuff with that which is divine,
> Thy lightning beames give lustre to the rest.
> > (ed. Hannay *et al.*, 1998, ll. 1–7)

Here is the 1623 published equivalent:

> To the pure Spirit, to the alone addrest
> Is this joynt worke, by double intrist thine,
> Thine by his owne, and what is done of mine
> Inspir'd by thee, thy secret powre imprest.
> My Muse with thine, it selfe dar'd to combine
> As mortall staffe with that which is divine:
> Let thy faire beames give luster to the rest.
> > (1998, ll. 1–7)

The divergent effects of 'coupled' and 'joynt' in the second lines may stand for the general difference, which is consistent throughout the two works. The Oxford editors detect merely a possible indication of 'time sequence as Sidney first began the work and then inspired her to complete it' (Hannay, Kinnamon and Brennan, eds, 1998, 1: 75), although that point appears to depend on, rather than mandate, the premise that the printed version is an earlier unrevised text. Arguably, 'joynt' better suits the grafting-on of new parts to an existing structure, while 'coupled' matches the active collaboration possible during Sidney's lifetime. Thus Coburn Freer was led, by a meticulous technical study of the Psalms, to conjecture that Sidney may have passed his translations on to his sister 'in an unfinished state, expecting her to revise them', but that 'During the initial stages of the work, the two poets were probably in touch with each other, for in her dedicatory poem to Sidney, Mary Herbert does refer to the psalter as "this coupled worke"' (1972, p. 89). Regardless of any chronological implication, 'coupled', with its inevitable sexual suggestion, evokes a more intimate and dynamic union than does 'joynt', a word whose applications in the period are commonly legal and technical. Whatever accounts for the distinction, a drastic deintensification and emotional diminishing can be traced between the manuscript and the published version. The personal and physical terms of the former ('rais'de by thy blest hand') contrast with the abstract ones of the latter ('Thine by his owne'), the active ('what is mine') with the passive ('what is done of mine'), the direct with the indirect (as in the word order of line five), the immediate ('Thy lightning beames give lustre') with the distant ('Let thy faire beames give luster').

The final stanza of the printed version is only five lines long and amounts to a formal *envoi*; the poet withdraws from the poem, as from its addressee, effacing herself in an image of abstract sorrow, borne aloft by prayer:

> Receive these Hims, these obsequies receive,
> (If any mark of thy secret spirit thou beare)
> Made only thine, and no name els must weare.
> I can no more deare soule, I take my leave,
> My sorrow strives to mount the highest Sphere.
> (1998, ll. 71–75)

By contrast, in the longer manuscript version, the poet not only evokes her brother's presence in her work ('... thy sweet sprite appeare'), instead of figuring his absent soul ('... thy secret spirit thou beare'), but goes on to project herself assertively, through the intensity of her grief, into an imaginative (re)union evocative of sexual fulfilment ('... would mount thy highest sphere'):

> Receive theise Hymnes, theise obsequies receive;
>   if any marke of thy sweet sprite appeare,
>   well are they borne, no title else shall beare.
> I can no more: Deare Soule I take my leave;
>   Sorrowe still strives, would mount thy highest sphere
>   presuming so just cause might meet thee there,
> Oh happie chaunge! could I so take my leave.
>   (1998, ll. 85–91)

To reduce these three final lines to the 'conventional wish in elegy that the mourner could join the departed' (Hannay, Kinnamon and Brennan, eds, 1998, 1: 325n.91) undervalues not only their erotic force but also the heterodoxy toward which that force is allowed to tend. When full weight is allowed to the use of 'chaunge' in the sense of 'death', the conclusion figures a bereaved lover desperate for reunion with her beloved and arrogating to herself a judgement about the value of life and death ('presuming so just cause') such as is normally reserved to God. Even in the context of highly personal and intense religious feeling, this makes an incongruous introduction to the Psalms: 'presuming' emerges as very much the operative word.

The incongruity is only enhanced by an echo of the farewell to Antoine that Garnier assigns his Cléopâtre, whose 'obsequies' (*Marc Antoine*, ed. Lebègue, 1974, l. 1881) convert to kisses, as the mourning queen anticipates – across the familiar trope for sexual climax and, intertextually, across Catullus 5 – expiring upon her lover's body:

> Que de mille baisers, et mille et mille encore,
> Pour office dernier ma bouche vous honore:
> Et qu'en un tel devoir mon corps affoiblissant
> Defaille dessur vous, mon ame vomissant.
>   (1974, ll. 1996–99)

It is the essence of my approach to *Antonius* that, even as she faithfully (if rather woodenly) renders the heroine's passion –

> A thousand kisses, thousand thousand more
> Let you my mouth for honors farewell give:
> That in this office weake my limmes may growe,
> Fainting on you, and fourth my soule may flowe.
>   (*Antonius*, 1998, ll. 2019–22)

– Herbert shies away from the same formal religious term ('obsequies') that she applies to her brother's soul in the Christian context: Garnier's 'obsequies' is flattened into 'due rites' (1998, l. 1904).

X

No responsible person could hold a brief for John Aubrey's scandal-sheet claim (1950, p. 139), citing local gossip, that Sidney and his sister slept together – indeed, produced a child. Some serious criticism, however, has followed the path thus signposted, if not to Wilton itself, at least back into the shadowy poetic groves of both Sidney and Herbert, thereby demonstrating at least that where there is smoke, there is smoke. Gary F. Waller now prefers, with particular regard to 'Angell Spirit', to shift the ground from 'the perils of historical psychoanalysis' (associated with the male gaze) to the text's 'cultural unconscious' (deemed to allow for female *jouissance*).[52] He still registers a sense of 'forbidden love', but the death of that love now constitutes 'a liberation into autonomy, into being more than a passive reader of the significance of her brother's life' (1990, p. 339). Meanwhile Jonathan Crewe (1986, pp. 82–88), approaching the question from Sidney's side, has elicited from *Astrophil and Stella* a double movement of revelation and concealment, appropriation and denial. Not surprisingly, a similar doubleness has been attached to Herbert's Cleopatra, and Janet MacArthur has usefully stressed the freedom from religious and moral strictures offered by that figure: 'The subliminal erotic aspect of Mary Sidney's love for her brother is articulated by Cleopatra who in a pagan and profane voice, safely distanced from the Countess' own, declares an intemperate, self-destructive yet constant love' (1990, p. 7). Of course, translation itself is another distancing factor, but one perhaps offering less safety, since the distance can, to some degree, be measured.

The manuscript version of 'Angell Spirit' may be read against its printed version according to a model of distancing translation. The sense of Herbert's 'love' for Sidney is so heavily eroticized in the manuscript text as to convey a strong sense of the relation, at least as re-imagined across the experience of loss, as profoundly amorous, entailing a love that does not simply flow in 'normal' channels:

> Oh, when to this Accompt, this cast upp Summe,
>> this Reckoning made, this Audit of my woe,
>> I call my thoughts, where so strange passions flowe;
>> Howe workes my hart, my sences striken dumbe?
>>> that would thee more, then ever hart could showe ...
>>> (1998, ll. 43–47)

As opposed to summoning 'thoughts, where so strange passions flowe' to supplement and complicate the 'Audit of my woe', the persona of the more disciplined printed version speaks more neutrally of 'swelling passions', which the same 'Audit' actually serves to calm:

O when from this accompt, this cast-up somme,
This reckning made the Audit of my woo,
Sometime of rase my swelling passions know ...
(1998, ll. 57–59)

The mysterious and organic processes of grief itself are, in the manuscript text, beyond even the power of the 'hart', not merely of 'words' (as in the printed version [1998, l. 61]) to 'show'. Moreover, this mystery puts Herbert's grief beyond conventional consolation: it can be neither Stoically mastered nor accommodated within Christian resignation. The manuscript version makes the production of 'thy praise' (1998, l. 49) an end in itself, which can have no end. The published text, by contrast, implicitly declares consolation to be achievable; 'praise' is transcended, transformed, contained: the focus of production becomes 'thy prayer' (1998, l. 63).

I will not dispute the consensus that the printed version of the dedicatory poem is chronologically prior to that of the manuscript, although the only evidence appears to be inferential, and editors may be overhasty in applying to the special case of 'Angell Spirit' the conclusion clearly warranted by the Psalms themselves – namely, that Herbert 'increasingly asserts herself as a poet' over time and with practice.[53] Conceivably, the eroticized spirituality in the dedicatory poem was liberated, rather than contained, by the process of revision. What is demonstrable in any case is that Herbert's translation of *Marc Antoine* tends in the contrary direction, flattening and restraining the more extravagant impulses of the original. The sense, in Garnier, of passion overflowing the approved categories of emotional response, the boundaries of the self and the expressive capacities of language matches the claim of the manuscript 'Angell Spirit' to a 'love' that cannot 'enough in world of words unfold' (1998, l. 28); Herbert's *Antonius*, by contrast, strongly tends, at least, to the sobriety of the dedicatory poem's printed version, which figures that love as 'justly here contrould' (1998, l. 42).

Much of this effect seems inadvertent, as if Herbert's verbal skills are simply not up to the challenge, although to say so goes very much against the trend of commentary. In fundamental reaction, no doubt, against Witherspoon (1968), a number of recent studies of *Antonius* have praised the translator's fidelity (Hannay, Kinnamon and Brennan, eds, 1998, 1: 151), commended her dexterity 'in the difficult exercise of converting Garnier's alexandrines into English blank verse' (Brennan, 1988, p. 67), or perceived an enhancement of the original. Thus the Countess 'amplifies', 'adds' and 'extends' (Hannay, Kinnamon and Brennan, eds, 1998, 1: 66); she 'embellishes metaphors developed incompletely by Garnier', even while achieving greater concision (Sanders, 1998, p. 109). Contrary to the aristocratic image, her language opens the text to 'a larger audience', and her characters are more vividly realized (Sanders, 1998, pp. 109, 112–13). Certainly, at some points such comments are warranted. My own comparisons, however, tend in a contrary direction and broadly support the view of Howard B. Norland that, in revisiting 'the tension between the moral and the romantic in Garnier's conception' (2009, p. 204), Herbert 'reduces the emotional intensity of the original' (2009, p. 208). As Norland documents (2009, pp. 204–11), several aspects of Garnier's Cléopâtre come under particular pressure through changes in vocabulary, syntax and versification: Herbert downplays the force of Cleopatra's beauty and takes a harsher moral line on the love affair; at the same time, she accentuates the queen's political and social rank and responsibility. These tendencies suggest an underlying ambivalence, whereby the Countess at once invests herself in her heroine and struggles to limit that investment, especially on the point of passion.[54]

XI

It is finally difficult to praise Herbert's translation without short-changing the original, explicitly or implicitly. In general, Garnier's rhetoric, however relent-less, is intricately structured, dramatically functional and richly evocative. Thus his Cléopâtre laments over the corpse of Antoine in terms first cosmic, then intensely personal, so that her guilt-ridden internalizing of the loss is strongly conveyed: 'O cruelle fortune! ô desastre execrable! / O pestilente amour! ô abominable torche ! [O cruel fortune! O execrable disaster! O pestilent love! O abominable torch!]' (*Marc Antoine*, 1974, ll. 1792–93); this is what gives point to the unusual verb 'infortune', as she proceeds, in apostrophe, to exalt the value 'De vous que j'infortune, et que de main sanglante / Je contrains devaler sous la tombe relante [Of you whom I make unfortunate, and whom with a bloody hand I force to descend into the odorous tomb]' (1974, ll. 1808–9). The queen's terrible sense of Antoine's blood on her hands thus modulates into conjuration of an atmosphere akin to that imagined by Juliet, who dreads waking in the 'foul mouth' of the Capulet tomb, reeking 'with loathsome smells', 'Where bloody Tybalt ... / Lies fest'ring in his shroud' (*Rom.*, IV.iii.34, 46, 42–43). This subtle progression is collapsed by the Countess into disconnected expletives more reminiscent of Shakespeare's lamenting Nurse – 'O cruell Fortune! ô accursed lott! / O plaguy love! ô most detested brand!' (*Antonius*, 1998, ll. 1815–16); it culminates in lines that not only leave fortune out of the picture but teeter (like a great many, in fact) on the brink of *Pyramus-and-Thisbe*-like parody: 'Of you, whom I have plagu'd, whom I have made / With bloudie hand a guest of mouldie Tombe' (1998, ll. 1831–32).

Such instances of the blunting of poetical impact – and dozens might be cited – are presumably quite unintentional, but in an exercise whose intention, precisely, appears provocatively conflicted, it becomes significant that they reinforce definite tendencies and apparent choices. When Antoine (speaking to himself) laments the unhappy day 'que te gaigna l'Amour' (*Marc Antoine*, 1974, l. 52), the Countess might simply be mistranslating when she inverts the syntax – 'that gained thee thy love' (*Antonius*, 1998, l. 53) – but she consistently downplays the agency of erotic passion. Hence, surely, the impression that she is 'much less taken by Cleopatra's charms than Garnier' (Norland, 2009, p. 208). The physical potency and danger of those charms are vividly realized when Antoine (again to himself) speaks of 'le visage aimé, dont le semblant moqueur, / Errant en ta mouëlle, envenime ton cœur [the beloved face, whose mocking semblance, straying in your deepmost self, empoisons your heart]' (1974, ll. 111–12); the colours fade in translation: 'Sight of that face whose guilefull semblant doth / (Wandring in thee) infect thy tainted hart' (1998, ll. 112–13). By the same token, while Cléopâtre's 'ardente jalousie' (1974, l. 464) must be acknowledged ('burning jealousie' [1998, l. 471]), since it is directly stated, the transfer of the possessive pronoun from 'Antoine' to 'absence' and the change in word order sap the force of the emotion and especially diminish her fear of being deserted, when 'Par-ce que, je craignois que mon Antoine absent / Reprint son Octavie, et m'allast delaissant [Because I feared that my absent Antoine should take back Octavie and depart, abandoning me]' (1974, ll. 465–66) becomes, 'Fearing least in my absence *Antony* / Should leaving me retake *Octavia*' (1998, ll. 472–73).

The most sensitive and suggestive points, however, are those that touch on divinity and eschatology. The active idolatry of Antoine's fixation – 'J'ay son idole faux en l'esprit nuict et jour [I have her false idol in my mind night and day]' (*Marc Antoine*, 1974, l. 911) – is softened into his pursuit by amorous remembrance: 'Each day, each night her Image haunts my minde' (*Antonius*, 1998, l. 922). And while the translator appears inclined to associate passion with hell ('horrible amour' [1974, l. 285] becomes 'hellish love' [1998, l. 289]), Cleopatra herself is stripped of the desire to follow her lover 'aux Enfers pallissans [to pale-shaded Hades]' (1974, l. 650): the phrase is simply omitted from the equivalent line (1998, l. 657).[55] At the points where Garnier allows for a positive quasi-religious power in Cleopatra's beauty, the translator's flattening hand is still more conspicuous. In arguing for Shakespeare's knowledge of *Antonius*, Schanzer has cited the speech of Diomed ('Nature by such a worke / Her selfe, should seme, in workmanship hath past … ' [*Antonius*, 1998, ll. 717 ff.]) as the basis for Enobarbus' wondrous evocation of Cleopatra in Rome (*Ant.*, II.ii.201 ff.),[56] although Norland rightly observes that 'Diomed's enthusiasm rather disappears in Sidney's prosaic rendering' (2009, p. 208). Indeed, an entire dimension of that enthusiasm is excised with special rigour. In Garnier's 'L'albastre qui blanchist sur son visage saint [The alabaster that gleamed white on her holy face]' (1974, l. 713), Herbert fails to translate 'saint' ('The Allablaster covering of hir face' [1998, l. 721]), while 'son esprit divin' (1974, l. 720) is made as anodyne as possible: 'her cælestiall Sp'rite' (1998, l. 728). At stake is Cleopatra's improbably carnal blessedness – hence, Shakespeare's apparent recourse to the source, not merely to the translation. Finally, while there is obviously no thwarting the structural momentum towards suicide, Herbert effaces the subtle suggestion that hope actually lies within the queen's despair – 'L'espoir de mes malheurs ne gist plus en la force [The hope of my miseries no longer lies in strength]' (1974, l. 428) is reduced to 'In striving lyes no hope of my mishapps' (1998, l. 435) – and strips the *Liebestod* of its Neoplatonic sacramentality; the reader relying on the line, 'And our true loves your dolefull voice commend' (1998, l. 665), would never suspect the lyrical claim to mystical transcendence that lies behind it, as Cléopâtre imagines the mourning of her women: 'Et nos saintes amours vostre voix benira [And your voice will bless our sacred loves]' (1974, l. 658).

XII

Suicide thus emerges across the Countess's translation as a more highly charged issue than Lamb's straightforward theory of a female 'heroics of constancy' would allow, and this realization imposes reconsideration of the play's original companion piece, which, indeed, received both priority of place in the 1592 volume and top billing (including larger type) in its title: '*A Discourse of Life and Death. Written in French by* Ph. Mornay. *Antonius,* A Tragœdie written also in French *by* Ro. Garnier. *Both done in English by the* Countesse of Pembroke.' There are two points to make at the outset: first, there could have been no better French Protestant counterweight than Mornay to the flawed religious and political credentials of Garnier; secondly, as Stoical as Mornay's treatise may be, with its insistence on the vanity of life and the reasons for welcoming death, it is hardly (and could hardly be, in Christian terms) an endorsement of suicide. On the contrary, as if he is anxious precisely to counteract any such impression, Mornay concludes by stressing that to seek death is 'temeritie' and 'despaire', as far from 'magnanimitie' as is over-fondness for life, and that 'there is nothing more uncertaine then the houre of death, knowen onlie to God, the onlie Author of life and death, to whom wee all ought endevour both to live and die' (ed. Hannay, Kinnamon and Brennan, 1998, 1: 254).

Seneca was the Renaissance's most popular philosopher, as he was its favourite tragedian, not least because his moral pronouncements lent themselves, selectively, to extraction from their pagan context and translation into Christian terms. In this there was continuity with medieval practice, given the early and wide diffusion of the pseudo-Senecan *Formula Vitae Honestae* or *De Quatuor Virtutibus*, which began to be attributed to Saint Martin of Braga only in editions well into the sixteenth century. The tragedies provided grist to the Christian mill thanks largely to Pierre Grosnet in France, who, beginning in 1539, published a collection of sentences shorn of all dramatic accompaniments but embroidered with moral commentary and enriched with biblical parallels. Seneca's insistence on personal spiritual development in the face of implacable destiny was at least as compatible with Reformed as with Catholic doctrine, and it is therefore not surprising that Mornay (like Pibrac) drew heavily on Seneca in dealing with death. But Mornay did more: he appended to the *Excellent discours* a substantial collection of excerpts from several works of Seneca, especially the *Epistulae Morales*, explaining in his preface that he considered Seneca's testimony regarding the vanity of life to be especially salutary because it came from natural judgement, learning and experience without the benefit of revelation.

The *Excellent discours* of Mornay held a noteworthy fascination for English translators (and presumably readers). The Countess's translation would establish itself as the dominant one, being reissued (without *Antonius*) several times in the early 1600s. The first edition, however, met with immediate competition in the form of *A Christian View of Life and Death*, produced by an unidentified 'A. W.' and published in 1593 by Richard Field. Moreover, the Countess herself must have been intimately familiar with the prior version of the prolific translator Edward Aggas. The Oxford editors, in documenting her divergences from this precursor, also establish that she made use of his work, to the point where 'some of her text exactly matches his' (Hannay, Kinnamon and Brennan, eds, 1998, 1: 223). Aggas, who specialized in strongly Protestant French texts, had produced the initial English version of the *Excellent discours* with evident haste. (It appeared in the same year as the original, 1576, and was reissued in 1577.) Yet, unlike the Countess and 'A. W.', Aggas retained the Senecan supplement, hence the shape and scope of Mornay's original volume, complete with introductory epistle.[57]

Thereby reproduced as well was an underlying tension, further highlighted by Aggas's one-sided title, *The Defence of Death*. Certainly, Mornay had deftly chosen his excerpts to illustrate the philosopher's more Christian-sounding counsels regarding mortality; together they amount to death's second 'defence' in a broadly compatible consolatory vein. They retain, nevertheless, the trace of their origin within a radically different metaphysics, which is not completely effaced by the regular transposition of 'fata' and 'dei' into 'God' (although

Seneca is also conveniently capable of invoking 'deum, quo auctore cuncta proveniunt [god, from whom, as author, all things derive]'[58]). Moreover, given the familiarity of the texts in question, the very principle of rigorous selection makes the omissions conspicuous.

The pivotal issue is precisely suicide, which for the philosopher constitutes the ultimate guarantee of personal freedom and power over adverse destiny, but which is forbidden to Christians as a denial of divine providence and, more essentially, as an affront to creation. Not only are all positive mentions of suicide avoided in the Senecan texts edited by Mornay, but the question is implicitly made the hinge between the treatise and its supplement. The opening of the Senecan excerpts, from Letter 24 of the *Epistulae Morales*, is carefully fashioned to dovetail with the pious conclusion of the treatise on the facing page. Omitted is the lengthy opening section of that letter, which moves from endurance of hardship to celebration of the archetypal Stoic suicide, that of Cato. The remainder is severely compressed, and the conclusion, which evokes the idea that, for many persons, life is merely pointless, is also dropped. Allowed to resonate instead is what might sound like an absolute stricture against suicide, although readers of the unexpurgated Seneca would have recognized it merely as an argument against making a premature and cowardly end:

> The wise and valiaunt man muste not flee from this life, but soberly departe with all, and abooue all thinges eschew this vicious passion which hath ouer come many: namely ouer greate desire of death. (*Defence*, 1976, sig. Cv^v)

XIII

Read against the precursor volume of Aggas – and many contemporaries would so have read it – the Countess's double translation of 1592 might appear not only to have substituted Garnier's *Marc Antoine* for Mornay's Senecan excerpts, but also to have modified the play's neo-pagan eschatology in an analogous way, and likewise imperfectly. The point is more notable because of an echo, which, fortuitous or not, is likely to have served as an intertextually evocative 'ungrammaticality' for contemporary readers (in this case readers only) of the Folio text of Shakespeare's *Antony and Cleopatra*. Schanzer (1960, p. 22) has also linked Shakespeare with Herbert's translation (though the point would work as well for Garnier's original) through the ghost character of 'Lucillius', named in the opening stage direction of Shakespeare's Act I, Scene ii, but never mentioned again. According to Plutarch (in *The Life of Julius Caesar*), Lucilius was Antony's trusted servant, who first made an impression with his courage by impersonating Brutus at Philippi; he accompanied Antony into Asia and 'ever after served him faithfullie, even to his death' (ed. Bullough, 1957–75, 5: 129). It was therefore natural for Garnier to use this name for the faithful friend of Antoine who, in Act III, attempts to console the hero for shamefully yielding to love and to dissuade him from suicide – an argument refuted thus:

> Allons, mon cher Lucile: hé! pourquoy plorez-vous?
> Cette fatalité commune est à nous tous,
> Nous devons tous mourir: chacun doit un hommage
> Au Dieu, qui les Enfers eut jadis en partage.

[Come, my dear Lucilius: ah, why do you weep? This destiny is common to us all. We must all die. Everyone owes a homage to the god who shares the rule of the underworld.] (1974, ll. 1242–45)

It is striking to a reader of Mornay's volume or Aggas's translation that the better part of the Senecan excerpts – the *Epistulae Morales*, certainly, but also the substantial extract from the *De Providentia* ('*De la Providence Divine*' for Mornay, '*Of God's Providence*' in Aggas's translation) – are directly addressed to the philosopher's own friend Lucilius, often naming him in the same familiar tone. While Mornay strove to Christianize these addresses, Garnier's paganism is nowhere more vivid than in Antoine's dark justification of suicide as a sacrifice to the god of the underworld, and here Herbert's translation is remarkably faithful:

> Come, deare *Lucill*: alas: why wepe you thus!
> This mortall lot is common to us all.
> We must all die, each doth in homage[59] owe
> Unto that God that shar'd the Realmes belowe.
>   (*Antonius*, 1998, ll. 1257–60)

In fact, the incantations of Garnier's Cléopâtre summon Antoine himself as the god of death to whom she will make a joyous sacrifice:

> Antoine je te pry' par nos amours fidelles,
> Par nos cœurs allumez de douces estincelles,
> Par nostre sainct hymen, et la tendre pitié
> De nos petits enfans, nœu de nostre amitié,
> Que ma dolente voix à ton oreille arrive,
> Et que je t'accompagne en l'infernale rive,
> Ta femme et ton amie.

[Antoine, I pray you by our faithful loves, by our hearts kindled by gentle sparks, by our sacred marriage, and the tender pity of our little children, the bond of our amity, that my grieving voice may arrive to your ear, and that I may accompany you to the infernal bank, your wife and your friend.] (1974, ll. 1944–50)

Here, at what might seem the least likely moment, Herbert dares in frank language ('holy', 'hellish') to reproduce that eschatology:

> *Antonie* by our true loves I thee beseche,
> And by our hearts swete sparks have sett on fire,
> Our holy mariage, and the tender ruthe
> Of our deare babes, knot of our amitie:
> My dolefull voice thy eare let entertaine,
> And take me with thee to the hellish plaine,
> Thy wife, thy frend.
>
> (1998, ll. 1967–73)

We are by no means remote from the ecstatic apotheosis of 'Husband, I come!' (*Ant.*, V.ii.286). The fact remains that Herbert chose to render a text in which the heroine's suicide is evoked but not actually accomplished.[60] It is, rather, deferred into an off-stage future – precisely the one that Daniel was then entrusted with supplying. Had she herself adapted the *Cléopâtre captive*, besides confronting the suicide itself (at least in narrative), Herbert would also have had to accommodate the very different representation of Antony. As has been seen, Jodelle's Antoine, far from undergoing a progression from self-loathing to loving reconciliation, simply deplores, from beyond the grave, his expense of spirit in a waste of shame and seeks nothing but his ex-lover's company in his eternal misery.[61]

Hardly could such an Antoine have stood in for an 'Angell Spirit' to whom the Countess might address herself, in the person of Cleopatra, to envisage a death recuperating Cato's philosophy in the cause of erotic union. Garnier, by contrast, offered a hero whose love, however conflicted and morally dubious, finally constituted 'so just cause' for just such a 'happy chaunge' on his lover's part:

> ... je suis heureuse en mon mal devorant,
> De mourir avec toy, de t'embrasser mourant,
> Mon corps contre le tien, ma bouche desseichee
> De soupirs embrasez, à la tienne attachee ...

> [... I am happy, in my consuming ill, to die with you, to embrace you as I die, my body against yours, my parched mouth enkindled with sighs, attached to yours ...] (1574, ll. 1962–65)

This pair will transcend death by what could not more clearly be a 'coupling' – or, it might be said, a 'mingling', to recall the terms with which Shakespeare's Mardian falsely announces to Antony Cleopatra's death but truly describes her life: 'My mistress loved thee and her fortunes mingled / With thine entirely' (IV.xiv.24–25). Yet still the translator resists the persona that she herself chose to speak for her. As in the passage from one version of the 'Angell Spirit' to another, this vivid *coupling* becomes a *joining*, which attaches a living body to an irrevocably dead one:

> ... most happie in this happles case,
> To die with thee, and dieng thee embrace:
> By bodie joynde with thine, my mouth with thine,
> My mouth, whose moisture burning sighes have dried ...
> (*Antonius*, 1998, ll. 1985–88)

Finally, however, despite what seem to have been her best efforts, Herbert's evident disavowal of Cleopatra on moral and religious grounds did not prevent her from effectively *translating* the transcendentally erotic grief that Garnier had devoted his full rhetorical resources to evoking. On the contrary, the very resistance of the translation throws that potent emotional amalgam into ambivalent relief. Equally revealing intertextually is the impact on the 1592 composite volume of allowing the heroine's suicidal momentum effectively to restore the major excision imposed on Seneca's Stoicism: the Countess thereby opened a discursive channel that flows around and beyond Mornay's stern containment operation, with sudden currents and (self-?)surprising eddies. Her own juxtaposition of texts, though proposing an even starker contrast between pagan and Christian perspectives, paradoxically produces, not a statically 'joynt worke', but a dynamically 'coupled' one.

XIV

One can only wonder whether the Countess would have envisaged her project in the first place had she been edified by the margins of the re-editions of Amyot's translations of the *Lives* that began to appear, as early as 1583, with Calvinistic moral commentary added by Simon Goulart.[62] When it comes to the Life of Antony, there is no mistaking Goulart's impulse to contain the tendencies towards heroic transcendentalism that might be attached to Cleopatra's mourning and suicide. Succinct proof that the most Roman of thoughts – and most extravagant of metaphors – could become grist for the Genevan mill are his marginal judgements presenting the death of Cleopatra as a token of divine retribution: 'Cleopatra ayant empoisonné si malheureusement Antonivs, & par tel moyen causé vn grand mal au monde, est estoufée de poison en vn instant, pour tesmoignage de la vengeance diuine sur les voluptueux, les plaisirs desquels s'esuanouïssent en vn moment [Cleopatra, having so miserably poisoned Antonius, and by such means caused great evil to the world, is snuffed out by poison in an instant to bear witness to the divine vengeance upon voluptuaries, whose pleasure fades away in a moment]' (*Les Vies des hommes illustres*, ed. Goulart, 1583, fol. 621ʳ). Her waiting-women likewise, far from attracting any sympathy, are said to get exactly what they deserve: 'Et quant à ses femmes, on void que les complices d'iniquité reçoyuent ordinairement leur salaire quand & les personnes qui ont vse de leur meschant seruice [And as for her women, one sees that the accomplices of wickedness ordinarily receive their payment at the same time as those persons who have made use of their evil service]' (1583, fol. 621ʳ). The Stoic exaltation of suicide as a supremely courageous assertion of human will – an idea that palpably attracted even Mornay's carefully hedged admiration and left the door ajar for the Countess to glance through with awe and fascination, if not longing – withers under Goulart's scornful glance into the most pathetic of human self-delusions.

Goulart's introductory sonnet, commonplace as it is, might seem at first to leave room for a neo-classically tragic reading:

> Ce liure est vn Theatre, où Plutarque le sage
> Ameine vn milion de mortels, reuestus
> De vestemens divers de vices & vertus,
> Qui iouent à leur honte ou à leur auantage.

[This book is a Theatre, where the wise Plutarch brings in a million mortals, clothed in diverse costumes of vices and virtues, who play to their shame or to their credit.]

The eyes of faith, however, reveal the grim framework of the divine comedy securely in place:

> Mais parmi tant de cas tragiquement diuers,
> Regarde ce grand Dieu, Iuge de l'vnivers,
> Qui garde verité, ruine le mensonge,
> Abat l'ambitieux, maintient le genre humain,
> Veut que petits & grands tremblent dessous sa main,
> Et leur dit par ceux-ci, que le monde est vn songe.

[But among such tragic and various cases, see that great God, Judge of the universe, who preserves truth, destroys lies, strikes down the ambitious, maintains the human race, wishes that small and great tremble beneath his hand, and tells them by these examples that the world is a dream.] (1583, sig. **iijʳ)

Far from conferring power over destiny through immortal fame, or even procuring liberty from mortal captivity, even the 'noblest' act of sacrificial self-destruction is revealed, in this light, as a dismal but banal sign of being pre-destined to be destroyed eternally.

Given this distinctly Protestant moralizing framework, which intriguingly made itself at home in sixteenth- and early seventeenth-century editions of Amyot in France,[63] the Countess's persistence in taking her Plutarch, if hardly straight, at least by way of Garnier seems all the more remarkable, whatever ambivalence the exercise reveals – and, to a large extent, conceals, thanks to the premise of translation. It may even say something about the Channel as a cultural buffer that, although Field's several re-editions of North's Plutarch increasingly included Goulart's contributions – beginning in 1603, with the latter's life of Octavius Caesar, in which Antony and Cleopatra are curtly dismissed as 'these wicked louers'[64] – they resisted Goulart's glossing intrusions on the text. Rather, the relatively neutral, page-marking marginalia that *The Life of Marcus Antonius* had carried since Vautrollier's first edition of 1579 – which already contained (without attribution) Goulart's 'The Comparison of Annibal with P. Scipio African' – continued to be reset well beyond Field's own time.[65]

That, of course, may well have been a function less of ideology than of printing-house economics. Less equivocal – to the point of comprising one of the rare instances where the playwright's personal judgement regarding his fiction may be measured with some confidence – is one resounding Shakespearean echo that has gone unnoticed, presumably because it has not occurred to scholars that he might have consulted a current edition of the 'original'. Certainly, the plethora of verbal borrowings from North in *Antony and Cleopatra* confirms Shakespeare's main indebtedness. But it is therefore especially revealing, with regard to his reading and compositional practices, to find that he also recalled Amyot's version as edited by Goulart.

Such a conclusion must be drawn from Cleopatra's first lines in the final act, as she decisively announces her progression beyond the cataclysmic renunciations of her initial mourning ('there is nothing left remarkable / Beneath the visiting moon' [IV.xv.69-70]; 'All's but nought' [82]; 'Our lamp is spent, it's out' [89]), to transcendent affirmation: 'My desolation does begin to make / A better life' (V.ii.1–2). That affirmation has no precedent in Plutarch, but its nearly precise mirror-image may be found in one of Goulart's marginal comments on Cleopatra's final state of mind. Demonstrably, at this moment, Shakespeare was refuting the dismissive judgement that had been handed down by the man from Geneva. The commentaries of the English editions neutrally signal Cleopatra's 'lamentation ouer Antonius tombe'. Goulart, by contrast, glosses fulsomely: 'En tous ces regrets on void la deplorable condition des personnes qui ne peuuent regarder plus loin que ceste vie. ... On ne lit que desespoir & desolation [In all these regrets one sees the deplorable condition of persons who cannot see farther than this life. ... One reads only despair and desolation]' (1583, fols 620ᵛ–21ʳ). Shakespeare evidently read these glosses and read more – at once more tragically and more generously. And his countervailing images hark back to Jodelle.[66] In evoking the 'better life' born of her 'desolation', Cleopatra first recasts the 'universal landlord' (III.xiii.76) as captive to a female deity ('he's but Fortune's knave, / A minister of her will' [V.ii.3–4]), then relegates that deity symbolically to subjection: the ending that 'shackles accidents and bolts up change' (6) finally renders captive captivity itself.

Notes

1 Grévin, a Protestant, modelled his work closely on the Latin *Julius Caesar* (pub. 1552) of Muret, his former professor. See Ginsberg, ed., 1971, pp. 20–26.

2 See Forsyth, 1994, as well as Jondorf, 1969, esp. pp. 105–10. Cf. my *French Origins*, 2010, pp. 37–39, 46–51.

3 Cited Jouanna *et al.*, eds, 1998, p. 113; on these events more generally, see pp. 100–41 and the entries on the three 'Triumvirs'. A rich perspective is also furnished by Romier's biography of Saint-André (1909).

4 Ginsberg, ed., 1971, pp. 22–23. There is uncertainty about the date of *César's* composition and publication. Ginsberg, who resists the temptation to read the play in militant Protestant terms, believes that it was first performed at the Collège de Beauvais in February 1561; even if this is so, the text might still have been revised before it received its *privilège* on 16 June 1561 (see Ginsberg, ed., 1971, pp. 18–19).

5 Garnier's plays were not performed at court, and, in this regard, Lestringant (1992, p. 232) notes – and cites André Thevet, the 'court cosmographer', as having noted at the time – that, besides implying Antoine's unfitness for governance, *Marc Antoine* shows Octave's potential for tyranny in his debate with Agrippe.

6 The innovatory comparisons of Muir (1969), who, however, does not insist on Shakespeare's knowledge of Jodelle, do not seem to have attracted the attention they deserve. My discussion revisits some of his points.

7 *Ant.* is cited throughout in the edition of Wilders (1995).

8 On *Ant.*, see, e.g., Yachnin, 1991. Kewes (2012) has attributed a pointed political project to Mary Sidney Herbert's translation of Garnier (*Antonius*) and Daniel's *The Tragedy of Cleopatra* – at the cost, perhaps, of skewing these texts and certainly of obscuring their French affiliations.

9 Cf. Stone: 'La diversité des œuvres de Montreux est si grande et si significative qu'on comprend mal pourquoi il est toujours peu connu [The diversity of the works of Montreux is so great and so significant that it is difficult to understand why he is still so little known]' (Montreux, *La Sophonisbe*, Stone, ed., 1976, p. 4). The most substantial study to date of Montreux (a priest who wrote under the anagrammatic pseudonym of 'Ollenix du Mont-Sacré') is by Daele (1946).

10 See Jouanna *et al.*, eds, 1998, pp. 1095–97 ('Mercœur, Philippe-Emmanuel de Lorraine, duc de'), as well as Croix, 1993, pp. 52–72.

11 See Buron, 2009, p. 243 and n. 18.

12   Consistent with Montreux's preoccupation with female virtue is the role in this
      victory attributed to the prayers of the household's women. On the battle of Craon
      in its political and military context, see Croix, 1993, p. 54.

13   The topical political application of Montreux's vast literary output during this
      period is often elusive. Witness his 1597 poem of 463 pp. (part one only!), *L'Es-*
      pagne conquise, par Charles le Grand, roy de France, whose retelling of Charlemagne's
      exploits for Christianity avowedly glorifies Mercœur's House of Lorraine (not
      forgetting his wife, 'sage, & rare en chasteté [wise and rare in chastity]' [1597, p.
      408]), in keeping with the standard propaganda. Yet the theme might also suggest
      a shift in attitude toward the Spanish, whose widely resented influence in Brittany
      needed to be broken as part of the Duke's reluctant reconciliation with the French
      king. The latter event was solemnized on 20 March 1998, whereupon Montreux
      duly published (this time in Paris) *La Paix au très-chrestien et très-victorieux roy de*
      France et de Navarre Henry IIII.

14   See Mouflard, 1961–64, 2: 237.

15   The relative dates of composition and performance (for Montreux's play, too, may
      have been staged) remain, it would seem, open to question. Almost certainly, in
      some measure and in ways informed by current religious politics, one of these
      treatments of Sophonisba was responding to the other, whether or not the rather
      tenuous verbal parallels carry much weight; see Montreux, *La Sophonisbe*, Stone,
      ed., 1976, pp. 7–10, and, for hints of the religious politics of Montchrestien's
      version, Charpentier, 1981, pp. 15–16, 18, and 18n.32: the first performance was
      attended by the wife of Caen's governor, Madame de la Vérune, and the first publi-
      cation, which is dedicated to her, was by a printer known for anti-League
      pamphlets. See also Aquilon, 1983, p. 360. Incidentally, if John Marston elsewhere
      reveals himself as a reader of Montreux's prose (see O'Connor, 1957), his private-
      theatre fantasia on the Sophonisba theme (1606) is not notably indebted to its
      stately French dramatic precursors.

16   A word on the difficult dating of these plays is in order, especially given the sugges-
      tive points of contact between Montreux's *Cléopâtre* and the version of Daniel,
      first published in 1594 but entered in the Stationers Register in October of the
      previous year. The earliest known edition of *Cléopâtre* was annexed to *Œuvre de la*
      chasteté (1595), but the play is not mentioned in the *privilège* following the *Œuvre*
      (dated 18 December 1594), and the text is set apart by separate (undated) title
      page, typography and pagination, so that its prior publication seems certain. On
      one surviving copy not currently bound with *Œuvre de la chasteté* (in the Biblio-
      thèque Carré d'Art, Nîmes), '1594' has been added in manuscript. *Cléopâtre*'s pre-
      existence would be consistent with the mention of a performance of the play at
      the end of *Œuvre de la chasteté*: the reference seems tacked onto the narrative as if
      to explain the composite volume.
           Daele (1946, p. 178) gives the year of *Cléopâtre*'s first performance as 1594,
      as is repeated by Grente, Simonin *et al.*, eds, 2001. Buron (2009, p. 243), who reads
      the play as a plea for leniency on the part of Henri IV, takes it to postdate the latter's

coronation on 27 February 1594. Yet Daele (1946, pp. 178–79, 213) accepts claims that *Isabelle*, too, was first staged in 1594 and that both plays were popular as performed by the Nouveaux Confrères de la Passion at the Hôtel de Bourgogne in Paris under the League. (If so, they could not have been long-running: Henri IV seized Paris on 22 March 1594.) This suggests (as is arguably more consistent with the texts) propaganda in favour of heroic resistance. Cf. Léris, 1763, p. 111, who identifies *Cléopâtre* as performed and printed in Lyons in 1594 – implicitly, as well, in the final stage of League influence. Given Montreux's relation to Mercœur, it would be surprising if both tragedies were not first staged in Nantes. Certainly, the conclusion of *Le Quatrième livre des Bergeries de Julliette ... ensemble la tragédie d'Isabelle* (1595) states that some of the author's Arcadian characters are about to perform before the Duke. A pre-1594 date for *Cléopâtre* thus appears plausible.

As Mouflard points out (1961–64, 1: 227–28), Montreux had apparently composed at least some version of *Isabelle*, together with a number of other tragedies (not *Cléopâtre*, however), before 1584, the date of La Croix du Maine's bibliography. She detects the influence of the earlier Garnier, on whom Ariosto's story of Isabella and Zerbino had also made an impression (1961–64, 3: 212–18, 235), and of aesthetic fashions in Le Mans (of which Montreux was a native). Whether or not he revised the piece substantially, it remains suggestive that Montreux chose it to supplement his 1595 volume, thereby integrating it into the tragic exaltations of heroic femininity associated with his League period.

17   Similar insinuations emerge in Nervèze's *Lettre consolatoire envoyée à Mme la duchesse de Mercœur* (1602), when the angelic spirit of Mercœur (whose death while engaged in anti-Turkish crusading was attributed in some quarters to poison) records his 'crainte que quelques vns d'entre les Chrestiens, eussent quelque impie fidelité pour les infidelles [fear lest certain Christians might have had a certain impious fidelity in favour of the infidels]' (pp. 13–14).

18   Despite the collapse of the League, which obviously imposed reticence, such virtues were to become the hallmarks of a larger-than-life Madame de Mercœur in some Catholic rhetoric until her death over twenty years later; thus the eulogy by Abra de Raconis (Bishop of Lavaur) endows her with the magnanimity and moral merit of a virtual Christian Cleopatra, uniting seemingly contradictory virtues (1625, pp. 36–37); the mercy and grandeur of the great Henri (Louis XIII's father, after all) are also duly acknowledged.

19   This motif, too, is anchored in Jodelle, whose Chorus credits her with 'un cœur plus que d'homme [a heart more than a man's]' (l. 1540).

20   Unless otherwise stated, I cite Daniel, *The Tragedy of Cleopatra* (1599), in Bullough, ed., 1957–75, vol. 5 (having verified the agreement of citations with the 1594 edition).

21   As the Countess's immortal fame will be assured by her translation of the Psalms,

so the works of Sidney and Spenser, Daniel asserts, will eternize Elizabeth by showing

> ... what great ELIZAS raigne hath bred.
> What musique in the kingdome of her peace,
> Hath now beene made to her, and by her might,
> Whereby her glorious fame shall neuer cease.
>
> (Daniel, *The tragedie of Cleopatra*, 1594, sig. H7^r)

This hardly encourages a reading of the play as the sort of attack on Elizabeth detected by Kewes (2012).

22 On these negotiations, which Mornay conducted half-heartedly, preferring a military solution, see Daussy, 2002, pp. 517–22.

23 On Robert Sidney's diplomatic mission to Henri IV, see Millicent V. Hay, 1984, pp. 145–51. On the variously successful English interventions in Brittany, see MacCaffrey, 1993, pp. 253–57, 259–62.

24 Cf. Greengrass, 2002, pp. 78–97.

25 On the tribulations of Protestants in Mercœur's Brittany, see Vaurigaud, 1870, 1: 316–44.

26 For Jodelle's influence on Garnier, see Mouflard, 1961–64, 3: 254–58, who, interestingly, credits Garnier with enriching his predecessor in terms that anticipate some critical views of the Countess of Pembroke's supplementation of Garnier himself ('donne de l'ampleur, du relief, un volume plastique [lends size, relief, dynamic volume]' [258]). My discussion of Daniel develops, extends, and refocuses that of Rees, 1952; see also Rees, 1964, pp. 43–61. By contrast, it diverges sharply from Sanders (1998, pp. 106–36 *passim*), in part perhaps because the latter does not seem familiar with Jodelle, who is mentioned (p. 129) only in passing. For a general discussion of Daniel's work in relation to Jodelle and Garnier, see also Norland, 2009, pp. 211–18.

27 Hence the recurrent choric laments of the Egyptians for their conquered state, which anticipate those singled out by Kewes (2012) as evidence of Daniel's critique of Elizabeth.

28 This was first observed by A. Müller (cited Rees, 1952, p. 4n.1).

29 Daniel, 1607, I.ii [fol. 12^r]; *Ant.*, IV.14.82–83. This is noted by Barroll, 1991, pp. 161–64.

30 This hypothesis has proved popular among editors of *Ant.*: first advanced by Case, ed., 1906, pp. xi–xii, it was adopted, e.g., by John Dover Wilson, ed., 1950, p. ix, and Neill, ed., 1994, pp. 21–22.

31 On these points see Schanzer, 1957, p. 380, and Bullough, ed., 1957–75, 5: 235–36.

32 Despite perceiving Daniel's use of Jodelle for *Cleopatra,* Rees (1964, pp.76–81) stresses his originality in the 'Letter'.

33 The edition of Charpentier, Beaudin and Sanchez (1990) retains 'ils' for 'elles', but I cannot make sense of the line in this way.

34   Cf. Stirling, 1964, as well as Neill, ed., 1994, n. to V.ii.153–54.

35   Bullough, ed., 1957–75, 5: 236; Neill, ed., 1994, n. to V.ii.164–70. Muir is more appreciative of Jodelle's dramaturgy here and of its affinity with Shakespeare's: 'It is the liveliest scene in *Cléopâtre captive*, and Jodelle conveys, as Shakespeare does, the theatrical violence of his heroine's behavior' (1969, p. 202).

36   Shakespeare's synthetic method stands out here. Unlike Daniel, he retained (V.ii.200–3) the three-day warning of Dolabella that Jodelle took over from Plutarch (ed. Bullough, 1957–75, 5: 314), but his depiction of Dolabella is inflected by that of Daniel, who, distractingly, has the Roman fall outright in love with Cleopatra (ed. Bullough, 1957–75, 5: ll. 723 ff.). At the same time, Shakespeare deepens mere amorousness into profound human sympathy: 'I do feel, / By rebound of yours, a grief that smites my very heart at root!' (V.ii.102–4). Plutarch says only that Dolabella 'did beare no evil will unto Cleopatra' (ed. Bullough, 1957–75, 5: 314); Jodelle does not bring him on stage but has Charmium refer to him as 'ce bon Dolabelle, ami de notre affaire [that good Dolabella, friend to our affair]' (1990, l. 1199).

37   See Neill, ed., 1994, n. to V.ii.308. Cf. also the suicide scene of Montreux's Sophonisbe, whose exaltant imagery in the presence of her Nurse (who will follow her in death) androgynously blends the poison she will drink, thereby acquiring masculine virtue, with the milk that nourished her:

> Sus, nourrice, aide-moy; au lieu de soupirer,
> Viens mon masle tombeau de lauriers honorer.
> Viens le couvrir de fleurs, et ne pleins pas dolente
> Le lait que tu donnas à ma bouche mourante,
> Puisque tu as nourry un cœur qui genereux
> Ne peut estre vaincu des hommes et des dieux.

[Onwards, nurse, assist me; instead of sighing, come honour my male tomb with laurels. Come cover it with flowers, and do not, grieving, lament the milk you gave to my dying mouth, since you have nourished a heart which, in its nobility, cannot be vanquished by either men or gods.] (ed. Stone, 1976, ll. 2519–24)

38   Herbert's works are cited from *The Collected Works*, ed. Hannay, Kinnamon and Brennan, 1998.

39   On the points mentioned, see Schanzer, 1956.

40   Little appears to be known about Virey, a native of Normandy, who died in 1597; he also wrote a tragedy on the Maccabees, likewise published posthumously in Rouen (1599). There were a number of original plays published in Rouen in the first years of the seventeenth century, and the resemblance of some of them to their English counterparts in the use of dramatic conventions leads Christian Biet, for one, to speculate about 'd'éventuels échanges littéraires entre la Normandie et une Angleterre si proche [possible literary exchanges between Normandy and an England so close by]' (1996, p. 551).

41   See my *Shakespeare, Marlowe and the Politics of France* (2002), *passim*, as well as the Introduction to my translation of Fronton Du Duc (2005), esp. pp. 21–22, 43–51, 173n.68. My discussion complements the interesting perception by Emrys Jones (1971, pp. 249–52) of a structural similarity between *1H6* and *Ant.*, including the 'witchcraft' imputed to Joan and Cleopatra.

42   There is the hint of a precedent in the fifteenth-century *Mystère du siège d'Orléans*, 2002, ll. 13639 ff., where Talbot's losses at Orléans produce suicidal despair and provoke attempts to cheer him up; for him, moreover, Jeanne is already a witch (ll. 12089–90). The *Mystère* had not been published, but a popular dramatic tradition is likely to have existed; see my Introduction to Fronton Du Duc, 2005, p. 20, and esp. 'The Pucelle and the "godons"' (forthcoming).

43   See Witherspoon, 1968, esp. pp. 65–83, and Beauchamp, 1957, as well as Spriet, 1968, pp. 344–49.

44   Brennan, 1988, pp. 78–83; Lamb, 1990, pp. 115–45.

45   See also Clarke, 2007, for a concise account of the 'Sidney Psalter' in its cultural and literary contexts.

46   The League-leaning tendency of *Les Juifves*, at least, is recognized by historians – see Jouanna *et al.*, eds, 1998, p. 940, and Constant, 1996, p. 173; the latter also makes it clear, however, to what extent the League was imposed by force in Le Mans, Garnier's city, in 1589 (1996, pp. 299–307). On Garnier's political evolution, with attention to his role as a royalist propagandist whose League leanings reflected a loss of faith in that solution, see Mouflard, 1961–64, 1: 168–89 and 358–408.

47   A parallel case is that of Catherine de Medici's Chancellor Michel de L'Hospital, whom posterity has sought to make a pioneering champion of religious toleration while obscuring his *Realpolitik*, his early adherence to the war party (with regard to Italy) and his initial close ties with the Guises; see Kim, 1989. Such questions of moral responsibility were not necessarily clearer for contemporaries; see the remarks regarding Pibrac after the 1572 massacre in Sidney and Languet, *Correspondence*, 1912, p. 100 (Letter 36). Prescott (2008, pp. 78–80) offers a balanced assessment of Pibrac in these terms.

48   See Spriet, 1968, pp. 107–8 (for Greville) and 154–58 (on Daniel's *Philotas*). Cf. Yachnin, 1991, pp. 8–9. Kewes, 2012, explains, in part, that the political analogizing of Herbert and Daniel functioned 'intermittently' and with 'parallels … so inexact' as to furnish 'plausible deniability'; she thereby comes close to undercutting her own argument.

49   See also Spriet, 1968, p. 348.

50   See, notably, Waller, 1990, p. 335, and Fisken, 1990, pp. 263–75.

51   For comparison on the premise of revision from the printed version to that of the manuscript, see Herbert, Hannay, Kinnamon and Brennan, eds, 1998, 1: 74–76.

52   See Waller, 1979, p. 100, and 1990, p. 336.

53   Hannay, Kinnamon and Brennan, eds, 1998, 1: 77. See 1: 303–4 for the transmission and authority of the poem's texts. The fact that the 'Angell Spirit' of the title

matches lines present only in the manuscript version cuts both ways. Indeed, it appears more likely that such a title would have been retained despite excision of the verses that gave rise to it than that Herbert would subsequently have added lines to match a pre-existing title. Nevertheless, as is attested by both Fisken (1990) and Waller (1990, pp. 334–40), critics are strongly inclined to presume her growth in poetical power and distinctiveness.

54 Here, as below, I come squarely up against the one-sided view of Sanders that, by comparison with the original, Herbert 'decoupled chastity from female virtue' (1998, p. 124) and celebrated Cleopatra's sheer sensuality, which in turn 'animated Shakespeare's complementary view' (1998, p. 136) of Cleopatra's numinous sexuality. The basis of Cleopatra's final scene remains self-blame in both translation and original: 'O hellish worke of heav'n [O ciel par trop funeste]' (*Antonius*, 1998, l. 1821; *Marc Antoine*, 1974, l. 1798)]; 'of mine the plague and poison I [je suis le poison et la peste des miens' (*Antonius*, 1998, l. 1825; *Marc Antoine*, 1974, l. 1802)]; 'O hurtfull woman! [O dommageable femme!]' (*Antonius*, 1998, l. 1835; *Marc Antoine*, 1974, l. 1812).

55 '[P]erhaps for theological reasons', as the Oxford editors suggest (Hannay, Kinnamon and Brennan, eds, 1998, 1: 151).

56 As well as for *Ant.*, V.ii.96 ff. – see Schanzer, 1963, p. 151.

57 Aggas's translation, while sometimes less elegant than Herbert's, is serviceable and generally accurate. I have compared his volume with the *Excellent discours* (1576).

58 Seneca, *Epistulae Morales*, ed. Reynolds, 1965, Letter 107.9 (p. 449); Letter 108 in Mornay, *Excellent discours*, 1576, followed by Aggas (*The Defence of Death*, 1576). Even here the Latin receives a Christian inflection, thanks to an idiomatic conversion that had became standard procedure. Seneca literally says that it is desirable to 'follow' or 'accompany' ('comitari') the divinity; the translation makes this into submission to the divine 'will' (*Defence*, 1576, sig. Gi^v).

59 '[I]n homage' should probably read 'an homage'.

60 This has seemed clear enough for commentators to take for granted but requires restating in light of Sanders, 1998, p. 118, who insists that Cleopatra's suicide by snakebite actually occurs without being mentioned. To pass over this spectacular event in silence would scarcely be credible even in a text meant for performance (as Garnier's evidently was), and its omission from the Arguments provided by both Garnier and Herbert is decisive evidence. Nor would such a reading have occurred to contemporaries who knew their Plutarch, where the scene at Antony's tomb is quite distinct from that of Cleopatra's suicide.

61 Given his dependence on Jodelle, this adds an ironic dimension to Daniel's statement, in his dedication to the Countess, that 'thy well grac'd *Anthony*' has 'Requir'd his *Cleopatras* company' (*The tragedie of Cleopatra*, 1594, sig. H5^r).

62 Hannay, Kinnamon and Brennan, eds, believe that, in writing her Argument, Herbert consulted Plutarch in Amyot's translation as well as North's (1998, 1: 148). The use of 'cordes' instead of 'ropes' is weak evidence, however, since the French word is naturally used by Garnier (*Marc Antoine*, 1974, ll. 1630, 1635,

1646) in the account of Antoine's raising. That Amyot's version was popular reading for Cambridge students at least prior to the publication of North's translation is attested by a letter of Gabriel Harvey conjecturally dating from the late 1570s (*Letter-book of Gabriel Harvey*, 1884, p. 79).

63   See the list of editions of Goulart's Amyot in Leonard Chester Jones, 1917, pp. 586–88, although Jones is obviously wrong in claiming (p. 293) that North's original translation was based on Goulart's edition.

Could Goulart have found favour with French licensing authorities because, in effect, his containment operation conveyed the message that Roman meanings were not simply up for grabs? Amyot's original address to the reader, maintained in North's translation, was a far more easy-going affair, giving delight its equal Horatian claim with profit, depicting history as composed of 'wonderfull aduentures & straunge cases' (Plutarch 1579, sig. *iii^v), and giving free reign to interpretation by allowing that, while the historian may be 'a register to set downe the iudgements and definitiue sentences of Gods Court', only some of the latter 'are geuen according to the ordinarie course and capacitie of our weake naturall reason, and other some goe according to Gods infinite power and incomprehensible wisedome, aboue and against all discourse of mans vnderstanding' (sig. *v^r).

64   Goulart, *The liues of Epaminondas, of Philip of Macedon, of Dionysius the elder, and of Octauius Caesar Augustus*, 1603, p. 59.

65   See, e.g., the edition of 1631.

66   Here again Daniel's tragedy is intertextually implicated. Although only Shakespeare's key line directly confronts, and succinctly transforms, Goulart's gloss, Daniel shapes Cleopatra's mourning as if he, too, knew that commentary – but agreed with it. The opening monologue of his *Cleopatra* has her lamenting,

> Yet do I live, and yet doth breath extend
> My life beyond my life? nor can my grave
> Shut up my griefes, to make my end my end?
> Will yet confusion have more then I have?
> Is th'honor, wonder, glory, pompe, and all
> Of *Cleopatra* dead, and she not dead?
> Have I out-liv'd my selfe, and seene the fall
> Of all upon me, and not ruined?
> Can yet these endure the ghastly looke
> Of Desolations darke and ougly face … ?
>   (Daniel, ed. Bullough, 1957–75, 5: ll. 1–10)

Cleopatra's last moments present even her honourable death as fitting retribution for lust ('And heere I sacrifice these armes to Death, / That Lust late dedicated to Delights' [ll. 1534–35]), while the concluding Chorus paints a picture of Egypt itself as bereft of hope

> That ever sweete repose
> Shall repossesse the Land,

> That Desolation fills,
> And where Ambition spills
> With uncontrouled hand,
> All th'issue of all those
> That so long rule have held:
> To make us no more us,
> But cleane confound us thus.
>   (ll. 1675–83)

(Still, Kewes distorts somewhat in citing ll. 1680–83 to show how the Chorus 'ruefully reflects on their queen's guilt' [2012]: the issue-spilling 'hand' of 'Ambition' in this passage clearly belongs to Octavius.)

'Rossillion' (*bis*) revisited: five minutes to midnight and *All's Well*

Some explanation seems needed for the conclusion of a study of tragedy with a long chapter on a comedy, and it seems an evasion to take refuge in the label of tragicomedy.[1] The explanation, however, can be brief – on the condition of its being somewhat reductive. In a previous study of soliloquies and other forms of 'self-speaking', I devoted extensive attention to a discursive phenomenon that I termed, on the model of Lacanian psychoanalysis, 'aphanisis' or 'fading', in which the experience of a character's 'self' is communicated to the audience through the signs of its own regression – much as the desire to hold on to anything is born of the sensation that it is slipping from one's grasp.[2] This phenomenon seemed to me useful in defining the illusion of subjectivity as produced on the early modern stage. Even when found within comedies, however, as it sometimes is, the tendencies of the procedure are insistently tragic; in Shakespeare, they are most conspicuously realized in the major soliloquies of the tragic protagonists, who tend to approach catastrophe through variations on the theme of 'All the world's a stage' (*AYL*, II.vii.139) – a theme proclaimed, of course, by a self-appointed wall-flower at the comic cotillion.

As Jaques' case confirms, such a sense of tragic subjectivity remains intrinsically individualizing, an expression of amputation from the social body. By contrast, the social bonds and structures typical of comic play-worlds, whatever resistance they may initially oppose to individual initiative – the pursuit of happiness as love or money, usually both – tend to advertise their incorporative potential, the capacity to be transformed and renewed. In tragedy, social bonds and structures remain non-renewable resources, and are consumed to the point of exhaustion by futile impulses towards fulfilment. Such futility is felt acutely when tragedies conclude with belated compensatory gestures: Capulet's and Montague's statues of their children, the bearing of Hamlet 'like a soldier to the stage', the promise to torture Iago into speech. It is always there, however, as early modern English tragedy's enabling condition – to the point where the genre virtually defines itself by illusions of meaning. The untenability of such illusions, which collectively stand in for the universal human delusion of immortality itself, is a 'mere' matter of time, and to this extent *Doctor Faustus* may be taken as generically archetypal, with its fifth-act soliloquy ticking aphanitically towards midnight and the apocalypse of the dawn of consciousness figured, according to human habit, diabolically: 'Ah, Mephistopheles!' (*Doctor Faustus, A-text [1604]*, ed. Bevington and Rasmussen, 1993, V.ii.115).

The unique interest of *All's Well* in these terms is that, positioned on the threshold of Shakespeare's sustained period of tragic composition (for I see no reason to abandon the most widely accepted dating of 1603–4[3]), it audibly sets the tragic clock ticking, even while also, by its formal comic ending, setting it back by a few minutes – or, through Helena's pregnancy, by a generation. (But then, to invoke its only precursor with a French setting, 'That's too long for a play' [*LLL*, V.ii.878].) The sense of futility, figured as universal entropy, weighs oppressively on the 'happy' ending, which eponymously bears *all* the burden of generic determination. The kicking foetus produced by the bed-trick finally seems as much of a mockery of the paradigm of joyous renewal as does the arrival of Fortinbras. Helena may realize, in a sense, Ophelia's revenge: a virgin blowing up men, miraculously returning from the undiscovered country to which repudiation by her lover had consigned her. But she can do so only at the cost of exempting Bertram from a confrontation with culpability in the form of her corpse. Versions of such confrontation, dress-rehearsed in *Much Ado* and quintessentially staged in *Hamlet*'s graveyard, pervade Shakespeare's post-1600 plays as emblems of the perverse eagerness of human beings to sacrifice those they love – that is, themselves – to their illusions. The distance between the tragedies and *All's Well* comes down to the difference between horizontal and vertical lifeless bodies.

Yet *All's Well* remains a comedy, not only formally, but also by its privileging of collective over individual experience, and this fact is arguably reflected in a collectivizing of aphanisis unique, I think, in the canon. The sense of living on borrowed time is diffused throughout its society and enacted through the medium of memory. Character after character effectively 'does a Hamlet' – 'How weary, stale, flat, and unprofitable / Seem to me all the uses of this world!' (I.ii.133–34) – renouncing the substantiality of the present by nostalgically conjuring the superior substance of the past, seeking out precisely the models that will slip through his or her fingers. Such aspirations to the Real through selective memory serve disingenuously to obscure both the past as it really was and the present as it really is. The experience of absence is exchanged for the illusion of presence. As the King puts it, endorsing Lafew's evocation of the supposedly expired Helena, 'Praising what is lost / Makes the remembrance dear' (V.iii.19–20);[4] he thereupon takes refuge from his inability to restore her by arrogating the power to restore Bertram – a miracle more achievable than getting the latter to love or (convincingly) to regret his wife:

> The nature of his great offence is dead,
> And deeper than oblivion we do bury
> Th'incensing relics of it. Let him approach
> A stranger, no offender.
>
> (23–26)

The King's miracle remains dependent on Helena's cure, which seems to have turned back the clock for him ('of as able body as when he number'd thirty' [IV.v.77–78]). The past thus conjured continually fades from view, like Prospero's spirit-actors, and the sense of absence is commensurately installed and universalized – darkness visible, the tragic ticking, audible to the King despite himself:

> All is whole.
> Not one word more of the consumed time;
> Let's take the instant by the forward top.
>
> (V.iii.37–39)

The more tightly woven such a tissue of illusions, the more vulnerable it is to a touch of reality, and this is what renders possible the quasi-miraculous triumph of Helena, the exception that proves the rule. In another of the provocative points of contact and contrast between *All's Well* and the closely contemporary *Hamlet*, Helena, who begins the play in an analogous situation, conspicuously refuses to 'do *her* Hamlet' and frees herself for present action by jettisoning remembrance of her father: 'What was he like? / I have forgot him' (I.i.79–80). The comic ending is spectacularly her creation, but her loss of virginity 'to her own liking' (I.i.147) finally fails to convince the off-stage audience of the future she has forged (in both senses). Even as she gives Bertram a lesson he will never forget, Helena finally re-inscribes herself close-to-tragically under the sign of the title. After all, the superficially reassuring proverb, 'All's well that ends well', is a thinly disguised injunction to separate events from causes, endings from beginnings – at once to forget the past and arbitrarily to foreclose the future (for who decides when things have ended?) – and it bears, like many proverbial consolations, the rueful trace of wishful thinking. Its universality ultimately makes a mockery of the King's analogous pronouncement ('*All* is whole') and rejoins that of the melancholy Jaques: '*All* the world's a stage'.

I

The pervasive nostalgia of this play-world is the standard stuff of criticism.[5] My argument is that the original impact would have depended, to a greater extent than is generally realized, on the historical materiality of the mechanisms of memory put on display and held up to scrutiny. The famous ambiance itself, that is, entails an aphanitic process, according to which seemingly 'real' images undergo a 'fading'. Those images stake their untenable claim to reality, I suggest, on an historical basis – to the point where this frank adaptation of a 'timeless' medieval romance (*Decameron*, Day III, Story 9, of Giletta of Narbonne) resonates along a chronological chain stretching backward to the Middle Ages from Shakespeare's age.

The material referentiality of the play depends on French intertexts. It has little to do, however, with the main 'French question' that has so far been raised regarding the play – namely, whether Shakespeare worked from William Painter's translation of Boccaccio in *The Palace of Pleasure* (1566–67) or the French version of Antoine Le Maçon (1545, multiply reprinted), or both. That question, introduced by Wright (1955), has been much debated and can never be settled, especially given Wright's own demonstration elsewhere that Painter himself drew freely on Le Maçon (Wright, 1951). Indeed, Le Maçon's translation of the complete *Decameron* might be supposed to have possessed a particular claim to attention from English Protestants: it was commissioned, as the introductory epistle announces, by Queen Marguerite of Navarre (herself the author, of course, of the Boccaccian *Heptaméron*[6]), who was widely viewed as sympathetic to the early French Reform movement. In any case, it is interesting to find Hunter's similar judgement about the inconclusiveness of particular 'French' sources rubbing shoulders with compelling intuitions of Frenchness: 'the atmosphere of the play is decidedly French'; 'Parolles, Lavatch, and Lafew seem to indicate a mind at work strongly imbued with a consciousness of French meanings' (*AWW*, Hunter, ed., 1959, p. xxv). Few critics, however – apart from Lambin[7] – have attempted to determine what those 'French meanings' might be.

Two recent exceptions are Lisa Hopkins and Deanne Williams, who both, in remarkably coincidental fashion, seize on Lafew's evocation of Charlemagne and Pepin (II.i.75–76) to define the text's central tension between history and legend (Hopkins, 2003, p. 371; Williams, 2008, pp. 165–66). More broadly, that tension extends between, on the one hand, the infinite possibility of fairy-tale romance and, on the other, the stubborn limitations of human nature, the latter reflecting what Susan Snyder terms the 'unromantic social realities of Early Modern Europe' (*AWW*, Snyder, ed., 1993, p. 5). This double alignment seems to me insistent in the text and will likewise guide my own approach. With regard to historical detail, however, I share little common ground with either Hopkins or Williams.

The former detects, on the one hand, a pointed allegory involving Henri II's initially childless marriage with Catherine de Medici and, on the other, an allusion to the early thirteeth-century Albigensian 'crusade' against the Cathars of the Midi. The first argument (in keeping with a veritable school of bottom's-up criticism) makes much of the King's fistula, locating it in his anus without clear textual warrant (such as might be expected, given the implications for staging) – and contrary to Boccaccio (a precedent likely to influence the assumptions of some spectators):[8]

> ... the French king had a swelling upon his breast, which by reason of ill cure was growen to be a Fistula, which did put him to marveilous paine and griefe. ... (*Decameron*, Day III, Story 9, trans. Painter [*The Palace of Pleasure*, Novel 38], ed. Bullough, 1957–75, 2: 390)

In any case, there is little reason to suppose that the play's forlorn and lacklustre King was calculated to evoke the energetic, athletically prodigious Henri.[9] As for the idea that the play somehow 'pokes fun at the French wars of religion and their complex interrelationships with questions of marriage and procreation' (Hopkins, 2003, p. 372), the point remains indefinite and seems questionable on the grounds of chronology, if not of tone. (Henri II died in 1559; the first War of Religion broke out three years later.)

The Cathars likewise remain elusive within Shakespeare's text. Indeed, this gesture at historicizing the first and original Roussillon tends to confirm that such an exercise offers limited footholds in itself and has limited potential for opening up the play as a whole. Lavatch's reference to the devil as 'the prince of this world' (IV.v.46), which might be supposed merely to be echoing Christ (John 14:30, 16:11), or, with Lambin, to be Puritan-tinged,[10] is stated by Hopkins to be 'strongly associated with Catharism', and since 'the historical Roussillon itself was famous for Catharism' (2003, p. 378) and Narbonne lies within it, the mere name of Gerard de Narbon emerges as a further Cathar allusion. No evidence is offered that a London playgoer in the first years of the seventeenth century would have picked up such allusions, much less recognized the dualism of Cathar theology as lying behind Lavatch's comment.

For her part, Williams summarizes the ethnic and political history of Roussillon to elaborate the notion that the region, '[f]ar from a peaceful French fiefdom', as Shakespeare would supposedly have it, 'is a major site of Catalan resistance to French incorporation' (2008, p. 169). The historical background furnished is sound enough, but, again, its application to the dramatic fable is fanciful. It seems that Shakespeare's ideological purpose of 'deliberately foregrounding [Roussillon's] French history and suppressing its Catalan history' (2008, p. 173) – apparently as a denial of Spanish hegemony – is subverted by Helena, who 'decisively demolishes' (with the support of Parolles) 'the construct of a French Roussillon' (2008, p. 172). Such arguments harden into near-allegory more reminiscent of the Old than of the New Historicism, and they do so, palpably, because the impulse to produce concrete 'French' meanings finds so little material to work with. As in the case of Hopkins, conspicuously missing are documents attesting to contemporary English – and French – ways of imagining political realities.

II

Although Hunter (1959, ed., pp. xxv–xxvi) suspects the punctual influence of the story of Boccaccio immediately following in Painter's collection – that of Tancred of Salerne (Day IV, Story 1) – All's Well remains a classic instance of what I have called the Myth of the Single Source.[11] Despite the play's invention of Parolles, Lafew and the key figure of the widowed Countess – not to mention the heroine's renaming – the dominant influence of the tale of Giletta of Narbonne is generally considered such an open-and-shut case that, as is rare indeed for the plays in the canon, Bullough includes nothing else in his collection.

Implicitly for him, therefore, as explicitly for Hunter (1959, ed., p. xxix), there is no point in pursuing the resemblance between Parolles' exposure as a coward, when he is duped into supposing himself captured, and that of the 'vgly mechanicall Captain' (1958, p. 217) in Nashe's *The Vnfortvnate Traveller*, whom Jack Wilton tricks into putting himself in the (French) enemy's power, whereupon he is terrified out of his 'glorious bragging humor' (1958, p. 223) and made a laughing-stock ('could not choose but mooue them all to laughter' [1958, p. 224]). Undoubtedly, in terms of source study, this amounts to a 'weak parallel' that fails to 'establish any necessary connection' (Hunter, ed., 1959, p. xxix) between the two works. The point may be pursued intertextually, however, on the premise that the resonance is initiated by the prescient dismissal of Parolles by Lafew – 'You are a vagabond and no true traveller' (II.iii.255–56) – and sustained by the variations of Lavatch and Lafew in Act V, Scene ii, on the theme of the braggart's fall into 'Fortune's displeasure' (6).

I have elsewhere related the same episode in Nashe's novel to the humiliating exposure of Pistol in *Henry V*.[12] To engage *All's Well* in this dynamic leads broadly in the same thematic direction – ironic commentary on heroic and chivalric values and pretensions – but shifts the historical accent from the

English in France to the French in Italy. Arguably at the imaginative core of *The Vnfortvnate Traveller*, after all, is the narrator's virtual vivisection of the ultimate glory of French arms under François I at Marignano (1515), an event literally dragged into the mud with a sordid physicality worthy of the late medieval art of the macabre:

> here vnweeldie *Switzers* wallowing in their gore, like an Oxe in his dung, there the sprightly *French* sprawling and turning on the stained grasse, like a Roach new taken out of the streame. ... In one place might you behold a heape of dead murthered men ouerwhelmed with a falling Steede in stead of a toombe stone, in another place a bundell of bodies fettered together in their owne bowells ... the halfe liuing here mixt with squeazed carcases long putrifide. (1958, p. 231)

The picture is thus already darkened by the shadow of France's future bloody losses, failures and humiliations in 'the *Sodom* of *Italy*' (Nashe, 1958, p. 327), as emblematized by François I's defeat and capture at Pavia ten years later.

To read these events back into *All's Well* is hardly to transpose Boccaccio's seemingly casual wars between Florence and Sienna to another time and place, any more than Shakespeare does. It is, however, to follow Shakespeare's lead in rendering considered and functional what was originally an arbitrary narrative device for getting Beltramo off the scene after his marriage:

> ... quand il fut monté à cheual, il ne s'en alla pas en son païs: mais s'en vint en Toscane, là ou, ayant sceu que les Florentins auoient guerre contre les Senoys, il se delibera d'estre de leur party: & y estant volontiers receu, & avec honneur faict capitaine de certain nombre de gens auec bon estat d'eux, il se mit en leur seruice & y fut long temps.

> [... when he had mounted on horseback, he did not head to his own country but went into Tuscany, where, having known that the Florentines were at war against the Siennese, he decided to take part with them; and being willingly accepted, and having honourably been made captain of a certain number of men of reputable condition among them, he put himself in their service and remained so for a long time.] (Boccaccio, trans. Le Maçon, 1558, p. 342)[13]

All's Well supplies meaningful context, if not historical precision: it sketches the French King's implication in the political situation (I.ii.4 ff. and perhaps II.i.12–14, though the latter passage is difficult);[14] it pointedly portrays Bertram as impatiently burning, even before the crisis over Helena, to join the other young Frenchmen in the pursuit of 'honour' (II.i.27 ff.). The latter is the watchword of the King himself, who gives it a distinct national spin:

> Farewell, young lords.
> Whether I live or die, be you the sons
> Of worthy Frenchmen; let Higher Italy ...

...

> ... see that you come
> Not to woo honour, but to wed it, when
> The bravest questant shrinks: find what you seek,
> That fame may cry you loud. I say farewell.
>
> (10–17)

Soldierly fellowship was the basis of the King's comradeship with Bertram's father; idealization of the latter as the epitome of noble manhood proceeds outward from this core towards a renewal of the chivalric ideal, with particular attention to the right relation of words and deeds:

> ... It much repairs me
> To talk of your good father; in his youth
> He had the wit which I can well observe
> Today in our young lords; but they may jest
> Till their own scorn return to them unnoted
> Ere they can hide their levity in honour.
> So like a courtier, contempt nor bitterness
> Were in his pride or sharpness; if they were,
> His equal had awak'd them, and his honour,
> Clock to itself, knew the true minute when
> Exception bid him speak, and at this time
> His tongue obey'd his hand. ...
>
> (I.ii.30–41)

Given the text's obsession with time past, it goes well beyond the commonplace of 'the music of men's lives', as expounded by Richard II (*R2*, V.v.44 ff.), to represent Bertram's father as clockwork incarnate, certainly 'Jack of the clock' (*R2*, V.v.60) to no one else. As the king's language ironically signals ('repairs me'), his loss in this sense, too, is irreparable.

For an audience attuned to Continental historical discourse, the overlay of the French wars in Italy would, I suggest, be palpable. Indeed, both the young men's dreams of glory and the old king's nostalgia have close counterparts in the autobiographical *Commentaires* of the famous commander Blaise de Monluc (or Montluc, c. 1500–77), first published in 1592 (and demonstrably known, to some extent, in contemporary England[15]). For Protestants, Monluc became infamous for cruelty on behalf of the Catholic cause during the Wars of Religion;[16] the other side of the coin, however, is his youthful image as the '[p]arfait représentant de ceux qui participèrent à l'épopée des guerres d'Italie [perfect representative of those who participated in the epic of the wars of Italy]'[17] – hence, his resemblance to the restless young men of *All's Well*:

... il me print envie d'aller en Italie, sur le bruit qui couroit des beaux faicts
d'armes qu'on y faisoit ordinairement. ... je me mis en chemin pour executer
mon dessein, remettant à la fortune l'esperance des biens et honneur que je
devois avoir. ... le sieur de Castelnau, vieux gentil'homme qui avoit longuement
praticqué l'Italie ... m'en dit tant de choses, et me raconta tant de beaux exploits
de guerre, qui s'y fasoient tous les jours, que, sans sejourner ny arrester en lieu
que pour repaistre, je passay les monts, et m'en allay à Milan, estant lors aagé de
dix-sept ans.

[... I was taken with a desire to go to Italy, given what was being said about the
splendid deeds of arms that were being accomplished there all the time. ... I set
out to execute my plan, leaving to fortune the hope of profit and honour that I
should obtain. ... Lord Castelnau, an old gentleman who had long experience
of Italy ... told me so many things about it, and recounted so many splendid
exploits of war, which took place there every day, that, without staying or stop-
ping anywhere except to take refreshment, I passed over the mountains and
headed for Milan, being then seventeen years of age.] (Monluc, ed. Courteault,
1964, p. 30)[18]

On a later famous occasion, when he was in a position of command, Monluc's
successful exhortation of the king (François I) to let him take the offensive in
Italy roused to enthusiasm the young nobles gathered round in the hope of
such a decision.[19] In fact, *All's Well's* presentation of the scions of great houses
as inflamed with ardour for Italian glory echoes a recurrent motif in the military
life of Monluc.[20]

Monluc's nostalgic reminiscence, although less romantically extravagant
than that of Shakespeare's King, leads him likewise to affirm his own generation's superiority to the present one, especially in the point of humility. In
his time, even great lords accepted places alongside those of lower rank ('il se
trouvoit de grands seigneurs, qui estoyent aux compaignies, et deux ou trois
en une place d'archier [great lords were found in the companies, and two or
three held the rank of bowman]' [1964, p. 30]); so of Bertram's father the King
recalls:

> Who were below him
> He us'd as creatures of another place,
> And bow'd his eminent top to their low ranks,
> Making them proud of his humility
> In their poor praise he humbled.
> (I.ii.41–45)

The two old soldiers agree that attitudes have changed for the worse, and their
modes of expression are remarkably similar:

Depuis tout s'est abastardy. Aussi tout s'en va à l'envers, sans que ceux qui vivent puissent esperer de voir les choses en meilleur estat.

[Since then all has degenerated. And so all goes backwards, without those who are alive being able to hope to see things in a better condition.] (Monluc, 1964, p. 30)

> Such a man
> Might be a copy to these younger times;
> Which, followed well, would demonstrate them now
> But goers backward.
> *(AWW*, I.ii.45–48)

They also agree – and it is, of course, a point of importance in the play – in admonishing young men against love affairs, which are considered a detriment to honour. The King warns,

> Those girls of Italy, take heed of them;
> They say our French lack language to deny
> If they demand; beware of being captives
> Before you serve.
> (II.i.19–22)

There is close accord with the experienced voice of Monluc, who, at the outset, cautions aspiring young soldiers against 'l'amour des femmes [the love of women]':

Ne vous y engagez pas. Cela est du tout contraire à un bon cœur. Laissez l'amour aus crochets, lorsque Mars sera en campagne. Vous n'aurez après que trop de temps. Je me puis vanter que jamais affection ny folie ne me destourna d'entre-prendre et executer ce qui m'estoit commandé. À ces hommes il leur faut une quenouille, et non une espée. Et outre la desbauche et perte de temps, ce mestier ameine une infinité de querelles, et quelquefois avec voz amis. J'en ay veu plus combattre pour ceste occasion que pour le desir de l'honneur. O la grand vilenie, que l'amour d'une femme vous desrobe vostre honneur et bien souvent vous face perdre la vie et diffamer!

[Do not get drawn into it. That goes thoroughly against a sound heart. Leave love hanging up when Mars is in the field. You will have only too much time later. I may boast that never did affection or folly prevent me from undertaking and executing what had been commanded me. Such men have need of a distaff, not a sword. And apart from the debauch and waste of time, that pursuit induces an infinity of quarrels, and sometimes with your friends. I have seen more of them combat for that cause than for the desire of honour. O what great shame, that the love of a woman should rob you of your honours and often cause you to lose your life and reputation.] (1964, p. 29)

Perhaps more surprisingly, lurking within Monluc's nostalgia for the glory of the Italian campaigns of his youth is disillusion, a sense of their issue in futile bloodshed and destruction that is equivalent to Nashe's dark underside of Marignano:

> La guerre recommença entre le roy François et l'Empereur, plus aspre que jamais, luy pour nous chasser de l'Italie et nous pour la conserver; mais ce n'a esté que pour y servir de tumbeau à un monde de braves et vaillans François. Dieu feit naistre ces deux grands princes ennemys jurez et envieux de la grandeur l'un de l'autre, ce qui a cousté la vie à deux cens mil personnes, et la ruyne d'un million de familles, et en fin l'un ny l'autre n'en ont rapporté qu'un repartir d'estre cause de tant de misères.

> [The war began again between the French king and the Emperor more bitterly than ever, he in order to chase us out of Italy, and ourselves to keep it. But it was for nothing but to furnish a tomb for a world of brave and valiant Frenchmen. God caused those two great princes to be born sworn enemies and each envious of the grandeur of the other, which cost the lives of two hundred thousand persons, and the ruin of a million families, and in the end neither one nor the other of them gained anything but the regret of having been the cause of so many miseries.] (1964, p. 30)

The strong insinuation here that the 'monde' remaining behind is diminished and tainted – in ruins and in mourning – turns out, in fact, to connect the dramatic universe of *All's Well* with that of *The Vnfortvnate Traveller* by a further intertextual bond.

III

To dispel any doubt that Nashe's apparent rhetorical insouciance is often calculated, it suffices to juxtapose the moment when *The Vnfortvnate Traveller* launches into its narrative, sounding the theme of Henry VIII's glorious wars in France, with another French text, one perhaps still better known in its time than the memoirs of Monluc. For Nashe reworks a resonant snippet of that text in a way that suggests an allusion he expected to be widely picked up:

> About that time that the terror of the world and feauer quartane of the French, *Henrie* the eight ... advanced his standard against ... *Turney* and *Turwin*, and had the Emperour and all the nobilitie of *Flanders, Holland & Brabant* as mercenarie attendants on his ful-sayld fortune ... (1958, p. 209)

> Au temps que le roy Henry d'angleterre vint bouter le siege devant la cité de Teroane, que les antiques appelloient Morini, ainsi que ceulx de Tornai furent appelés Nervii, le roy Loys de france, douziesme de ce nom, regnoit pour lors,

lequel estoit desjà sur l'eaige, et avoit les goutes merveilleuses, et se faisoit pourter en litiere.

[At the time when King Henry of England came to lay siege before the city of Térouanne, which the ancients called Morini, as those of Tornai were called Nervii, King Louis of France, the twelfth of that name, was then reigning, who was already well on in age, and suffered terribly from gout, and had himself carried in a litter.] (Champier, ed. Crouzet, 1992, p. 177 [Bk. II, Ch. 11])

Immediately striking here is the contrast between the 'ful-sayld fortune' of the English king, as vaunted by Nashe's travelling page, and the age-enfeebled and chronically diseased condition of the French adversary – a condition that broadly coincides with that of the King in *All's Well*.

The French text in question is by Symphorien Champier (c. 1472–c. 1539). It is commonly known as *La vie de Bayard* (1524) – the life, that is, of Pierre Terrail, seigneur de Bayard (c. 1474–1524), who, with the support of a second biography by Jacques de Mailles (1527) became a legend in sixteenth-century (and later) France under the sobriquet of the 'chevalier sans peur et sans reproche [knight without fear and without reproach]'.[21] Champier's mouthful of a title is *Les Gestes, ensemble la vie du preulx chevalier Bayard, avec sa genealogie; comparaisons aulx anciens preulx chevaliers: gentilx, israélitiques et chrestiens; ensemble oraisons, lamentations, epitaphes dudit chevalier Bayard. Contenant plusieurs victoyres des roys de France Charles VIII, Loys XII et Francoys, premier de ce nome* [The deeds, together with the life of the bold knight Bayard, with his genealogy, comparisons with the ancient bold knights, Gentiles, Israelites and Christians, together with prayers, lamentations and epitaphs of the said knight Bayard. Containing many victories of the kings of France Charles VIII, Louis XII and François, first of that name].[22] The author (from Lyons) was a physician, antiquarian and historian – in fact, an extremely prolific writer in these and other fields (the Bibliothèque Nationale de France lists about one-hundred-and-sixty editions of his various works) – who had soldiered together with his subject and apparently married into the family.

My main point here is the one developed by Denis Crouzet, in richly reveal-ing fashion, in the Introduction to his edition of Champier's hagiographic biography (1992): for a France caught up in the spiralling throes of civil and religious strife, the legend of the pure heroism, unquestioning devotion to his king and flawless (Catholic) piety of the chevalier Bayard filled a profound cultural and spiritual need. Champier ignores, among many other things, the burgeoning dissent and unrest with which the historical Bayard would have had to deal – as he evidently did to general satisfaction – during his term (1516–21) as the king's Lieutenant-Général in Dauphiné.[23] Rather, as the title itself might suggest, *Les Gestes* combines the structure of a saint's life with a revival of the Arthurian warrior ethos, the whole deeply informed by the nostalgic sense that the world left behind at the death of Bayard – when the very incarnation of chivalric tradition was struck down by an ordinary soldier's musket-shot – is a lesser one, the values he exemplified lost beyond recovery. As Jean Jacquart puts it:

> En ce sens, notre héros est presque anachronique, témoin dépassé d'un monde révolu. C'est peut-être pour cela que tout un groupe social a voulu se reconnaître en lui. Et que sa mémoire a traversé les siècles.

> [In this sense, our hero is almost anachronistic, the witness left behind of a world thoroughly changed. That is perhaps why an entire social group wished to recognize itself in him. And why his memory has passed across the centuries.] (1987, p. 12)

The recuperative work of memory began immediately, moreover, and with a self-consciousness worthy of that faculty's operations in *All's Well*.

IV

The principal battlefields on which Bayard's valour and values were exemplified were precisely those of the Italian wars. The acme of his honour was achieved at Marignano, where the young François I himself requested Bayard to confer knighthood on him (Champier himself was also knighted [Champier, Crouzet, ed., 1992, p. 72]). Appropriately, Bayard's death – as sublime an apotheosis of pious chivalry as might be imagined – took place during a retreat (from Rebecco, 30 April 1524), one of the string of defeats that heralded the ultimate French disaster at Pavia.[24] He expires in a haze of sanctity, lamented by friends and enemies alike – not least by the soldier who shot him, who experiences a virtual curse of Cain 'd'avoir, par ung engin dyabolique, tué le plus noble et vertueulx chevalier de toute chevalerie [for having, with a devilish engine, killed the most noble and virtuous knight of all chivalry]' (Champier, 1992, p. 210); the soldier then disappears – perhaps, it is conjectured, to take to religion.

What is left of Bayard himself is at once larger and smaller than life – an image of greatness that can be measured only imperfectly by abstract comparisons with ancient heroes. It is also fragmentary: the narrative is reduced to enumerating his surviving followers and family connections. The whole truth is acknowledged by Champier to be beyond restoration, even subject to contradictory testimony, as is proof of humain frailty: 'Et pour ce, doibvent les liseurs supplir et excuser les hystoriographes, si du tout il ne sont semblables, car il n'y a riens perfaict soubz le ciel de la lune, qui est le ciel des actions et passions humaines [And therefore must the readers supplement and excuse the writers of history, if they are not entirely the same, for there is nothing perfect beneath the sky of the moon, which is the sky of actions and human passions]' (1992, p. 257). Proof, too, is the fading of the author's own memory, which has a *de-authorizing* effect – transforming him virtually before our eyes, at the close of his story, from a narrator from whom we expect closure to a subject indefinitely in production across the speech of the Other: 'Plusieurs aultres proverbes moraulx disoit, lesquelz pour le present sont dehors ma memoire [Many other moral proverbs he spoke, which for the present have gone out of my memory]' (1992, p. 241). By such means does the world of Champier's narrative come to resemble the Shakespearean dramatic one, although the proverb conditioning the latter was presumably not part of Bayard's repertoire.

As the inconclusive conclusion of Champier demonstrates, Bayard's chivalric perfection consisted in a fusion of words and deeds manifesting, above all, his thorough knowledge of his *place* – at once within society and within the divine creation. His bearing as a young chivalric apprentice ('paige') exemplified what Shakespeare's King recalls about Bertram's father: unfailing self-control, gracious modesty towards inferiors, 'wit' without 'levity' (I.ii.32, 35), indeed a 'good melancholy' that seemingly 'oft began / On the catastrophe and heel of pastime, / When it was out' (56–58); he conformed to the counsel of both the King and Monluc with respect to true humility – and resistance to the charms of women. Here is Book V, Chapter 2 (in its entirety):

> Le noble Bayard, en sa jeunesse, fust honteulx, doulx et gracieulx, humble, courtoys à ung chescun; nul oncques ne le veist en fureur ny en yre grande. Il estoit soubre sur tous aultres paiges. Oncques ne fust abusé de femme, que pour elle il delaissast ses affaires ny choses licites. Et si tenoit quelque peu de la nature melancholique, si estoit il à toutes gens joyeulx, aymant compaignie, esbatemens et choses plaisantes. Quant à sa gravité, elle estoit toujours meslée de doulceur et affabilité, et en tout gardoit ordre. Il estoit bening, humain et charitable.

> [The noble Bayard, in his youth, was modest, gentle, gracious, humble, courteous to everyone; no one ever saw him in fury or great anger. He was more serious than all the other pages. Never was he so abused by a woman as to neglect for her his business or lawful affairs. And if he tended a bit towards the melancholic nature, still he was joyful towards all persons, fond of company, amusements and pleasant things. As for his gravity, it was always mingled with sweetness and affability, and he kept order in everything. He was kind, humane and charitable.]
> (1992, p. 238)

Even the down-to-earth Monluc, hardly inclined to chivalric illusions (although capable of lip-service to the ignoble levelling effect of firearms[25]), finds a way implicitly to invoke Bayard as a model – and with some credibility. For it was under the latter's command that the old soldier had begun his career:

> Ayant esté nourri en la maison du duc Antoine de Lorraine et mis hors de page, je fuz pourveu d'une place d'archier de sa compaignie, estant monsieur de Bayard son lieutenant.

> [Having been brought up in the house of the Duke Antoine de Lorraine and passed beyond the position of page, I was furnished with a place as bowman in his company, Monsieur de Bayard being his lieutenant.] (1964, p. 30)[26]

Distinctions are to be made here, however. The Gascon Monluc had been placed as a page at the ducal court in Nancy for practical and family reasons, although his attempts to capitalize on the connection later in his career did not prove notably successful. By contrast, Bayard's affiliation with the House of Lorraine, like everything about the man, was richly symbolic. For while Bayard's association with his native Dauphiné, for which he latterly served as royal governor, grounds his identity as mythologized by Champier – a point, in fact, that I will shortly be reading back into *All's Well* – the biographer also insistently develops the link with Lorraine. It spans Bayard's story from the beginning (the coronation of François I, '[a]uquel couronnement alast monseigneur de Lorraine, bien à mille chevaulx moult bien acoustrés [to whose coronation my lord of Lorraine journeyed, with a good thousand horse well appointed]' [Champier, 1992, p. 187]) to the end: 'Cy finist les faictz et gestes du noble chevalier capitaine Bayard, en son temps lieutenant du daulphiné et de monseigner de Lorraine [Thus conclude the feats and deeds of the noble knight Bayard, in his time lieutenant of Dauphiné and of my lord of Lorraine]' (1992, pp. 256–57). Encoded here, as in the comparison of Bayard with Godefroy de Bouillon (1992, p. 232) – the current Duke's ancestor and one of the Nine Worthies, who 'recovered' Jerusalem in 1099 – is the entire crusading heritage of the House of Lorraine: the image of selfless service to God against infidels and heretics that became the stock-in-trade of the Guises during the Wars of Religion.[27]

V

To return briefly to Nashe, it would have been obvious to a contemporary reader familiar with Champier's Bayard – and Nashe must have been counting on some – that the flagrant appropriation of that narrative to open *The Vnfortvnate Traveller* is part of an assertion of Englishness over and against Frenchness. After all, Nashe's imitation makes of the invading Henry VIII 'the terror of the world and feauer quartane of the French', transforms the emperor and other grandees into his 'mercenarie attendants', substitutes his robust health for the decrepitude of Louis XII and – not least – writes Bayard himself quite out of the story. The episode recounted in *La vie de Bayard* naturally has a different focus and direction; it involves the knight's surprising encounter with both the emperor (here Maximilian I) and the English king, when he decides quite deliberately, on the occasion of the so-called 'journée des esperons [day of the spurs]', to allow himself to be captured instead of joining the fleeing French. He asks to be taken to the emperor, who recognizes him at once and treats him in a friendly and respectful way; Henry VIII then casually happens along, with this upshot:

> Quant le roy entendit que c'estoit Bayard, si le print par la main et l'embrassa comme s'il eust esté ung prince; mais Bayard bouta le genoulx à terre, et le roy le print et luy dist: Capitaine, je suys joyeulx de vous veoir et vouldroye, pour vostre honneur et proffit, vous veoir aultrement que prisonnier. Sire, dict Bayard, je suys vrayment prisonnier voluntayre, car il [*sic*] ne me ont pas prins prisonnier, mais libéralement me suys donné à eulx; car je avoye grant desir aussi de veoir la majesté imperiale et aussi la vostre, laquelle je voys à présent, et je n'ay voulu fouyr commes les aultres, car oncques ne fustz à escolle pour aprendre à fouyr.
> ... Et leur raconta comment il s'estoit rendu. Adonques l'empereur et le roy se boutarent plus fort à rire. Or se dict Bayard, sire empereur et vous sire roy, je proteste que ne me vueillés traicter en prisonnier prins par force, car si je eusse voulu, ne fusse prisonnier; mais je loue dieu de ce que n'ay heu vouloir à fouyr comme les aultres, car oncques ne fouys en guerre, ne feray, à l'ayde du createur du monde; mais vueillés moy traicter en capitaine, comme vous, sire empereur, m'avés aultresfoys congneu. Certes, dict l'empereur, si serés traicté non seulement en capitaine prisonnier, mais en amy.

> [When the king heard that it was Bayard, he so took him by the hand and embraced him as if he had been a prince. But Bayard put his knee to the ground, and the king took him and said: Captain, I am delighted to see you and would wish, for your honour and profit, to see you other than a prisoner. Sire, said Bayard, I am truly a voluntary prisoner, for they did not take me prisoner, but I freely rendered myself to them. For I also had a great desire to see your Imperial Majesty and your Majesty as well, whom I behold at present, and I did not wish to flee like the others, for I was never at school to learn how to flee.
> ... And he told them how he had yielded himself. Then the emperor and the king set themselves laughing more heartily. Now, said Bayard, Sire Emperor and you, Sire King, I protest that you should not treat me like a prisoner taken by force, for if I had wished, I would not be a prisoner. But I praise God that I had no desire to flee like the others, for never have I fled in war, nor will do, with the help of the Creator of the world. But may you be pleased to treat me as a captain, such as you, Sire Emperor, have previously known me. Indeed, said the emperor, but you shall be treated, not only as a captain prisoner, but as a friend.] (1992, p. 182)

Nashe did more, it would seem, in the apparent cause of exclusively glori-fying Henry VIII than eliminate Bayard's jaunty (but unfailingly respectful) upstaging of the emperor and king. In producing the original of Parolles' expo-sure, he parodically transformed both Champier's episode and its hero: the 'vgly mechanicall Captain' (1558, p. 217) with the 'glorious bragging humor', duped into presenting himself in the enemy camp, grotesquely stands in for the knight 'sans peur et sans reproche', whose exquisite poise uniformly matches modest words with deeds that speak for themselves. Each of them, it may be added, receives his due recompense.

By this intertextual route too, then, the figure of Bayard makes his way into *All's Well*, accompanied by the image of a decrepit French king reduced to discriminating among the dregs of heroism. The very absence of Bayard muddles the contrast between the lost emblem of chivalric perfection that was Bertram's father and the son, supposedly 'misled with a snipp'd-taffeta fellow … whose villainous saffron' – and yellow is still the colour of cowardice – 'would have made all the unbak'd and doughy youth of a nation in his colour' (IV.v.1–4). As has often been noted, *all* is made *well* in Shakespeare's play with the conspicuous assistance of that scapegoat: Parolles' unforgettable disgrace enables selective forgetting in Bertram's case; the latter is redeemed through the 'good liv'ry of honour' (IV.v.95–96) he displays on his final appearance, though that too, as Lavatch points out, may be mere appearance:

> O madam, yonder's my lord your son with a patch of velvet on's face; whether there be a scar under't or no, the velvet knows; but 'tis a goodly patch of velvet. (90–93)

Finally, however, *The Vnfortvnate Traveller*'s narrative excision of the French epitome of knighthood – the vehicle by which ancient Worthiness extended into the present age – to proclaim the heroic monopoly of '*Henrie* the eight (the onely true subject of Chronicles)' (1958, p. 209) is conspicuously self-subverting. At the distance of fifty years, Henry's knightly image would have shone all the more dimly because of Nashe's vigorous polishing: apart from the tarnish applied by internal and domestic politics, the great English exploits in France conspicuously came to nothing. If Monluc's *mémoire* – in the double sense – was capable of cutting through the nostalgic haze to gauge the collateral damage produced by François I and Charles V, so surely were Nashe's more perspicuous readers, including Shakespeare, with regard to Henry VIII. And to assist them in that process, Nashe furnished a narrator who was a 'page' of a very different order from Bayard and Monluc, one who writes, and writes himself into, a 'chronicle' that proves unremitting in exposing idealistic preten-sion.[28] It is the horrific reality of Marignano, renewed in the living dissection of Cutwolfe, whose god is Revenge, that gets the last laugh, or scream, and at the narrator's own expense. The sobered Jack Wilton, who once gloried in giving the braggart 'Iacke Drums entertainment' (1958, p. 218), comes close to illustrating the moral that Lafew applies to Parolles:

> A good traveller is something at the latter end of a dinner, but one that lies three thirds and uses a known truth to pass a thousand nothings with, should be once heard and thrice beaten. (II.v.27–30)

Nashe's 'last laugh' resounds hollowly along the halls of history until it resonates with the beaten hollowness of Parolles, 'Good Tom Drum' (V.iii.315).

VI

In Nashe and Shakespeare alike, then, the insistent materiality of history is set off against the idealism of which the unmentioned Bayard may be taken as the transcendental signified. The contrast makes its way to the very core of *All's Well*, I suggest, by way of those marriages between the miraculous and the contrived that are multiply effected by Helena in recuperating a thwarted marriage of her own. Her first and critical step, of course, is to cure the king. As has often been remarked, her quasi-magical power of restoration is figured in sexual terms by Lafew, whose very name helps to project the waning 'fire' of his old age into his hopeful imagery. Sexuality here figures an essential union of desire and memory, with the impossible gift to the king of his past youth couched in terms of the resurrection of ancient French worthies:

> I have seen a medicine
> That's able to breathe life into a stone,
> Quicken a rock, and make you dance canary
> With sprightly fire and motion; whose simple touch
> Is powerful to araise King Pippen, nay,
> To give great Charlemain a pen in's hand
> And write to her a love-line.
> (II.i.71–77)

Such necromancy was not beyond the reach of the better sort of Renaissance magician, and it could take on nationalist overtones – witness, for instance, the contest between Vandermast and Friar Bacon in Robert Greene's play. I propose another analogue – more to the point, as I hope to demonstrate, but superficially more remote, for it comes from a poem published in 1569 (and again in the following year) by the same incorrigibly prolix François de Belleforest responsible for the *Histoires tragiques* and other works with more serious historical pretensions. Belleforest's *La pastorale amovrevse*, by contrast, is at least superficially modest in scope – a personal and local act of homage to the author's current patrons, the noble family of Tournon in Dauphiné, whose most illustrious member was the great Cardinal François de Tournon (1489–1562). The latter was a prominent supporter of the 'Triumvirate' backed by the Guises; he served as the Papal emissary at the Colloquy of Poissy.[29] As has been suggested previously, these events of the early 1560s were ones about which Shakespeare seems to have been reading, and perhaps hearing, around the time of his composition of *Hamlet*.

The greater part of *La pastorale amovrevse* is devoted to the reanimation, performed by the wise magician Sydéré in his grot, if not of Pepin and Charlemagne, at least of the great heroes of the House of Tournon, past, present and to come, 'Qui doiuent pour la Foy & pour le Roy mourir [Who must die for the Faith and the King]' (*La pastorale amovrevse*, ed. Gaume, 1980, p. 52).[30] Their images ('maint viuant simulachre [many a living simulacre]' [1980, p. 51]) are animated by a wave of the magic wand ('en le [baston] maniant ces images qu'ay dit / Se remuoyent ainsi qu'vn corps plein de l'esprit [in manipulating (the wand) those images I have mentioned stirred themselves like bodies full of spirit]' [1980, p. 52]), and when the watching shepherd feels faint with terror, he himself is restored – indeed, transformed – by a drink from the medicinal spring that pours forth from the rock:

> ... le viellard expert me restaura le cœur
> Et me remit en force auecques la liqueur
> De l'eau de la fontaine, & sentis ne sçay comme
> Que changé il m'auoir du tout en vn autre homme.

[... the skilled old man refreshed my heart and restored me to strength with the liquor of the water of the fountain, and I felt, I know not how, as if he had changed me entirely into another man.] (1980, pp. 52–53)

Magically curative fountains are also the standard stuff of Renaissance pastoral romance, but this one particularly resembles Helena's medicine, not merely in its tonic force and divine association, but in its power to cure melancholy – not the 'good melancholy' based on sober reflection, but that produced by frustrated desire – through the union of memory and desire virtuously channelled:

> ... nature en ce lieu
> Monstre son artifice, & la force de Dieu.
> Que souhaiterois tu plus saint qu'vne fontaine
> Qui est dans ce pourpris sourdant à grosse veine
> Laquelle oultre le chault, & la soif qu'elle estaint
> Elle guerist encor, tout homme estant attaint

De fieure, & de transport de sens, & de folie:
Elle fait oublier toute melancolie
Et efface en vn rien les douleurs de l'esprit:
Ie sçay bien quil i'estois, & sçay comme il m'en prist
Et le iouir i'en benis, la memoire en honore
Lors que i'en beuz à gré, il me souuient encore.
Quand iamais i'y entray, & sentis la vigueur
Et sainteté du lieu & de ceste liqueur:
Et ne pense pasteur, que le pied de pagase
Ayt iamais bouïllonné vn si excellent vase
Pour nourir les espritz, que ce canal heureux
Nourrissier de vertu, & mort des vicieux.

[... Nature in that place shows its artifice, and the force of God. What would you wish more sacred than a fountain which within that enclosure gushes forth in a strong pulse, which, apart from the heat and the thirst that it extinguishes, moreover, heals every man touched with fever, and transported senses, and folly? It causes all melancholy to be forgotten, and in a trice does away with the pains of the spirit. I well know what I was, and I know how it took hold of me, and I bless the day and honour its memory when I drank my fill of it. I still remember when I had never yet entered there and felt the vigour and the holiness of the place and of that liquor. And I do not think there is a shepherd for whom the hoof of Pegasus has ever caused to bubble up[31] such an excellent mist to nourish spirits as that happy channel, nourisher of virtue, death of the vicious.] (1980, p. 51)

This seems much the sort of universal cure that Helena has in mind when she tells the King, 'Great floods have flown / From simple sources' (II.i.138–39), and its power to quicken 'melancholy' spirits will finally be exercised, not only on the King, taught that expectation 'oft ... hits / Where hope is coldest and despair most fits' (143–44), but on the frigid Bertram, whose fundamental disease Lavatch diagnoses, most interestingly, as melancholy (III.ii.3 ff.).

As for the line of heroes whose 'memoires sans fins, & diuines images [eternal memories and divine images]' (1980, p. 53) are magically brought to life in *La pastorale amovrevse*, it begins (almost inevitably, given the family name[32]) with the Rutilian king Turnus, who is represented as the fountainhead of perfect chivalry – 'courtois aux petitz, & aux orgueilleux fier [courteous towards the small, and proud towards the arrogant]' (1980, p. 53), like Bayard and Bertram's father. The admixture 'du saint Lys, & de la croix insigne [of the holy Lily and the illustrious cross]' (1980, p. 55) then introduces the double theme of royal affiliation and Catholic militancy – the latter leading from Saint Just (the fourth-century Bishop of Lyons, whose name remained prominent in the family) to the Cardinal de Tournon, whose struggle against the Huguenots is developed at length. Meanwhile, the family's thirst for honour in the king's cause finds grim but glorious fulfilment in the Italian wars. Singled out in the pageant are Just I, the cardinal's brother, killed at Pavia in 1525, and two of his sons, Antoine and Jacques, who fell three years later at the siege of Naples (1980, pp. 56–57 and p. 126nn.). The narrative then decisively shifts focus to that new enemy of God and country, the 'sanglier sanguinaire [bloody wild boar]' (1980, p. 59) of Protestantism, whose evil is elaborated in the usual terms of hypocrisy, poison, treachery and destruction.

The long line of family heroes ends with the one who will put down that monster once and for all, the still-youthful Just-Louis I, destined to follow the double example of valiant father and resolute mother ('Illustré des haults faicts, & vertuz de son pere / Et armé du cerueau, & bon sens de sa mere [Distinguished by the high deeds and virtues of his father, and armed with the intelligence and good sense of his mother]' [1980, p. 63]). The former, Just II, had already perished in that noble cause, having been killed during the successful siege of nearby Saint Agève, held by the Huguenots, in 1563. His glorious eldest son, Just III, had in turn died (in Italy, as it happens, though of natural causes[33]), leaving two daughters, in 1568, the year before Belleforest's poem (in which Just II barely figures, albeit as a 'demy-Dieu [demi-god]' [1980, p. 64]).[34] It is quite clear, therefore, that the immediate occasion of Belleforest's 1569 eulogy is the succession of Just-Louis to the ancestral titles.

This point is relevant because Just-Louis was not only seigneur of Tournon but Count of Roussillon, as his widowed mother, Claude de La Tour-Turenne, was the Countess. The volume contains a dedicatory sonnet (by Jean Willemin, a medical doctor who was the young count's tutor) addressed 'À treshavte, et heroiqve dame, Claude de Turaine, Dame de Tournon, & Contesse de Roussillon [To that most high and heroic lady, Claude de Turaine, Lady of Tournon and Countess of Roussillon]' (*La pastorale amovrevse*, ed. Gaume, 1980, p. 38). Belleforest, a friend of Willemin, seems to have become associated with the family recently, and a year later he would, in his turn, dedicate 'À tres-illustre et tres-vertvevse dame, Madame Clavde de Tvraine, Dame de Tournon, & Comtesse de Roussillon [To the highly illustrious and greatly virtuous lady, Madame Claude de Turenne, Lady of Tournon and Countess of Roussillon]', not a volume of his *Histoires tragiques*,[35] but nothing less than *L'histoire universelle du monde* in 318 folios. For a Shakespearean, the evocation of the family situation is resonant; Belleforest assures the Countess of

> … celle mienne deuotion à vous faire seruice, conceuë en mon esprit dès le temps que i'ay cest honneur que de cognoistre Monsieur vostre fils le Comte de Roussillon, les traitz de la vertu naissante duquel me donnent vn grand espoir de le voir vn iour le filz digne du Seigneur de Tournon, & de celle Claude de Turaine, qui en vn corps feminin porte vne vertu si remarquable, que peu d'hommes la

surpassent en magnanimité, & nul en desir de seruir Dieu, l'Eglise, le Roy, & la Patrie.

[… my devotion to do you service, conceived in my mind from the time when I had the honour of making the acquaintance of your son the Count of Roussillon, whose traits of budding virtue give me great hope to see him one day the worthy son of the Lord of Tournon, and of that Claude de Turenne who, in a female body, bears virtue so distinguished that few men surpass her in magnanimity, and none in the desire to serve the Church, the King and the Nation.] (Belleforest, *L'histoire universelle du monde*, 1570, sig. †ij^v)

VII

The Roussillon in question, a *seignurie* granted the status of *comté* by Louis IX and centred on a village in Dauphiné lying fifty kilometres to the south of Lyons, has nothing in common, except the name (and a location within the vast territory called by the Romans Gallia Narbonensis), with the Catalan region where Boccaccio set his tale of Giletta of Narbonne (modern Pyrénées-Orientales). Indeed, the latter was a virtual never-never land, as far as sixteenth-century France was concerned, having been returned to Spanish control, after a long back-and-forth struggle, in 1493. Or, rather, it was a particularly appropriate locale to become a symbol of lost – or transposed – glory, having originally been annexed by the same Louis XI responsible for thoroughly integrating Dauphiné into the kingdom of France.[36] Roussillon was finally ceded by Charles VIII, however, in exchange, amongst other things, for the Spanish promise not to impede the French in Italy, and Count of Roussillon became one of the titles claimed by the Emperor Charles V (Rodriguez-Salgado, 1988, p. 33). On the one hand, the Catalan Roussillon made as fitting a setting for fairy-tale romance as, say, Illyria. On the other hand, in terms of French nationhood, the new-found Roussillon in Dauphiné takes the place of the lost one. By manipulating this symbolic equation in the background, *All's Well* arguably does something with its setting akin to the doubleness of Arden/Ardennes.

In so far as Shakespeare and his audiences were concerned, then, the title of Count of Roussillon was a real one, pertaining to the perfectly material Roussillon of Dauphiné. Moreover, two formally proclaimed Edicts of Roussillon had further applied the stamp of historicity. They memorialize the extended stay of Charles IX in the family's château during the summer of 1564 – a lengthy pause (from 17 July to 15 August) in the grand tour of his realm undertaken at his mother's initiative during 1564–66 in the cause of reimposing the royal authority. (It is notable that the King's presence at Roussillon for the climax is among Shakespeare's additions to the story.) The first edict, issued on 4 August

1564, severely restricted Protestant freedom of worship and banned all synods – an apparent response to reports of seditious talk at the gathering at La Ferté in late April.[37] This proclamation is accordingly celebrated as an event honouring the region by the conservative Catholic historian Hilarion de Coste (to whose local knowledge I will have further recourse).[38]

Perhaps curiously, the anti-Protestant edict is not mentioned in a dispatch of the same date by the English ambassador, Sir Thomas Smith (*CSPF, 1564–65*, No. 592, p. 184 [4 August 1564, Smith to Cecil]), despite his previous detailed reporting to Cecil with regard to the controversial synod.[39] No doubt the printed declaration spoke for itself, but neither were the English interested at this point in stirring up controversy. At the outset of the royal journey (12 April 1564), the English and the French had concluded a solemn peace and renewal of their alliance – a second (highly symbolic) Treaty of Troyes involving the definitive return (for compensation) of Calais to the French. At any rate, the English were very much a friendly presence on this tour, and, despite the menace of plague, the stay in Lyons just prior to crossing the Rhone ('qui est le commencement de Daulphiné' [Jouan, 1979, p. 88][40]) on 9 July had been rendered agreeable by entertainments and a formal exchange of honours between the two nations, at which Henry Carey, Lord Hunsdon, was present.[41] (This is an intriguing fact, given that Hunsdon [d. 1596] was to become a notable patron of the theatre and eventually, as Lord Chamberlain, of Shakespeare's company.) Smith's report that in early August the court was 'yet at Roussillon', seemingly constrained by fear of the plague throughout the region, suggests a certain languor, somewhat relieved by courtly comings-and-goings: 'The Duke of Ferrara is in the Court and the Duke of Florence is looked for' (*CSPF, 1564–65*, No. 592, p. 184 [4 August 1564, Smith to Cecil]).[42] Incidentally, the professional diplomat, at least, had no difficulty in keeping the two Roussillons apart – and presumed that his royal mistress could do so: in a routine report to the Queen during the following January, he matter-of-factly mentioned a location in the south-west as being within 'King Philip's jurisdiction in Roussillon' (No. 915, p. 280 [7 January 1565]).

At least as pertinent, however, may be the second so-called Edict of Roussillon, issued five days after the first, by which the king fixed the beginning of the French New Year on 1 January (as opposed to 25 March, as remained the case in England).[43] After all, the thematic prominence of time in *All's Well* extends to the ostentatious royal arrogation of power over it. The King's quick series of edicts burying Bertram's offence 'deeper than oblivion', razing 'the consumed time' from the register and presuming to 'take the instant by the forward top' ironically announces the fact that starting over again is beyond the royal power. In line with Charles's edict leaping into the New Year, the

King's impulse is to speed up the clock, to avoid remembrance, even as Helena is beating him at his game with a leap into the new generation.

That Charles's highly symbolic and meticulously chronicled grand tour may lie dimly in the background to *All's Well* would match the abrupt removal of the play's king from Marseilles (IV.iv.8–10) to Roussillon (V.i.22 ff.), where Helena must hasten to catch up with him. Marseilles was, in fact, a major destination and place of sojourn on Charles's subsequent itinerary (he arrived there in early November), after which the royal entourage made its way by stages to Montpellier. It is the latter, not Marseilles (and not with the king present), that figures in Boccaccio's source-tale. For the royal household to remove from Marseilles to Roussillon (*bis*) would be, by the pattern of Charles's movements, to go backwards. On the contrary, those movements described a vast circle on the southern geography of France in a resolutely clockwise direction, with Paris serving as the point of origin and return – high noon and midnight.[44]

But more broadly and less fancifully associated with Roussillon for the English would have been political realities involving the central issues of French statehood over the sixteenth century, as they impinged on the concerns of England: the wars of Italy, followed by the Wars of Religion and the intrigues of more radical French Catholics, especially the House of Guise, on behalf of Mary, Queen of Scots. For Tournon was also, like Pont-à-Mousson in Lorraine and, more notoriously, Douai and Reims, the centre of an important and controversial university, which had every reason to interest the English government. That university had been founded by the cardinal and remained closely associated with his family. When, in 1561, just before the outbreak of the first civil war, the institution showed signs of openness to Protestant ideas, the cardinal took the definitive and effective counter-measure of handing it over to Jesuit control.[45]

The Jesuits did not always have an easy time at Tournon (any more than elsewhere); apart from various natural disasters, the official history of the institution speaks of riots in 1581 (sparked by the rumour that they had distributed poisoned hosts) and again on 26 May 1583 (Massip, 1890, p. 35). The latter occurred only a month after the lavish 'entrée solennelle [ceremonial entry]' arranged to welcome Count Just-Louis back from Paris with his bride of some nine weeks, and although, curiously, the historian does not mention this occasion, not only were the Jesuits extensively involved in the affair, but they were responsible for publishing the official account, under the title of *La triomphante entree de tresillvstre dame madame Magdeleine de La Rochefocavd, Espouse de hault et puissant Seigneur Messire Just-Loys de Tournon … faicte en la Ville, & Vniversité de Tournon, le dimenche vingtquatriesme du moys d'Auril 1583* (1583). This text is attributed to Honoré d'Urfé, one of their scholars at the time and someone destined far to eclipse Belleforest as a composer of pastoral romance. In the circumstances, it is difficult not to suspect the Jesuits of seeking to obliterate the recent stain on the image of communal harmony. Certainly, the document evinces a particular insistence on the combatting of heresy – a response in part, perhaps, to the bride's somewhat suspect religious credentials (her father, Count François III de La Rochefoucauld, had been killed in the Saint Bartholomew massacre, while her half-brother François would fall in the cause of Henri IV in 1591).[46]

Regardless of any flaws in solidarity among the local population, all the surviving documentation points to a thorough and enduring community of interest between the family of Tournon-Roussillon and the Jesuits. Count Just-Louis himself remained a staunch defender of the Catholic cause on and off the battlefield, and he further put himself at risk when he stood up for the Order against the repressive measures taken by the *Parlement* of Paris after the attempted assassination of Henri IV by Jean Chastel in December 1594.[47] Thus in 1598 Just-Louis found himself the object of a published *Arrêt de Parlement* ordering the seizure of his property and his destitution from titles and offices, although a private accommodation with the king was subsequently reached.[48] The Count of Roussillon (*bis*) had thus been controversially 'in the news' until just a few years before the writing of *All's Well*.

As for the University of Tournon itself, there is nothing in the official history of the institution to indicate international 'missionary' activity comparable to that of Reims or of Pont-à-Mousson, but it can hardly have failed to attract the notice of English intelligence – a possible source of information for Shakespeare. Certainly, there were English and Scottish students (Lambin, 1954, p. 29); there was also a particularly controversial faculty member, thanks to whom Tournon became a centre of production for Catholic propaganda in French and English. The Scottish Jesuit John Hay, who had been on the faculty at Pont-à-Mousson (where his brother Edmund was rector until undertaking secret negotiations with King James in 1582[49]), was based at Tournon from at least late 1583, and formally as professor of theology from 1584.[50] The French translation of Hay's exhortation to Scottish ministers (*Demandes faictes aux ministres d'escosse*, 1583) contains a dedication to 'Madame Claude de Turenne, dame de Tournon ctesse de Roussillon', dated 1 November 1583 (sigs A2ʳ– 3ᵛ).[51] There the author speaks of having himself sojourned in Scotland five years earlier – supposedly for health reasons (his physicians having prescribed exposure to his native climate) – where he busied himself in countering the nefarious practices of the Protestant clergy. He then returned initially to 'notre College de Paris [our College in Paris]', where he pursued his efforts by writing his book, now translated for the benefit of the ministers of Nîmes and elsewhere in the region, whose equal stubbornness he has witnessed over the last two years (this serves as a rough marker for his move to the South of France). The dedication, Hay stipulates, is due to the Countess's singular piety and unflinching constancy in defence of the Catholic religion, as God has seen fit to preserve it in France; the signature reads: 'A Tournon en *vostre* College [In Tournon at your College]' (my emphasis). Along the same lines, Hay's 1588 controversial pamphlet *L'Antimoine*, written in response to an attack by Théodore de Bèze and again addressing the situation in Scotland, was among the first works actually printed in Tournon – on presses offered to the university by the Count.[52]

VIII

Within very recent memory, then, the region could lay claim to something notably missing from Boccaccio's Roussillon but present in Shakespeare's: a strong-willed widowed Countess, bent on bringing up her son in his father's noble image. Still, by comparison with this possible original (she lived until 1591), Shakespeare's Countess has had her hard edges smoothed out in the benign climate of fairy-tale. The actual Countess, although by all accounts intellectually inclined and remarkably learned, was notoriously made of sterner stuff. Belleforest's praise of her in *La pastorale amovrevse* centres on her successful defence of Tournon against the threat of Huguenot attack in 1567 – a feat celebrated in the same year by Willemin, functioning as a sort of local court poet, in Latin verses subsequently translated by Belleforest.[53] By the time of the dedicatory preface to *L'histoire universelle* (1570), she had virtually repeated the exploit by deterring the Admiral Coligny himself from a further assault. So Belleforest records with admiration, and in language that strikes a chord with *All's Well*, for he contrasts her determined and effective actions with 'la vertue qui ne gist que en *parolles*, & n'est painte que en la brauade sans effait [the virtue that does not merely lie in words, and is not merely painted in ostentation without effect]' (1570, sig. †ij^v, my emphasis). (Indeed, Shakespeare's *miles gloriosus* might have done well to take warning from the point that 'ceux qui ne payent ceux, à qui ils sont obligez, que de simples *parolles* ... donnent moyen à l'ennemy de se preualoir de leur paresse [those who do not pay those to whom they are indebted except in simple words ... give means to the enemy to prevail over their lassitude]' [1570, sig. †iij^r, my emphasis].)

The Countess's celebrated heroism was, predictably, of the uncompromising Catholic kind, bound up with militant piety, aggressive royalism (grounded in ancestral tradition) and (perhaps more than incidentally) largess towards the Church. It is in these terms that she was due to be eulogized by the Reverend Coste in *Les éloges et les vies des reynes, des princesses et des dames illustres en piété*, *en courage et en doctrine* (first published 1630), who cites the tributes of both Willemin and Belleforest ('dont tous les sçavans en l'Histoire honorent la memoire [whose memory is honoured by all the learned in history]') in recounting her anti-Huguenot exploits (1647, 1: 481–82). Also insistent is the regional orientation: for Coste, the illustrious history of the Counts of Rous-sillon is bound up with that of Dauphiné, and as in *Les éloges de nos rois*, his discourse consolidates the integration of that relatively recent royal acquisition into the central idea of the French Catholic nation.[54]

As for the Countess's son, who still held the title of Count of Roussillon when Shakespeare's play was first performed (he lived until 1617), he did indeed distinguish himself according to his parents' example and Belleforest's hopes, not only in letters and learning (again in quite specifically Catholic terms[55]), but as a *Ligueur* combatting the Protestants on all possible occasions. There is reason to think that Just-Louis began his courtly career as one of Henri III's lesser *mignons* – a satirical poem of 1577 dismisses him as a 'Cigalle [cicada]'.[56] His rigour towards Huguenots in his region attracted notice in 1579, however, and his marriage took place in the Hôtel de Guise, even if the great duke had a more important engagement elsewhere.[57] His notable campaigns included another siege of Saint Agève (Belleforest, *La pastorale amovrevse*, Gaume, ed., 1980, p. 129, n. to p. 67), which, one may confidently conjecture, he would have viewed as symbolic revenge for his father's death.

To the extent that such an image of the Count of Roussillon hovered behind the youthful Bertram for Shakespeare and his audience, it is easier to appreciate that character's resistance to the erotic fable in which Helena engages him, with the support of a far less Amazonian mother than Claude de Turenne. The young man who vows eternal devotion at the conclusion of *All's Well*, accepting his dramatic destiny on the graceless condition that Helena has met the terms of his rash promise – 'If she, my liege, can make me know this clearly / I'll love her dearly, ever, ever dearly' (V.iii.309–10) – has proven notoriously difficult for audiences and critics to swallow as a romantic hero. That is perhaps finally because, like Hamlet (if in fewer dimensions), he is anamorphically misshapen, discernibly the product of intertextual *bricolage*. And in his case, too, the perspective that ironically deflates the heroic role imposed on him by the fiction depends on historical actuality. To ears attuned to Parolles' hollowness, Bertram's extravagant last *words* come close to parodically echoing his scape-goat's rationalization of entrapment: 'Who cannot be crush'd with a plot?' (IV.iii.314).

IX

Even apart from its presumed borrowing from his previous eulogy of the Countess, Belleforest's *La pastorale amovrevse* is not a notably original work; on the contrary, it is a close imitation of the second Eclogue (first published 1549) of the Spanish poet Garcilaso de la Vega, which likewise deploys its pastoral and amatory machinery in celebration of a noble family (the House of Alba).[58] In both, a similar pageant is produced by a magician adept in the cure of lovesick shepherds; both landscapes possess a restorative fountain. The treatment of the fountain, however, also signals a major difference – to the point of suggesting the source (the word is unavoidable) of Belleforest's inspiration. Here is its presentation at the opening of Garcilaso's poem:

> En medio del invierno está templada
> el agua dulce desta flara fuente,
> y en el verano más que nieve helada.

[In the midst of winter it is warm, the sweet water of that clear fountain, and in summer chillier than the snow.] (Garcilaso de la Vega, 1972, ll. 1–3)

The point here, as shortly appears, is to emblematize the Petrarchan lover's conventional capacity for freezing and burning at the same time, but the fountain itself could not be simpler and more straightforward, well within the scope of the (pastorally inflected) natural.

By comparison, the erotic paradox developed by Belleforest at the opening of *La pastorale amovrevse* depends on a fountain endowed with unusual properties indeed:

> Av plvs froid de l'hyuer, comme espris tout en feu
> Les Nymphes de ce mont tant nuit que iour m'ont veu
> Arresté, sur le bord pierreux d'vne fontaine
> Contemplant le surgeon clerluisant de sa veine,
> Laquelle en plein hiuer ressent le feu en soy,
> Et en l'ardeur brillant d'esté à [sic] ne sçay quoy
> Qui non moins l'enfroidist que si de glace esprise
> La terre se vestoit d'vne gelée grise
> Herissonnant le tout des horreurs de l'hiuer.

[In the coldest of winter, as if seized all in fire, the Nymphs of that mountain both night and day have seen me seated on the stony edge of a fountain, contemplating the clear-gleaming pulsation of its jet, which in the midst of winter retained fire within it, and in the shimmering heat of the summer had I know not what that rendered it no less cold than if, seized by ice, the ground clothed itself with a grey frost, all bristling with the horrors of winter.] (1980, pp. 1–2)

Conspicuously preternatural here is the water's quality of harbouring 'le feu' in the depth of winter – a point that might also have struck Shakespeare, when he sought a name for the lively old lord who introduces 'sprightly fire and motion' into the winter world of the French king's decrepitude, with the capacity 'to breathe life into a stone' and 'Quicken a rock'.[59]

It turns out that in adapting Garcilaso's dynastic encomium, Belleforest had local conditions very much in mind, and these were rather particular in the matter of the fountain. He may well have had further sources of information, but he need not have gone beyond Champier. In aid of establishing its hero's local identity, the opening of *La vie de Bayard* consists of 'La description des pays du Daulphiné [The description of the regions of Dauphiné]', beginning with its symbolic link to the Dolphin/Dauphin. Just as the dolphin is 'le poisson de mer le plus noble et charitable [the fish of the sea the most noble and charitable]', so Dauphiné is the natural centre of the chivalric ethic: 'terre noble domestique, laquelle produit les gens les plus humbles, courtoys, nobles, domesticques, piteables, humains, hardys et preulx en guerre, en paix charitable que gens ny nations qui soyent entres les Allobroges et gaules [a noble and homely soil, which produces the most humble, courteous, noble, homely, humane, bold, and valiant in war of the peoples and nations found between the Allobroges and the Gauls]' (Champier, 1992, p. 122). (Arguably, there is latent ethnic and geographical, as well as sexual, content in Lafew's image for the French king's revival: 'your dolphin is not lustier' [II.iii.26].) We are then given an account of four marvellous 'singularités [singularities]' of Dauphiné, including a heaven-sent medicine known as manna, 'de laquelle ordinairement sans aulcune sophistication usent tous les medecins de France et aultres provinces [which with no sophistication is used by all the physicians of France and other regions]' – and why not, then, a physician's daughter? It is 'ung don celeste, lequel dieu donne aulx provinces par especial priviliege [a heavenly gift, which God bestowed upon regions by special privilege]', and it was abundantly supplied to the French in Italy (Champier, 1992, pp. 128–29).

The first and foremost marvel, however, is 'la fontaine qui brusle [the fountain that burns]', which is invested at once with irreproachable materiality and mystical authority:

> c'est une fontaine ardante laquelle est située entre la cité de Grenoble et la cité de Dye, de laquelle parle sainct Augustin au .VII. chapitre du .XXI. Livre de la cité de Dieu disant ainsi. … je n'ay pas trouvé gens qui dient avoir veu la fontaine en epire, laquelle ont dict que les torches alumées sont esteinctes et ceulx qui sont pas alumées se alument, mais bien une telle avons ouy par certain estre en Gaule au près d'une cité nommée Grenoble; ce sont les propres paroles de sainct

Augustin. Ceste fontaine, à la toucher, est froide, et si on boute dedans de la paille ou chandelle, elle se alume comme si c'estoit flambe de feu.

[It is a burning fountain that is situated between the city of Grenoble and the city of Die, of which Saint Augustine speaks in the seventh chapter of the twenty-first book of *The City of God*, pronouncing thus: … 'I have not found anybody who claims to have seen the fountain in Epirus where it is said that lighted torches are extinguished and those which are not lit enkindle themselves. But we have heard tell that such a one indeed exists in Gaul near a city named Grenoble.' These are the very words of Saint Augustine. This fountain is cold to the touch, and if you put in it straw or candle-wick it alights as if it had been flamed with fire.] (Champier, 1992, p. 123)[60]

Champier adds that he will not dwell on the phenomenon because it has been examined 'très scientifiquement [very scientifically]' by 'ung jeusne et docte docteur nommé maistre [a young and learned doctor named master] Hieralume de montuis' (1992, p. 123). In fact, although this young doctor's name might seem too well suited to the subject to be real, the reference is to the very well-published and well-connected Hierosme de Monteux, also a native of Dauphiné, who served (with less than spectacular success, a cynic might note) as court physician to Henri II and François II; the treatise in question – an impressively intricate mixture of scholastic disputation and dithyrambic rapture – figures as the first item in a collection of his juvenilia published in 1556. The intertextual effect is to situate the fountain squarely at the junction of the marvellous and the real that conditions the approach of both Champier and Belleforest. And if the latter thus implicitly reinvokes the 'sprightly fire and motion' of Bayard to 'Quicken [the] rock' of the Dauphiné landscape on behalf of his own local heroes, he does so with Champier's all but explicit encouragement, for 'la maison de tornon' (1992, p. 222) figures prominently among those noble houses of Dauphiné enumerated by Champier in summing up the purpose of his story.

That purpose concerns making the most of the present, palpably diminished by Bayard's loss:

car le noble Bayard, à ceste heure, n'a aulcun vouloir ny indigence de nostre louange ny gloire, car nostre hystoire ny commendation de luy ne servent de riens à son ame au royaulme celeste, mais pourra servir à nous et à ceulx qui après nous viendront en ce monde.

[for the noble Bayard, at this hour, has no desire or need of our praise or glory, for our history and commendation of him may serve for nothing to his soul in the celestial realm, but it may serve for us and for those who shall come to this world after us.] (Champier, 1992, p. 223)

Champier has just described the hero's funeral and entombment in Grenoble – or rather, he has chosen not to describe them, lest his description impinge on the magnificence enshrined in memory:

> Et furent les obseques et funerailles faictes, comme s'il eust esté, non un lieu-tenant ou gouverneur, mais ung prince, et furent faictes si solempnelles que à cause que ne soye reputé avoir diminué d'icelles, m'en desporte pour le present.
>
> [And the obsequies and funerals were done, as if he had been not a lieutenant or a governor, but a prince, and they were done so solemnly that, lest I be accused of having diminished them, I defer speaking of them for the present.] (1992, p. 211)

The reverently nostalgic tone resembles that of the King in praising Bertram's father. The only possible consolation would be that offered by Bertram – 'His good remembrance, sir, / Lies richer in your thoughts than on his tomb' (I.ii.48–49) – despite the certainty of the reply, 'Would I were with him!' (52).

X

Helena's stock-in-trade is the miraculous, generated out of the ordinary. By deftly applying the 'remedies' that 'in ourselves do lie' (I.i.212) in the cause of impossible desire ("twere all one / That I should love a bright particular star / And think to wed it' [83–85]), she produces an escalating series of offers impossible to refuse. In precociously aligning himself with that project, Lafew is the first to be reanimated, in terms that echo Hamlet's affirmation to Horatio of 'more things in heaven and earth ... / Than are dreamt of in your philosophy' (*Ham.*, I.v.174–75):

> They say miracles are past; and we have our philosophical persons to make modern and familiar, things supernatural and causeless. Hence is it that we make trifles of terrors, ensconcing ourselves into seeming knowledge when we should submit ourselves to an unknown fear. (*AWW*, II.iii.1–6)

The miraculous defines itself precisely by defying normal logic. Thus if it seems out of Helena's way to be passing through Florence en route to Compostella (although the journey to Italy is notably shorter from Dauphiné, as Lambin pertinently calculated), that same symbolic destination has proved at least as difficult for Bayard's 'modern and philosophical' biographers to work into his known itinerary. Yet there it miraculously is, in a story recounted uniquely by Champier (though acknowledged as imaginatively 'tentant [tempting]' by Jacquart [1987, pp. 211–12]) – a detour somehow to be accommodated between Italian sojourns:

comme pelerin, sans se donner à congnoistre, ala à sainct Jaques en Galice, là où
il demeura aulcun temps pour veoir le pays jusques à sainct Saulvadour, retorna
à saint Jaques, et par la mer retourna en france.

[as a pilgrim, without letting himself be known, he went to Saint Jacques in
Galacia, where he remained a certain time to see the country as far as Saint
Salvador, returned to Saint Jacques, and by sea returned to France.] (Champier,
1992, p. 239)

But of course the most dramatically functional miracle staged by Helena,
the key to making *all well* at the ending she imposes, is her fictional return from
the 'undiscover'd country, from whose bourn / No traveller returns'. Together
with the invention of the Countess, this is also Shakespeare's most notable addition to the story of Giletta, and as a flagrant but symbolically charged
contrivance it pulls the play further in its contrary directions: at once towards
fairy-tale and towards demystification. In fact, a contemporary audience might
have recognized more reasons for this double movement than critics have done
– even including Lambin, who identified the underlying 'true story'.

For the story is evidently a true one, in its broad outline, although all
published versions derive from Marguerite de Valois, who decided to incorpo-
rate it in her *Mémoires* on the grounds that it was 'si remarquable, je ne puis
omettre à la raconter, faisant cette digression à mon discours [so remarkable, I
cannot omit to recount it, making this digression in my discourse]' (Viennot,
ed., 1999, p. 159). The tragic tale Marguerite recounts concerns the daughter
of one of her *dames d'honneur*, a girl 'agréable et aimable (car elle était plus que
belle, sa principale beauté étant la vertu et la grâce) [pleasant and attractive
(for she was more than lovely, her principal beauty consisting in her virtue and
grace)]' (1999, p. 159), who, while staying in the household of her sister,
married to the Seigneur de Balançon, was courted by the latter's brother, the
Marquis de Varambon, who wished to marry her. His brother, however, was
determined that he should go into the Church, and so the girl's mother
removed her from the situation. Marguerite relates the sequel – and there is no
alternative to citing her powerful narrative at length:

Et comme elle était femme un peu terrible et rude, sans avoir égard que cette fille
était grande et méritait un plus doux traitement, elle la gourmande et la crie sans
cesse, ne lui laissant presque jamais l'œil sec, bien qu'elle ne fît nulle action qui
ne fût très louable – mais c'était la sévérité naturelle de sa mere.
    Elle, ne souhaitant que de se voir hors de cette tyrannie, reçut une extrême
joye quand elle vit que j'allais en Flandre, pensant bien que le marquis de Varembon [sic] s'y trouverait, comme il fit, et qu'étant lors en état de se marier, ayant
du tout quitté la robe longue, il la demanderait à sa mere, et que par le moyen de
ce mariage elle se trouverait délivrée des rigueurs de sa mère. À Namur, le marquis

de Varembon et le jeune Balançon son frère s'y trouvèrent, comme j'ai dit. Le jeune de Balançon, qui n'était pas (de beaucoup) si agréable que l'autre, accoste cette fille, la recherche; et le marquis de Varembon, tant que nous fûmes à Namur, ne fait pas seulement semblant de la connaître ... Le dépit, le regret, l'ennui lui serrent tellement le cœur – elle s'étant contrainte de faire bonne mine tant qu'il fut présent, sans montrer de s'en soucier – soudain qu'ils furent hors du bateau où ils nous dirent adieu, qu'elle se trouve tellement saisie qu'elle ne pût plus respirer qu'en criant, et avec des douleurs mortelles. N'ayant nulle autre cause de son mal, la jeunesse combat huit ou dix jours la Mort, qui, armée du dépit se rend enfin victorieuse, la ravissant à sa mere et à moi, qui n'en fîmes moins de deuil l'une que l'autre. Car sa mere, bien qu'elle fût fort rude, l'aimait uniquement.

Ses funérailles étant commandées, les plus honorables qu'il se pouvait faire – pour être de grande maison comme elle était, même appartenant à la reine ma mere – , le jour venu de son enterrement, l'on ordonne quatre gentilshommes des miens pour porter le corps, l'un desquels était La Bussière, qui l'avait durant sa vie passionnément adorée sans le lui avoir osé découvrir, pour la vertu qu'il connaissait en elle et pour l'inégalité, qui lors allait portant ce mortel faix et mourant autant de fois de sa mort qu'il était mort de son amour. Ce funeste convoi étant au milieu de la rue qui allait à la grande église, le marquis de Varembon, coupable de ce triste accident, quelques jours après mon partement de Namur s'étant repenti de sa cruauté, et son ancienne flamme s'étant de nouveau rallumée (ô étrange fait!) par l'absence, qui par la présence n'avait pu être émue, se résout de la venir demander à sa mère, se confiant peut-être à la bonne fortune qui l'accompagne d'être aimé de toutes celles qu'il recherche – ... Et se promettant que la faute lui serait aisément pardonnée de sa maîtresse, ... prie don Juan lui donner une commission vers moi; et venant en diligence, il arrive justement sur le point que ce corps, aussi malheureux qu'innocent et glorieux en sa virginité, était au milieu de cette rue. La presse de cette pompe l'empêche de passer. Il regarde que c'est. Il avise de loin, au milieu d'une grande et triste troupe de personnes en deuil, un drap blanc couvert de chapeaux de fleurs. Il demande que c'est. Quelqu'un de la ville lui répond que c'était un enterrement. Lui, trop curieux s'avance jusques au premier du convoi et importunément presse de lui dire de qui c'est. Ô mortelle réponse! L'Amour ainsi vengeur de l'ingrate inconstance veut faire éprouver à son âme ce que, par son dédaigneux oubli, il a fait souffrir au corps de sa maîtresse: les traits de la Mort. Cet ignorant qu'il pressait lui répond que c'était Mademoiselle de Tournon. À ce mot, il se pâme et tombe de cheval, il le faut emporter en un logis comme mort. Voulant plus justement, en cette extrémité, lui rendre l'union en la mort que trop tard en la vie il lui avait accordée, son âme, que je crois, allant dans le tombeau requérir pardon à celle que son dédaigneux oubli y avait mise, le laissa quelque temps sans aucune apparence de vie; d'où étant revenu l'anima de nouveau pour lui faire éprouver la Mort qui, d'une seule fois, n'eût assez puni son ingratitude.

[And since she was a woman rather ferocious and harsh, without considering that that daughter was grown-up and deserved gentler treatment, she kept after her and yelled at her incessantly, hardly ever leaving her a dry eye, although she did nothing that was not wholly praiseworthy; but such was the natural severity of her mother.

She, wishing nothing but to see herself out of that tyranny, experienced intense joy when she saw that I was going into Flanders, considering that the Marquis de Varambon would be found there, as he was, and that, being then in a condition to marry, having finally given up all idea of the priesthood, he would ask her of her mother, and by means of that marriage she might be delivered from her mother's rigours. At Nemours the Marquis de Varambon and the young Balançon, his brother, were present, as I said. The young Balançon, who was not nearly as agreeable as the other, approached the girl, pursued her; and the Marquis de Varambon, as long as we were at Nemours, never so much as pretended to know her. The bitterness, the regret, the pain so pressed on her heart (she being constrained to put on a cheerful countenance when he was present, without showing that she cared) that as soon as they were out of the boat where they had said good-bye to us, she found herself so seized that she could no longer breathe without crying out, and with mortal pains. Having no other cause of affliction, her youth fought for eight or ten days against death, which, armed with the pain of disappointment, finally rendered itself victorious, ravishing her from her mother and from me, neither of us mourning less than the other, for her mother, although she was very harsh, loved her only.

Her funeral ceremonies being provided for as honourably as could be done, given the great house involved, indeed one that depended on the Queen my mother, the day having come for her burial, four gentlemen of mine were arranged to carry the body, one of whom was La Bussière, who, while she lived, had passionately adored her without daring to reveal it to her, on account of the virtue he knew to be in her and the inequality, and who then carried those mortal remains, dying as often from her death as he had died of his love. This mournful procession being in the middle of the street which led to the great church, the Marquis de Varambon, responsible for this sad occurrence, a few days after my departure from Namur, having repented for his cruelty, and his former flame being enkindled anew (O strange phenomenon!) by her absence, which by her presence could never be moved, resolved himself to come and ask her of her mother, having confidence perhaps in that good fortune that follows him to be loved by all women he seeks, ... and telling himself the fault would readily be pardoned by his mistress, ... asked Don Juan to send him on an errand to me, and, arriving in the carriage just at the moment when that corpse, as unfortunate as innocent, and glorious in its virginity, was in the middle of the street, the crowd of the ceremony prevented him from passing. He looked to see what was going on. He became aware from afar, amidst a large and sad troupe of people in mourning, of a white cloth covered with wreaths of flowers. He asked what the occasion was. Someone from the town told him that it was a burial. He, too curious, advanced to the person at the head of the procession and importunately asked him to tell him whose it was. O mortal answer! Love, thus avenging his ungrateful inconstancy, wished to have his soul feel what by his disdainful negligence he had caused the body of his mistress to suffer: the strokes of death. The unknowing man whom he pressed replied that it was Mademoiselle de Tournon. At that word he fainted and fell from his horse. They had to carry him to a chamber as if dead. Wishing more justly, in that extremity, to render her the union in death which in life he had granted her too late, his soul, as I believe, going forth into the tomb to ask pardon of her whom his disdainful neglect put there, left him a certain time without any appearance of life; and being thence returned, revived him in order to make him again experience Death, which, by one occurrence alone, would not have sufficiently punished his ingratitude.] (1999, pp. 160–62)

It goes without saying that the 'Mademoiselle de Tournon' in question was the daughter of the Countess of Roussillon, who in her widowhood had entered the Queen of Navarre's service (apparently much to the credit of both); and although Marguerite does not actually say so, at least in any of the extant texts, of course the daughter's name was Hélène.[61]

How and when Shakespeare encountered this story – as he assuredly did, given the double overlap with *All's Well* and *Hamlet* – are questions intriguing in the extreme but probably never to be answered. (I remain unconvinced by Lambin's leap of faith: 'Nous le saurons sans doute un jour ou l'autre [We shall undoubtedly know some day]' [1954, p. 29].) As with some of the material bearing on Antoine de Bourbon, however, it is difficult to exclude the possibility of access to Navarrois manuscripts (see above, pp. 34–35, 42–43). Marguerite's *Mémoires*, although not published until 1628, thirteen years after her death (and in incomplete form), were composed during her years of exile at Usson in Auvergne (1587–1605). They seem to have circulated in manuscript and were evidently known to the English-connected Brantôme, to whom they are dedicated.[62] Moreover, *pace* the Lefranc-Lambin school, with its vested interest in the playwright's (that is, Derby's) personal contact with the family of Tournon, it is arguably the filtering effect of Marguerite's narrative that distinctly colours the two plays clearly in question. It is she who places herself in the position of substitute mother taken up by Shakespeare's Countess in relation to Helena, Gertrude in relation to Ophelia. It is her terms of praise, however commonplace ('sa principale beauté étant la vertu et la grâce'), that resonate as Helena's keynotes: 'it was the death of the most virtuous gentlewoman that ever nature had praise for creating' (IV.v.8–10); 'she was … the herb of grace' (15–16);[63] 'by grace itself I swear' (I.iii.215); 'The greatest Grace lending grace' (II.i.159). Such elements, which serve to shape and direct the story, make simple verbal gossip an unlikely source.

It is tempting to date Shakespeare's acquaintance from at least 1594–95 – that is, not long after Marguerite began work on her *Mémoires* (Viennot, ed., 1999, p. 23).[64] For apart from Helen of Troy – and an association with the latter has also found its place in criticism of *All's Well*, with the encouragement of Lavatch (I.iii.67 ff.)[65] – Shakespeare otherwise gave the name Helen(a) only to the maiden of *A Midsummer Night's Dream*, likewise love-sick and repudiated.[66] In any case, there is surely no disputing the significant parallel with *Hamlet*: the protagonist's fraught encounter with the funeral procession of Ophelia, whom he had courted then spurned, has no such precedent elsewhere.[67] It is in this context that Parolles' dismissive banter – 'virginity murthers itself, and should be buried in highways out of all sanctified limit, as a desperate offendress against nature' (I.i.136–39) – resonates most meaningfully with the Gravediggers' discussion and the Priest's retort to Laertes:

> Her death was doubtful;
> And but that great command o'ersways the order,
> She should in ground unsanctified been lodg'd
> Till the last trumpet: for charitable prayers
> Shards, flints, and pebbles should be thrown on her.
> Yet here she is allow'd her virgin crants,
> Her maiden strewments, and the bringing home
> Of bell and burial.
>
> (*Ham.*, V.i.220–27)[68]

For his part, Laertes effectively demands for his sister the rites accorded Hélène de Tournon, likewise 'glorieu[se] en sa virginité' and with 'un drap blanc couvert de chapeaux de fleurs'. When Gertrude adds flowery 'Sweets to the sweet' (V.i.236), feelingly mourns Ophelia and regrets the thwarting of her marriage with Hamlet (a puzzling detail for some critics), her passing resemblance to the bereft Countess of *All's Well* takes on further intertextual depth:

> I hop'd thou shouldst have been my Hamlet's wife:
> I thought thy bride-bed to have deck'd, sweet maid,
> And not have strew'd thy grave.
>
> (237–39)

Finally, if Laertes' curse – 'O, triple woe / Fall ten times treble on that cursed head / Whose wicked deed thy most ingenious sense / Depriv'd thee of' (239–42) – seems short-circuited first by Hamlet's aggression, then by his quick and 'accidental' end, that impression gains from the inward affliction visited on the unkind marquis – specifically, again, according to Marguerite's narrative.

XI

When he grafted the true-to-life *histoire tragique* of Hélène of Tournon onto
the fairy-tale of Giletta, Shakespeare retained the latter's basic family situation,
except in introducing the figure of the Countess. He came as close as possible,
moreover, to making the latter into a mother-figure for Helena, inverting the
real Countess's character from severe and tyrannical to indulgent and nurturing.
It is precisely as a sympathetic mother that the Countess actively presents
herself at the outset ('You know, Helen, / I am a mother to you ... ' [I.iii.
132–33]), as well as in her profound mourning at Helena's supposed death: 'If
she had ... cost me the dearest groans of a mother I could not have owed her
a more rooted love' (IV.v.10–12). Indeed, when the Countess pursues the point
in her opening conversation with Helena – and thereby triggers the horrified
reaction, 'The Count Rossillion cannot be my brother' (I.iii.150) – it is hard
not to suspect a teasing of the audience, as if by evoking a situation in which
such was precisely the case. There could not be a more graphic figure for the
initial impossibility of Helena's love, hence for the transition she effectively
manages from one narrative to another ('My mother greets me kindly ... '
[II.iv.1]).

Intertextually, then, we are returned to the starting point of this discussion:
the fairy-tale fulfilment of that love as enacting Ophelia's revenge, the invention
of 'a military policy how virgins might blow up men'. Still, however much forgetting is imposed upon the characters, the audience is never allowed to forget
that, in the patriarchal 'real world', virginity is not a strong card to play. It is one
that can be played only by keeping it forever in one's hand – at the cost, in some
sense, of life itself – or by discarding it. Parolles' words (as is hardly surprising)
have truth in them too: 'Virginity, by being once lost, may be ten times found;
by being ever kept it is ever lost' (I.i.128–29). So Helena acknowledges in reck-
oning her chances (and speaking truer than she knows, at least intertextually):
'I will stand for't a little, though therefore I die a virgin' (131–32). Parolles is
also putting into words the unspoken assumptions behind the warnings to
Ophelia by her brother and father regarding her 'chaste treasure', her 'maiden
presence' (*Ham.*, I.iii.31, 121); stereotypically, they regard virginity as a prize
of combat rather than a weapon: 'Set your entreatments at a higher rate / Than
a command to parlay' (122–23).

Such a discourse of patriarchal power-relations resounds churlishly against
All's Well's background of fairy-tale possibility:

> ... follows it, my lord, to bring me down
> Must answer for your raising? I know her well:
> She had her breeding at my father's charge –

> A poor physician's daughter my wife! Disdain
> Rather corrupt me ever!
> (II.iii.112–16)

But then even the quasi-magical power of the King on fairy-tale's behalf is subsumed within the material game: "Tis only title thou disdain'st in her, the which / I can build up' (117–18). The resemblance to Lear, who presumes the omnipotence of his pronouncements – and who gives the game away by doing as much tearing down as building up of title – bespeaks tragic self-delusion.

From many quarters of the world around them, on the contrary, contemporaries would have recognized not only the unyielding discourse of social relations but its propensity to assimilate and appropriate romance. Certainly, the combination resounded around the nobility of Tournon-Roussillon – from *La pastorale amovrevse* of 1569 (with its immediate re-edition), to the 1583 entry celebrating the incorporation (and reduction to orthodoxy) of the House of Rochefoucauld by loss of virginity under the standard controlled conditions. Thus the 'Ode' that constitutes the virtual centrepiece of Urfé's published record gathers up all the familiar elements of the family myth – the heroic lost father, the indomitable mother, the latter's association with the Queen of Navarre, the glorious ancestral sacrifices in Italy (Pavia itself is all but painted as a triumph – a fairy-tale triumph indeed!) – and notably adds the resplendent marriages of Just-Louis's two (surviving) sisters:

> Vn tant deuot Pere il eut,
>   Si vertueux, & si sage,
>   Que de Iustice il reçeut
>   Le nom de IVST en partage.
> Dieu Mere luy a donné
>   Vne CLAVDE de Turene,
>   Qui tant dextre a gouuerné
>   De Nauarre la grand Reine. ...
> Que dirons nous de ses sœurs
>   CADAROVSSE ET BALANCONNE.
>   Iointes aux plus grands Seigneurs
>   D'Auignon, & de Bourgongne?
> De ce TOVRNON les Ayeux
>   A Naples, & à Pauie,
>   Par leur fer victorieux
>   Feirent trembler l'Italie.

[Such a devout father he had, so virtuous, and so wise, that in justice he received as his lot the name of Just. God give him as a mother Claude de Turenne, who so ably served as governess to the great Queen of Navarre. ... What shall we say of his sisters, Caderousse and Balançon, joined to the greatest lords of Avignon and Burgundy? The ancestors of this Tournon, at Naples and at Pavia, by their victorious swords, caused Italy to tremble.] (Urfé, ed. Gaume, 1976, pp. 35–36)

Such a synthetic formulation, with its implicit claim to completeness, might well have seemed a challenge to a wry-minded playwright to furnish a supplement on behalf of the present-absence, the unmentioned and eternally virginal third sister whose memory is suppressed – symbolically, Cordelia in relation to Goneril and Regan. From this perspective, Hélène effectively makes her own surprise triumphant entry in the place of the dynastically suitable bride anticipated by the hero. Intertextually, one might say, this is the bed-trick to end (well?) all bed-tricks. And since it is Lafew's daughter who, in the dazzling light of Helena's sun/son, is consigned to the shadows, this is where it becomes actively functional that Shakespeare uses for that daughter, uniquely in the canon, the actual name of the current Count of Roussillon's bride: Madeleine.[69]

XII

Shakespeare's Helena succeeds where the King has failed by exploiting her position as an outsider. She knows that she must perform her illusion on a cosmic scale, loving as she does 'a bright particular star / ... so above' her that 'In his bright radiance and collateral light / Must I be comforted, not in his sphere' (I.i.84–87). And she has the privilege of refashioning and reapplying the precepts of a dead father – in a basic sense, of forgetting him – rather than having the perspective of impossibility reinforced by a living one:

> ... I went round to work,
> And my young mistress thus I did bespeak:
> 'Lord Hamlet is a prince out of thy star.
> This must not be.'
> (*Ham.*, II.ii.139–42)

Within the patriarchal structure, the corollary of remembrance is, finally, rue (cf. *Ham.*, IV.v.173 ff.), the daughter's obligatory drowning – as it were, in her own tears – when her father dies.

To produce the illusion that the stars have changed places, Helena effectively uses her father's remedy – whether or not miraculous in itself – as if it were the magic wand of the aptly named Sydéré. When she disappears from this world, she might as well be entering the magical cave. It is as if she manipulates the underground mechanisms of memory so as to inscribe herself as the Countess of Roussillon within the family pageant. The model of Claude de la Tour is, after all, not so far removed – the 'Amazonne' (Belleforest, *La pastorale amovrevse*, ed. Gaume, 1980, p. 63) who, far from transgressing femininity, exalts it by uniting to it the courage of manhood. In defence of the citadel that manifests at once her perfect chastity and her entitlement, the Countess literally devised 'a military policy' to 'blow up men':

> ... honorée en tout lieu
> Excellente en beauté, admirable en sagesse,
> Des hommes imitant le cœur & la proüesse
> Des femmes la douceur, la pitié, la bonté
> Aymant le simple cœur, l'honneur, la chasteté
> Et pour ses grandz vertuz, de chacun estimée.
> Elle donc se voyant si fortement armée,
> De soldatz, de deuoir, de Iustice, & de droit
> Fait braquer le canon, & ses enseignes reuoit,
> Visite toutz les lieux des Tours, de la muraille
> Despite l'ennemy, met ses gens en bataille.

[... honoured in every place, excellent in beauty, admirable in wisdom, imitating the heart and prowess of men, of women the mildness, the pity, the goodness; loving the simple heart, honour, chastity, and for her great virtues, by each esteemed. Thus seeing herself so strongly armed, with soldiers, duty, justice and right, she has the cannon aimed and sees to her banners, visits all the places of the towers, of the rampart, in spite of the enemy sets her men in battle-order.] (1980, p. 64)

If the perfect synthesis of feminine and masculine here also evokes 'le chevalier sans peur et sans reproche', we are thereby reminded that Bayard's very significance is inextricable from his inability to reproduce himself in posterity, his confinement to memory. Precisely the contrary is the message of *La pastorale amovrevse*, as it is the condition of Helena's renunciation of the eternal virginity of Hélène de Tournon and return from the dead as the Countess of Roussillon. The Countess, Belleforest affirms, was the 'femme d'vn demy-Dieu' (1980, p. 64) – an epithet perhaps better adapted to the Bayard that was Bertram's father, as he is remembered. In any case, the latter is now revived in a virtual pageant extending into the future. Helena need only become, like Belleforest's Countess, the 'Mere de beaux enfans ... [Mother of beautiful children]' (1980, p. 64), which is indeed where the play chooses to end. It is a pageant in which Bertram's place has been pre-defined – 'Be thou bless'd, Bertram, and succeed thy father / In manners as in shape!' (I.i.57–58) – and he is compelled to take it by the revelation that he has been taken at, and by, his word; in a reversal of the Parolles 'plot', the authority of fairy-tale has changed the stars in their spheres, and the shadows conjured by Helena have become substance, emerging, if not from Plato's, at least from Sydéré's, cave in material form:

> Diana.   ...
>   Dead though she be she feels her young one kick.
>   So there's my riddle: one that's dead is quick,
>   And now behold the meaning.
>
>   [Re-]enter Widow [with] Helena.
>
> King.   Is there no exorcist
>   Beguiles the truer office of mine eyes?
>   Is't real that I see?
>
> Helena.   No, my good lord;
>   'Tis but the shadow of a wife you see;
>   The name and not the thing.
>
> Bertram.   Both, both. O pardon!
>   (V.iii.296–302)

Thus indeed is Bertram's promise (in both senses) fulfilled despite himself. Thus is Helena's father's 'knowledge' finally 'set up against mortality' (I.i. 28–29).

But 'kick' and 'quick' stubbornly rhyme with 'trick' (as in 'bed-trick'), and if Helena recreates herself as more than natural, she is materially destined to remain, like Rosalind ('I have, since I was three year old, convers'd with a magician' [*AYL*, V.ii.59–60]), the sorcerer's apprentice rather than the sorcerer – much less the sorcerer's source. Her very pregnancy, psychoanalysis would probably maintain, is proof that the 'baguette magique' is invariably masculine, and it is certainly true that both heroines' magical ability to provide the transcendental solution to all the riddles is an illusion. The illusion depends on inventing riddles to which there is no solution but only an imposed 'meaning'. Ultimately, that meaning must be incarnated in female and contingent 'true' identities – versions of 'To you I give myself, for I am yours' (*AYL*, V.iv.116–17, 118). In these terms, the audience, which after all is in on the secret, is likely to supply an answer of its own that enfolds the surprised 'wonder' of the dazzled characters into something like the rueful jadedness of Lavatch.

Epilogue

Modern French has a colloquial expression – more or less humorous but always with a bitter edge – which, while not precisely translatable, quite precisely translates such a response: 'Ah, la vache!' In a similar way, English idiom is capable of conflating local discovery with the impossibility of ultimate knowledge ('I might have known!', 'Wouldn't you know it!', 'What do you know!'), or of assimilating speech to muteness ('You don't say so!'), or of recording wonder by denying it ('No wonder!'), or of diffusing it through a prismatic expletive ('Damn!'). Such expressions serve equally whether the 'news' is good or bad, and so straddle optimism and pessimism – as does, for that matter, the proverb, 'All's well that ends well'. These are all possible translations, depending on the context, of 'Ah, la vache!' It is arguably such a response that an audience, privy to the manipulations that precede, supplies as an overlay on the discoveries of both Parolles ('Who cannot be crush'd with a plot?') and Bertram ('Both, both. O pardon!'). 'Ah, la vache!' amounts to a bitter and petty shrug on a cosmic scale; it is the anagnorisis of aporia, the recognition of the tragedy of absent meaning as 'always already' present within the human comedy.

The special match between Lavatch's character as 'a shrewd knave and an unhappy' (IV.v.60) and the entropic society of the play has rightly attracted much attention. Nowhere does he better exemplify that point than by his 'answer that will serve all men' or 'fits all questions' (II.ii.13, 15–16), and always from below or behind – namely, 'O Lord, sir!' (40–56, *passim*). Beyond the obvious satire against the pretentious at a loss for words – and Parolles' comments on Helena's 'miracle' cure immediately come in as illustration (II.iii.11 ff.) – the joke expresses the essential helplessness of the human condition in the face of, or at least when seated upon, its most banal vicissitudes. Lafew calls for greater accommodation of mystery, but that is to play Helena's game by keeping the category apart. The foolish wisdom of the Clown knows better, and his universal answer takes to heart the empirical evidence that 'miracles are past' (1), while withholding judgement as to whether they ever existed. His doubt extends, significantly, to the 'miracle' of love: 'I begin to love as an old man loves money, with no stomach' (III.ii.15–16). Humanity is going through the *motions*, puppet-like, but the clock is running down.

The less-than-convincing stabs taken by criticism at explaining the name of *All's Well*'s relentlessly worldly-wise fool (these include, in my judgement, 'la vache à Colas') make it tempting to suppose that the connotations of 'Ah, la vache!' might have been accessible to the play's first audiences, ready to be triggered by the unique mention of that name, when the fallen Parolles addresses him in the final act: 'Good Master Lavatch, give my Lord Lafew this letter ... ' (V.ii.1–2). Prudence is in order, however. I cannot track the expression, whose origin remains mysterious, farther back than the nineteenth century; neither can several far more accomplished French-language scholars than I. Let me, therefore, in concluding both this chapter and this book, retain the spirit but return the letter to more certain territory.

To consult Cotgrave's fascinating and remarkably accomplished French-English dictionary of 1611[70] is to be struck by the prominence and broad significance attributed to the expression, 'manger de la vache enragée' (literally, 'eat mad cow'). The phrase refers literally to being desperate enough to consume the meat of a rabid animal, and 'vache enragée' is still virtual shorthand for 'hardship', but the lexicographer confirms that the senses of *enrager* itself extended to human distraction of various kinds,[71] including folly – witness his citation of the proverb, 'Vn fol vn enragé': '*Once a foole euer madde; or there's little difference between a foole & a madde man*' (Cotgrave, 1611, s.v. 'enragé'). More immediately to the point, Cotgrave elaborates English equivalents for 'Il a mangé de la vache enragée' that evoke the universe of *All's Well* generally, and the crushed Parolles in particular:

> *He hath drunke of many waters, passed many pikes, tryed many experiments; he hath beene well practised in, or beaten vnto, the course of the world.* (1611, s.v. 'vache')

It is certainly not anachronistic, then, and hardly seems far-fetched, to suppose that a range of related 'French meanings' (I cite Hunter once more [1959, ed., p. xxv]) might be set in play when Parolles names the comedy's formal incarnation of folly, whose services as intermediary he is reduced to humbly begging:

> Good Master Lavatch, give my Lord Lafew this letter; I have ere now, sir, been better known to you, when I have held familiarity with fresher clothes; but I am now, sir, muddied in Fortune's mood, and smell somewhat strongly of her strong displeasure. (V.ii.1–5)

It is now the prerogative of Lavatch to fob off the fallen courtier with words, sustaining the intersection with Cotgrave's images of attrition through privation ('fall'n into the unclean fish-pond of [Fortune's] displeasure' [20–21]), and when Lafew offers succour, he does so on the understanding that Parolles has taken on the (double) identity of the Clown by whose means he now pursues survival. '[T]hough you are a fool and a knave you shall eat' (50) harks back to the lord's previous attempt to resolve the Clown's nature: 'Whether dost thou profess thyself – a knave or a fool?' (IV.v.20–21). Beyond this, it recalls Parolles' confident discovery and dismissal, which were immediately turned back prophetically against him:

> *Parolles.* Away! Th'art a knave.
>
> *Clown.* You should have said, sir, 'Before a knave th'art a knave'; that's 'Before me, th'art a knave'. This had been truth, sir.
>
> *Parolles.* Go to, thou art a witty fool; I have found thee.

> *Clown.* Did you find me in your self, sir, or were you taught to find
> me? ... The search, sir, was profitable; and much fool may
> you find in you, even to the world's pleasure and the increase of
> laughter.
>
> (II.iv.27–35)

Parolles, then, is finally forced wretchedly and desperately to acknowledge his
adversary by name, and so to come into the open as having not only to eat but
thoroughly to digest 'de la vache enragée'. And again there is a parallel with the
newly penitent Bertram, who behaved, according to the King, 'As mad in folly'
when he 'lack'd the sense' (V.iii.3) to recognize Helena's excellence.

This point returns us to *All's Well* as poised on the Shakespearean tragic
threshold (probably facing forwards). To cross that threshold, as with *Macbeth*
and especially *King Lear*, is to privilege apocalypse at midnight, the horror of
seeing the devil in the face (God having turned His face away). Here, it is not
yet midnight (and it will never be), but five minutes to, thanks to the rear-guard
action fought on behalf of the retreat, or 'fading', of comedy by two unlikely
heroes: a virgin who blows up men and a clown who deflates them – and who
invokes the 'prince of darkness' (IV.v.39) in familiar, not fearful, terms. But to
fight the good fight for comedy is inevitably to problematize it, as criticism of
Shakespeare's late comedies has made all but official ('Problem Plays'), and
precisely because the aphanisis enacted in *All's Well* is diffused across an entire
society and endlessly self-renewable, the figuration of subjectivity as absence
and loss may have more disquieting implications.

Most fundamentally, an audience is thereby cut off from catharsis. Whatever
precise meaning that term may legitimately carry for early modern tragedy, it
corresponds to a species of satisfaction that something is thoroughly over and
done with. An audience may be exempt from the tragic reflexes of pity and fear
(again, whatever meaning those terms possess in the cultural context), but at
the cost of experiencing its own susceptibility to being 'crush'd with a plot', like
Parolles or Bertram, in that the inescapable contingency of the self on the Other
is thereby starkly projected. There is arguably no more terrifying revelation of
human insubstantiality than Parolles' ultimate fall-back position: 'Simply the
thing I am / Shall make me live' (IV.iii.322–23). It is a supremely self-undoing
affirmation, which, by begging the question (what 'thing' is he?), prepares us
to see him as a perpetual beggar, doomed to be unendingly 'found' and 'lost'
(II.iii.204–5, V.ii.41–42) – and, perhaps most disturbingly of all, noisily finding
religion: 'I praise God for you' (V.ii.52). On the same principle as Puck's superficially reassuring, 'Think but this, and all is mended ... ' (*MND*, V.i.424), such
is precisely the ball thrown into the audience's court by the distinctive Epilogue:
'*The king's a beggar, now the play is done*' (*AWW*, Epi.1). As the macabre excesses

of Jacobean tragedy may confirm, physical, perhaps even metaphysical horror, and even when conceived in Christian terms – 'Ah, Mephistopheles!' – is finally more *vivable* than *horror vacui*, however mediated by laughter: 'Ah, la vache!'

Notes

1 Nevertheless, the label is applied by an increasing number of scholars – Wilcox, 2008, for one – for reasons that generally match my own thinking.

2 See my *Self-Speaking*, 1997, esp. Ch. 1 (pp. 1–34).

3 The Oxford editors offer none for their re-assignment of the play to 1606–7 in the second edition of *The Complete Works* (2005), but such late dating – which would again place it on the tragic threshold, though facing in the other direction – has had sporadic precedent. Given that the only evidence is inferential, I would accord most weight to the stylistic and thematic links with the rest of the canon. Cf. the recent rethinking of the issue by Leggatt in his Introduction to the updated New Cambridge edition (Fraser and Leggatt, eds, 2003); Leggatt notes that the other Shakespearean plays that *AWW* 'echoes (or anticipates)' (p. 10) date from 1604 or earlier and concludes, 'if we place it in 1603, we may not be far wrong' (p. 11).

4 Used for *AWW* citations in this chapter is Hunter, ed., 1959.

5 Witness the evocative comments of Anne Barton in her *Riverside Shakespeare* Introduction:

> *All's Well That Ends Well* is a play filled with nostalgia for the past, concerned to evoke the remembrance of better times. Rossillion, where the action begins and ends, is a Chekhovian backwater, elegiac and autumnal, a world preserved in amber. (1997, p. 534)

The invocation of Chekhov bears witness to the tendency to transcendentalize, rather than historicize, such nostalgia. For a stimulating approach in terms of desire, identity and social relations, see Sullivan, 2005, pp. 44–64.

6 A copy of the 1560 edition of the *Heptaméron* was owned by Elizabeth's ambassador to France, Sir Thomas Smith – see http://www2.lib.virginia.edu/rmds/port folio/gordon/literary/marguerite/heptameron.html (accessed March 2011).

7 See above, pp. 9–11.

8 Strangely, the closest French royal case seems never to have been brought to bear by criticism – that of François I, who, for several years before his death suffered from a lower-body (though not anal) abscess, which seems to have aged him prematurely. Neglected, too, is the very recent 'notorious' (*AWW*, I.i.33) instance of Henri III, who suffered from childhood from a chronic fistula; it was situated, however, between his nose and his eye.

9 Nothing in the thorough English-language biography by Baumgartner (1988) appears to support Hopkins's association of that notably vigorous monarch, much given to violent exercise, with the portrait offered by Shakespeare. Cf. Romier, 1909, pp. 16–19, *passim*. In fact, although there had been talk of a

fertility-inhibiting deformity in Henri until he produced a child by a mistress at nineteen, the prolonged lack of fecundity in the marriage made in 1533 between Catherine and Henri when they were both fifteen (Henri would not even become Dauphin until two years later) was at least as widely attributed to her as to him, and a divorce was being actively considered. See Sournia, 1981, pp. 90–91, and Erlanger, 1955, pp. 115–31, 148–49, 173–74. The first of Catherine de Medici's ten children, François, was born on 16 January 1544, more than three years before Henri succeeded to the throne.

10   See above, p. 20.

11   See my *French Origins*, 2010, pp. 8–11.

12   *Shakespeare, Marlowe and the Politics of France*, 2002, p. 40.

13   I cite Le Maçon's translation, which Shakespeare may have consulted, mainly because Painter's is widely available elsewhere.

14   Wilcox perhaps goes a bit far in stating simply that 'the cause does not concern the French' (2008, p. 85); the monarch's declaration that his subjects may 'stand on either part' (I.ii.15) signals a formal stance of neutrality.

15   See my *French Origins*, 2010, p. 91n.1.

16   On the 'myth' of Monluc's brutality, see Sournia, 1981, pp. 376–84.

17   Jouanna *et al.*, eds, 1998, p. 1114. For a politically astute, if somewhat partisan, biography, largely based on Monluc's own account, see Sournia, 1981.

18   All citations from Monluc in the present chapter are taken from Courteault's admirable variorum edition of the *Commentaires* (1964) and appeared in the first printed version of 1592; I do not reproduce the typographical distinction of the different textual states.

19   Sournia, 1981, pp. 72–73; the upshot was the French victory at Cerisole in Piedmont. The dramatic arousal of enthusiasm evoked by Montluc himself (1964, p. 149) is confirmed by other memorialists (Martin Du Bellay, Tavannes), who report that some of the young men left without even taking leave of the king (Romier, 1909, p. 30 and n.2).

20   Cf. Sournia, 1981, pp. 97 and esp. 153 regarding the siege of Volpiano during the campaign of 1555: 'Encore une fois, à l'annonce d'un beau fait de guerre, on vit arriver de Paris la jeunesse de la cour. ... Ils ne recevaient pas de commandement, ils venaient pour voir, pour se battre, et pourvoir ensuite en parler. [Yet again, at the news of an attractive occasion to make war, the young courtiers were seen arriving from Paris. ... They received no orders; they came in order to observe, to fight, and to be able to talk about it afterwards.]'

21   A modern historical biography of Bayard, containing valuable documentation of the development of the myth, is by Jacquart (1987).

22   For that matter, the equally prolix title of Jacques de Mailles (1527) is even more richly evocative of the already-nostalgic ambiance surrounding Bayard and soldiership in the period more generally: *La trèsioyeuse plaisante & recreatiue hystoire composée par le loyal seruiteur, des faiz, gestes, triumphes et prouesses du bon cheualier sans paour et sans reprouche le gentil seigneur de Bayart, dont humaines louenges sont*

espandues par toute la chrestiente. De plusieurs autres bons, vaillans et vertueux cappi-
taines qui ont esté de son temps. Ensemble les guerres, batailles, rencontres et assauls
qui de son vivant sont survenues, etc. [The joyous, pleasant and recreative history
composed by (his) faithful servant of the feats, exploits, triumphs and deeds of
prowess of the good knight without fear and without reproach, the noble seigneur
of Bayar(d) … of many other good, valiant and virtuous captains who were in his
time, together with the wars … that took place during his lifetime, etc.]. It is noteworthy that the chapter (fols lvvvii^v–lvvvvi^r [Ch. 57]) in which Mailles narrates
Bayard's encounter with Henry VIII and the emperor does not begin with wording
recalling Champier, hence anticipating Nashe.

23   On Bayard's administrative function, see Jacquart, 1987, pp. 239–62.

24   On the historical situation, see Monnet, 1970; for François I's struggle with the
side-changing Duke of Bourbon and the events leading up to Pavia, see Knecht,
1994, pp. 211–25.

25   See Sournia, 1981, pp. 23–24, who makes it clear that Monluc eagerly availed
himself of military innovations; Sournia actually cites the courtier scorned by
Hotspur (*1H4*, I.iii.59–64) to illustrate the commonplace chivalric attitude to
firearms, although (almost inevitably) the attitude is presumed to be Shakespeare's
own. On the contrary, even the honour-obsessed Hotspur cherishes no such illusions.

At least equally to the cultural point is the commentary by the chronicler
Edward Hall on the slaying of John Talbot, Earl of Shrewsbury, at the battle of
Castillon in 1453, which marked the end of English hopes in the Hundred Years
War:

> But his enemies hauing a greater company of men, a more abundaunce of
> ordinaunce then before had bene sene in a battayle, fyrst shot him through
> the thighe with a handgonne, and slew his horse, & cowardly killed him
> lyenge on the grounde, whome they neuer durste loke in the face, whyle he
> stode on his fete. (1550, fol. 84^r)

Talbot is the closest equivalent in English national mythology to Bayard as a
vehicle of chivalric nostalgia – an element exploited, of course, in *1H6*, although
there the tragedy of his death is blamed rather on English dissension and fantasti-
cally associated with Jeanne d'Arc (IV.vii).

26   A reader of Monluc's *Commentaires* with an imperfect knowledge of persons and
events might also have taken 'le chevalier sans peur et sans reproche' to have been
(posthumously) present when Monluc roused the courtiers of François I to enthusiasm for Italian combat in 1544, although the 'monsieur de Bayart' (1964, p. 149)
mentioned at that point is Gilbert Bayard, the secretary of finance.

27   See Taveneaux, 1986, pp. 256–63. Cf. the particularly intricate symbolic knot
woven – quite consciously ('par vraye simbolisation [by true symbolization]') –
by Champier at the conclusion of Bk. II, Ch. 11 (the section imitated by Nashe):

> Et si le noble Bayard estoit prudent en guerre, de bonne nature, aymoit

dieu, si estoit le chief de sa compagnie monseigneur le duc de lorraine, qui
est et a esté tousjours vertueulx, saige et devot prince entre tous les aultres
princes de son temps, qui moult bien a tousjours entretenue sa terre en paix.
Et si ses ancestres, comme Godefroy roy de Jherusalem et le roy Baudoin
son frere et son pere le roy Regné de Cecile ont esté princes vertueulx entre
tous aultres de leurs temps, si est aussi, par vraye simbolisation, ce duc à
présent Lorrain vertueulx entre tous princes vivans, lequel a bien merité en
son temps avoir ung lieutenant l'ung des plus hardys et chevaleureulx, je ose
bien dire et affermer que, non seulement de son temps, mais aussi qui fut
oncques entre tous chevaliers chrestiens.

[And if the noble Bayard was prudent in war, good-natured, and loved God,
so it was the chief of his company, my lord of Lorraine, who is and always
was a virtuous, wise and devout prince among all the princes of his time,
who has always greatly maintained his land in peace. And if his ancestors,
such as Godefroy King of Jerusalem, and King Beaudoin his brother, and
René of Sicily were virtuous princes amongst all others of their time, so is
also, by true symbolization, that present duke of Lorraine virtuous amongst
all living princes, who has well deserved in his time to have one of the
boldest and most knightly lieutenants, I dare well say and affirm, not only
of his time, but also who ever was amongst all Christian knights.] (1992,
pp. 183–84)

28   Cf., from the point of view of French-English and Protestant-Catholic issues, my
     Shakespeare, Marlowe and the Politics of France, 2002, pp. 30–46.
29   See Jouanna *et al.*, eds, 1998, pp. 90, 100.
30   The pages of the original were not numbered, and I cite using the pagination super-
     imposed on the facsimile by Gaume, ed., 1980; references to editorial matter use
     the regular page numbers of this edition.
31   The fountain of Hippocrene sprang forth at the touch of the hoof of Pegasus.
32   Not quite inevitably, since there was a strong competing impulse (promoted by
     Ronsard in the *Franciade*, among others) to invent a Trojan descent for the family
     – hence, the statue of Aeneas in front of the chateau of Tournon. Both legends
     figure in *La triomphante entree* scripted by Honoré d'Urfé; see the instructive
     discussion in Urfé, Gaume, ed., 1976, pp. 8–10.
33   He was Charles IX's ambassador to Rome (*La pastorale amovrevse*, Gaume, ed.,
     1980, p. 113, n. to the dedication).
34   The relative dearth of references to Just II supports the idea that he was 'impopu-
     laire [unpopular]' (Urfé, Gaume, ed., 1976, p. 11).
35   One collection of the *Histoires*, however, was dedicated to Claude de Turenne's
     sister Antoinette (Simonin, 1992, pp. 112–13).
36   Louis XI is closely identified with Dauphiné by Champier (1992, pp. 123, 125,
     127). For extended discussion of both Dauphiné and the Catalan Roussillon, see
     Favier, 2001, esp. pp. 115–63, 431–34, 670; see also Jacquart, 1987, p. 55.

37 Kingdon, 1967, p. 160; Jouanna *et al.*, eds, 1998, p. 876. Cf. *CSPF, 1564–65*, No. 358, pp. 119–20 (27 April 1564, 'Complaint made against the Synod at Ferté-sous-Jouarre').

38 Coste, 1643, p. 303.

39 On 12 July 1564 he sent Cecil the acts of the synod to be shared with English ecclesiastics, as well as information about its 'calumniation' (*CSPF, 1564–65*, No. 553, p. 175).

40 Abel Jouan's contemporary account first appeared in 1566.

41 See Jouan, 1979, p. 88 and n. 78, and Jouanna *et al.*, eds, 1998, p. 137.

42 On 12 July, Smith had reported that the imminent arrival of the Duke of Ferrara and the Duke of Florence's son was anticipated (*CSPF*, 1564–65, No. 553, p. 175). Cf. *AWW*: 'Florence is denied before he comes' (I.ii.12).

43 Lambin (1962, pp. 29–30) mentions this edict, together with Marie de Medici's visit in 1600, as a reason why Roussillon was well known. See also Champion, 1937, p. 119.

44 See the map in Jouanna *et al.*, eds, 1998, p. 138.

45 See Mazon, 1994, 1: 128–38.

46 See Urfé, Gaume, ed., 1976, pp. 11–12.

47 On the assassination attempt and the consequent anti-Jesuit sentiment, see Jouanna *et al.*, eds, 1998, pp. 792–94 ('Chastel, Jean').

48 *Arrest de la Cour de parlement, du 18 aoust 1598, contre le sieur de Tournon, contenant aussi défenses à toutes personnes d'envoyer escholiers aux collèges des jésuites.* This decree, which was republished in the following year in a compilation by Goulart (*Le sixiesme et dernier recueil, contenant les choses plvs memorables auenues sovs la Ligue*, 1599, pp. 691–94), singles out Tournon (p. 4) as still receiving pupils for indoctrination in the Jesuits' dangerous doctrines, like Pont-à-Mousson. See Mazon, 1994, 4: 135–41, on the protracted controversy over the Jesuits at Tournon; Just-Louis's defence of them effectively permitted them to resist, uniquely in France, until the legal re-establishment of the Order in 1603.

49 On these political developments and the English interest in them, see my Introduction to Fronton Du Duc, 2005, pp. 30–35, 45.

50 Massip, 1890, p. 71. On Hay's career, cf. Prat, 1876, pp. 108–15, whose avoidance of political questions, however, tends to obscure chronology. Hay seems to have remained at Tournon until 1590, when he took up a chair in theology in Lyons; he died, however, in Pont-à-Mousson in 1609.

51 Jean Pillehotte, the Lyons publisher of this work, as of Urfé's Jesuit-sponsored *La triomphante entrée*, is associated with Catholic propaganda; see Pallier, 1983, pp. 335, 346.

52 See Prat, 1876, p. 114 and p. 114n.1, who asserts that this was the first book published at Tournon; the BnF catalogue is less definite on the point.

53 Jean Willemin, *Historia belli quod cum hoeriticis rebellibus gessit, anno 1567, Claudia de Turaine* (Paris, 1569). This work has not survived; neither has Belleforest's

translation, which, however, is reliably attested and figures in Simonin's bibliography (1992) as No. 47 under the heading of *Discours de la brave resistance faite aux rebelles l'an 1567 par Madame de Tournon Contesse de Roussilon nommee Claude de Turaine, escrit premierement en vers latins par Iean Willemin, et depuis traduit en vers François par ledit Belleforest* (Paris: Jean Hulpeau, 1569). Simonin (1992, p. 245) reasonably presumes that the account of the confrontation given in *La pastorale amovrevse* derives from this earlier work. On the facts and the legends, see also Mazon, 1994, 1: 33–41.

54 See Coste, 1647, 1: 475–76.

55 See Coste, 1647, 1: 480–81.

56 See L'Estoile, 1992–2003, 2: 146.

57 For these details, see, respectively, L'Estoile, 1992–2003, 3: 73 and 4: 72. The marriage is mentioned in an English dispatch of late January as one of several pleasant events likely to be postponed because of the ill-fortune of the Duke of Anjou (presumably his debacle at Antwerp); see *CSPF, January–June 1583 and Addenda*, No. 54, p. 62 (20 January 1583, Cobham to Walsingham). Nonetheless, it took place on 13 February.

58 See Belleforest, *La pastorale amovrevse*, Gaume, ed., 1980, pp. 10–15.

59 It would not be beyond Shakespeare's familiarity with French, it seems to me, to be punning as well on the adjective 'feu' meaning 'late', 'defunct'. The character is thus poised nominally between the shadows of the past and the Helena-quickened spirits of the present.

60 The 'fountaine ardente' is real enough, if not notably medicinal, and still popularly classed among the 'merveilles du Dauphiné', having been restored after the damage done by futile attempts at commercial exploitation of its combustible gases.

61 Obviously, no secrets are involved on such a point. Coste takes up Marguerite's narrative word-for-word and matter-of-factly names Hélène, likewise praising her for 'sa sagesse, sa beauté et ses mérites [her wisdom, her beauty and her merits]' (1647, 1: 478).

I have nowhere else seen mention, incidentally, of a very curious episode sardonically recounted in a 1582 report from Henry Brook, Lord Cobham, to Walsingham – evidence, perhaps, that amorous entanglements ran in the family:

Count de Tournon of Savoy has lately slain a gentleman called 'd'Ayella', whereon his sister, who attends on the Queen Mother, has taken so great displeasure that she would profess herself a nun. This humour is found very strange in this Court. (*CSPF, 1581–82*, No. 572, p. 511 [3 March 1582, Cobham to Walsingham])

The index to this volume of the *CSPF* lists the Count simply as 'Just', but Just-Louis must be intended, and Tournon is often loosely assimilated to Savoy in contemporary English references. By all accounts, Just-Louis had only three sisters, so the reference must be to one of the honourably married ones.

62 See above, p. 42 and p. 87n.46.

63   Cf. the mad Ophelia:

> There's rue for you. And here's some for me. We may call it
> herb of grace a Sundays. You must wear your rue with
> a difference.
>
> (*Ham.*, IV.v.178–81)

64   Conjectural as any connection must be, at least one potential channel of information was open at this point between Marguerite and certain English milieux: it
was around this time that she entered into friendly and frequent correspondence
with Philippe de Mornay (the close acquaintance of the Sidney family), who
conducted negotiations over her divorce from Henri IV on behalf of the king. See
her *Correspondance*, 1998, Letter 252 (p. 344) *et passim*, as well as Mornay and
Arbaleste, 1824–25, 1: 271–73.

65   See esp. Snyder, 1992, 271–72.

66   Lefranc's early venture into the territory of Derby-Shakespeare encodings (*Sous
le masque de 'William Shakespeare'*, 1918–19) also made the reported death of
Katherine's love-stricken sister in *LLL* (V.ii.14–15) an allusion to Hélène of
Tournon, given an identification of that play's princess with Marguerite de Valois.
Such a reading could hardly be definitive, given the commonplace involved (cf.
TN, II.iv.107 ff.), although Lefranc subsequently claimed that his 'démonstration
... a été accueillie par l'unanimité des critiques compétents [demonstration ...
was favourably received unanimously by competent critics]' (1926, p. 20), while
Lambin, nearly thirty years later, pronounced Lefranc's 'déchiffrement ...
aujourd'hui presque universellement adopté [decoding ... almost universally
adopted today]' (1954, p. 13).

67   See Lefranc, 1926, pp. 25–33. The slightly earlier *Ado* (1598) has an abundance
of possible sources of its own – including another adaptation of Bandello by Belleforest (from the third volume of *Histoires tragiques*) – for the more generally analogous death and revival of the repudiated Hero (see Bullough, ed., 1957–75, 2:
61–139). Nor is there any need to seek beyond historical fact for the name of its
villainous bastard 'Don John'. In fact, however, Don John of Austria, in whose
service Marc de Rye, marquis de Varambon, was employed, was prominent in the
events related to Marguerite's diplomatic mission to the Low Countries in June-
September 1577. He entertained her lavishly at a banquet and ball. See Marguerite
de Valois, *Mémoires*, ed. Cazaux, 1986, pp. 111, 311–12, n. 2 to p. 109, and Viennot,
1993, pp. 94–100. In the previous year, Don John had travelled incognito across
France to take up his governorship of the Netherlands; on that occasion, according
to Brantôme, he encountered Marguerite for the first time at a masked ball and
opined (as Brantôme paraphrases his Spanish), 'Combien que ceste beauté de
reyne soit plus divine que humaine, elle est plus pour perdre et damner les
hommes que les sauver [Although that queenly beauty was more divine than
human, it was made rather for losing and damning men than for saving them]'
(Brantôme, ed. Lalanne, 1864–82, 8: 26; cf. *Mémoires*, ed. Cazaux, 1986, p. 313,

n. 2 to p. 111). Especially given the masked ball and the substitution of Margaret for Hero, it seems possible, then, that Don John finds his way into *Ado* by way of the stories associating him with Marguerite de Valois. Lambin (1962, p. 31; 1954, p. 21) takes it for granted that he is the historical figure behind 'our cousin Austria' (I.iii.5) mentioned by the King of *All's Well*.

68 The resonance between *AWW* and *Ham.* has often been noted; see, e.g., Hopkins, 2003, p. 376.

69 Shakespeare might have gleaned this fact from *La triomphante entrée* itself, where the name is prominent and recurrent. Madeleine de La Rochefoucauld was also known for her relief efforts on behalf of the Jesuits after the 1594 order issued against them; that she died in the following year is recorded by Massip, 1890, p. 48, who terms her 'le plus influent et le plus dévoué des apôtres de la charité à Tournon [the most influential and the most devoted of the apostles of charity at Tournon]' (also cited Mazon, 1901–4, 4: 135). Hopkins (2003, p. 374) mentions that Madeleine was the name of Catherine de Medici's mother, but it is not clear how this fact might be relevant.

70 See the appreciative analysis of this work on its own terms, and in particular relation to Rabelais, by Prescott, 1998, pp. 48–49, 51–55.

71 See Cotgrave, 1611, s.v. 'enrager': '*To rage; raue, storme, play the Bedlam, fare like a madde-man, be starke madde.*'

Works cited

Early texts and editions

Abra de Raconis, Charles-François d' (évêque de Lavaur). *La vie et la mort de feu Mme de Mercoeur.* Paris: Lovys Boulanger, 1625.

Albret, Jeanne d'. *Ample Declaration des lettres precedentes* [*Mémoires*]. *Histoire de nostre temps, contenant vn recveil des choses memorables passées & publiées pour le faict de la Religion & estat de la France, depuis l'edict de paciffication du 23. iour de Mars, 1568 iusques au iour présent.* Ed. Christophe Landré and Charles Martel (attrib.). [n.p.]: [n.pub.], 1570. 172–238.

———. *Mémoires. Mémoires et poésies de Jeanne d'Albret, publiés par le baron de Ruble.* Ed. Alphonse de Ruble. Paris: E. Paul, Huart et Guillemin, 1883.

Arnauld, Antoine. *Libre discours sur la delivrance de la Bretagne.* [n.p.]: [n.pub.], 1598.

———. *A trve discovrse concerning the deliuerie of Brittaine, in the yeare 1598. An historical collection, of the most memorable accidents, and tragicall massacres of France, vnder the raignes of Henry. 2. Francis. 2. Charles. 9. Henry. 3. Henry. 4. now liuing.* Ed. Simon Goulart (attrib.) or Jean de Serres (attrib.). London: Thomas Creede, 1598. Sigs Bbb3^r–4^v.

Arrest de la Cour de parlement, du 18 aoust 1598, contre le sieur de Tournon, contenant aussi défenses à toutes personnes d'envoyer escholiers aux collèges des jésuites. Paris: M. Pattisson, 1598.

Aubigné, Agrippa d'. *Histoire universelle,* 11 vols. Ed. André Thierry. Textes littéraires français. Geneva: Droz, 1981–99.

Aubrey, John. *Aubrey's Brief Lives,* 2nd ed. Ed. Oliver Lawson Dick. London: Martin Secker and Warburg, 1950.

Belleforest, François de. *Le cinquiesme tome des Histoires tragiques, etc.* Paris: J. Hulpeau, 1572.

———. *Discours des presages et miracles advenuz en la personne du Roy et parmy la France.* Paris: R. Le Mangnier et V. Norment, 1568.

———. *Les Grandes Annales et histoire générale de France, dès la venue des Francs en Gaule jusques au règne du Roy très-chrestien Henry III,* 2 vols. Paris: G. Buon, 1579.

———. *Histoire des neuf roys Charles de France, contenant la fortune, vertu et heur fatal des*

Roys, qui sous ce nom de Charles ont mis à fin des choses merveilleuses, le tout comprins en dix-neuf livres, avec la table sur chacune histoire de roy. Paris: P. L'Huillier, 1568.

———. *Hist. Troisiesme [d'Amleth]. Le cinquiesme tome des Histoires tragiques, etc. The Sources of Hamlet, with Essay on the Legend*. Ed. Israel Gollancz. London: Humphrey Milford, Oxford University Press, 1926. 164–310.

———. *L'histoire universelle du monde: contenant l'entière description & situation des quatre parties de la terre, la division & estendue d'une chacune region & provinces d'icelles: Ensemble l'origine & particulières moeurs, loix, coustumes, religion, & ceremonies de toutes les nations, et peuples par qui elles sont habitées. Divisée en quatre livres*. Paris: G. Mallot, 1570.

———. *The Hystorie of Hamblet* (1608). Trans. anon. *The Sources of Hamlet, with Essay on the Legend*. Ed. Israel Gollancz. London: Humphrey Milford, Oxford University Press, 1926. 165–311.

———. *L'innocence de la très illustre, très chaste et débonnaire princesse Madame Marie, royne d'Escosse, etc*. [n.p.]: [n.pub.], 1572.

———. *La pastorale amovrevse, contenant plvsieurs discours non moins proufitables que recreatifs. Auec des descriptions de Paisages. La pastorale amoureuse (Jean Hulpeau, 1569), La Pyrénée (Gervais Mallot, 1571)*. Introduction, Notes and Index by Maxime Gaume. Images et témoins de l'âge classique, 8. Fac. rpt. Saint-Étienne: Publications de l'Université de Saint-Étienne, 1980. 33–131.

———. *Remonstrance au peuple de Paris, de demeurer en la foy de leurs ancestres*. Paris: R. Le Mangnier and V. Norment, 1568.

Bèze, Théodore de (attrib.). *Histoire ecclésiastique des églises réformées du Royaume de France*, 3 vols. Ed. G. Baum and E. Cunitz. 1883–89; rpt. Nieuwkoop: B. De Graaf, 1974.

The Bible and Holy Scriptvres Conteyned in the Olde and Newe Testament. Geneva: [n.pub.], 1562 [i.e., 1561]. STC 2095.

Biet, Christian (ed.) *Théâtre de la cruauté et récits sanglants en France: XVIe–XVIIe siècle*. Paris: R. Laffont, 2006.

Boccaccio, Giovanni. *Le Decameron*. Trans. Antoine Le Maçon. Lyons: Guillaume Rouille, 1558.

———. *Decameron (Day III, Story 9, of Giletta of Narbonne)*. Trans. William Painter. (*The Palace of Pleasure*, Novel 38.) *Narrative and Dramatic Sources of Shakespeare*. Ed. Geoffrey Bullough, vol. 2. London: Routledge and Kegan Paul; New York: Columbia University Press, 1958. 389–96.

Bordenave, Nicolas de. *Histoire de Béarn et Navarre par Nicolas de Bordenave (1517–1572), historiographe de la maison de Navarre. Publiée pour la première fois, sur le manuscrit original pour la Société de l'Histoire de France*. Ed. Paul Raymond. Paris: Veuve J. Renouard, 1873.

Bourbon, Antoine de, and Jeanne d' Albret. *Lettres d'Antoine de Bourbon et de Jehanne d'Albret publiées pour la Société de l'Histoire de France par le marquis de Rochambeau*. Ed. Achille Lacroix de Vimeux, marquis de Rochambeau. Paris: Librairie Renouard, 1867.

Brantôme, Pierre de Bourdeille, abbé de. *Œuvres complètes*, 11 vols. Ed. Ludovic Lalanne. Paris: La Société de l'Histoire de France, 1864–82.

Bullough, Geoffrey (ed.). *Narrative and Dramatic Sources of Shakespeare*, 8 vols. London: Routledge; New York: Columbia University Press, 1957–75.

Calendar of State Papers, Foreign Series, of the Reign of Elizabeth, 1558–59, Preserved in the State Paper Department of Her Majesty's Public Record Office. Ed. Joseph Stevenson. London: Longman, Green, Longman, Roberts, and Green, 1863.

Calendar of State Papers, Foreign Series, of the Reign of Elizabeth, 1560–61, Preserved in the State Paper Department of Her Majesty's Public Record Office. Ed. Joseph Stevenson. London: Longman, Green, Reader, and Dyer, 1865.

Calendar of State Papers, Foreign Series, of the Reign of Elizabeth, 1561–1562, Preserved in the State Paper Department of Her Majesty's Public Record Office. Ed. Joseph Stevenson. London: Longman, Green, Longman, Roberts, and Green, 1866.

Calendar of State Papers, Foreign Series, of the Reign of Elizabeth, 1581–82, Preserved in the Public Record Office. Ed. Arthur John Butler. London: HMSO, 1907.

Calendar of State Papers, Foreign Series, of the Reign of Elizabeth, January–June 1583 and Addenda, Preserved in the Public Record Office. Ed. Arthur John Butler and Sophie Crawford Lomas. London: HMSO, 1913.

Calendar of State Papers, Foreign Series, of the Reign of Elizabeth, August 1584–August 1585, Preserved in the Public Record Office. Ed. Sophie Crawford Lomas. London: HMSO, 1916.

Calvin, Jean. *The institution of Christian religion written in Latine by M. John Caluine, and translated into English according to the authors last edition, by Thomas Norton, etc.* Trans. Thomas Norton. London: Thomas Vautrollier for William Norton, 1578. STC 4418.

Capilupi, Camillo. *Le Stratagème, ou la ruse de Charles IX, Roy de France, contre les Huguenots rebelles à Dieu et à luy. Archives curieuses de l'histoire de France.* Ed. L. Cimber and C. Danjou. Ser. 1, vol. 7. Paris: Beauvais, Membre de l'Institut Historique, 1835. 401–71.

Champier, Symphorien. *Les gestes ensemble la vie du preulx Chevalier Bayard*. Ed. Denis Crouzet. Acteurs de l'histoire. Paris: Imprimerie Nationale Éditions, 1992.

Chantelouve, François de. *La tragédie de feu Gaspard de Colligny*. Ed. Keith Cameron. Exeter: University of Exeter Press, 1971.

____. *The Tragedy of the Late Gaspard de Coligny. The Tragedy of the Late Gaspard de Coligny and The Guisiade* [by Pierre Matthieu]. Trans. with Introduction and Notes by Richard Hillman. Carleton Renaissance Plays in Translation, 40. Ottawa: Dovehouse Editions, 2005.

Chappuys, Gabriel. *L'Histoire du royaume de Navarre, contenant, de roy en roy, tout ce qui y est advenu de remarquable dès son origine, et depuis que les roys d'Espagne l'ont usurpé, etc.* Paris: N. Gilles, 1596.

Coste, Hilarion de. *Les éloges de nos rois, et des enfants de France, qui ont esté daufins de Viennois ... . A Monseigneur le Dauphin. Avec des remarques curieuses du Pais & de la Noblesse de Daufiné, etc.* Paris: Sébastien Cramoisy, 1643.

____. *Les éloges et les vies des reynes, des princesses et des dames illustres en piété, en courage et en doctrine*, 2 vols. Paris: Sébastien Cramoisy, 1647.

Cotgrave, Randle. *A Dictionarie of the French and English Tongues (1611)*. Anglistica and Americana, 77. Fac. rpt. Hildesheim: Georg Holms, 1970.

Daniel, Samuel. 'A Letter sent from *Octauia* to her husband Marcus Antonius *into Egypt*.' *Certaine Small Workes heretofore Divulged by Samuel Daniel, one of the Groomes of the Queenes Maiesties priuie chamber, & now againe by him corrected and augmented*. London: I[ohn] W[indet] for Simon Waterson, 1607. Fols 1ʳ–6ᵛ (begins new folio sequence within volume). STC 6240.

____. *The Tragedie of Cleopatra. Certaine Small Workes heretofore Divulged by Samuel Daniel, one of the Groomes of the Queenes Maiesties priuie chamber, & now againe by him corrected and augmented*. London: I[ohn] W[indet] for Simon Waterson, 1607. Fols 7ʳ–36ʳ (in second folio sequence within volume). STC 6240.

____. *The tragedie of Cleopatra. Delia and Rosamond augmented, Cleopatra*. London: [James Roberts and Edward Allde for] Simon Waterston, 1594. STC 6243.4.

____. *The Tragedy of Cleopatra* [1599]. *Narrative and Dramatic Sources of Shakespeare*, vol.5. Ed. Geoffrey Bullough. London: Routledge; New York: Columbia University Press, 1964. 406–49.

La destinée de Gaston Fébus. Archives Départementales des Hautes-Pyrénées, 2005. www.passion-bigorrehp.org/febus.html (accessed October 2011).

Frederick III, Elector Palatine. *Briefe Friedrich des Frommen, Kurfürsten von der Pfalz*, 2 vols. Ed. August Kluckhohn. Brunswick: C. A. Schwetschke und Sohn, 1868–70.

Froissart, Jean. *Here begynneth the thirde and fourthe boke of sir Iohn Froissart of the crony-cles of Englande, Fraunce, Spaygne, Portyngale, Scotlande, Bretayne, Flaunders, and other places adioynyng, translated out of Frenche in to englysshe by Iohan Bourchier knyght, lorde Berners, etc.* Trans. John Bourchier, Lord Berners. London: Richard Pynson, 1525. STC 11397.

Fronton Du Duc. *L'histoire tragique de la Pucelle de Dom-Rémy*. Ed. Marc André Prévost. Théâtre français de la Renaissance. *La tragédie à l'époque d'Henri III*, 2nd ser., vol. 2. Florence: Leo S. Olschki; Paris: Presses Universitaires de France, 2000.

____. *The Tragic History of the Pucelle of Domrémy Otherwise Known as the Maid of Orléans*. Trans. with Introduction and Notes by Richard Hillman. Carleton Renaissance Plays in Translation, 39. Ottawa: Dovehouse Editions, 2005.

Garcilaso de la Vega. *Garcilaso de la Vega y sus comentaristas. Obras completas del poeta acompañadas de los textos íntegros de los comentarios de El Brocense, Fernando de Herrera, Tamayo de Vargas y Azara*, 2nd ed. Ed. Antonio Gallego Morell. Biblioteca Románica Hispánica. Madrid: Editorial Gredos, 1972.

Garnier, Robert. *Antonius*. Trans. Mary Sidney Herbert. *The Collected Works of Mary Sidney Herbert, Countess of Pembroke*, 2 vols. Ed. Margaret P. Hannay, Noel J. Kinnamon and Michael G. Brennan. Oxford: Clarendon Press, 1988. 1: 152–207.

____. *Hymne de la Monarchie. Robert Garnier, sa vie, ses poésies inédites avec son véritable portrait et un facsimile de sa signature*. Ed. Henri Chardon. 1905; rpt. Geneva: Slatkine Reprints, 1970.

_____. *Marc Antoine. Œuvres complètes de Robert Garnier: Marc Antoine, Hippolyte.* Ed. Raymond Lebègue. Les textes français. Paris: Les Belles Lettres, 1974.

_____. *Porcie. Œuvres complètes de Robert Garnier: Porcie, Cornélie.* Ed. Raymond Lebègue. Les textes français. Paris: Les Belles Lettres, 1973.

_____. *Porcie, tragédie françoise, représentant la cruelle et sanglante saison des guerres civiles de Rome, propre et convenable pour y voir dépeincte la calamité de ce temps.* Paris: R. Estienne, 1568.

Goulart, Simon (attrib.), Jean de Serres (attrib.), Pierre Matthieu *et al. Histoire des choses mémorables avenues en France, depuis l'an 1547 jusques au commencement de l'an 1597, sous le règne de Henri II, François II, Charles IX, Henri III et Henri IV, contenant infinies merveilles de notre siècle. Dernière édition.* [n.p.]: [n.pub.], 1599.

_____ (attrib.), Jean de Serres (attrib.), Pierre Matthieu *et al. An historical collection, of the most memorable accidents, and tragicall massacres of France, vnder the raignes of Henry. 2. Francis. 2. Charles. 9. Henry. 3. Henry. 4. now liuing.* Trans. anon. London: Thomas Creede, 1598. STC 11275.

_____. *The liues of Epaminondas, of Philip of Macedon, of Dionysivs the elder, and of Octavivs Cæsar Avgvstvs: collected out of good Authors. Also the liues of nine excellent Chieftaines of warre, taken out of Latine from Emylivs Probvs, by S. G. S. By whom also are added the liues of Plutarch and of Seneca: Gathered together, disposed, and enriched as the others.* Trans. Thomas North. *The liues of the noble Grecians and Romaines, etc.* London: Richard Field for Thomas Wright, 1603. STC 20068 (separate pagination within volume).

_____ (ed.). *Le sixiesme et dernier recueil, contenant les choses plvs memorables auenues sovs la Ligue, depuis le commencement de l'an M.D.XCIIII. jusques à la paix accordee entre les Rois de France & d'Espagne, l'an M.D.XCVIII.* [n.p.]: [n.pub], 1599.

Granvelle, Antoine Perrenot, cardinal de. *Papiers d'État du cardinal de Granvelle, d'après les manuscrits de la bibliothèque de Besançon,* 9 vols. Ed. Charles Weiss, Clément Duvernoy and Charles Duvernoy. Collection de documents inédits sur l'histoire de France, publiés par ordre du roi, et par les soins du ministre de l'instruction publique. Ser. 1, Histoire politique. Paris: Imprimerie Royale, [later] Imprimerie Nationale, 1841–52.

Grévin, Jacques. *César.* Textes littéraires français. Ed. Ellen S. Ginsberg. Geneva: Droz; Paris: Minard, 1971.

Hall, Edward. *The vnion of the two noble and illustre famelies of Lancastre & Yorke, beyng long in continuall discension for the croune of this noble realme: with al the actes done in both the tymes of the princes, both of the one linage & of the other, etc.* London: Richard Grafton, 1550. STC 12723.

Harvey, Gabriel. *Letter-book of Gabriel Harvey, A.D. 1573–1580, Edited from the Original Ms. Sloane 93, in the British Museum.* Ed. Edward John Long Scott. Camden Society, New Series. Westminster: for the Camden Society, 1884.

Hay, John. *L'Antimoine aux responses que Th. de Beze faict à trente sept demandes de deux cents et six proposées aux ministres d'Ecosse.* Tournon: Claude Michel, 1588.

_____. *Demandes faictes aux ministres d'escosse touchant la religion Christienne, par M. Iean*

Hay escossois, de la compagnie de Iesus, professeur en theologie, en l'vniversité de Tournon. Trans. Michel Coyssard. Lyons: Jean Pillehotte, 1583.

Herbert, Mary Sidney, Countess of Pembroke. *The Collected Works of Mary Sidney Herbert, Countess of Pembroke,* 2 vols. Ed. Margaret P. Hannay, Noel J. Kinnamon and Michael G. Brennan. Oxford: Clarendon Press, 1998.

Histoire de notre temps, contenant vn recveil des choses memorables passées et publiées pour le faict de la Religion & estat de la France, depuis l'Edict de paciffication du 23 iour de Mars, 1568. iusques au iour présent. Ed. Christophe Landré and Charles Martel (attrib.). [n.p.]: [n.pub.], 1570.

L'histoire prodigieuse du doctor Fauste. Trans. Pierre-Victor Palma-Cayet. Ed. Yves Cazaux. Textes littéraires français, 313. Geneva: Droz, 1982.

The historie of the damnable life, and deserued death of Doctor Iohn Faustus Newly imprinted, and in conuenient places imperfect matter amended: according to the true copie printed at Franckfort, and translated into English, by P. F. Gent. (1592). *The Sources of the Faust Tradition from Simon Magus to Lessing.* Ed. Philip Mason Palmer and Robert Pattison More. New York: Oxford University Press, 1936. 134–236.

Hotman, François (attrib.). *Epistre envoiée au tigre de la France.* [Paris]: [n.pub.], [1560].

Jodelle, Étienne. *Cléopâtre captive.* Ed. Françoise Charpentier, Jean-Dominique Beaudin and José Sanchez. Mugron: J. Feijóo, 1990.

Jouan, Abel. *The Royal Tour of France by Charles IX and Catherine de' Medici: Festivals and Entries 1564–6.* Ed. Victor E. Graham and W. McAllister Johnson. Toronto: University of Toronto Press, 1979. 71–143.

Languet, Hubert. *Huberti Langueti, … Epistolae secretae ad principem suum Augustum, Sax. ducem … Primus e museo edit Jo. Petr. Ludovicus,* 3 parts in 1 vol. Ed. Johann Peter von Ludewig [pseud. Lud. Patr. Giovanni and Peter von Hohenhard]. Arcana seculi decimi sexti. Halae Hermunduror [Halle an der Saale]: impensis J. F. Zeitleri, 1699.

La Place, Pierre de (d'Angoulême). *Commentaires de l'estat de la religion et republique soubs les rois Henry et François seconds, & Charles neufieme.* [n.p.]: [n.pub.], 1565.

———. *The fyrst parte of commentaries, concerning the state of religion, and the common wealthe of Fraunce, vnder the reignes of Henry the second, Frauncis the second, and Charles the ninth.* Trans. Thomas Tymme. London: Henrie Bynneman for Francis Coldocke, 1573. STC 22241.

———. *Rervm in Gallia ob religionem gestarvm libri tres, regibvs Henrico secundo, ad illivs quidam regni Finem, Francisco secvndo, et Carolo nono.* [n.p.]: [n.pub.], 1570.

L'Estoile, Pierre de. *Registre-journal du règne de Henri III,* 6 vols. Ed. Madeleine Lazard and Gilbert Schrenck. Geneva: Droz, 1992–2003.

Mailles, Jacques de. *La trèsioyeuse plaisante & recreatiue hystoire composée par le loyal seruiteur, des faiz, gestes, triumphes et prouesses du bon cheualier sans paour et sans reprouche le gentil seigneur de Bayart, dont humaines louenges sont espandues par toute la chrestiente. De plusieurs autres bons, vaillans et vertueux cappitaines qui ont esté de son temps. Ensemble les guerres, batailles, rencontres et assauls qui de son vivant sont survenues, tant en France, Espaigne que Ytalie.* Paris: Galliot Du Pré, 1527.

Marlowe, Christopher ('and his collaborator and revisers'). *Doctor Faustus, A-text (1604). Doctor Faustus, A- and B-texts (1604, 1616).* Ed. David Bevington and Eric Rasmussen. The Revels Plays. Manchester: Manchester University Press, 1993.

Matthieu, Pierre. *La Guisiade.* Ed. Louis Lobbes. Textes littéraires français. Geneva: Droz, 1990.

____. *The Guisiade. The Tragedy of the Late Gaspard de Coligny* [by François de Chantelouve] *and The Guisiade.* Trans. with Introduction and Notes by Richard Hillman. Carleton Renaissance Plays in Translation, 40. Ottawa: Dovehouse Editions, 2005.

Medici, Catherine de. *Lettres de Catherine de Médicis,* 11 vols. Ed. Hector La Ferrière-Percy, Gustave Baguenault de Puchesse *et al.* Paris: Imprimerie Nationale, 1880–1943.

Monluc, Blaise de (Lasseran de Massencome de). *Commentaires 1521–1576.* Ed. Paul Courteault. Preface by Jean Giono. Bibliothèque de la Pléiade. Paris: Gallimard, 1964.

____. *Commentaires et lettres de Blaise de Monluc, maréchal de France. Édition revue sur les manuscrits et publée avec les variantes pour la Société de l'Histoire de France,* 5 vols. Ed. Alphonse de Ruble. Paris: Veuve J. Renouard, 1864–72.

Montaigne, Michel de. *Les Essais de Michel de Montaigne. Édition conforme au texte de l'exemplaire de Bordeaux avec les additions de l'édition posthume, l'explication des termes vieillis et la traduction des citations, une étude sur Montaigne, une chronologie de sa vie et de son œuvre, le catalogue de ses livres et la liste des inscriptions qu'il avait fait peindre dans sa librairie, des notices, des notes, un appendice sur l'influence des Essais, et un index,* 3rd ed., 2 vols. Ed. Pierre Villey and V.-L. Saulnier. Paris: Presses Universitaires de France, 1978.

____. *Montaigne's Essays.* Trans. John Florio. Ed. L. C. Harmer. Everyman's Library. London: Dent; New York: Dutton, 1965.

Montchrestien, Antoine de. *Sophonisbe. Tragédie.* Caen: Veuve Jacques Lebas, 1596.

Monteux, Hierosme de. *Opuscula juvenilia.* Lyons: Ioan. Tornaesium and Guliel. Gazeium, 1556.

Montreux, Nicolas de [pseud. 'Ollenix du Mont-Sacré']. *Cléopâtre. Œuvre de la chasteté, qui se remarque par les diverses fortunes, adventures et fidelles amours de Criniton et Lydie. Livre premier, ensemble la tragédie de Cléopâtre, le tout de l'invention d'Ollenix du Mont-Sacré.* Paris: G. Des Rues, 1595 [?].

____. *L'Espagne conquise, par Charles le Grand, roy de France.* Nantes: Pierre Doriou, 1597.

____. *L'Heureuse et entière victoire, obtenue … sur les ennemis de Dieu à Cran, par le grand, victorieux et catholique prince Philippes Emanuel de Lorraine, duc de Mercoeur et de Peinthièvre, etc.* Nantes: N. Des Marestz and F. Faveyrne, 1592.

____. *La miraculeuse délivrance de Monseigneur le duc de Guise Henry de Lorraine, naguère prisonnier au château de Tours.* Nantes: Nicholas des Marestz and François Faverie, 1591.

____. *La Sophonisbe: tragédie*. Ed. Donald Stone, Jr. Textes littéraires français. Geneva: Droz, 1976.

____. *La Sophonisbe tragedie, par le sieur du Mont-Sacré, Gentilhomme du Maine*. Rouen: Raphaël Du Petit Val, 1601.

____. *La tragédie d'Isabelle. Le Quatrième livre des Bergeries de Julliette ... ensemble la tragédie d'Isabelle*. Paris: G. Des Rues, 1595.

Mornay, Philippe de, seigneur du Plessis-Marly. *A Christian View of Life and Death*. Trans. A. W. London: Richard Field, 1593. STC 18135.

____. *The Defence of Death, Contayning a moste excellent discourse of life and death, etc.* Trans. Edward Aggas. London: John Allde for Edward Aggas, 1576. STC 13136.

____. *A discourse of life and death. Written in French by Ph. Mornay. Antonius, a tragoedie written also in French by Ro. Garnier. Both done in English by the Countesse of Pembroke*. London: [John Windet] for William Ponsonby, 1592. STC 18138.

____. *Excellent discours de la vie et de la mort*. [n.p.]: [n.pub.], 1576.

____, and Charlotte Arbaleste. *Mémoires et correspondance de Duplessis-Mornay pour servir à l'histoire de la Réformation et des guerres civiles et religieuses en France sous les règnes de Charles IX, de Henri III, de Henri IV et de Louis XIII, depuis l'an 1571 jusqu'en 1623*, 12 vols. Ed. Pierre-René Auguis and André-Désiré de La Fontenelle de Vaudoré. Paris: Treuttel et Würtz, 1824–25.

Mystère du siège d'Orléans. Ed. Gérard Gros. Lettres gothiques. Le livre de poche. Paris: Librairie générale française, 2002.

Nashe, Thomas. *The Vnfortvnate Traveller. Or, The life of Iacke Wilton. The Works of Thomas Nashe*, 5 vols. Ed. Ronald B. McKerrow and F. P. Wilson. Vol. 2. Oxford: Blackwell, 1958. 187–328.

Nervèze, Antoine de. *Lettre consolatoire envoyée à Mme la duchesse de Mercœur sur le trespas de Mgr le duc de Mercœur*. Paris: Antoine de Breuil, 1602.

Olaus Magnus. *Historia Olai Magni, ... gentium septentionalium variis conditionibus stat-ibusve et de morum, rituum, superstitionum ... diversitate, item de bellis ... item de mineris metallicis et variis animalium generibus in illis regionibus degentium, etc.* Basel: ex officina Henricpetrina, 1567.

Olhagaray, Pierre. *Histoire de Foix, Béarn et Navarre, diligemment recveillie, tant des prece-dens historiens, que des Archiues desdites maisons. En laqvelle est exactement monstrée l'origine, accroissemens, alliances ... d'icelles, jusques à Henri IIII, Roy de France & de Nauarre ... à présent regnant*. Paris: David Douceur, 1609.

Plutarch. *The Life of Julius Caesar. Narrative and Dramatic Sources of Shakespeare*, vol. 5. Trans. Thomas North. Ed. Geoffrey Bullough. London: Routledge; New York: Columbia University Press, 1964. 58–140.

____. *The Life of Marcus Antonius. Narrative and Dramatic Sources of Shakespeare*, vol. 5. Trans. Thomas North. Ed. Geoffrey Bullough. London: Routledge; New York: Columbia University Press, 1964. 254–321.

____. *The liues of the noble Grecians and Romanes, compared together by that graue learned philosopher and historiographer, Plutarke of Chaeronea: translated out of Greeke into*

French by Iames Amyot ... and out of French into Englishe, by Thomas North. Trans. Thomas North. London: Thomas Vautroullier, 1579. STC 20065.

———. *The liues of the noble Grecians and Romaines, etc.* Trans. Thomas North. London: Richard Field for Thomas Wright, 1603. STC 20068.

———. *The liues of the noble Grecians and Romains, etc.* Trans. Thomas North. London: George Miller for Robert Allott, 1631. STC 20070.

——— [Plutarque]. *Les Vies des hommes illustres ... translatees par M. Jacques Amyot, ... enrichies en cette derniere edition ... d'annotations morales en marge qui monstrent le profit qu'on peut faire en la lecture de ces histoires. ... Le tout disposé par S.G.S.* Trans. Jacques Amyot. Ed. Simon Goulart. [Dijon]: Ieremie Des Planches, 1583.

Régnier de La Planche, Louis [pseud. 'François de l'Isle']. *Histoire de l'estat de France, tant de la république que de la religion, sous le règne de François II.* [n.p.]: [n.pub.], 1576.

———. *A legendarie conteining an ample discovrse of the life and behauiour of Charles Cardinal of Lorraine, and of his brethren, of the house of Guise. Written in French by Francis de L'isle.* [n.p.]: [n.pub.], 1577. STC 20855.

———. *La Legende de Charles, Cardinal de Lorraine, et de ses freres, de la maison de Guise, descrite en trois livres, par François de l'Isle.* Reims: Pierre Martin, 1576.

———. *Response à l'épistre de Charles de Vaudémont, cardinal de Lorraine, jadis prince imaginaire des royaumes de Jerusalem et de Naples, duc et conte par fantaisie d'Anjou et de Provence, et maintenant simple gentilhomme de Hainault.* [n.p.]: [n.pub.], 1565.

Ronsard, Pierre, Amadis Jamyn and Robert Garnier. *Le Tombeau du feu Roy Tres-Chrestien Charles IX, etc.* Paris: F. Morel, 1574.

Seneca, Lucius Annaeus. *L. Annaei Senecae ad Lucilium Epistulae Morales.* Ed. L. D. Reynolds. Oxford: Clarendon Press, 1965.

———. *Les Tragédies très-éloquentes du grans Philosophe Seneque diligentement traduictes de Latin en Françoy. Avec plusieurs épitaphes, épigrammes, dictz moraulx et aultres choses mémorables nouvellement adjoustées.* Trans. and ed. Pierre Grosnet. Lyons: [n.pub.], 1539.

Serres, Jean de, Pierre Matthieu *et al. A general inuentorie of the history of France from the beginning of that monarchie, vnto the treatie of Veruins, in the year 1598. Written by Ihon de Serres. And continued vnto these times, out off the best authors which haue written of that subiect.* Trans. Edward Grimeston. London: George Eld, 1607. STC 22244.

Shakespeare, William. *All's Well That Ends Well,* rev. edn. Ed. Russell Fraser and Alexander Leggatt. New Cambridge Shakespeare. Cambridge: Cambridge University Press, 2003.

———. *All's Well That Ends Well.* Ed. G. K. Hunter. The Arden Shakespeare (2nd ser.). London: Routledge, 1959.

———. *All's Well That Ends Well.* Ed. Susan Snyder. The Oxford Shakespeare. Oxford: Clarendon Press, 1993.

———. *Antony and Cleopatra.* Ed. R. H. Case. The Arden Shakespeare (1st ser.). London: Methuen, 1906.

____. *Antony and Cleopatra*. Ed. John Wilders. The Arden Shakespeare (3rd ser.). London: Routledge, 1995.

____. *Antony and Cleopatra*. Ed. John Dover Wilson. The New Shakespeare. Cambridge: Cambridge University Press, 1950.

____. *The Complete Works*, 2nd edn. Ed. John Jowett, William Montgomery, Gary Taylor and Stanley Wells. The Oxford Shakespeare. Oxford: Clarendon Press, 2005.

____. *Hamlet*. Ed. Harold Jenkins. The Arden Shakespeare (2nd ser.). London: Methuen, 1982.

____. *Hamlet*. Ed. Ann Thompson and Neil Taylor. The Arden Shakespeare (3rd ser.). London: Thompson Learning, 2006.

____. *The Merry Wives of Windsor*. Ed. David Crane. New Cambridge Shakespeare. Cambridge: Cambridge University Press, 1997.

____. *The Riverside Shakespeare*, 2nd edn. Ed. G. Blakemore Evans, J. J. M. Tobin *et al.* Boston: Houghton Mifflin, 1997.

____. *The Tragedy of Anthony and Cleopatra*. Ed. Michael Neill. The World's Classics. Oxford: Oxford University Press, 1994.

Sidney, Philip. *An Apology for Poetry*. Ed. Geoffrey Shepherd. Manchester: Manchester University Press; New York: Barnes and Noble, 1973.

____, and Hubert Languet. *The Correspondence of Sir Philip Sidney and Hubert Languet*. Trans. Steuart A. Pears. Ed. William Aspenwall Bradley. The Humanist's Library. Boston: Merrymount Press, 1912.

Sleidanus, Johannes. *Frossardi, nobilissimi scriptoris gallici, historiarum opus omne: iamprimum et breviter collectum et latino sermone redditur* ['Epitome']. Paris: Simon de Colines, 1537.

____. *Recueil diligent et profitable auquel sont contenuz les choses plus notables à remarquer de toute l'histoire de Jean Froissart ... abrégé et illustré de plusieurs annotations, par François de Belle-Forest*. Trans. François de Belleforest. Paris: Guillaume de la Noue, 1572.

Suriano, Michele. *Discours de Michel Soriano, Venentien, traduit de son ambassade de France. Histoire de l'estat de France, tant de la république que de la religion, sous le règne de François II, etc.* [by Louis Régnier de la Planche]. Ed. Édouard Mennechet. Paris: Techener, 1836. 349–96.

Thou, Jacques-Auguste de. *Histoire universelle de Jac.-Aug. de Thou, avec la suite, par Nic. Rigault, les mémoires de la vie de l'auteur, un recueil de pièces concernant sa personne et ses ouvrages, y comprises les notes et principales variantes, etc.* 11 vols. Ed. Casaubon, Du Plessis Mornay, G. Laurant *et al.* The Hague: Henri Scheurleer, 1740.

La tragédie française du bon Kanut, roi de Danemark. La tragédie à l'époque d'Henri III (1574–1579). Ed. Christiane Lauvergnat-Gagnière. Théâtre français de la Renaissance, 2nd ser., vol. 1. Florence: Leo S. Olschki; Paris: Presses Universitaires de France, 1999.

Urfé, Honoré d'. *La triomphante entree de tresillvstre dame madame Magdeleine de La Rochefocavd, Espouse de hault et puissant Seigneur Messire Just-Loys de Tournon, Seigneur & Baron dudict lieu, Comte de Roussillon, &c., faicte en la Ville, & Vniuersité de Tournon, le dimenche vingtquatriesme du moys d'Auril 1583*. Ed. Maxime Gaume. Images et témoins de l'âge classique, 4. Fac. rpt. Saint-Étienne: Presses de l'Université de Saint-Étienne, 1976.

Valois, Marguerite de. *Correspondance 1569–1614*. Ed. Éliane Viennot. Textes de la Renaissance, 23. Paris: H. Champion, 1998.

____. *Mémoires et autres écrits 1574–1614*. Ed. Éliane Viennot. Textes de la Renaissance, 31. Paris: H. Champion, 1999.

____. *Mémoires et autres écrits de Marguerite de Valois, la reine Margot*, 2nd ed. Ed. Yves Cazaux. Paris: Mercure de France, 1986.

Virey, Jean de, seigneur Du Gravier. *Tragedie de Jeanne-d'Arques, dite la Pucelle d'Orléans, native du village d'Emprenne, pres Voucouleurs en Lorraine*. Rouen: Raphaël du Petit Val, 1600.

Critical and historical scholarship

Aquilon, Pierre. 'Les réalités provinciales.' *Histoire de l'édition française*, 3 vols. Ed. Henri-Jean Martin and Roger Chartier. Vol. 1. Paris: Promodis, 1983. 351–63.

Barroll, J. Leeds. *Politics, Plague, and Shakespeare's Theater: The Stuart Years*. Ithaca, NY: Cornell University Press, 1991.

Barthold, Wilhelm Friedrich. *Deutschland und die Hugenotten, Geschichte des Einflusses der Deutschen auf Frankreichs kirchliche und bürgerliche Verhältnisse von der Zeit des schmalkaldischen Bundes bis zum Gesetze von Nantes 1531–1598*. Vol.1. Bremen: F. Schlodtmann, 1848.

Barton, Anne. 'Introduction to *All's Well That Ends Well.*' *The Riverside Shakespeare*. Ed. G. Blakemore Evans, J. J. M. Tobin *et al.*, 2nd ed. Boston: Houghton Mifflin, 1997. 533–37.

Baumgartner, Frederic J. *Henry II, King of France, 1547–1550*. Durham, NC: Duke University Press, 1988.

Beauchamp, Virginia Walcott. 'Sidney's Sister as Translator of Garnier.' *Renaissance News* 10 (1957): 8–13.

Brennan, Michael. *Literary Patronage in the English Renaissance: The Pembroke Family*. London: Routledge, 1988.

Brioist, Pascal, Hervé Drévillon and Pierre Serna. *Croiser le fer. Violence et culture de l'épée dans la France moderne (XVIe–XVIIe siècle)*. Époques. Seyssel: Champ Vallon, 2002.

Brown, Elizabeth. 'La Renaudie se venge: l'autre face de la conjuration d'Amboise.' *Complots et conjurations dans l'Europe moderne. Actes du colloque international, Rome, 30 septembre–2 octobre 1993*. Ed. Yves-Marie Bercé and Elena Fasano Guarini. Rome: École Française de Rome, 1996. 451–74.

Buron, Emmanuel. 'Chronique d'une soumission. Lecture historique de *Cléopâtre* et *Sophonisbe* de Nicolas de Montreux.' *Le duc de Mercœur. Les armes et les lettres (1558–1602)*. Ed. Emmanuel Buron and Bruno Méniel. Rennes: Presses Universitaires de Rennes, 2009. 237–57.

Cazaux, Yves. *Jeanne d'Albret*. Paris: Éditions Albin Michel, 1973.

Champion, Pierre. *Catherine de Médicis présente à Charles IX son royaume (1564–1566)*. Paris: Grasset, 1937.

Charpentier, Françoise. *Les débuts de la tragédie héroique: Antoine de Montchrestien (1575–1621)*. Lille: Service de Reproduction des Thèses, Université de Lille III, 1981.

Chéruel, Adolphe. *Marie Stuart et Catherine de Médicis: étude historique sur les relations de la France et de l'Écosse dans la seconde moitié du XVIe siècle*. Geneva: Slatkine-Megariotis Reprints, 1975.

Clarke, Danielle. 'Mary Sidney Herbert and Women's Religious Verse.' *Early Modern English Poetry: A Critical Companion*. Ed. Patrick Cheney, Andrew Hadfield and Garrett A. Sullivan, Jr. Oxford: Oxford University Press, 2007. 184–94.

Constant, Jean-Marie. *La Ligue*. Paris: Fayard, 1996.

Crewe, Jonathan. *Hidden Designs: The Critical Profession and Renaissance Literature*. New York: Methuen, 1986.

Croix, Alain. *L'âge d'or de la Bretagne, 1532–1675*. Paris: Éditions Ouest-France, 1993.

Crouzet, Denis. *Les guerriers de Dieu: la violence au temps des troubles de religion (vers 1525–vers 1610)*, 2 vols. Seyssel: Champ Vallon, 1990.

Daele, Rose-Marie. *Nicolas de Montreulx, Ollenix du Mont-Sacré, Arbiter of European Literary Vogues of the Late Renaissance*. New York: Moretus Press, 1946.

Dareste, R. 'Hotman, sa vie et sa correspondance.' *Revue Historique* 1.2 (1876): 1–59.

Daussy, Hugues. *Les Huguenots et le roi: le combat politique de Philippe Duplessis-Mornay (1572–1600)*. Travaux d'humanisme et Renaissance, 364. Geneva: Droz, 2002.

De Grazia, Margreta. *Hamlet without Hamlet*. Cambridge: Cambridge University Press, 2006.

Demonet, Marie-Luce. *'À plaisir'. Sémiotique et scepticisme chez Montaigne*. L'Atelier de la Renaissance. Orléans: Paradigme, 2003.

Dorsten, Jan Adrianus van. *Poets, Patrons, and Professors: Sir Philip Sidney, Daniel Rogers, and the Leiden Humanists*. Publications of the Sir Thomas Browne Institute, Leiden, General Series. Leiden: University Press (for the Sir Thomas Browne Institute), 1962.

Duvernoy, Émile. *Chrétienne de Danemark, duchesse de Lorraine*. Nancy: Humblot, 1940.

Ellrodt, Robert. 'Self-Consciousness in Montaigne and Shakespeare.' *Shakespeare Survey* 28 (1975): 37–50.

Erlanger, Philippe. *Diane de Poitiers*. Paris: Gallimard, 1955.

Farnham, Willard. *The Medieval Heritage of Elizabethan Tragedy*. Berkeley: University of California Press, 1936.

Favier, Jean. *Louis XI*. Paris: Fayard, 2001.

Feis, Jacob. *Shakespeare and Montaigne: An Endeavour to Explain the Tendency of Hamlet from Allusions in Contemporary Works*. 1884; rpt. New York: AMS, 1970.

Findlay, Alison. *Illegitimate Power: Bastards in Renaissance Drama*. Manchester: Manchester University Press, 1994.

Fisken, Beth Wynne. '"To the Angel spirit …": Mary Sidney's Entry into the "World of

Words"'. *The Renaissance Englishwoman in Print: Counterbalancing the Canon*. Ed. Anne M. Haselkorn and Betty S. Travitsky. Amherst: University of Massachusetts Press, 1990. 263–75.

Forbes, Patrick. *A Full View of the Public Transactions in the Reign of Q. Elizabeth, or a Particular Account of All the Memorable Affairs of that Queen*, 2 vols. London: G. Hawkins, 1740–41.

Forsyth, Elliott. *La tragédie française de Jodelle à Corneille (1533–1640): le thème de la vengeance*. Études et essais sur la Renaissance. 1962; rpt. Paris: H. Champion, 1994.

Freer, Coburn. *Music for a King: George Herbert's Style and the Metrical Psalms*. Baltimore, MD: Johns Hopkins University Press, 1972.

Fröbe, Walter. *Kurfürst August von Sachsen und sein Verhältnis zu Dänemark bis zum Frieden von Stettin (1570): Inaugural-Dissertation zur Erlangung der Doktorwürde einer Hohen Philosophischen Fakultät der Universität Leipzig*. Leipzig: E. Glausch, 1912.

Geisendorf, Paul-Frédéric. *Théodore de Bèze*. Geneva: Alexandre Jullien, 1967.

Greengrass, Mark. 'Informal Networks in Sixteenth-Century French Protestantism.' *Society and Culture in the Huguenot World: 1559–1685*. Ed. Raymond A. Mentzer and Andrew Spicer. Cambridge: Cambridge University Press, 2002. 78–97.

Grente, Georges, Michel Simonin *et al.* (eds). *Dictionnaire des lettres françaises. Le XVIe siècle*, new ed. La Pochotèque. Encyclopédies d'aujourd'hui. Paris: Fayard, 2001.

Hadfield, Andrew. *Shakespeare and Republicanism*. Cambridge: Cambridge University Press, 2005.

Hampton, Timothy. *Literature and Nation in the Sixteenth Century: Inventing Renaissance France*. Ithaca, NY: Cornell University Press, 2001.

Hannay, Margaret P. *Philip's Phoenix: Mary Sidney, Countess of Pembroke*. New York: Oxford University Press, 1990.

Hauser, Henri. 'Antoine de Bourbon et l'Allemagne (1560–1561)'. *Revue Historique* 16 (1891): 54–61.

Hay, Millicent V. *The Life of Robert Sidney, Earl of Leicester (1563–1626)*. Washington, DC: The Folger Library; London: Associated University Presses, 1984.

Heinrich, Christoph Gottlob. *Teutsche Reichsgeschichte*, 9 vols. Leipzig: Weidmanns Erben und Reich, 1797–1805.

Hildebrandt, Esther. 'Christopher Mont, Anglo-German Diplomat.' *Sixteenth Century Journal* 15 (1984): 281–92.

Hillman, Richard. 'Des *Champs faëz* de Claude de Taillemont au labyrinthe du *Songe* shakespearien, en passant par le *Proumenoir de Monsieur de Montaigne*.' *Studi Francesi* 48.1 (2004): 3–18.

——. *French Origins of English Tragedy*. Manchester: Manchester University Press, 2010.

——. 'Hamlet and Death: A Recasting of the Play within the Player.' *Essays in Literature* 13 (1986): 201–18.

——. 'Marlowe's Guise: Offending against God and King.' *Notes and Queries* 55.2 (2008): 154–59.

____. 'A Midsummer Night's Dream and La Diane of Nicolas de Montreux.' *Review of English Studies* 61 (2010): 34–54; doi: 10.1093/res/hgp030.

____. 'The Pucelle and the *Godons* in the *Mistère du Siège d'Orléans*: Civic Pageant and Popular Tradition.' *Les Mystères: Studies in Text, Theatricality and Urban Drama.* Ed. Peter Happé and Wim Hüsken. Amsterdam: Rodopi, forthcoming: 169–90.

____. *Self-Speaking in Medieval and Early Modern English Drama: Subjectivity, Discourse and the Stage.* Basingstoke, Hampshire: Macmillan; New York: St. Martin's, 1997.

____. *Shakespearean Subversions: The Trickster and the Play-text.* London: Routledge, 1992.

____. *Shakespeare, Marlowe and the Politics of France.* Basingstoke, Hampshire: Palgrave, 2002.

____. 'The Tragic Channel-Crossings of George Chapman, Part I: *Bussy D'Ambois* and *The Conspiracy and Tragedy of Byron.' Cahiers Élisabéthains* 45 (2004): 25–43.

Honoré-Duvergé, Suzanne. 'L'origine du surnom de Charles le Mauvais.' *Mélanges d'histoire du moyen-âge dédiés à la mémoire de Louis Halphen.* Ed. Charles-Edmond Perrin. Paris: Presses Universitaires de France, 1951. 345–50.

Hooker, Elizabeth Robbins. 'The Relation of Montaigne to Shakespeare.' *PMLA* 17 (1902): 302–66.

Hopkins, Lisa. *The Cultural Uses of the Caesars on the English Renaissance Stage.* Studies in Performance and Early Modern Drama. Aldershot: Ashgate, 2008.

____. 'Paris is Worth a Mass: *All's Well That Ends Well* and the Wars of Religion.' *Shakespeare and the Culture of Christianity in Early Modern England.* Ed. Dennis Taylor and David N. Beauregard. Studies in Religion and Literature, 6. New York: Fordham University Press, 2003. 369–81.

Jacquart, Jean. *Bayard.* Paris: Fayard, 1987.

Johannesson, Kurt. *The Renaissance of the Goths in Sixteenth-century Sweden: Johannes and Olaus Magnus as Politicians and Historians.* Trans. and ed. James Larson. Berkeley: University of California Press, 1991.

Jondorf, Gillian. *Robert Garnier and the Themes of Political Tragedy in the Sixteenth Century.* Cambridge: Cambridge University Press, 1969.

Jones, Emrys. *Scenic Form in Shakespeare.* Oxford: Clarendon Press, 1971.

Jones, Leonard Chester. *Simon Goulart (1543–1628). Étude biographique et bibliographique.* Geneva: Georg; Paris: H. Champion, 1917.

Jouanna, Arlette, Jacqueline Boucher, Dominique Biloghi *et al.* (eds). *Histoire et dictionnaire des Guerres de Religion.* Paris: Robert Laffont, 1998.

Kelley, Donald R. *François Hotman: A Revolutionary's Ordeal.* Princeton, NJ: Princeton University Press, 1973.

Kewes, Paulina. '"A Fit Memorial for the Times to Come …": Admonition and Topical Application in Mary Sidney's *Antonius* and Samuel Daniel's *Cleopatra.' Review of English Studies* (forthcoming 2012).

Kim, Seong Hak. 'Michel de l'Hôpital.' *Proceedings of the Annual Meeting of the Western Society for French History* 17 (1989): 106–12.

Kingdon, Robert M. *Geneva and the Consolidation of the French Protestant Movement,*

1564–1572: A Contribution to the History of Congregationalism, Presbyterianism and Calvinist Resistance Theory. Travaux d'humanisme et Renaissance, 92. Geneva: Droz, 1967.

Knecht, Ronald J. *Renaissance Warrior and Patron: The Reign of Francis I*. Cambridge: Cambridge University Press, 1994.

La Croix du Maine, François Grudé, seigneur de. *Premier volume de la Bibliothèque du sieur de La Croix Du Maine, qui est un catalogue général de toutes sortes d'autheurs qui ont escrit en françois depuis cinq cents ans et plus jusques à ce jour d'huy, etc*. Paris: A. L'Angelier, 1584.

Lamb, Mary Ellen. *Gender and Authorship in the Sidney Circle*. Madison: University of Wisconsin Press, 1990.

Lambin, Georges. *Shakespeare et Tournon*. Tournon: Aux Amis des Arts, 1954.

——. *Voyages de Shakespeare en France et en Italie*. Travaux d'humanisme et Renaissance, 53. Geneva: Droz, 1962.

Lee, Sidney. *A Life of William Shakespeare*, rev. and enl. edn. London: Smith, Elder, 1915.

Lefranc, Abel. *Hélène de Tournon, celle qui mourut d'amour, et l'Ophélie d'Hamlet*. Drawings by Daniel Némoze. Collection du Pigeonnier, 15. Paris: Maison du Livre Français, 1926.

——. *Sous le masque de 'William Shakespeare': William Stanley, VIe comte de Derby*, 2 vols. Paris: Payot, 1918–19.

Le Hir, Yves. Rev. of *La Soltane*, by Gabriel Bounin, ed. Michael Heath (1977). *Bibliothèque d'Humanisme et Renaissance* 41 (1979): 192–93.

Léris, Antoine de, ed. *Dictionnaire portatif historique et littéraire des théâtres, etc.*, 2nd ed. Paris: A. Jombert, 1763. Electronic version http://cesar.org.uk/cesar2/ books/leris/ (accesssed July 2010).

Leroy, Béatrice. *Le royaume de Navarre au Moyen Âge: les hommes et le pouvoir, XIIIe– XVe siècle*. Biarritz: J. et D. Éditions, 1995.

Lestringant, Frank. 'Deux vies parallèles: Henri III et Dom Sébastien 1er de Portugal.' *Henri III et son temps: actes du colloque international du Centre de la Renaissance de Tours, octobre 1989*. Ed. Robert Sauzet. De Pétrarque à Descartes, 56. Paris: Librairie Philosophique J. Vrin, 1992. 227–37.

Levin, Harry. *The Question of Hamlet*. Alexander Lectures, 1958. New York: Oxford University Press, 1959.

Limbrick, Elaine. '"Ce dernier tour d'escrime".' *Cahiers de l'Association Internationale des Études Françaises* 33 (mai, 1981): 53–64.

MacArthur, Janet. 'Ventriloquizing Comfort and Despair: Mary Sidney's Female Personae in *The Triumph of Death* and *The Tragedy of Antony*.' *Sidney Newsletter and Journal* 11 (1990): 3–13.

MacCaffrey, Wallace. *Elizabeth I*. London: Arnold, 1993.

Maguin, Jean-Marie, and Angela Maguin. *William Shakespeare*. Paris: Fayard, 1996.

Mallin, Eric S. *Inscribing the Time: Shakespeare and the End of Elizabethan England*. The New Historicism. Studies in Cultural Poetics, 33. Berkeley: University of California Press, 1995.

Margolin, Jean-Claude. 'Rasse des Noeux et la Saint-Barthélemy.' *Actes du colloque 'L'amiral de Coligny et son temps' (Paris, 24–28 octobre 1972)*. Paris: Société de l'Histoire du Protestantisme Français, 1974. 489–513.

Massip, Maurice. *Le Collège de Tournon en Vivarais, d'après les documents originaux inédits*. Paris: A. Picard, 1890.

Masson, Gustave. 'Mort de Gaspard de Heu, seigneur de Buy, 1er septembre 1558.' *Bulletin de la Société d'Histoire du Protestantisme Français* 25 (1876): 164–80.

Maxwell, Julie. 'Counter-Reformation Versions of Saxo: A New Source for *Hamlet*?' *Renaissance Quarterly* 57 (2004): 518–60.

Mazon, Albin. *Notes et documents historiques sur les huguenots du Vivarais par le Dr Francus*, 4 vols. 1901–4; fac. rpt. Valence: Éditions de la Bouquinerie, 1994.

Monnet, Camille. *Petite histoire véridique des faits et gestes du capitaine Bayard avant et pendant les guerres d'Italie*. Grenoble: R. Félix, 1970.

Mouflard, Marie-Madeleine. *Robert Garnier (1545–1590)*, 3 vols. La Fierté Bernard: R. Bellanger; later La Roche-sur-Yon: Imprimerie Centrale de l'Ouest, 1961–64.

Mueller, Martin. 'From *Leir* to *Lear*.' *Philological Quarterly* 73 (1994): 195–217.

Muir, Kenneth. 'Elizabeth I, Jodelle, and Cleopatra.' *Renaissance Drama* ns 2 (1969): 197–206.

Muntz, A. 'Entrevue de Christophe duc de Würtemberg avec les Guise, à Saverne, peu de jours avant le massacre de Vassy, 1562. Relation autograph du duc de Würtemberg.' *Bulletin de la Société de l'Histoire du Protestantisme Français* 4 (1856): 184–96.

Naef, Henri. *La conjuration d'Amboise et Genève*. Geneva: A. Jullien, Georg; Paris: Édouard Champion, 1922.

Nicollier-De Weck, Béatrice. *Hubert Languet (1518–1581): un Réseau politique international de Melancthon à Guillaume d'Orange*. Travaux d'humanisme et Renaissance, 293. Geneva: Droz, 1995.

Norland, Howard B. *Neoclassical Tragedy in Elizabethan England*. Newark: University of Delaware Press, 2009.

O'Connor, John J. 'Chief Source of Marston's *Dutch Courtezan*.' *Philological Quarterly* 54 (1957): 505–15.

Pallier, Denis. 'La réponse catholique.' *Histoire de l'édition française*. Ed. Henri-Jean Martin and Roger Chartier. Paris: Promodis, 1983. 327–47.

Pariset, Jean-Daniel. *Les relations entre la France et l'Allemagne au milieu du XVIe siècle: d'après des documents inédits*. Publications de la Société Savante d'Alsace et des Régions de l'Est. Grandes publications. Strasbourg: Librairie ISTRA, 1981.

Prat, J.-M. *Recherches historiques et critiques sur la Compagnie de Jésus en France du temps du P. Coton (1564–1626)*, 3 vols. Vol. 1. Lyons: Briday, 1876.

Prescott, Anne Lake. *Imagining Rabelais in Renaissance England*. New Haven, CT: Yale University Press, 1998.

_____. 'Mary Sidney's French Sophocles: The Countess of Pembroke Reads Robert Garnier.' *Representing France and the French in Early Modern English Drama*. Ed. Jean-Christophe Mayer. Newark: University of Delaware Press, 2008. 68–89.

Rahlenbeck, Charles. *Metz et Thionville sous Charles-Quint*. Brussels: M. Weissenbruch, 1880.

Rees, Joan. *Samuel Daniel: A Critical and Biographical Study*. Liverpool: Liverpool University Press, 1964.

———. 'Samuel Daniel's *Cleopatra* and Two French Plays.' *Modern Language Review* 47 (1952): 1–10.

Richard, Alfred. *Un diplomate poitevin du XVIe siècle. Charles de Danzay, ambassadeur de France en Danemark*. Poitiers: Blais et Roy, 1910.

Rigolot, François. 'D'une *théologie* "pour les dames" à une *apologie* "per le donne"?' *Montaigne, 'Apologie de Raimond Sebond'. De la Theologia à la Théologie*. Ed. Claude Blum. Études montaignistes, 6. Paris: H. Champion, 1990. 261–90.

Robertson, John M. *Montaigne and Shakespeare, and Other Essays on Cognate Questions*, 2nd ed. London: Adam and Charles Black, 1909.

Rodriguez-Salgado, Mia J. *The Changing Face of Empire: Charles V, Philip II and Habsburg Authority, 1551–1559*. Cambridge Studies in Early Modern History. Cambridge: Cambridge University Press, 1988.

Romier, Lucien. *Jacques d'Albon de Saint-André, maréchal de France (1512–1561). La carrière d'un favori*. Paris: Perrin, 1909.

———. *Les origines politiques des guerres de religion. D'après des documents originaux inédits*, 2 vols. 1913–14; rpt. Geneva: Slatkine-Megariotis, 1974.

Ruble, Alphonse de. *Antoine de Bourbon et Jeanne d'Albret, suite de Le mariage de Jeanne d'Albret*, 4 vols. Paris: A. Labitte, 1881–86.

Sanders, Eve Rachele. *Gender and Literacy on Stage in Early Modern England*. Cambridge Studies in Renaissance Literature and Culture. Cambridge: Cambridge University Press, 1998.

Schanzer, Ernest. '*Antony and Cleopatra* and the Countess of Pembroke's *Antonius*.' *Notes and Queries* 3.4 (1956): 152–54; doi:10.1093/nq/3.4.15.

———. 'Daniel's Revision of His *Cleopatra*.' *Review of English Studies* 8 (1957): 375–81; doi:10.1093/res/VIII.32.375.

———. *The Problem Plays of Shakespeare: A Study of* Julius Caesar, Measure for Measure, Antony and Cleopatra. London: Routledge and Kegan Paul, 1963.

———. 'Three Notes on *Antony and Cleopatra*.' *Notes and Queries* 7.1 (1960): 20–22; doi:10.1093/nq/7.1.20.

Schoenbaum, Samuel. *William Shakespeare: A Documentary Life*. New York: Oxford University Press, in assoc. with The Scolar Press, 1975.

Seward, Desmond. *Henry V: The Scourge of God*. New York: Viking Penguin, 1987.

Shaheen, Naseeb. *Biblical References in Shakespeare's Plays*. Newark: University of Delaware Press; London: Associated University Presses, 1999.

Simonin, Michel. *Vivre de sa plume au XVIe siècle, ou, La carrière de François de Belleforest*. Travaux d'humanisme et Renaissance, 268. Geneva: Droz, 1992.

Sitzmann, J. Édouard. *Dictionnaire de biographie des hommes célèbres en Alsace*, 2 vols. Rixheim: F. Sutler, 1909–10.

Snyder, Susan. 'Naming Names in *All's Well That Ends Well.' Shakespeare Quarterly* 43 (1992): 265–79.

Sournia, Jean-Claude. *Blaise de Monluc: soldat et écrivain (1500–1577)*. Paris: Fayard, 1981.

Spriet, Pierre. *Samuel Daniel (1563–1619), sa vie – son œuvre*. Études anglaises, 29. Paris: Didier, 1968.

Stirling, Brents. 'Cleopatra's Scene with Seleucus: Plutarch, Daniel, and Shakespeare.' *Shakespeare Quarterly* 15 (1964): 299–311.

Stone, Donald, Jr. 'Belleforest's Bandello: A Bibliographical Study.' *Bibliothèque d'Humanisme et Renaissance* 34 (1972): 489–99.

Sullivan, Garrett A., Jr. *Memory and Forgetting in English Renaissance Drama: Shakespeare, Marlowe, Webster*. Cambridge Studies in Renaissance Literature and Culture, 50. Cambridge: Cambridge University Press, 2005.

Sutherland, Nicola Mary. 'Queen Elizabeth and the Conspiracy of Amboise, March 1560.' *Princes, Politics and Religion, 1547–1589*. London: Hambledon Press, 1984. 97–112.

Taveneaux, René. 'L'esprit de croisade en Lorraine aux XVIe et XVIIe siècles.' *L'Europe, l'Alsace et la France, problèmes intérieurs et réactions internationales à l'epoque moderne. Études réunies en l'honneur du Doyen Georges Livet pour son 70e anniversaire*. Publications de la Société Savante d'Alsace et des Régions de l'Est. Grandes publications, 28. Colmar: Les Éditions d'Alsace, 1986. 256–63.

Tucoo-Chala, Pierre. *Gaston Fébus, prince des Pyrénées (1331–1391)*. Pau: J. et D. – Deucalion, 1993.

Vaurigaud, Benjamin. *Essais sur l'histoire des églises réformées de Bretagne, 1535–1808*, 3 vols. Paris: J. Cherbuliez, 1870.

Viennot, Éliane. *Marguerite de Valois: histoire d'une femme, histoire d'un mythe*. Paris: Payot, 1993.

Vogler, Bernard. 'Le rôle des électeurs palatins dans les guerres de Religion en France.' *Cahiers d'histoire* 10 (1965): 51–85.

Waddington, Albert. 'La France et les Protestants allemands sous Charles IX et Henri III. Hubert Languet et Gaspard de Schomberg.' *Revue Historique* 42 (1890): 241–77.

Waller, G. F. 'The Countess of Pembroke and Gendered Reading.' *The Renaissance Englishwoman in Print: Counterbalancing the Canon*. Ed. Anne M. Haselkorn and Betty S. Travitsky. Amherst: University of Massachusetts Press, 1990. 327–46.

____. *Mary Sidney, Countess of Pembroke: A Critical Study of Her Writings and Literary Milieu*. Salzburg Studies in English Literature, Elizabethan and Renaissance Studies, 87. Salzburg: Institut für Anglistik und Amerikanistik, Universität Salzburg, 1979.

Wells, Stanley, Gary Taylor *et al. William Shakespeare: A Textual Companion*. New York: Norton, 1997.

Wilcox, Helen. 'Drums and Roses? The Tragicomedy of War in *All's Well That Ends Well.'*

Shakespeare and War. Ed. Ros King and Paul J. C. M. Franssen. Basingstoke, Hampshire: Palgrave Macmillan, 2008. 84–95.

Williams, Deanne. 'Roussillon and Retrospection in *All's Well That Ends Well.*' *Representing France and the French in Early Modern English Drama.* Ed. Jean-Christophe Mayer. Newark: University of Delaware Press, 2008. 161–77.

Wilson, Richard. *Secret Shakespeare: Studies in Theatre, Religion and Resistance.* Manchester: Manchester University Press, 2004.

___. 'To Great St Jaques Bound: *All's Well That Ends Well* in Shakespeare's Europe.' *Shakespeare et l'Europe de la Renaissance: Actes du congrès organisé par la Société Française Shakespeare.* Ed. Yves Peyré and Pierre Kapitaniak. Paris: Société Française Shakespeare, Institut du Monde Anglophone, Université de Paris III – Sorbonne Nouvelle, 2004. 273–90.

Witherspoon, Alexander Maclaren. *The Influence of Robert Garnier on Elizabethan Drama.* Yale Studies in English, 65. 1924; rpt. Hamden, CT: Archon Books, 1968.

Wright, Herbert G. 'How Did Shakespeare Come to Know the *Decameron*?' *Modern Language Review* 50 (1955): 45–48.

___. 'The Indebtedness of Painter's Translations of Boccaccio in *The Palace of Pleasure* to the French version of Le Maçon.' *Modern Language Review* 40 (1951): 431–35.

Yachnin, Paul. '"Courtiers of Beauteous Freedom": *Antony and Cleopatra* in its Time.' *Renaissance and Reformation/Renaissance et Réforme* ns 15.1 (1991): 1–20.

Index

Abra de Raconis, Charles-François, d'
    (bishop of Lavaur) 143n.18
Aesop 114
Aggas, Edward 134
    Defence of Death, The (trans. of
        Mornay, *Excellent discours*) 134,
        135, 147n.57, 147n.58
Agnès de Navarre (wife of Gaston III,
    Count of Foix; c.1337–96) 65, 67
Alba, House of 177
Albon de Saint-André, Jacques d' *see*
    Saint-André, Jacques d'Albon de
Albret, Jeanne d', Queen of Navarre
    (1528–72) 28, 33, 35, 37, 53, 62
    Mémoires 28, 30, 31, 84n.22, 84n.23,
        85n.31, 86n.40
Alençon, François-Hercule, Duke of
    (latterly Duke of Anjou) 59,
    91n.89, 96, 199n.57
Alexander the Great 18–20, 22, 83n.6
Aliénor de Comminges (mother of
    Gaston III, Count of Foix; 1329–
    1402) 65
Amboise, Conspiracy of (1560) 29, 35,
    44, 50, 85n.28, 85n.30, 89n.77
Ample Declaration des lettres précédentes
    see Albret, Jeanne d', *Mémoires*
Amyot, Jacques 4, 6, 8, 105, 138, 140,
    147–48n.62, 148n.63
Anjou, Duke of *see* Alençon, François-
    Hercule, Duke of; Henri III, King
    of France; René, Duke of Anjou
Anna of Denmark, Electress/Duchess
    of Saxony (1532–85) 47

Anna of Denmark, Queen of Scotland,
    later of England (1574–1619) 47
Antoine, Duke of Lorraine (1489–
    1544) 164, 197n.27
Antony, Marc [Marcus Antonius] 9,
    91n.93, 94–95, 100, 101, 104,
    117, 118, 120, 135–36
Aquilon, Pierre 142n.15
Arbaleste, Charlotte (wife of Philippe
    de Mornay; *Mémoires et correspon-
    dance*) 102
Arc, Jeanne d' *see* Jeanne d'Arc
Ariosto, Lodovico (*Orlando Furioso*)
    98–99, 143n.16
Arnauld, Antoine (*Libre discours sur la
    delivrance de la Bretagne*) 97–98
Arthur (legendary King of Britain) 63,
    162
Aubigny, Agrippa d' (*Histoire
    universelle*) 86n.32
Aubrey, John (*Brief Lives*) 129
Augsburg, Confession of (1530) 47,
    88n.58
Augsburg, Peace of (1555) 46
August I, Elector/Duke of Saxony
    (1526–86) 45, 47, 49, 53, 85n.29
Augustine, Saint (*The City of God*)
    178–79
Augustus, Caius Octavius, Emperor of
    Rome 9, 12n.15, 95, 100, 103,
    108, 110, 118
Aumale, Duke of *see* Guise, Charles Ier
    de, Duke of Aumale

Balançon, Philibert de Rye, Baron of
    181, 182, 183
Bandello, Matteo (*Novelle*) 65, 200n.67
Barroll, J. Leeds 144n.29
Barthold, Wilhelm Friedrich 88n.69,
    89n.73
Bartholomew's Day massacre, Saint (24
    August 1572) 29, 57, 59, 63, 64,
    95, 124, 174
Barton, Anne 194n.5
Baumgartner, Frederic J. 194n.9
Bayard, Gilbert, baron de La Font
    (minister of François I) 196n.26
Bayard, Pierre Terrail, seigneur de
    (c.1474–1524) 161–66, 167, 169,
    179–80, 189, 195n.21, 195–
    96n.22, 196n.23, 196n.25,
    196n.26, 196–97n.27
Beauchamp, Virginia Walcott 146n.43
Beaudin, Jean-Dominique 144n.33
Beaudoin de Boulogne, King of
    Jerusalem (c.1065–1118)
    197n.27
Belleforest, François de 1, 55, 56, 57,
    62, 65, 91n.101, 170, 175, 176
    *Discours de la brave resistance faite
        aux rebelles l'an 1567* 175, 176,
        198–99n.53
    Discours des presages et miracles 56
    *Grandes Annales et histoire générale de
        France, Les* 59, 64–65, 70,
        91n.102, 92n.104, 92n.109
    *Histoire des neuf roys Charles de
        France* 60–62
    Histoires tragiques 2–3, 11n.3, 11n.4,
        16–17, 22–24, 25, 33, 36, 37,
        54–81 *passim*, 83n.16, 87n.45,
        90n.85, 90n.86, 90n.87,
        90–91n.88, 91n.89, 91n.94,
        92n.106, 92n.110, 92n.112,
        92–93n.113, 93n.115, 93n.119,
        170, 197n.35, 200n.67

    L'histoire universelle du monde
        170–71, 175, 176
    *L'innocence de … Marie, royne
        d'Escosse* 57, 91n.90
    Hystorie of Hamblet, The (anon.
        translation) 2, 36, 83, 87n.45
    pastorale amovrevse, La 167–70, 175,
        177–78, 179, 187, 188–90,
        197n.30, 197n.34, 199n.53,
        199n.58
    *Recueil diligent et profitable … Frois-
        sart abrégé* 63–64, 66, 92n.106,
        92n.109
    Remonstrance av peuple de Paris 56
Belyard, Simon (*Le Guysien*) 12n.6
Berners, Lord *see* Bourchier, John, Lord
    Berners
bestrafte Brudermord, Der 82n.5, 90n.86
Beza, Theodore *see* Bèze, Théodore de
Bèze, Théodore de 28, 31, 35, 50,
    86n.33, 175
    *Histoire ecclésiastique des églises réfor-
        mées* 28, 84n.24, 86n.33
Bible, The 16, 25–28, 31, 36, 82n.3,
    83n.13, 83–84n.17, 84n.18,
    84n.21, 145n.40
Biet, Christian 145n.40
Biloghi, Dominique 86n.33, 86n.34,
    87n.55, 91n.96, 91n.98, 141n.3,
    141n.10, 146n.46, 195n.17,
    197n.29, 198n.37, 198n.41,
    198n.44, 198n.47
'Black Prince, The' *see* Edward of
    Woodstock, Prince of Wales
Boccaccio, Giovanni (*Decameron*) 4,
    153, 154, 155, 156, 171, 173, 175,
    181, 186
Bodley, Thomas 51
Bolwiller, Nicolas de (*bailli* of Hague-
    nau) 46, 51, 87n.54
Bordeille, Pierre de *see* Brantôme,
    Pierre de Bourdeille, abbé de

Bordenave, Nicolas de (*Histoire de Béarn et Navarre*) 35–41, 53, 86n.38, 86.40

Boucher, Jacqueline 86n.33, 86n.34, 87n.55, 91n.96, 91n.98, 141n.3, 141n.10, 146n.46, 195n.17, 197n.29, 198n.37, 198n.41, 198n.44, 198n.47

Boulogne, Beaudoin de *see* Beaudoin de Boulogne

Bourbon, Antoine de, Count of Vendôme, King of Navarre (1518–62) 25–54 *passim*, 58, 61, 62, 81, 84n.25 84n.26, 85n.29, 85n.31, 85–86n.32, 86n.33, 86n.36, 86n.41, 87n.44, 87n.47, 87n.55, 87n.58, 88n.62, 88n.66, 89n.75, 89n.76, 89–90n.77, 184

Bourbon, Catherine de 83n.11

Bourbon, Charles III de Montpensier, Duke of (1490–1527) 196n.24

Bourbon, House of 27, 81
see also Bourbon, Antoine de, Count of Vendôme, King of Navarre; Bourbon, Catherine de; Condé, Louis Ier de Bourbon, Prince of; Henri IV, King of France and Navarre

Bourbon, Louis Ier, Prince of Condé *see* Condé, Louis Ier de Bourbon, Prince of

Bourchier, John, Lord Berners (translator of Froissart) 66, 92n.105

Braga, Saint Martin of 134

Brantôme, Pierre de Bourdeille, abbé de 42–43, 53, 61, 87n.46, 87n.47, 184, 200

Brennan, Michael 123, 127, 128, 130, 146n.44, 146n.51, 146–47n.53, 147n.55, 147n.62

Brioist, Pascal 83n.13

Brissac, Charles Ier de Cossé, Count of (Marshal of France; 1505–63) 84n.25

Brooke, Henry, Lord Cobham *see* Cobham, Henry Brooke, Lord

Brooke, Lord *see* Greville, Fulke, Lord Brooke

Brown, Elizabeth 85n.28

Brutus, Marcus Junius 9, 24, 50, 135

Bullough, Geoffrey 8, 9, 12n.14, 54–55, 93n.118, 105, 144n.31, 145n.35, 155, 200

Burghley, Lord *see* Cecil, Willam, Lord Burghley [or Burleigh]

Buron, Emmanuel 141n.11, 142–43n.16

Caesar, Augustus *see* Augustus, Caius Octavius

Caesar, Julius 9, 12n.15, 18–19, 94, 97–98, 103

Calvin, Jean 31
Calvinism/Calvinists 4, 28, 47, 49, 56, 87n.58, 88n.62
Institution of the Christian Religion 27, 84n.20

Canute IV, King of Denmark (c.1042–86) 56, 57

Capilupi, Camillo (*Le Stratagème, ou la ruse de Charles IX*) 57

Carey, Henry, Baron Hunsdon *see* Hunsdon, Henry Carey, Baron

Carlos, Prince of Asturias ['Don Carlos'] (1545–68) 88n.64

Case, R. H. 144n.30

Cateau-Cambrésis, Peace of (1559) 33–34, 37, 44, 46, 49, 52, 89–90n.77

Catharism/Cathars 154

Catiline [Lucius Sergius Catilina] 98

Cato, Marcus Porcius 135, 137

Catullus, Valerius 128

Cazaux, Yves 5, 12n.7, 12n.8, 53,
    87n.52, 200–1n.67
Cecil, Willam, Lord Burghley [or
    Burleigh] 46, 49, 87n.54, 88n.65,
    88n.69, 88n.70, 172, 198n.39
Champier, Symphorien 161, 162
    vie de Bayard, La 160–66 *passim*,
    178–81 *passim*, 196n.22,
    196–97n.27
Champion, Pierre 198n.43
Chantelouve, François de (*La tragédie
    de feu Gaspard de Colligny*) 59
Chapman, George 2, 9, 87n.46
Chappuys, Gabriel (*L'histoire du
    royaume de Navarre*) 86n.41
Charles II ['the Bad'], King of Navarre
    (1332–87) 58–75 *passim*, 81,
    91n.92, 91n.94, 91n.102,
    92n.106, 92n.108, 92n.109
Charles III, Duke of Lorraine
    (1543–1608) 48, 49, 51, 52,
    88n.71
Charles V, Holy Roman Emperor
    (1500–58) 45, 166, 171
Charles V ['the Wise'], King of France
    (1338–80) 58, 60, 91n.92
Charles VIII, King of France
    (1470–98) 171
Charles IX, King of France (1550–74)
    32, 34, 46, 48, 56, 57, 58, 59,
    85n.27, 91n.94, 95, 171–73,
    197n.33
Charpentier, Françoise 142n.15,
    144n.33
Chastel, Jean 174, 198n.47
Châtillon *see* Coligny
Chaucer, Geoffrey 8
Chekhov, Anton 194
Chéruel, Adolphe 88n.64, 88n.66
Christian II, King of Denmark
    (1481–59) 48–52
Christian III, King of Denmark
    (1503–59) 48

Christina of Denmark, Duchess of
    Lorraine (1521–90) 48 52 *passim*,
    88n.68, 89n.76
Christoph, Duke of Württemberg
    (1515–68) 88n.58
Cinthio, Giambattista Giraldi
    (*Cleopatra*) 8
Clarke, Danielle 146n.45
Claude de France *see* Valois, Claude de
Cleopatra, Queen of Egypt 91n.93, 94,
    97–114 *passim*, 122, 143n.18,
    145n.36, 147n.60
Cobham, Henry Brooke, Lord
    (ambassador to France) 199n.57,
    199n.61
Coligny, Gaspard de [also Châtillon],
    Admiral of France (1519–72) 59,
    91n.101, 95, 175
Comminges, Aliénor de *see* Aliénor de
    Comminges
Condé, Louis Ier de Bourbon, Prince of
    (1530–69) 29, 32, 38, 85n.30, 95
Constant, Jean-Marie 146n.46
Coste, Hilarion de 172
    éloges de nos rois, Les 176, 198n.38
    *Éloges et les vies … des dames illustres,
    Les* 175–76, 199n.54, 199n.55,
    199n.61
Cotgrave, Randle (*A Dictionarie of the
    French and English Tongues*) 3,
    192, 201n.70, 201n.71
Courteault, Paul 195n.18
Crane, David 3
Crewe, Jonathan 129
Croix, Alain 141n.10, 142n.12
Crouzet, Denis 56, 59, 91n.97, 161

Daele, Rose-Marie 141n.9, 142–43n.16
Daniel, Samuel 104, 124, 126, 144n.30
    Cleopatra 1, 8, 97, 101–25 *passim*,
    137, 141n.8, 142n.16,
    143–44n.21, 144n.26, 144n.27,
    144n.28, 144n.29, 144n.31,

144n.32, 145n.34, 145n.36,
146n.48, 147n.61, 148–49n.66
Letter sent from *Octauia, A* 105–7,
144n.32
Philotas 125, 146n.48
Dareste, R. [Rodolphe Dareste de la
Chavanne] 87n.53
Daussy, Hugues 144n.22
De Grazia, Margreta 2, 6–7, 12n.10
Demonet, Marie-Luce 82n.2
Derby, Earl of *see* Stanley, William, Earl
of Derby
destinée de Gaston Fébus, La (Internet
document) 92n.107
Dio Cassius (*Roman History*) 103
Dorothea of Denmark, Electress
Palatine (1520–80) 48, 49, 52
Dorsten, Jan Adrianus van 90n.82
Drévillon, Hervé 83n.13
Du Bellay, Martin 195n.19
Duchesne, Léger 56
Duvernoy, Émile 49, 51, 52, 88n.68,
89n.76

Edward of Woodstock, Prince of Wales
('the Black Prince') 65
Elizabeth I, Queen of England 44, 46,
48, 51, 52, 88n.63, 89–90n.77,
101, 123, 125, 144n.21, 144n.27,
172
Ellrodt, Robert 14, 82n.1
Erlanger, Philippe 195n.9
Escars [des Cars], François Pérusse,
Count of (d. 1595) 81
Escluse, Charles d' 8
Essex, Robert Devereux, Earl of 125

Farnham, Willard 125
*Faustbuch see L'histoire prodigieuse du
Docteur Fauste; historie of the
damnable life, and deserued death
of Doctor Iohn Faustus, The*
Favier, Jean 197n.36

Feis, Jacob 82n.4
Ferdinand I, Holy Roman Emperor
(1503–64) 45, 46–47
Ferdinand II, King of Aragon
(1452–1516) 33
Ferté-sous-Jouarre, Synod of (1564)
172, 198n.37, 198n.39
Field, Richard 8, 11n.1, 134, 140
Findlay, Alison 93n.119
Fisken, Beth Wynne 146n.50, 147n.53
Florio, John 4, 14, 15, 16, 22, 81–82n.1,
83n.8
Foix, Gaston, Count of *see* Gaston III
('Phoebus'), Count of Foix
Forsyth, Elliott 141n.2
François I, Duke of Lorraine
(1517–45) 48
François I, King of France
(1494–1547) 156, 158, 161, 162,
164, 166, 194n.8, 195n.9,
195n.19, 196n.24
François II, King of France (1544–60)
27–34 *passim,* 35, 38, 42–43, 44,
48, 52, 85n.31, 85–86n.32, 179
Frederick I, King of Denmark
(1471–1533) 48
Frederick II, Elector/Count Palatine
(1482–1556) 48
Frederick II, King of Denmark
(1534–88) 47–53 *passim,* 88n.63,
88n.64, 88n.69, 88n.70
Frederick III, Elector/Count Palatine
(1515–76) 33, 45, 47, 52, 85n.29,
87n.58, 90n.78
Freer, Coburn 127
Fregoso, Battista ['Fulgose'] 65–66
Fröbe, Walter 89n.73
Froissart, Jean (*Chronicles*) 63, 65–66,
91n.92, 92n.105, 92n.108
Fronton Du Duc (*L'histoire tragique de
la Pucelle de Dom-Rémy*) 119,
198n.49
Fulgose *see* Fregoso, Batista

Garcilaso de la Vega (Eclogue) 177–78
Garnier, Robert 123–24, 141n.5,
    143n.16, 146n.46
  Cornélie 95–96, 124–25
  Hymne de la Monarchie 95, 123–24
  Juifves, Les 124, 146n.46
  Marc Antoine 1, 94, 96–97, 98, 99,
    101, 103, 104, 108, 112, 115–18,
    119, 120, 122–25, 128, 130–33,
    135–38, 140, 141n.5, 141n.8,
    144n.26, 147n.54, 147n.55,
    147n.60, 147–48n.62
  Porcie 94–95, 96, 124–25
  Tombeau du feu Roy Tres-Chrestien
    Charles IX, Le 123–24
Gaston III ['Phoebus'], Count of Foix
    (1331–91) 56, 57 60, 61, 63, 65
    80 passim, 81, 91n.91, 92n.104,
    92n.106, 92n.107, 92–93n.113
Gaume, Maxime 176, 197n.30,
    197n.32, 197n.33, 197n.34,
    198n.46, 199n.58
Geisendorf, Paul-Frédéric 84n.24,
    86n.33
Giannetti, Guido (English intelligence
    agent) 90n.77
Ginsberg, Ellen S. 141n.1, 141n.4
Godefroy de Bouillon 164, 197n.27
Gollancz, Israel 54–55, 90n.86
Goulart, Simon 12n.5
  Histoire des choses mémorables
    avenues en France 28, 41
  historical collection, of the most memo-
    rable accidents, and tragicall
    massacres of France, An 28, 29, 97
  Plutarch's Lives (trans. North),
    additions to 8, 140, 148n.64
  sixiesme et dernier recueil, contenant
    les choses plvs memorables auenues
    sovs la Ligue, Le 198n.48
  Vies des hommes illustres, Les
    (Plutarch, trans. Amyot), edition
    of 4, 138–40, 148n.63

Granvelle, Antoine Perrenot, Cardinal
    of (1517–86) 47, 89n.77
Greene, Robert (Friar Bacon and Friar
    Bungay) 167
Greengrass, Mark 144n.24
Grente, Georges 142n.16
Gresham, Thomas (financier, royal
    agent, c.1519–79) 88n.65
Greville, Fulke, Lord Brooke 54, 123,
    125, 146n.48
Grévin, Jacques (César) 94, 95, 141n.1,
    141n.4
Grimeston, Edward 84
Grosnet, Pierre 134
Grumbach, Wilhelm von (soldier-of-
    fortune; 1503–67) 50–52, 54,
    89n.72, 89n.73, 89n.74, 89n.75
Guise, Charles, Cardinal of see
    Lorraine, Cardinal Charles de
Guise, Charles de, Duke of Mayenne
    see Lorraine, Charles de, Duke of
    Mayenne
Guise, Charles Ier de, Duke of Aumale
    (1554–1611) 10
Guise, Duke of see Lorraine, Henri de,
    Duke of Guise; Lorraine, François
    de, Duke of Guise
Guise, House of 27–54 passim, 56, 81,
    84n.25, 84–85n.26, 85n.27,
    86n.41, 86n.43, 88n.58, 88n.69,
    89n.73, 89n.74, 89–90n.77, 96,
    146n.47, 164, 168, 173
  see also Lorraine, House of;
    individual names
Gustave Vasa, King of Sweden
    (1496–1560) 50, 51

Hadfield, Andrew 11n.3
Hakluyt, Richard (Voyages) 87n.51
Hall, Edward (Chronicle) 196n.25
Hamblet, The Hystorie of see Belleforest,
    François de, Hystorie of Hamblet,
    The

Hampton, Timothy 1
Hannay, Margaret P. 123, 127, 130, 146n.51, 146–47n.53, 147n.55, 147n.62
Harvey, Gabriel 148n.62
Hauser, Henri 46, 87n.53, 89n.72
Hay, Edmund (Scottish Jesuit) 174, 198n.49
Hay, John (Scottish Jesuit) 174–75, 198n.50, 198n.51
Hay, Millicent V. 90n.83, 144n.23
Heinrich, Christoph Gotlob 87n.56
Henri II, King of France 27, 32, 33–34, 45, 48–49, 51, 86n.36, 89n.77, 154, 179, 194–95n.9
Henri III, King of France (previously Duke of Anjou) 59, 91n.89, 96, 125, 176
Henri IV, King of France and Navarre 5, 35, 43, 58–65 *passim*, 80, 86n.32, 86n.41, 97–98, 99, 102, 142–43n.16, 143n.17, 143n.18, 144n.22, 144n.23, 174, 198n.47, 200n.64
Henry IV, King of England 62
Henry V, King of England 62–63
Henry VIII, King of England 53, 160–61, 164–66, 196n.22
Herbert, Mary Sidney, Countess of Pembroke 101–2, 122–26 *passim*, 129, 147n.61, 200n.64
    Antonius 1, 97, 101, 104, 117, 118, 119, 122–26, 128, 129, 130–33, 135–38, 140, 141n.8, 144n.26, 146.48, 147n.54, 147n.55, 147n.56, 147n.59, 147n.60, 147n.61, 147n.62
    Discourse of life and death, A 125, 133–35, 138, 139, 147n.57
    Psalms (translations, with Philip Sidney) 123, 125, 126–28, 130, 143n.21, 146n.45

'To the Angell spirit of the most excellent Sir Philip Sidney' 126–30, 138, 146n.51, 146–47n.53
Heu, Gaspard de, seigneur de Buy (c.1517–58) 89–90n.77
Hildebrandt, Esther 90n.81
Histoire de notre temps, contenant vn recveil des choses memorables passées et publiées pour le faict de la Religion & estat de la France 30, 84n.23, 85n.31
    see also Albret, Jeanne d', *Mémoires*
Histoire ecclésiastique des églises réformées see Bèze, Théodore de, *Histoire ecclésiastique des églises réformées*
L'histoire prodigieuse du Docteur Fauste 5–6, 12n.7
historie of the damnable life, and deserued death of Doctor Iohn Faustus, The 5–6
Holinshed, Raphael (*et al.*) (*Chronicles*) 54, 55
Holy League *see* League, Holy
Honoré-Duvergé, Suzanne 91n.94
Hopkins, Lisa 12n.15, 153–54, 155, 194n.9, 201n.68, 201n.69
L'Hospital, Michel de, Chancellor of France (c.1505–73) 146n.47
Hotman, François (1524–90) 45–46, 50, 87n.53, 89n.74, 89n.77, 90n.82
    Epistre envoyée au tigre de la France 89n.77
Hotman, Jean (son of above; 1552–1636) 90n.82
Hunsdon, Henry Carey, Baron (1525–96) 172
Hunter, G. K. 4, 153, 155, 192

Isabella [of Austria], Queen of Denmark (1501–26) 48

Jacquart, Jean 162, 180, 195n.21,
    196n.23, 197n.36
James VI, King of Scotland; later James
    I of England 47, 174
Jamyn, Amadis (*Le Tombeau du feu Roy
    Tres-Chrestien Charles IX*) 124
Jeanne d'Arc 119, 196n.25
Jenkins, Harold 2, 11n.4, 16, 68, 82n.1,
    82n.4, 82n.5, 83n.6, 83n.7,
    83n.15, 84n.19, 86n.39, 91n.93,
    92n.111, 93n.114
Joan of Arc *see* Jeanne d'Arc
Joan of Navarre *see* Navarre, Joan of
Jodelle, Étienne
    Cléopâtre captive 1, 94, 96–97, 98,
        99, 100, 103–15 *passim*, 122, 124,
        125, 137, 141, 141n.6, 143n.19,
        144n.26, 144n.27, 144n.28,
        144n.32, 144n.33, 145n.35,
        145n.36, 147n.61
    Dido se sacrifiant 99
Johannesson, Kurt 88n.67
John Frederick II, Duke of Saxony/
    Saxe-Weimar (1529–95) 49
John, Don [of Austria] 182, 183,
    200–1n.67
Jondorf, Gillian 141n.2
Jones, Emrys 146n.41
Jones, Leonard Chester 148n.63
Jouan, Abel (*The Royal Tour of France
    by Charles IX and Catherine de'
    Medici*) 172, 198n.40, 198n.41
Jouanna, Arlette 86n.33, 86n.34,
    87n.55, 91n.96, 91n.98, 141n.3,
    141n.10, 146n.46, 195n.17,
    197n.29, 198n.37, 198n.41,
    198n.44, 198n.47
Jowett, John 194n.3
Just, Saint (4th cent.) 169

Kelley, Donald R. 87n.53
Kewes, Paulina 101, 141n.8, 144n.21,
    144n.27, 146n.48, 149n.66

Kim, Seong Hak 146n.47
Kingdon, Robert M. 198n.37
King Leir (anonymous play) 76
Kinnamon, Noel J. 127, 130, 146n.51,
    146–47n.53, 147n.55, 147n.62
Knecht, Ronald J. 196n.24
Kyd, Thomas
    Cornelia 124
    Spanish Tragedy, The 16, 17, 92n.110
    '*Ur-Hamlet*' 2, 16, 17, 54, 68

Lacan, Jacques 150
La Croix du Maine, François Grudé,
    seigneur de (bibliographer)
    143n.16
La Ferté-sous-Jouarre, Synod of (1564)
    172, 198n.37
Lalanne, Lodovic 42, 87n.47
Lamb, Mary Ellen 123, 125, 133,
    146n.44
Lambin, Georges 9–11, 13n.19, 153,
    154, 180, 181, 184, 194n.7,
    198n.43, 200n.66, 201n.67
Landré [Landrin], Christophe (*Histoire
    de notre temps*) 84n.23
Languet, Hubert 47, 49–50, 53–54,
    88n.59, 88n.71, 90n.79, 90n.80,
    146n.47
La Place, Pierre de [d'Angoulême]
    *Commentaires de l'estat de la religion
    et république* 29, 85n.29, 87n.58,
    89n.77
    fyrst parte of commentaries, The 29,
        47, 85n.29, 87n.58, 88n.60
    *Rervm in Gallia ob religionem
    gestarvm libri tres* 29, 85n.29
La Ramée, Pierre de *see* Ramus, Petrus
La Renaudie, Jean du Barry, seigneur
    de (d. 1560) 85n.28, 89n.77
La Rochefoucauld, François III, Count
    of 174
La Rochefoucauld, Madeleine de,

dame de Tournon 10, 187, 188, 199n.57, 201n.69

La Tour d'Auvergne (family) *see* La Tour-Turenne; Roussillon

La Tour-Turenne, Antoinette de 197n.35

Lauvergnat-Gagnière, Christiane 91n.89

League, Holy [*Sainte Ligue*] 96, 97, 99, 124, 142n.15, 143n.16, 143n.18, 146n.46, 176

Lee, Sidney 12n.13

Lefranc, Abel 10, 12n.17, 12–13n.18, 184, 200n.66, 200n.67

Leggatt, Alexander 194n.3

Le Hir, Yves 91n.89

Leicester, Earl of *see* Leicester, Robert Dudley, Earl of; Sidney, Robert, Viscount De l'Isle, Earl of Leicester

Leicester, Robert Dudley, Earl of 90n.82

Le Maçon, Antoine (translator of Boccaccio, *Decameron*) 153, 195n.13

Le Masle, Jean (*Chant d'allégresse sur la mort de … Colligny*) 91n.101

Lepidus, Marcus Aemilius 95

Léris, Antoine de 143n.15

Leroy, Béatrice 91n.92

L'Estoile, Pierre de (*Registre-journal du règne de Henri III*) 199n.56, 199n.57

Lestringant, Frank 141n.5

Levin, Harry 82n.2

Limbrick, Elaine 83n.13

Lorraine, Cardinal Charles de (also Cardinal of Guise; 1525–74) 27–54 *passim*, 84–85n.26, 85n.27, 85n.31, 86n.32, 86n.33, 86n.37, 86n.41, 86n.43, 87n.54, 88n.58, 88n.64, 88n.69, 89n.73, 89n.74, 89–90n.77

Lorraine, Charles de, Duke of Guise (son of Henri de Lorraine, Duke of Guiss) (1571–1640) 98

Lorraine, Charles de, Duke of Mayenne (1554–1611) 10
see also Guise, House of; Lorraine, House of

Lorraine, Duchess of *see* Christina of Denmark; Valois, Claude de

Lorraine, Duke of *see* Antoine, Duke of Lorraine; Charles III, Duke of Lorraine; François I, Duke of Lorraine

Lorraine, François de, Duke of Guise (1519–63) 27–54 *passim*, 84n.26, 85n.27, 85n.31, 85–86n.32, 86n.33, 86n.34, 86n.37, 86n.41, 86n.43, 88n.58, 88n.69, 89n.73, 89n.74, 89–90n.77, 95, 96, 168

Lorraine, Henri de, Duke of Guise (1550–88) 36, 65, 86n.43, 96, 176

Lorraine, House of 88n.58, 142n.13, 164, 196–96n.27
see also Guise, House of; individual names

Lorraine, Louis, Cardinal of (also Cardinal of Guise) (1555–88) 36, 96, 86n.43

Lorraine, Philippe-Emmanuel de *see* Mercœur, Philippe-Emmanuel de Lorraine, Duke of

Louis IX, King of France 171

Louis XI, King of France 171, 197n.36

Louis XII, King of France 160–61, 165, 166

Louis XIII, King of France and Navarre 143n.18

Lutheranism/Lutherans 46, 47, 49, 56, 88n.62

Luxembourg, Marie de, Duchess of Mercœur *see* Marie de Luxembourg

MacArthur, Janet 129
MacCaffrey, Wallace 144n.23
Machiavelli, Nicolò 25
Maguin, Angela 11n.1
Maguin, Jean-Marie 11n.1
Mailles, Jacques de (biographer of
    Bayard) 161, 195–96n.22
Mallin, Eric S. 7
Margaret of Parma, Governor of the
    Low Countries (1522–86) 34
Margolin, Jean-Claude 91n.101
Marguerite de Navarre [d'Angoulême],
    Queen of Navarre (1492–1549)
    87n.46, 153
    Heptaméron 153, 194n.6
Marie de Luxembourg, Duchess of
    Mercœur (1562–1623) 97, 98,
    102, 142n.13, 143n.17, 143n.18
Marlowe, Christopher 2, 5, 6
    Doctor Faustus 5–6, 12n.9, 151, 194
    Massacre at Paris, The 5, 9, 12n.6, 65,
    86n.43
    Tamburlaine 56
Marston, John
    Dutch Courtesan, The 142n.15
    Sophonisba 142n.15
Martel, Charles (*Histoire de notre
    temps*) 84n.23
Mary Stuart, Queen of Scots (also
    Queen of France 1559–60) 38, 44
    48, 53, 88n.64, 173
Mary Tudor, Queen of England 44
Massip, Maurice 173, 198n.50, 201n.69
Masson, Gustave 89n.77
Matthieu, Pierre (*La Guisiade*) 59–60,
    86n.43
Maximilian I, Holy Roman Emperor
    (1459–1519) 165, 166, 196n.22
Maximilian II, Holy Roman Emperor
    (1527–76) 46–47, 53
Maxwell, Julie 87n.51
Mayenne, Duke of *see* Lorraine,
    Charles de, Duke of Mayenne

Mazon, Albin 198n.45, 198n.48,
    199n.53, 201n.69
Medici, Catherine de, Queen of France,
    then regent 29, 32, 34, 45, 46, 47,
    48, 57, 59, 84n.25, 88n.64,
    88n.66, 95, 146n.47, 154, 171,
    195n.9, 201n.69
Medici, Marie de, Queen of France
    198n.43
Melancthon, Philip 47, 49
Mercœur, Duchess of *see* Marie de
    Luxembourg
Mercœur, Philippe-Emmanuel de
    Lorraine, Duke of (1558–1602)
    97–98, 102, 142n.12, 142n.13,
    143n.16, 143n.17, 144n.22,
    142n.25
Monluc [Montluc], Blaise [de Lasseran
    de Massencome], seigneur de
    (c. 1501–77) 34, 91n.103, 158,
    195n.16, 195n.17, 195n.19,
    196n.25
    Commentaires 157–60, 163–64, 166,
    195n.17, 195n.18, 195n.19,
    196n.26
Monnet, Camille 196n.24
Montaigne, Michel Eyquem de (*Essais*)
    4, 7, 14–22, 33, 57, 72, 80, 81,
    81–82n.1, 82n.2, 82n.4, 83n.8,
    83n.9, 83n.11, 83n.12, 83n.13,
    83n.14, 86n.35
Montchrestien, Antoine de (*Sophon-
    isbe*) 98, 142n.15
Monteux, Hierosme de (*Opuscula
    juvenilia*) 179
Montgomery, William 194n.3
Montluc, Blaise de *see* Monluc
Montmorency, Anne de, Constable of
    France (1492–1567) 27, 32, 37,
    95, 168
Montmorency, House of 27
Montpensier, Charles III de *see*

Bourbon, Charles III de Mont-
pensier, Duke of
Montreux, Nicolas de ['Ollenix du
Mont-Sacré'] 97, 98, 141n.9,
143n.16
Cléopâtre 1, 97–105 *passim*, 107,
111–12, 142n.14, 142–43n.16
*L'Espagne conquise, par Charles le
Grand, roy de France* 142n.13
*L'Heureuse et entière victoire obtenue
... à Cra[o]n* 98, 142n.12
Isabelle 98–99, 100, 142–43n.16
*miraculeuse délivrance de Monseigneur
le duc de Guise, La* 98
Œuvre de la chasteté 98, 142n.16
*Paix au très-chrestien et très-victorieux
roy ... Henry IIII, La* 142n.13
*Quatrième livre des Bergeries de Julli-
ette, Le* 143n.16
Sophonisbe, La 98, 142n.15, 145n.37
Mornay, Philippe de, seigneur du
Plessis-Marly 102, 144n.22,
200n.64
Christian View of Life and Death, A
(trans. 'A.W.') 134
Defence of Death, The (trans. Edward
Aggas) 134, 135, 136, 147n.57,
147n.58
Discourse of life and death, A (trans.
Mary Sidney Herbert) 125–26,
133, 134, 135, 138, 147n.57
*Excellent discours de la vie et de la
mort* 125, 133, 134, 135, 136, 138,
139, 147n.57, 147n.58
Mémoires et correspondance 200n.64
Mouflard, Marie-Madeleine 99,
142n.14, 143n.16, 144n.26,
146n.46
Mueller, Martin 93n.117
Muir, Kenneth 141n.6, 145n.35
Müller, A. 144n.28
Mundt [Mont], Christopher (English

intelligence agent) 46, 49, 53,
87n.54, 88n.65, 88n.69, 90n.81
Muntz, A. 88n.58
Muret, Marc-Antoine (*Julius Caesar*)
95, 141n.1, 141n.4
Mystère du siège d'Orléans 146n.42

Naef, Henri 31, 85n.28, 89n.74
Nantes, Edict of (1598) 80
Nashe, Thomas
Preface to *Menaphon* (by Robert
Greene) 16
Vnfortvnate Traveller, The 155–56,
160–61, 164–67, 196n.22,
196n.27, 197n.28
Navarre, Agnès de *see* Agnès de Navarre
Navarre, Henri de *see* Henri IV, King of
France and Navarre
Navarre, House of 58–66 *passim*, 80–
81
see also individual names
Navarre, Joan of, Queen of England
(1370–1437) 62–63
Navarre, King of *see* Bourbon, Antoine
de; Henri IV, King of France and
Navarre; Louis XIII, King of
France and Navarre
Navarre, Queen of *see* Albret, Jeanne d';
Marguerite de Navarre; Valois,
Marguerite de
Neill, Michael 144n.30, 145n.34,
145n.35, 145n.37
Nervèze, Antoine de (*Lettre consola-
toire*) 143n.17
Nicollier-De Weck, Béatrice 50, 53,
88n.59, 88n.69, 88n.71, 89n.72,
89n.73, 89n.75, 90n.79, 90n.80
Norland, Howard B. 131, 132, 144n.26
Norris [Norreys], John (c.1547–97)
102
North, Thomas 4, 6, 8, 101, 105, 106,
140, 147–48n.62, 148n.63,
148n.64, 148n.65

Norton, Thomas (*Gorboduc*, with
    Thomas Sackville) 125

O'Connor, John J. 142n.15
Octavius Caesar ('Augustus') *see*
    Augustus, Caius Octavius
Olaus Magnus (*Historia*) 87n.51
Olhagaray, Paul (*Histoire de Foix, Béarn
    et Navarre*) 35–36, 67, 86n.40

Painter, William (*The Palace of Pleas-
    ure*) 153, 154, 155, 195n.13
Palatine, Elector/Count *see* Frederick
    II; Frederick III
Pallier, Denis 198n.51
Palma-Cayet, Pierre-Victor 5
    *see also L'histoire prodigieuse du
    Docteur Fauste*
Pariset, Jean-Daniel 89n.73, 89n.77
Parthenay, Catherine de, Duchess of
    Rohan 102
Paul III [Alessandro Farnese], Pope
    (from 1534 to 1549) 48
Paulet [Poulet], Amyas (ambassador to
    France; c.1536–88) 90n.82
Pembroke, Countess of *see* Herbert,
    Mary Sidney
Perrenot, Antoine *see* Granvelle,
    Antoine Perrenot, Cardinal of
Petit Val, Raphaël du (printer in
    Rouen) 119, 145n.40
Philip II, King of Spain 32, 33–34, 38,
    45, 46, 47, 51, 87n.54, 101, 172
Pibrac, Guy du Faur de 124, 134,
    146n.47
Pillehotte, Jean (printer in Lyons)
    198n.51
Pius IV [Giovanni Angelo Medici],
    Pope (from 1559 to 1565) 46,
    90n.77, 168
Plessis-Marly *see* Mornay, Philippe de
Plutarch (*Lives*) 4, 6, 8, 12n.13, 54, 55,

96, 100–22 *passim*, 135–41
    passim, 145n.36, 147n.60,
    147–48n.62, 148n.63
    see also Field, Richard; Goulart,
        Simon; North, Thomas;
        Vautrollier, Thomas
Poissy, Colloquy of (September-
    October 1561) 47, 85n.29,
    87n.58, 168
Polwiller, Nicolas de *see* Bolwiller
Prat, J.-M. 198n.50, 198n.52
Prescott, Anne Lake 101, 146n.47,
    201n.70
Preston, Thomas (*Cambyses*) 125

Rabelais, François 201n.70
Rahlenbeck, Charles 89n.77
Ramus, Petrus [Pierre de La Ramée]
    (1515–72) 85n.29
Ranty, Jacques de 28, 30
Rees, Joan 110, 144n.26, 144n.28,
    144n.32
Régnier de La Planche, Louis
    ['François de L'Isle'] 27, 29,
    85n.27
    *Histoire de l'estat de France, tant de la
        république que de la religion, sous le
        règne de François II* 27–35 *passim*,
        41
    *legendarie conteining an ample
        discovrse of the life and behauiour of
        Charles Cardinal of Lorraine, and
        of his brethren, of the house of
        Guise, A* 84–85n.26, 85n.27,
        87n.44, 87–88n.58, 89n.77
    *Legende de Charles, Cardinal de
        Lorraine, et de ses freres, de la
        maison de Guise, La* 84–85n.26,
        85n.27, 87–88n.58, 89n.77
    *Response à l'épistre de Charles de
        Vaudémont, cardinal de Lorraine*
        84n.26

René, Duke of Anjou and Lorraine, King of Sicily and Naples (1409–80) 197n.27
Rigolot, François 83n.13
Robertson, John M. 81n.1
Rodriguez-Salgado, Mila J. 171
Rohan, Duchess of *see* Parthenay, Catherine de
Romier, Lucien 44–45, 87n.55, 141n.3, 194n.9, 195n.19
Ronsard, Pierre de
  Franciade, La 197n.32
  Tombeau du feu Roy Tres-Chrestien Charles IX, Le 124
Roussillon, Claude de La Tour-Turenne, Countess of 170–71, 174, 175–76, 181–89 *passim*, 197n.35, 198–99n.53
Roussillon, Edicts of (1564) 171–72, 198n.38, 198n.43
Roussillon, Just I, Baron of Tournon, Count of (d. 1525) 170
Roussillon, Just II, Baron of Tournon, Count of (d. 1563) 170, 187, 197n.34
Roussillon, Just III, Baron of Tournon, Count of (d. 1568) 170, 197n.33
Roussillon, Just-Louis I, Baron of Tournon, Count of 170–76 *passim*, 186, 187, 188, 198n.48, 199n.55, 199n.56, 199n.57
Ruble, Alphonse de 34, 45, 46, 47, 48, 84n.22, 84n.23, 86n.40

Sackville, Thomas (*Gorboduc*, with Thomas Norton) 125
Saint-André, Jacques d'Albon de (Marshal of France; c.1505–62) 38, 84n.25, 87n.55, 95, 141n.3, 168
Sainte Ligue see League, Holy
Sanchez, José 144n.33

Sanders, Eve Rachele 130–31, 144n.26, 147n.54, 147n.60
Saint Bartholomew's Day massacre *see* Bartholomew's Day massacre, Saint
Saulnier, V.-L. 83n.11, 83n.12, 83n.14
Saulx-Tavannes, Gaspard de *see* Tavannes, Gaspard de Saulx, seigneur de
Saxo 'Grammaticus' (*Historiae Danicae*) 16, 17, 22, 54, 57, 68, 87n.51
Scaliger, Julius Caesar [Giulio Cesare delle Scala] 91n.103
Schanzer, Ernest 104, 132, 135, 144n.31, 145n.39, 147n.56
Schoenbaum, Samuel 11n.1
Seneca, Lucius Annaeus 17, 92n.110, 94, 96, 115, 125, 133–34, 141n.2
  De Providentia 135, 136, 138
  Epistulae Morales 134–35, 136, 138, 147n.58
Serna, Pierre 83n.13
Serres, Jean de (*Inventaire général de l'histoire de France*) 84n.25
Seward, Desmond 91n.99
Shaheen, Naseeb 83–84n.17
Shakerley, Thomas (English intelligence agent) 45, 46, 87n.50
Shakespeare, William 2–4, 6, 8, 11, 11n.1, 11n.3, 13n.19, 34–35, 42, 47, 54–55, 84n.18, 140–41, 151, 168, 184, 185, 199n.59, 201n.69
  All's Well That Ends Well 1, 2, 3–4, 9–11, 35, 65, 150–94, 194n.1, 194n.3, 194n.4, 194n.5, 194n.9, 195n.14, 199n.59, 200n.65, 201n.67, 201n.68
  Antony and Cleopatra 1, 4, 8, 9, 11, 12n.13, 95–141, 141n.6, 141n.7, 141n.8, 144n.29, 144n.30, 144n.31, 145n.34, 145n.35, 145n.36, 145n.37, 145n.39,

146n.41, 146n.48, 147n.56,
    148n.66
As You Like It 84n.18, 84n.21, 150,
    152, 190
First Tetralogy 119
Hamlet 1, 2–3, 6–7, 9, 11, 11n.3,
    11n.4, 12n.10, 12n.12, 14, 81, 81–
    82n.1, 82n.4, 82n.5, 83n.6, 83n.7,
    83n.8, 83n.9, 83n.10, 83n.15,
    83–84n.17, 84n.19, 85n.30,
    86n.39, 86n.42, 87n.51, 90n.77,
    90n.86, 91n.93, 92n.110,
    92n.111, 93n.114, 119, 150, 151,
    152, 168, 176, 180, 184–85, 186,
    188, 200n.63, 201n.68
Henry IV, Part 1 196n.25
Henry V 3, 9, 10, 24, 80, 155
Henry VI, Part 1 119, 146n.41,
    196n.25
Julius Caesar 9, 24
King Lear 3, 17, 42, 76–80, 93n.117,
    93n.118, 93n.119, 188, 193
Love's Labour's Lost 151, 200n.66
Macbeth 193
Measure for Measure 82n.4
Merry Wives of Windsor, The 3
Midsummer Night's Dream, A 131,
    185, 193
Much Ado About Nothing 151, 200–
    1n.67
Othello 98, 150
'Problem Plays' 193
Richard II 11, 113, 157
Romeo and Juliet 131, 150
Second Tetralogy 119
Tempest, The 152
Twelfth Night 200n.66
Sidney, Mary *see* Herbert, Mary Sidney
Sidney, Philip 53–54, 90n.82, 102, 123,
    125–27, 129, 144n.21, 200n.64
    Apology for Poetry, An 122, 125,
        146n.43
    Arcadia 76–77, 80, 93n.117, 123

Astrophil and Stella 129
    Correspondence (with Hubert
        Languet) 146n.47
    Psalms (translations, with Mary
        Sidney Herbert) 123, 125–27,
        146n.45
Sidney, Robert, Viscount De l'Isle, Earl
    of Leicester 54, 90n.82, 90n.84,
    102, 144n.23, 200n.64
Simonin, Michel 55, 62, 90n.85,
    90n.87, 91n.88, 91n.89, 91n.90,
    91n.100, 142n.16, 197n.35, 198–
    99n.53
Sitzmann, J. Édouard 87n.54
Sleidanus, Johannes 63
    Epitome (of Froissart) 63–64, 66, 67,
        91n.100, 92n.106, 92n.109
Smith, Thomas (ambassador to France)
    172, 194n.6, 198n.39, 198n.42
Snyder, Susan 4, 153, 200n.65
Sournia, Jean-Claude 91n.103, 195n.9,
    195n.16, 195n.17, 195n.19,
    195n.20, 196n.25
Spenser, Edmund 144n.21
Spriet, Pierre 146n.43, 146n.48,
    146n.49
Stanley, William, Earl of Derby 11,
    13n.19, 184, 200n.66
Stirling, Brents 145n.34
Stone, Donald, Jr. 90n.85, 141n.9,
    142n.15
Stuart, Mary *see* Mary Stuart, Queen of
    Scots
Sturm, Jean [Johannes] (Protestant
    educator and activist; 1507–89)
    89n.74
Sullivan, Garrett A., Jr. 194n.5
Suriano, Michele [Michel] (Venetian
    ambassador to France) 33, 47
Sutherland, Nicola Mary 87n.49

Talbot, John, Earl of Shrewsbury
    (1387–1453) 196n.25

Tavannes, Gaspard de Saulx, seigneur de 195n.19
Taveneaux, René 196n.27
Taylor, Gary 82n.5, 194n.3
Taylor, Neil 11n.4
Terrail, Pierre *see* Bayard, Pierre Terrail, seigneur de
Thevet, André (1516–90) 141n.5
Thompson, Ann 11n.5
Thou, Jacques-August (*Histoire universelle*) 86n.32
Throckmorton, Nicholas (ambassador to France) 44, 45, 46, 48, 52, 87n.48, 87n.50, 88n.63, 88n.70, 89–90n.77
Tournon, Claudine de, Baroness of Balançon (1540–1600) 187–88, 199n.61
Tournon, François, Cardinal of (1489–1562) 168, 169, 170, 173
Tournon, Hélène de (d. 1577) 9, 10, 181–85, 186, 188, 189, 199n.61, 200n.66, 200n.67
Tournon, House of 168, 169–70, 187–88, 197n.32
    see also La Rochefoucauld; La Tour-Turenne; Roussillon
Tournon, Madeleine de, dame de Caderousse 187–88, 199n.61
tragédie française du bon Kanut, roi de Danemark, La 91n.89
Troyes, (second) Treaty of (1564) 172
Tucoo-Chala, Pierre 65, 91n.91, 92n.107, 92n.108
Turnus, King of the Rutuli 169, 197n.32
Tymme, Thomas (translator of La Place, *Commentaires*) 85n.29

Urfé, Honoré d' 173–74
    triomphante entrée de Magdeleine de La Rochefocaud, La 173–74, 187–88, 197n.32, 198n.51

'Ur-Hamlet' *see* Kyd, Thomas, 'Ur-Hamlet'

Valois, Claude de, Duchess of Lorraine (1547–75) 48–49, 88n.71
Valois, House of 59
Valois, Marguerite de [Marguerite de France], Queen of Navarre, then of France (1553–1615) 21, 59–60, 65, 83n.11, 83n.13, 87n.46, 184, 187, 200n.64, 200n.66, 200–1n.67
    Correspondance 200n.64
    Mémoires 35, 181–85, 199n.61, 200–1n.67
Varambon, Marc de Rye, marquis de 181–84, 185, 200n.67
Vassy *see* Wassy
Vaurigaud, Benjamin 144n.25
Vautrollier, Thomas 8, 11n.1
Vervins, Treaty of (1598) 80
Viennot, Éliane 200n.67
Villey, Pierre 83n.11, 83n.12, 83n.14
Virey, Jean de, seigneur Du Gravier 145n.40
    Machabée, La 145n.40
    Tragedie de Jeanne-d'Arques 119–22
Virgil (*Aeneid*) 99, 197n.32
Vogler, Bernard 87n.57, 87n.58

Waddington, Albert 89n.73
Waller, Gary F. 129, 146n.50, 146n.52, 147n.53
Walsingham, Francis 199n.57, 199n.61
Wassy, massacre of (1 March 1562) 31, 35, 46, 85n.27, 86n.34, 88n.58
Wells, Stanley 82n.5, 194n.3
Wilcox, Helen 194n.1, 195n.14
Willemin, Jean 170, 175, 176, 198–99n.53
Williams, Deanne 153–55
Wilson, John Dover 144n.30
Wilson, Richard 13n.19

Witherspoon, Alexander 122, 130, 146n.43
Woodstock, Edward of *see* Edward of Woodstock
Worms, Colloquy of (1557) 47
Wright, Herbert G. 4, 153

Yachnin, Paul 141n.8, 146n.48

CPSIA information can be obtained
at www.ICGtesting.com
Printed in the USA
FFOW04n0301260116
20675FF